Instructor's Guide and Solutions Manual

Bernard Gillett
University of Colorado at Boulder

Using and Understanding Mathematics
A Quantitative Reasoning Approach

Fourth Edition

Jeffery O. Bennett
University of Colorado at Boulder

William L. Briggs
University of Colorado at Denver

PEARSON

Addison
Wesley

Boston San Francisco New York
London Toronto Sydney Tokyo Singapore Madrid
Mexico City Munich Paris Cape Town Hong Kong Montreal

D0869022

Reproduced by Pearson Addison-Wesley from electronic files supplied by the author.

Copyright © 2008 Pearson Education, Inc.
Publishing as Pearson Addison-Wesley, 75 Arlington Street, Boston, MA 02116.

ISBN-13: 978-0-321-46496-5
ISBN-10: 0-321-46496-6

2 3 4 5 6 BRR 10 09 08 07

PEARSON
Addison
Wesley

Table of Contents

About the Instructor's Material

You are reading the Instructor's Guide of *Using and Understanding Mathematics*.

Table of Contents

Using This Book

This book is designed to be useful in a variety of general education mathematics courses, including but not limited to the following:

- Core mathematics requirements for liberal arts or fine arts students at two- and four-year colleges and universities.
- General mathematics courses for business students at two- and four-year colleges and universities.
- General mathematics courses for pre-service and in-service teachers at two- and four-year colleges and universities.
- Senior-level mathematics courses for high school students.

A Quantitative Reasoning Approach

The subtitle of this book advertises "a Quantitative Reasoning Approach." But what exactly is this?

The idea of "quantitative reasoning" goes back at least to the early 1980s (possibly much earlier), when it was raised as a catch-all phrase for the kinds of mathematical skills needed by all Americans. It has since been defined in greater detail by a number of different groups, including:

- the Mathematical Association of America (MAA), in its report *Quantitative Reasoning for College Graduates: A Complement to the Standards* (1995).
- the American Mathematical Association for Two-Year Colleges (AMATYC), in its report *Crossroads in Mathematics: Standards for Introductory College Mathematics before Calculus* (D. Cohen, ed., 1995).
- the College Board, in its report *Why Numbers Count: Quantitative Literacy for Tomorrow's America* (Lynn Steen, ed, 1997)
- the National Council on Education and the Disciplines, in its report *Mathematics and Democracy: The Case for Quantitative Literacy* (Lynn Steen, ed, 2001)

Our own definition of quantitative reasoning largely overlaps the MAA and AMATYC definitions, but originally grew out of discussions during 1987 by an interdisciplinary faculty committee at the University of Colorado, Boulder (author Jeffrey Bennett was an advisory member of the committee). This committee recommended the creation of a new type of college mathematics course, which was instituted at Boulder in 1988 under the direction of author Bennett. Our current definition of quantitative reasoning emphasizes the following four broad content areas:

1. **Logic, Critical Thinking, and Problem Solving**: Students should learn skills that will enable them to construct a logical argument based on rules of inference and to develop strategies for solving quantitative problems.
2. **Number Sense and Estimation**: Students should become "numerate," or able to make sense of the numbers that confront them in the modern world. For example, students should be able to give meaning to a billion dollars, and to distinguish it from a million dollars or a trillion dollars. Developing number sense involves being able to make simple calculations and estimates to put numbers in perspective. Other crucial aspects of number sense include being able to interpret the many different uses and abuses of percentages in the media, understanding the role of uncertainty in most real problems, and understanding issues of personal finance.
3. **Statistical Interpretation and Basic Probability**: Reports about statistical research are ubiquitous in the news. Students must have the tools needed to *interpret* this research. In particular, they should understand the basic ideas behind statistical research, how to interpret statistical graphics, and the difference between correlation and causality. At a slightly higher level they should understand the difference between various measures of central tendency (e.g., mean, median, mode), the meaning of variation, the importance of the normal distribution, and basic ideas of statistical inference. Probability is important both because of its use in statistical inference and because it is involved in so many topics of relevance to most Americans, including lotteries, casino gambling, and risk assessment.
4. **Interpreting Mathematical Models**: Many major issues today are studied through mathematical models; for example, economic models underlie much of the political wrangling over budgetary and tax policies, while climate models form the basis for controversies over potential impacts of global warming. While the creation of such models generally requires much more advanced mathematics than we can cover in general education courses, we can easily teach students how to interpret what they read or hear about models. The skills required for interpreting models include understanding the difference between linear and exponential growth, understanding the concept of a function and its domain of applicability, and understanding how to put together a simple linear or exponential function.

Core Quantitative Reasoning Content: Chapters 1–10

This textbook is designed to help instructors teach the four content areas described above. The first nine chapters of this book parallel these content areas quite closely:

- Chapters 1 and 2 emphasize content area (1): Chapter 1 focuses on logic and critical thinking, while Chapter 2 builds problem solving skills.
- Chapters 3 and 4 emphasize content area (2): Chapter 3 covers basic ideas of number sense and estimation, while Chapter 4 focuses on personal and government finance.
- Chapters 5–7 emphasize content area (3): Chapter 5 covers basic concepts needed for interpreting statistical research, Chapter 6 covers the slightly higher level skills described above (central tendency, variation, normal distribution, and statistical inference), and Chapter 7 covers probability.
- Chapters 8–10 emphasize content area (4): Chapter 8 covers the difference between linear and exponential growth. Chapter 9 discusses more general ideas of functions and their use in linear and exponential models. Chapter 10 covers geometric thinking and modeling, including a section on fractals.

Further Applications: Chapters 11–13

The final three chapters of the book go somewhat beyond the core topics of quantitative reasoning to give students a greater appreciation for the role that these topics play in modern society. In particular:

- Chapter 11 emphasizes the connections between mathematics and the arts, and should be of special interest to fine arts majors.
- Chapter 12 emphasizes the connections between mathematics and politics, with units on voting methods, voting theory, apportionment, and redistricting.
- Chapter 13 emphasizes the use of network theory (graph theory) in modern business, and should be of special interest to business majors.

Prerequisite Mathematical Background

This book is designed primarily as a college-level text, so we generally assume that students have taken at least one course in high school algebra. Note, however, that the book includes *Brief Review* boxes that remind students of key mathematical skills as they arise, so it should be possible for students to cover this text even if they enter with very weak memory of their high school mathematical skills. In addition, because of the book's modular structure (see below), it is possible for instructors to pick and choose among topics in accordance with the skill level of students.

Modular Structure of the Book

This book has a modular structure designed to allow you maximum flexibility in creating a course that meets your particular needs. The twelve chapters are organized broadly by mathematical topics. Each chapter, in turn, is divided into a set of self-contained *units* that focus on particular issues or applications. Because the units are largely self-contained, you can pick and choose among them in designing a course. The chapter-by-chapter guide that follows (p. G–22) lists the prerequisites, if any, for each unit.

Pedagogical Features

Besides the main narrative of the text, this book contains a number of pedagogical features designed to enhance student learning. You can find a complete list of the features, with descriptions, in the book's Preface (p. xi). Here, we describe a few ways in which you might use the features as you teach:

- Use the *Chapter Overview* and *Chapter Summary* to help you decide which units you intend to cover in class.
- Use the *summary boxes* and the many *examples and case studies* as the basis for class presentations; you may also wish to cover material in the *Brief Review* boxes if your students need the review.
- Use the *Time Out to Think* questions as starting points for classroom discussions.
- Ask your students to use the end-of-unit *Quick Quiz* and *Review Questions* as study aids.
- Assign homework by drawing from the end-of-unit questions under *In the News* and *Exercises*; because answers to odd-numbered exercises appear in the back of the book, you may wish to assign only even-numbered exercises while suggesting that students use the odd-numbered ones for additional practice.
- If you wish to have students work on extended projects, choose from among the *Web Projects* that appear at the end of each unit.

Additional Resources for Instructors

The following additional resources may also be of use to you in teaching:

Themes of the Times (ISBN 978-0-321-48725-4)
This collection of articles from *The New York Times* includes a series of follow-up questions for homework or class discussion.

Instructor's Testing Manual (ISBN 978-0-321-45922-0)
The Testing Manual includes three alternative tests per chapter. These items may be used as actual tests or as references for creating tests.

TestGen® (ISBN 978-0-321-47181-9)
TestGen is a computerized test generator with problems organized specifically for this textbook. For more information, see the Preface.

PowerPoint Lecture Presentation
Classroom presentation slides are geared specifically to the sequence and philosophy of this textbook. Available within MyMathLab or at www.aw-bc.com/irc

MyMathLab
MyMathLab is a series of text-specific, easily customizable online courses for Addison-Wesley textbooks in mathematics and statistics. MyMathLab gives you the tools you need to deliver all or a portion of your course online. For more information, see the Preface, www.mymathlab.com or contact your Addison-Wesley sales representative.

A Handout on Homework Quality

One of the most frustrating aspects of teaching can be grading papers that look shabby and show little effort. We have found that the quality of student work can be greatly enhanced by telling them exactly what you expect papers to look like. To that end, we encourage you to ask students to follow the guidelines that appear on the next page; you may freely photocopy this handout (with its credit line) and distribute it to your students.

Presenting Homework and Writing Assignments*

All work that you turn-in should be of *collegiate quality*: neat and easy to read, well-organized, and demonstrating mastery of the subject matter. Future employers and teachers will expect this quality of work. Moreover, although submitting homework of collegiate quality requires "extra" effort, it serves two important purposes directly related to learning.

1. The effort you expend in clearly explaining your work solidifies your learning. In particular, research has shown that writing and speaking trigger different areas of your brain. By writing something down — even when you think you already understand it — your learning is reinforced by involving other areas of your brain.

2. By making your work clear and self-contained (that is, making it a document that you can read without referring to the questions in the text), it will be a much more useful study guide when you review for a quiz or exam.

The following guidelines will help ensure that your assignments meet the standards of collegiate quality.

- Always use proper grammar, proper sentence and paragraph structure, and proper spelling.

- All answers and other writing should be fully self-contained. A good test is to imagine that a friend is reading your work, and asking yourself whether the friend would understand exactly what you are trying to say. It is also helpful to read your work out loud to yourself, making sure that it sounds clear and coherent.

- In problems that require calculation:
  - Be sure to *show your work* clearly. By doing so, both you and your instructor can follow the process you used to obtain an answer.
  - *Word problems should have word answers.* That is, after you have completed any necessary calculations, any problem stated in words should be answered with one or more *complete sentences* that describe the point of the problem and the meaning of your solution.
  - Express your word answers in a way that would be *meaningful* to most people. For example, most people would find it more meaningful if you express a result of 720 hours as 1 month. Similarly, if a precise calculation yields an answer of 9,745,600 years, it may be more meaningful in words as "nearly 10 million years."

- Finally, pay attention to details that will make your assignments *look* good. For example:
  - Use standard-sized white paper with clean edges (e.g., do not tear paper out of notebooks because it will have ragged edges).
  - *Staple* all pages together; don't use paper clips or folded corners because they tend to get caught with other students' papers.
  - Use a ruler to make straight lines in sketches or graphs.
  - Include illustrations whenever they help to explain your answer.
  - Ideally, make your work look professional by using a word processor for text and equations and by creating graphs or illustrations with a spreadsheet or other software.

Activity

The following activity can be used in many different ways, but we have found it particularly effective if you use it early in your course as a way for students to get to know each other and to get comfortable with ideas of mathematics. Many instructors have reported good results using this activity on the first day of class. It works best with groups of between about 20 and 50 students; with fewer than 20, you may not see the probabilistic patterns emerging, while it can become unwieldy with more than 50 students. If you have a large class of more than 50 students, you can still do the activity if you first break the class into smaller groups.

Mathematical Objective: The mathematical objective of the activity is to simulate the transmission and spread of a infectious disease among a group of people.

Social Objective: Students will meet each other, which should help "break the ice" for future class discussions and group work (if you plan any).

Materials Required:
  – Standard six-sided dice: enough to give one die to each student.
  – A photocopy for each student of the Record Sheet that appears on the next page.

Concept: The basic idea is that students will introduce themselves to each other in one-on-one "encounters." Each encounter simulates an interaction in which a person may be exposed to an infectious disease. The simulation works as follows:
  • One student will be randomly assigned as the initial "carrier" of the disease; however, so that no one knows the carrier's identity during the encounters, you should wait to assign the carrier's identity until after all the encounters are complete. (In fact, you may wish to keep your students in the dark about the entire purpose of the simulation until after the encounters are completed.)
  • In each one-on-one encounter, each student rolls his or her die. The sum determines whether the encounter is one in which the disease may have been transmitted.
  • The encounters proceed through a series of stages. Each student should have 3 to 6 encounters in each stage, and the activity should continue for at least five stages. At the end, the class analyzes how the disease spreads through each stage from its start with a single initial carrier.

Procedure:

Step 1: Hand Out Record Sheets and Dice: Each student should get one die and a copy of the Record Sheet that appears on the next page.

Step 2: Assigning ID Numbers. Each student needs a unique ID number for this activity. Two possible approaches to the ID numbers are the following:
  • you assign ID numbers in advance; e.g., ID numbers 1–30 for 30 students. In this case you can write the ID numbers on the Record Sheets before handing them out.
  • students choose their own 3-digit ID numbers by rolling their die 3 times; e.g., a student rolling 3 then 2 then 6 gets ID number 326. Any students getting duplicate numbers will need to roll again until they have unique numbers. Students write their ID numbers on their Record Sheets.

Step 3: Make a master list of all the ID numbers on a chalkboard or overhead transparency.

Step 4: Announce to students the following rules for the encounters:
  • Upon your command, the activity will commence with Stage 1. Each student should quickly introduce him or herself to another student. After brief personal introductions (suggest a 1 minute time limit), each student rolls his or her die.

- Each student writes the other's ID number in the Stage 1 column of his or her own Record Sheet, then circles or does not circle this ID number depending on the sum of the two dice:
  - Circle the ID if the sum is 5 or less.
  - Do not circle the ID if the sum is 6 or more.

  Example: If Student 5 meets Student 21, Student 5 writes "21" in the Stage 1 column of his or her sheet, while Student 21 writes "5" in the Stage 1 column of his or her sheet. If their dice roll gives a sum of 5 or less, then they circle the ID numbers recorded; if the dice roll gives a sum of 6 or more, they leave the recorded ID numbers uncircled.
- As soon as they're finished, the two students part and look for another partner, repeating the process; emphasize that they should continue to record results in the Stage 1 column until you call an end to the stage.
- After you call an end to Stage 1, you'll take a few seconds break and then start Stage 2, which works the same way except students record results in the Stage 2 column. The activity will continue through up to 6 stages. Ask students to strive for 3 to 6 encounters within each stage, trying to avoid multiple encounters with the same person (to the extent possible, which depends on group size).

Step 5: As soon as the rules are clear, begin the activity. You should allow 3–5 minutes for each Stage, with perhaps a bit of extra time for the first stage as students get the hang of the activity.

Step 6: After 5 or 6 stages, ask students to return to their seats. Then choose one student's ID number at random, using any technique you wish. (If your students chose 3-number ID's by rolling a die, you might roll your die 3 times and select the student ID that is numerically closest to whatever you roll.) On your master list of ID numbers on the board or overhead, circle the selected ID number.

Step 7: Now you inform the students that the selected ID number represents a student carrying an infectious disease. Encounters that are circled (i.e., those that had a sum of 5 or less on the two rolled dice) represent "risky encounters" in which a disease would have been transmitted if either student was a carrier. Ask students to raise their hands if they had a risky encounter with the carrier in Stage 1. All those with raised hands are now infected as well, so circle their ID numbers on your master list. Then ask students to look at their encounters in Stage 2. They should raise their hands if they had a risky encounter with any of the infected ID numbers circled on your master list. Again, all those with raised hands get added to your list of infected ID numbers. Continue this process until you've been through all the stages.

Analysis: You should find that the number of infected students at the end of each stage rises approximately exponentially, with perhaps some leveling out in the later stages if most students have already been infected. You can then generate some discussion of how this activity models the spread of a real disease.

Record Sheet

Your Personal ID Number _____

Instructions:
1. During each stage, record the ID number of each student you meet in the column for that stage.
2. Roll your die with each person you meet; circle the person's ID number (which you've already written down) if the sum of the two dice is 5 or less; if the sum is greater than 5, leave the ID number uncircled.

Stage 1	Stage 2	Stage 3	Stage 4	Stage 5	Stage 6

Sample Course Outlines

Unless you have a full-year course (which is quite rare for general education mathematics), you will need to pick and choose among topics in the book. Roughly speaking, you'll need to consider three main dimensions when designing your course: the prerequisite background of your students; the length of your course; and any special area of emphasis you intend to use. For simplicity in developing sample course outlines, we've identified the following choices for the three dimensions:

Course Grid		
Dimension 1: **Student Level**	**Dimension 2:** **Course Length**	**Dimension 3:** **Course Emphasis**
Level 1: No algebra prerequisite.	**Q**: 1 quarter course	**G**: General — a taste of many topics.
Level 2: Elementary algebra prerequisite.	**S**: 1 semester course	**SP**: Statistics and probability
Level 3: Intermediate algebra prerequisite	**S2**: 2 semester course	**BF**: Business, finance, and economics
		NS: Preparation for core natural science courses

Here we offer sample course outlines (or notes) for the following combinations of these dimensions:

1. (Level 1, Q, G): General one-quarter course for students with only one or two years of high school mathematics.
2. (Level 1, S, G): Similar to (1) above, but for one semester rather than one quarter.
3. (Level 2, S, SP): One-semester course for liberal arts/math survey students with emphasis on statistics and probability, and prerequisite of high school algebra.
4. (Level 2, S, NS): One-semester course for liberal arts/math survey students with emphasis on preparation for core natural science classes, and prerequisite of high school algebra.
5. (Level 3, S, BF): A business/finance oriented course for students with three solid years of high school mathematics.
6. Notes on full-year (two-semester) courses, especially those aimed at pre-service teachers or senior-level high school students.

Suggested Outline for Level 1, One Quarter, General Emphasis

General Notes:
- This outline assumes a pace of approximately 2 units per week, which should be realistic for Level 1 students.
- Note that we have chosen to focus on parts of chs. 1–5 and 8. If you wish to cover other topics, you might consider reducing the coverage of logic from chapter 1 or the coverage of finance in chapter 4.
- We recommend assigning 5 to 10 exercises for each unit. You may also want to assign one of the *In the News* questions for each unit.

Week	Suggested Topics	Reading
1	Introduction: welcome, including discussion of course content and expectations regarding work load; you may wish to conduct the activity described on p. G–7 of this guide. Cover the Prologue and Units 1A and 1B.	Prologue, Units 1A, 1B
2	Cover sets and Venn diagrams in Unit 1C; to keep the time on this topic reasonable, you may wish to stop before the Venn diagrams for three sets in Unit 1C. Then cover basic ideas of problem solving through unit analysis in Unit 2A.	Unit 1C, 2A
3	Continue problem solving with Unit 2B; discuss the four-step problem solving process in Unit 2C, but skip the rest 2C and assign homework only from Units 2A and 2B.	Unit 2B, 2C (4-step process only)
4	Spend this week on uses and abuses of percentages (Unit 3A) and putting numbers in perspective (Unit 3B).	Units 3A, 3B
5	Skip past unit 3C and focus instead on index numbers and the CPI in Unit 3D. Then begin financial management with Unit 4A.	Units 3D, 4A
6	Cover basic financial understanding, but possibly skip the material on investment types in Unit 4C.	Units 4B, 4C, 4D
7	Introduce fundamental ideas of statistics (Unit 5A), but devote most time to the question of whether to believe a statistical result as discussed in Unit 5B.	Units 5A, 5B
8	Cover statistical tables and graphs in Units 5C and 5D.	Units 5C, 5D
9	Conclude coverage of statistics by discussing the difference between correlation and causality in Unit 5E. Then begin discussion of linear versus exponential growth (Unit 8A).	Units 5E, 8A
10	For the final week, discuss doubling time and half-life (Unit 8B) and then wrap-up with discussions of real population growth (Unit 8C).	Units 8B, 8C

Suggested Outline for Level 1, One Semester, General Emphasis

General Notes:
- This outline is quite similar to the previous outline, except that it assumes a semester of 15 weeks rather than a quarter of 10 weeks.
- We have included topics only for the first 14 weeks, on the assumption that the last week may be devoted to review.

Week	Suggested Topics	Reading
1	Introduction: welcome, including discussion of course content and expectations regarding work load; you may wish to conduct the activity described on p. G–7 of this guide. Cover the Prologue and Units 1A and 1B.	Prologue, Units 1A, 1B
2	Cover sets and Venn diagrams in Unit 1C; to keep the time on this topic reasonable, you may wish to stop before the Venn diagrams for three sets in Unit 1C. Then cover basic ideas of problem solving through unit analysis in Unit 2A.	Unit 1C, 2A
3	Continue problem solving with Unit 2B; discuss the four-step problem solving process in Unit 2C, but skip the rest of 2C and assign homework only from Units 2A and 2B.	Unit 2B, 2C (4-step process only)
4	Spend this week on uses and abuses of percentages (Unit 3A) and putting numbers in perspective (Unit 3B).	Units 3A, 3B
5	Continue Chapter 3 with discussion of uncertainty in Unit 3C and index numbers and the CPI in Unit 3D.	Units 3C, 3D
6	Begin full coverage of the financial management chapter with personal finance (Unit 4A), compound interest (Unit 4B), and savings plans and investments (Unit 4C).	Units 4A, 4B, 4C
7	Cover loan payments (Unit 4D) and income taxes (4E).	Units 4D, 4E
8	Conclude finance with government budget issues in Unit 4F. Then begin discussing basic ideas of statistics (Unit 5A).	Units 4F, 5A
9	Continue statistics with Units 5B and 5C.	Units 5B, 5C
10	Conclude statistics with Units 5D and 5E.	Units 5D, 5E
11	Give a brief introduction to probability with Units 7A and 7B.	Units 7A, 7B
12	Discuss the law of averages (Unit 7C), then begin discussion of linear versus exponential growth (Unit 8A).	Units 7C, 8A
13	Continue discussion of exponential growth with Units 8B and 8C.	Units 8B, 8C
14	Discuss issues of voting and voting theory, and the important topic of congressional redistricting.	Units 12A, 12B, 12D
15	Class wrap-up.	—

Suggested Outline for Level 2, One Semester, Statistics/Probability Emphasis

General Notes:

- This outline places emphasis on topics most directly related to statistics and probability, which includes covering all of Chapters 1, 3, and Chapters 5–7. This set of material means that roughly 1/2 to 2/3 of your course will focus on issues directly related to statistics and probability, while still giving students exposure to other important quantitative reasoning topics.
- This outline assumes a more rapid pace through the early units in the book, which should be reasonable for Level 2 students. The pace slows as we move into the more advanced material.

Week	Suggested Topics	Reading
1	Introduction: welcome, including discussion of course content and expectations regarding work load; you may wish to conduct the activity described on p. G–7 of this guide. Cover the Prologue and Units 1A and 1B.	Prologue, Units 1A, 1B
2	Complete coverage of logic and critical thinking in Chapter 1.	Units 1C–1E
3	Cover problem solving through unit analysis in Units 2A and 2B; discuss the four-step problem solving process in Unit 2C, but skip the rest of 2C and assign homework only from Units 2A and 2B.	Units 2A–2B, 2C (4-step process only)
4	Begin coverage of number sense issues with the first three units of Chapter 3.	Units 3A–3C
5	Complete coverage of Chapter 3.	Units 3D, 3E
6	Begin full coverage of Chapter 5 on statistical reasoning; take plenty of time to emphasize the fundamental ideas in Unit 5A, then discuss the guidelines in Unit 5B.	Units 5A, 5B
7	Complete coverage of Chapter 5. Unit 5C should go quickly for Level 2 students, so devote most of the time to Units 5D and 5E.	Units 5C–5E
8	Begin full coverage of Chapter 6 with about a class period each devoted to Units 6A through 6C, respectively. Note that Unit 6B is particularly short and should be easy to cover in less than one full class period.	Units 6A–6C
9	Cover statistical inference (Unit 6D), then begin discussion of probability.	Units 6D, 7A, 7B
10	Continue discussion of probability with the law of averages (Unit 7C) and risk analysis (Unit 7D).	Units 7C, 7D
11	Conclude probability with Unit 7E. Spend some time summarizing your extensive coverage of statistics and probability, then begin discussion of linear versus exponential growth (Unit 8A).	Units 7E, 8A
12	Conclude discussion of exponential growth; emphasize the use of logarithmic scales (Unit 8D), which are arguably important to statistics.	Units 8B–8D
13	Discuss issues of voting, apportionment, and redistricting, with emphasis on the statistical nature of many of the controversies.	Units 12A–D
14	Choose a final week topic of interest to your students, such as selections from Chapter 4 on financial management or Chapter 11 on mathematics and the arts. If you choose chapter 11, be sure to include 10A as well on fundamentals of geometry.	choice
15	Class wrap-up.	—

Suggested Outline for Level 2, One Semester, Natural Science Emphasis

General Notes:

- This outline places emphasis on topics that will be particularly useful to students in their core natural science classes. It goes into greater depth on problem solving than earlier outlines by including Unit 2C, and also covers Chapter 9 on modeling.
- This outline assumes a more rapid pace through the early units in the book, which should be reasonable for Level 2 students. The pace slows as we move into the more advanced material.

Week	Suggested Topics	Reading
1	Introduction: welcome, including discussion of course content and expectations regarding work load; you may wish to conduct the activity described on p. G–7 of this guide. Cover the Prologue and Units 1A and 1B.	Prologue, Units 1A, 1B
2	Complete coverage of logic and critical thinking in Chapter 1. The discussion of inductive versus deductive logic in Unit 1D is particularly important as preparation natural science courses (because understanding this distinction underlies the scientific method).	Units 1C–1E
3	Cover problem solving through unit analysis in Units 2A and 2B; spend plenty of time covering the units of energy, density, and concentration in Unit 2B.	Units 2A, 2B
4	Cover Unit 2C and its examples in some depth. Then move quickly through Unit 3A on uses and abuses of percentages, leaving more time for putting numbers in perspective (Unit 3B). Be sure to cover the energy comparisons and scaling issues in Unit 3B.	Units 2C, 3A, 3B
5	Complete coverage of Chapter 3. Emphasize Unit 3C, especially significant digits (which are always important in natural science classes), and types and sizes of errors. If necessary for time reasons, skip Unit 3D on index numbers and the CPI.	Units 3C–3E
6	Begin full coverage of Chapter 5 on statistical reasoning; take plenty of time to emphasize the fundamental ideas in Unit 5A, then discuss the guidelines in Unit 5B.	Units 5A, 5B
7	Complete coverage of Chapter 5. Unit 5C should go quickly for Level 2 students, so devote most of the time to Units 5D and 5E.	Units 5C–5E
8	Begin full coverage of Chapter 6 with about a class period each devoted to Units 6A through 6C, respectively. Note that Unit 6B is particularly short and should be easy to cover in less than one full class period.	Units 6A–6C
9	Cover statistical inference (Unit 6D), then begin discussion of probability.	Units 6D, 7A, 7B
10	Continue discussion of probability with the law of averages (Unit 7C) and risk analysis (Unit 7D).	Units 7C, 7D
11	Conclude probability with Unit 7E. Then begin discussion of linear versus exponential growth with Units 8A and 8B; emphasize the bacteria in the bottle parable in Unit 8A and the ideas of doubling time and half-life in Unit 8B.	Units 7E, 8A, 8B
12	Move quickly through Unit 8C on real population growth, then devote necessary time to the logarithmic scales in Unit 8D (because all of them are used in natural science courses). Then begin discussion of functions in Unit 9A.	Units 8C, 8D, 9A
13	Cover linear and exponential modeling (Units 9B and 9C, respectively); the latter has many important natural science applications.	Units 9B, 9C
14	Cover basic ideas of geometry and applications (Units 10A and 10B). Fractal geometry is finding some application in the natural sciences. Consider covering 10C as time allows.	Units 10A, 10B
15	Class wrap-up.	—

Suggested Outline for Level 3, One Semester, Business/Finance Emphasis

General Notes:
- This outline places emphasis on topics that will be particularly useful to students planning to study business or finance, including full coverage of financial issues (Chapter 4) and network theory (Chapter 13).
- This outline assumes Level 3 students, which means a more rapid pace and more in-depth coverage is possible than assumed in previous outlines.

Week	Suggested Topics	Reading
1	Introduction: welcome, including discussion of course content and expectations regarding work load; you may wish to conduct the activity described on p. G–7 of this guide. Cover the Prologue and Units 1A and 1B; note the importance of fallacies in advertising.	Prologue, Units 1A, 1B
2	Complete coverage of logic and critical thinking in Chapter 1. Emphasize the critical thinking issues in Unit 1E, as many of them have importance to business.	Units 1C–1E
3	Cover problem solving through unit analysis in Units 2A and 2B; spend plenty of time covering the units of energy, density, and concentration in Unit 2B.	Units 2A, 2B
4	Cover Unit 2C and its examples in some depth. Then begin full coverage of Chapter 3 with Unit 3A on uses and abuses of percentages, and Unit 3B on putting numbers in perspective.	Units 2C, 3A, 3B
5	Complete coverage of Chapter 3. Emphasize Unit 3D on index numbers and the CPI.	Units 3C–3E
6	Begin full coverage of Chapter 4 on financial management; take plenty of time to discuss investment types in Unit 4C.	Units 4A, 4B, 4C
7	Continue coverage of Chapter 4, moving relatively slowly so you can go into plenty of depth on topics like home mortgages and subtleties of income taxes.	Units 4D, 4E, 4F
8	Cover government finance in depth (Unit 4E), then begin coverage of statistical reasoning.	Units 4E, 5A, 5B
9	Complete coverage of statistical reasoning with emphasis on media graphics (Unit 5D) and correlation versus causality (Unit 5E). If possible, include graphic creation (e.g., bar graphs and pie charts) with spreadsheets.	Units 5C–5E
10	Devote one week to Chapter 6, emphasizing material in Units 6A through 6C but at least briefly discussing statistical inference in 6D.	Chapter 6
11	Devote one week to probability. Have students read the entire chapter, but Units 7A and 7B should be relatively easy for Level 3 students. Emphasize expected values in Unit 7C and risk analysis in 7D.	Chapter 7
12	Devote one week to Chapter 8 on exponential astonishment, with emphasis on understanding doubling times and half-lives.	Chapter 8
13	Cover linear and exponential modeling; the material in Unit 9A on functions and 9B on linear modeling should be almost entirely review for Level 3 students.	Chapter 9
14	Cover network theory applications in Chapter 13. If time remains, also cover voting and other political issues in Chapter 12.	Chapter 13 (Chapter 12)
15	Class wrap-up.	—

Notes on Two-Semester Courses

If you are among the lucky few instructors with a full-year course in quantitative reasoning, it should be possible to cover the entire book while also having time for extensive problem solving and projects. Rather than giving a specific outline here, we give just a few general notes.

General Notes:

- The 13 chapters in the book contain a total of 57 units. Thus, in typical full-year course consisting of 30 contact weeks, you can cover the entire book at a pace between 1.5 to 2 units per week.
- For a course aimed at pre-service elementary teachers, emphasize class discussions about how each topic could be addressed within the elementary curriculum. Assign many of the *In the News* questions so the teachers will see how important this mathematics really is to everyday life.
- For senior-level high school courses, emphasize discussions of key issues and, if Web access is available, plenty of the Web Projects.

Suggestions on Teaching Strategies

If you are new to teaching "a quantitative reasoning approach," it may at first seem a daunting challenge. The material is much more interdisciplinary than that in traditional mathematics classes (such as algebra or calculus), and student assessment involves grading a lot more writing rather than just straightforward calculations. Nevertheless, the potential rewards are equal to the challenges, as your students will appreciate the relevance of this material to their lives. Moreover, unlike other mathematics classes which stay the same from term to term, teaching this course can be much more dynamic and exciting if you work to incorporate events from the news. Below, we offer a few general suggestions that may be of use to you in teaching this course.

Creating Your Syllabus

Perhaps the single most important thing you can do to help your students achieve success in mathematics is to lay out clearly what it takes for them to succeed in your class. Preparing a detailed syllabus is a crucial first step in this process, as it then becomes the reference for students whenever they have questions about class logistics or if they begin to struggle or fall behind. We believe that an ideal syllabus should include all of the following:

- General background information, including:
  - Your name, office location, office hours, e-mail address, and personal web address (if any).
  - Similar information for your teaching assistants, if any.
  - A brief, bulleted list of topics you will cover in your course.
- Detailed description of your grading policies, including:
  - A clear list of all work required in the course, such as homework assignments. E.g., do you intend to assign homework daily or weekly? Where and when must each assignment be turned in? (See below for a discussion of homework and testing strategies.)
  - A clear description of how you will determine final grades. E.g., percentage weighting of exams, homework, class participation, etc. Also be sure to list penalties for late homework, failure to attend an exam, or etc.
- A detailed schedule that lists the reading to be completed prior to each class period, the due dates for all written assignments, and the dates of all exams. E.g., fill in a grid similar to the following sample:

Mondays		Wednesdays		Fridays	
Mar 4	Reading: Units 5A, 5B *Homework 7 due*	Mar 6	Reading: Unit 5C	Mar 8	*Midterm Exam*

Besides the items listed above, you *may* wish to include some of the following additional items on your syllabus:
- To ensure that students understand your expectations regarding assignments that they turn in, you may wish to include the handout titled "Presenting Homework and Writing Assignments," which you can find on p. G–6 in this Instructor's Material.
- It would be nice if we could assume that all students would treat each other and you with proper respect — but we all know that this does not occur automatically these

days. We therefore suggest that you include on your syllabus, *and enforce in class*, the following guidelines; you may feel free to modify these guidelines or to copy them verbatim:

Common Courtesy Guidelines

For the benefit of your fellow students and your instructors, you are expected to practice common courtesy with regard to all course interactions. For example:

- Show up to class on time; turn off cell phones and other electronic devices.
- Do not leave class early, and do not rustle papers in preparation to leave before class is dismissed.
- Be attentive in class: stay awake, don't read newspapers, etc.
- If you must be late or leave or early on any particular day, please inform your instructor or TA in advance.

Students who do not practice common courtesy should expect their grades to be reduced substantially.

Homework and Testing

It is always a challenge to decide how to assess your students' learning, and in this course much depends on your number of students and the resources (if any) you have available to help you with grading. Nevertheless, as a general guideline, we recommend basing grades on some combination of the following:

1. Homework sets consisting of selections from the *Exercises* at the end of each unit. We generally recommend weekly homework assignments, because it makes it possible for students to budget their time in this and other courses.
2. Some set of quizzes and/or exams. E.g., you might choose short weekly quizzes, or two longer midterms, plus a final exam.
3. One or more projects, selected from the Web Projects at the end of each unit. You may wish to let students choose their own projects from the ones listed in the book.

Choosing Problems to Assign

This book has far more exercises and problems than you could reasonably assign to your students. In selecting problems for assignment, you may wish to consider the following:

- The "How to Succeed" section in the Preface of the Students Guide recommends that students in a 3-credit class expect about 3 to 5 hours per week on homework (i.e., on working problems; not counting time for reading the text). Thus, we suggest you seek to assign homework that you believe will take the average student about 4 hours to complete.
- The following guidelines can help you estimate the appropriate length for a homework assignment:
  - *Exercises* will generally take an average student roughly 4 times as long as they take you. E.g., if you can do a set of 10 exercises in 1/2 hour, the same set will take an average student about 2 hours.
  - *Web Projects* are fairly open ended and therefore may vary significantly in the time required; you should try a Web Project for yourself to estimate how long it will take your students.
  - *In the News* questions should take an average student roughly 1/2 hour each, with about half this time for finding a good article and half for writing up the answer.

Of course, these guidelines may vary depending on the level of your students and your own speed of work, so adjust accordingly from experience.

- Within the Exercise sets, the problems generally follow the order in which material is presented in the Unit; this should make it easy for you to identify exercises based on topics you wish to emphasize. The Exercises also tend to build from easier ones near the beginning to more difficult ones near the end.
- You may also wish to use homework resources on the MyMathLab site for this book.

Selective Homework Grading

Homework is often the best way for students to learn, but in many cases you will find yourself unable to grade as much homework as you would like to assign. In such cases, we recommend a selective grading strategy, implemented as follows:

- Tell students in advance that you will grade only a fraction (say, 10% to 20%) of the problems that you assign each week. Although some students will complain about turning in "extra" work that you do not grade, most will recognize that you are assigning this work for their benefit.
- Hand out detailed solutions to all the exercises you assign, so that students can check for themselves whether they did ungraded exercises correctly. You can find solutions to all the exercises in the Instructor's Guide and Solutions Manual.
- Make sure that some of the exercises that you do *not* grade appear verbatim on the exams. In that way, students will feel that working the exercises was beneficial because it helped them to do better on particular exam questions.

Homework Help and Preventing Procrastination

We encourage you to find ways to provide your students with plenty of homework help upon request. We have found that one good way is to offer unlimited help — providing that students have already tried the problems for themselves. We tell students that, if necessary, we'll even help them work until they write down a correct solution (in reality, it will rarely come to this point). This policy also has the effect of helping to prevent procrastination, because if students wait until the night before homework is due to try it, it will be too late for them to take advantage of your offer of help. (Note: if you need extra resources for homework help, your students may be eligible to make use of the Addison Wesley tutor center; consult your Addison Wesley Sales Consultant for more information.)

Projects

Projects (such as the end-of-unit *Web Projects*) can be very valuable in showing students the broad applicability of the material they learn in this course. Many of the Web projects are short and self-contained, requiring only a couple of hours of research and a short report. Others are more in-depth, such as using the Web to track a set of stocks over the course of many weeks. A few instructors have made their course almost entirely project-based — which can be great for select groups of students, as long as you can still get them to learn the more basic quantitative reasoning concepts.

Testing Strategies

In an ideal world, test questions would be as open-ended as homework assignments. However, to increase the number of concepts you can test on and to keep your grading load reasonable, you may wish to make your tests a mix of multiple choice and short answer questions. Here are a few hints:

- You can find many sample test questions in the Instructor's Testing Manual. If you write your own questions, try to write questions that serve as checks on student understanding of the particular homework problems you've assigned. This helps you justify the selective grading policy above and also gives you a way to make sure students understood their homework (and did not copy it from others). You may also wish to use testing resources on the MyMathLab site for this book.
- Short weekly quizzes (of 15 to 20 minutes each) can be very beneficial in forcing students to keep up with the class, if you are able to spare the class time. If you choose to give weekly quizzes, make solutions available immediately after the quiz so that students can think about their answers while the quiz is still fresh in their minds.
- If you choose to give weekly quizzes, we recommend that you still give at least one midterm in addition to a final exam. You may wish to have the midterm and final consist largely of questions repeated from the quizzes, as that will help students focus their studying and ensure that they learn what you consider to be the most important concepts in your course.
- If you do not give weekly quizzes, we recommend at least two midterms in addition to a final exam; otherwise, there is too much pressure concentrated on individual testing days.

Quizzes for Basic Skills

If your students are particularly weak in their mathematical skills, you might consider having them review basic skills on a "parallel track" with the regular course material. For example, you might assign a few of the book's Review Boxes (and associated exercises) each week. For each set of skills, you could then give a "must pass" quiz: if a student fails the quiz on the first try, the student must continue to take the quiz (with different questions) until passing. Adopt a grading policy whereby the grading scale declines with each subsequent try; e.g., a student getting a 95 on the first try earns an A for the quiz, but a student who fails the first time and gets 95 on the second try earns a B, and so on. The advantage of this "parallel track" approach to basic skills is that it forces students to review material that they should have learned in high school without requiring you to take class time for this material.

If you decide to follow a parallel track for skills, the following list of the book's Review Boxes will prove useful:

Review Topic	Page
Sets of Numbers	37
(e.g., natural numbers, integers, real numbers)	
Working with Fractions	86
Powers of 10	105
Percentages	135
What is a Ratio?	140
Working with Scientific Notation	153
Rounding	170
Three Rules of Algebra	223
(basic operations on both sides of an equation)	
Algebra with Powers and Roots	236
The Multiplication Principle	433
Factorials	477
Logarithms	505
The Coordinate Plane	535
Algebra with Logarithms	559

Preparing for Class

Many mathematics instructors are at first intimidated by the interdisciplinary nature of the material in this book, because it is often new to them as well as to students. However, you can easily stay ahead of your students and be prepared to conduct outstanding class sessions. We recommend the following, in particular:

- Always reread the material carefully before class, so that you will understand any student questions that might arise.
- While teaching this class, follow the news closely to look for current events that you can bring in as examples of quantitative reasoning in practice. Perhaps the most valuable news resource is the *New York Times*, but almost any good newspaper will do.
- Within your department, hold weekly meetings of all the instructors teaching this course, at which you can share resources, teaching ideas, and plans for homework assignments.

The First Day of Class

Spend some time on the first day of class going over your syllabus and the Prologue, with emphasis on the section called "How to Succeed in Mathematics" (pp. 10-11). This section emphasizes that students should expect to study 2-3 hours outside class for each hour in class. We have found that most students are *not* accustomed to this much studying in their classes, but it is crucial to success in mathematics. Thus, your students will be unaware that your class requires this much work unless you tell them so explicitly.

Structuring Class Sessions

The structure of each class period will depend on how frequently you meet and how long the class lasts. Nevertheless, we recommend a few general strategies:
- Try to begin each class by bringing in some example from current news that is relevant to the course material. You can almost always find examples having to do with statistical studies or ongoing political battles over the federal budget; if you are creative, you may find many other interesting news topics that can be tied to mathematics.
- *Expect* your students to do the assigned reading, and show that you expect it by avoiding direct repetition of what is in the book during your lectures and by asking questions of your students that check whether they have read the material. If you find that they are not doing the reading, threaten (and implement if necessary) pop quizzes on the reading.
- Use your class time to cover some of the more difficult concepts and to work through examples and case studies.
- Always spend a few minutes at the beginning of each class (after any presentation of news events) reviewing where you are in the syllabus, and save the last few minutes to review the topics covered that day.

Self-Evaluation

We recommend that instructors always ask their students for feedback on what is working and not working in their teaching, and it is especially important if you are new to this type of course. There are many ways to get this feedback; for example, you could create a midterm evaluation for students to complete. But one method we have found very effective is to include the following question on every homework assignment:

> "Comments (Please answer, but this will not be graded): How long did this homework assignment take you? Please comment on the assignment and the class in general. E.g., do you feel you are understanding the material? Do you feel that what you are learning will be beneficial to you? Other comments or suggestions?"

We have found that many students will offer extensive comments in response to this question (perhaps because they are already writing extensively for the homework). To the authors, this feedback has proven invaluable in improving teaching (and textbooks).

Chapter-By-Chapter Guide

We now present a brief overview of teaching issues related to each chapter. Following an introduction for each chapter, we list prerequisites and other comments for each unit within the chapter.

Chapter 1 Thinking Critically

This first chapter focuses on logic and critical thinking, primarily as a means of building skills that will help students solve quantitative problems later. Indeed, we have found that the primary reason students have difficulty with so-called "word problems" is not the mathematics, but rather a lack of skill at making sense of the words. Notes:

- This chapter is Chapter 1 because we have found it useful to begin with this material in a quantitative reasoning class. However, while critical thinking skills are used throughout the text, Chapter 1 is *not* an explicit prerequisite to any of the other chapters in the book. Thus, you can feel free to skip this chapter (or cover it later) if you prefer to spend your class time on other topics.
- Before you begin teaching this chapter, ask your students whether and when they have studied logic in the past. In many cases, you may be surprised to find that your students have little or no prior training in logic. For example, many college students have never used a truth table or a Venn diagram, and even more are unaware of the distinction between deductive and inductive arguments.
- A good way to introduce the logic in class is to ask students to hold an argument about the death penalty or some other controversial topic. Ask students to separate their emotional arguments from their logical arguments. Students should be able to discover the value of logic for themselves in this way. You can then discuss how the same "organized thinking" is useful in mathematics.

Unit 1A: Recognizing Fallacies

Prerequisite Units: None.
Overview: This unit is designed to give students a nonmathematical, "user friendly" introduction to logic by focusing on the analysis of common fallacies. It should go quite easily for most students, while helping them understand the idea of looking for a logical flow from premises to conclusions.
Specific Comments:

- This unit presents only a few basic concepts, then proceeds primarily with a set of 10 examples illustrating common fallacies. We urge you not to expect students to memorize the names of the fallacies, and instead only to concentrate on distinguishing reasonable from fallacious arguments.
- It should be easy to find examples of fallacies in the daily barrage of advertisements, and asking your students to look for such examples is a good topic either for assignment or discussion.

Unit 1B: Propositions and Truth Tables

Prerequisite Units: None, but 1A recommended.
Overview: This unit introduces the formal idea of a proposition and develops truth tables as a tool for analyzing propositions.
Specific Comments:
- We introduce truth tables because we believe that they help students learn to analyze propositions, and hence to build critical thinking skills. However, we do not expect students to use truth tables in their everyday lives, and therefore do not go into any more detail than is required to get the basic idea of truth tables across.

Unit 1C: Sets and Venn Diagrams

Prerequisite Units: None, but 1B recommended.
Overview: This unit focuses on defining the idea of sets and on illustrating relationships with Venn diagrams.
Specific Comments:
- For a basic overview of sets and Venn diagrams, cover only the sections of the unit through Example 5; i.e., skip the material beginning with the section head "Venn diagrams with Three Sets."
- If your students need a review of the meaning of natural numbers, integers, and etc., be sure to cover the Brief Review box and Example 3.

Unit 1D: Analyzing Arguments

Prerequisite Units: The basic ideas of deductive versus inductive argument can be covered without prerequisite; to cover the Venn diagram tests of arguments, you need the basic introduction to Venn diagrams in Unit 1C as prerequisite.
Overview: This unit covers the distinction between deductive and inductive arguments, then covers techniques for analyzing the validity of deductive arguments.
Specific Comments:
- The techniques we present for analyzing deductive validity are not the most general known, but were chosen because they are relatively easy for students to learn. We focus much of the attention on conditional deductive arguments for this reason.
- More advanced students may be particularly interested in the last section on induction and deduction in mathematics, as well as in the proof of the Pythagorean theorem that appears in the Thinking About box.

Unit 1E: Critical Thinking in Everyday Life

Prerequisite Units: None, but 1A recommended
Overview: This unit is structured as a series of hints that are useful in thinking critically, each illustrated by example.
Specific Comments:

- It is the last unit in the chapter, because it serves as a good capstone to the other units. However, it can be covered independently of the earlier units if you so choose.
- You could potentially engage in long discussions about any of the examples in this unit. Example 5 (Which Airline Ticket to Buy?) has proven to be a particular student favorite.

Chapter 2: Approaches to Problem Solving

This chapter turns to quantitative problem solving. Most of the chapter (Units 2A and 2B) focus on skills of unit analysis — one of the few problem solving skills that is actually "teachable." We discuss more general problem solving strategies in Unit 2C, but here we can proceed only by example, since there are no hard and fast rules for problem solving. Hopefully, the skills and problem solving practice developed in this chapter will enable your students to perform better at problem solving in the future. Notes:

- Unit analysis is not often covered in mathematics courses, but it is a very powerful technique for problem solving. It is a technique that will be used throughout this book, and also is used extensively in natural and social sciences.
- For these reasons, we believe it is important for all students to be familiar, at a minimum, with the techniques discussed in Unit 2A. Unit 2B is equally important if you are preparing students for core natural science courses, because it extends the discussion to standard metric units and units for energy, density, and concentration — all of which are used frequently in natural science courses.
- Nevertheless, like Chapter 1, this chapter is not an explicit prerequisite for later chapters. Thus, it is possible to skip this chapter, especially if your students are already familiar with techniques of unit analysis.

Unit 2A: The Problem-Solving Power of Units

Prerequisite Units: None.
Overview: This unit focuses on unit analysis as a valuable tool for problem solving.
Specific Comments:

- The techniques described in Unit 2A are used throughout the book. If you choose not to cover this unit, you should still make sure your students understand the basic ideas; for example, point them to the summary boxes on p. 85 ("Reading Units") and p. 93 ("Working with Units").
- Note that Example 13 tends to be a particular student favorite, because it shows the surprising effect on sea level that would occur if polar ice melted.

Unit 2B: Standardized Units: More Problem Solving Power

Prerequisite Units: 2A.
Overview: Unit 2B reviews the metric system and then focuses on units commonly used in sciences, especially units of energy, density, and concentration.
Specific Comments:

- The applications in Unit 2B are among the most practical and relevant in the entire book. In particular, your students are likely to be very interested in:
  – Example 8, which will help students understand electric bills.
  – Example13, which shows how little alcohol it takes to reach legal limits of sobriety. [Note: as indicated in the Technical Note with Example 13, we use a somewhat simplified definition of blood alcohol concentration, rather than the more common legal definition of "blood alcohol *content*." The legal definition is

somewhat easier to measure in roadside tests (one reason why it is used), but is much more difficult to work with in calculations (which is why we use the simplified definition). The two definitions differ by about 25%.]

Unit 2C: Problem Solving Guidelines and Hints

Prerequisite Units: None, but 2A recommended.
Overview: In this unit we offer a four-step procedure for problem solving modeled after Polya (Polya, G., *How to Solve It*, Princeton University Press, 1957), but also concede that there is no single process that works all the time. For the most part we proceed by example and espouse mastery through practice.
Specific Comments:
- This unit provides valuable practice at problem solving, but may be skipped without repercussions to the rest of the book. However, even if you are skipping the mechanics in this unit, we urge you to have students read and discuss the four-step procedure in the summary box on p. 119.
- Students tend to be very interested in Example 7 on China's population policy.
- More advanced students will find the discussion of Zeno's Paradox (in the Thinking About box on p. 122) to be particularly interesting.

Chapter 3: Numbers in the Real World

In some ways, this may be the most important chapter in the book. It shows students how numbers *really* are used in the media and the world around them, as opposed to the way they are *ideally* used in mathematics. Moreover, this material is virtually never covered in other mathematics courses, and thus is almost entirely new to students despite its great importance.

Unit 3A: Uses and Abuses of Percentages

Prerequisite Units: None.
Overview: This unit shows students some of the surprisingly subtle ways in which percentages can be used and misused.
Specific Comments:
- Please note that this is *not* a remedial unit on the calculation of percentages! Rather, it involves some sophisticated thinking about the meaning of percentages in the many different ways we encounter them in society.
- Note also that many instructors overestimate their students' facility with understanding statements involving percentages. For example, many students have difficulty interpreting a phrase like "up 44 percent, to 10.4 percent," and even more have trouble understanding why the fact that Car A costs 25% more than Car B means that Car B costs 20% less than Car A. This unit should alleviate these difficulties.
- Re: the cartoon on p. 143. Not everyone gets this one immediately, so in case you don't see it: Fridays and Mondays are 40% of the days in the work week, so the boss's initial statement shows that he does not recognize this fact — which is why the employee assumed he was kidding.

Unit 3B: Putting Numbers in Perspective

Prerequisite Units: None.

Overview: Students are constantly confronted with large numbers, such as $1 billion or $1 trillion. This unit shows students strategies for putting such numbers in perspective.
Specific Comments:

- We urge everyone to cover this unit. The ability to put numbers in perspective is a crucial skill in the modern world.
- Many students find the energy comparisons and the scale model solar system examples to be of particular interest. The case studies at the end of the unit also should engage your students.
- FYI: The 1 to 10 billion scale of the solar system described in Example 7 is, in fact, the scale used in a solar system exhibit on the National Mall (Washington, DC). One of the authors (Bennett) proposed this project and served as a consultant throughout its development by NASA, the Smithsonian Institution, and the Challenger Center for Space Science Education. Replicas of the exhibit are being created for many colleges and science centers around the world; if you are interested in such a replica at your institution, contact the Challenger Center's corporate office in Alexandria, VA.

Unit 3C: Dealing With Uncertainty

Prerequisite Units: None.
Overview: The topics in this unit are rarely covered in traditional mathematics classes, but they are crucial both to: (1) making sense of the many uncertain numbers we encounter in the real word; and (2) understanding the treatment of errors in significance that will be expected of students in their core natural science classes.
Specific Comments:

- The topic of significant digits, in particular, is heavily emphasized in science classes. Thus, it is important to cover if one of your goals is preparing students for such courses.
- Example 4 and the later Case Study concerning the census may prove to be of particular interest to students and may stimulate discussion about the political nature of even such a supposedly simple task as counting the population.

Unit 3D: Index Numbers: The CPI and Beyond

Prerequisite Units: None.
Overview: The primary purpose of this unit is to explain the meaning of the Consumer Price Index (CPI) and its use as a measure of inflation.
Specific Comments:

- Price comparisons across time are extremely common in the news; this unit provides the necessary background to understand such comparisons.

Unit 3E: How Numbers Deceive: Polygraphs, Mammograms, and More

Prerequisite Units: None, but 3A recommended and 3D needed for Example 5.
Overview: This unit covers several common numerical paradoxes including: Simpson's paradox; how mammogram results can be misinterpreted; how a 90% accurate polygraph test can yield false positives in far more than 10% of the cases; and how the same tax data can be given different spins by Democrats and Republicans.
Specific Comments:

- The various paradoxes discussed in this unit are in some sense independent, so you can pick and choose among the examples if you wish to cover only part of the unit.

Chapter 4: Managing Your Money

For students concerned with money — especially nontraditional students dealing with work, mortgages, taxes, or children — Chapter 4 will be their favorite chapter. It covers what we believe are all the basics of modern financial management: personal budgeting; understanding compound interest; savings plans and investments (including retirement plans); loans including mortgages and credit cards; and income taxes. It also includes a unit on government finance, with emphasis on issues of importance to everyone, such as Social Security. Please note that this chapter does *not* do "consumer math" such as balancing a checkbook — it is sophisticated financial management that should have immense practical value to your students.

When deciding if/how to present this chapter in class, keep in mind the following important notes:

- Beginning with Unit 4B, this chapter takes a noticeable jump in its algebraic sophistication compared to earlier chapters. However, we have found students are generally able to deal with this change because of the practical utility of the subject matter. The necessary algebraic skills are covered in Brief Review boxes within the chapter.
- This chapter has no prerequisites in the book, nor is it prerequisite for any later chapters. Thus, you can feel free to cover this chapter out of order. However, if you are following our book in a somewhat linear fashion, you will find its current placement effective — it comes after students have had exposure to the more basic quantitative reasoning concepts in chapters 1–3, but still early to be useful in convincing students of the practical importance of mathematics (since financial issues are so obviously practical).
- We are sometimes asked why this chapter *precedes* our chapters that cover exponential growth more generally (Chapters 8 and 9). The answer is two-fold:
  1. The financial topics covered in this chapter are immediately relevant to nearly all students; other applications of exponential growth are also important, but of somewhat less general relevance to students in non-technical majors. Thus, we placed this chapter ahead of other exponential growth topics because it should take higher priority in the event you are unable to cover both.
  2. Students can actually learn general ideas of exponential growth more easily if they have already covered this chapter: by first teaching the context of financial matters, students are much more likely to be engaged when you show them how some of the same principles can be applied more generally through the mathematics of exponential growth.

Unit 4A: Taking Control of Your Finances

Prerequisite Units: None.
Overview: This unit introduces basic principles of budgeting, emphasizing how to create your own personal budget.
Specific Comments:
- This unit is new to the fourth edition.
- Students should find this unit very useful, especially if you have them do some work with their own budgets as part of their assignments. However, since some students will not want to reveal personal data, be sure you give an option that allows them either to use fictional data or to describe their findings without giving specifics.

Unit 4B: The Power of Compounding

Prerequisite Units: None.
Overview: This unit introduces the concept of compound interest and teaches students how to use the compound interest formula.
Specific Comments:
- Note that we give students several variations on the compound interest formula: We begin with the general compound interest formula, which can be applied to all later cases. However, we then restate the formula for the common cases of interest paid annually, interest paid multiple times per year, and interest paid continuously.
- Note also that we have tried to select variables that make their meaning easier to remember, such as using *Y* for the number of years and *APR* for the annual percentage interest rate.
- The Using Your Calculator box assumes only an inexpensive scientific calculator. If your students have graphing or business calculators, or access to a spreadsheet (such as *Excel*), you may wish to show them how to do compound interest calculations with this technology.

Unit 4C: Savings Plans and Investments

Prerequisite Units: 4B.
Overview: This unit has two major sections: First, it shows how to calculate the growth of savings plans (such as retirement plans), to which periodic (usually monthly) contributions are made. Second, it covers various investment types (e.g., stocks, bonds, cash) in which savings plans are often invested; note that it also includes discussion of how to read the financial tables that appear in newspapers.
Specific Comments:
- The formula that we call the *savings plan formula* is more commonly called the *ordinary annuity formula*. However, the term *savings plan* is much more familiar to students. In addition, use of this term allows us to separate the units on investment annuities and installment (amortized) loans, which we have found to be a good way to present this material to students.
- Perhaps the most difficult part of this unit for many students will be button pushing on their calculators. And again, we provide a step-by-step procedure that will work on basic scientific calculators. If your students have access to more sophisticated calculators or computer spreadsheets, you may want to teach the use of such tools.
- In the main text, we motivate but do not derive the savings plan formula; the derivation appears in the Thinking About box on p. 230. This gives you the flexibility to choose whether you want to cover the derivation in class or simply to have students use the formula without derivation.
- When covering the material on investment types, we urge you to bring in examples from financial pages. Our favorite sources are the New York Times Business section and the Wall Street Journal.
- Figure 4.4 shows the historical values of the Dow through the end of 2003. As this book goes to press in mid-2004, the stock market has fallen spectacularly from its earlier high levels. It will surely be interesting to discuss how the stock market has changed since the book was printed.

Unit 4D: Loan Payments, Credit Cards, and Mortgages

Prerequisite Units: 4B, 4C.

Overview: This unit builds on the work with compound interest, but turns attention to loans on which interest is charged. Specifically, this unit covers installment (amortized) loans, credit cards, and mortgages.

Specific Comments:
- Note that what we call an *installment loan* is also called an *amortized loan*. We believe the term *installment* is much more accessible and descriptive for students.
- We start this unit with the rather uncommon example of *equal* principal payments on a loan. We believe this approach helps remove some of the mystery that usually accompanies the loan payment formula.
- As with the savings plan formula in Unit 4B, we give the loan payment formula without derivation in the text; however, the derivation appears in the Thinking About box on p. 255 for those instructors who wish to cover it.
- The sections on credit cards and mortgages can engender a lot of class discussion about dealing with debt. If you have older, nontraditional students, the section on mortgages may be of particular interest.

Unit 4E: Income Taxes

Prerequisite Units: None.
Overview: This unit provides an overview of how federal income taxes work, as well as discussions of FICA taxes, tax deductions, and issues of tax fairness.
Specific Comments:
- For most mathematics teachers, this unit may be as "non-traditional" as any in the book; indeed, we've found that a substantial fraction of mathematics professors are unfamiliar with the income tax issues covered in this unit. Nevertheless, we believe it is also among the most practical units in the book: for the vast majority of students, who generally have relatively simple tax returns, this unit should provide the confidence they need to do their own taxes rather than paying fees for tax preparation help.
- Note that all the calculations in this unit are based on 2006 tax tables. Tax laws and rates change frequently. Nevertheless, the basic ideas of tax law appear unlikely to change in a major way, so the unit should still be relevant. If you want your students to work with more up-to-date tax tables, they are available on the IRS Web site.
- Many topics in this chapter can stimulate in-class discussions, particularly on fairness issues. For example, would a flat tax be fairer than our current progressive tax? Is it fair that Social Security tax effects low-income people much more than high-income people? Is the marriage penalty fair, and if not, how could it be changed? Are deductions such as the mortgage income deduction fair? Should capital gains be taxed at a different rate from ordinary income?

Unit 4F: Understanding the Federal Budget

Prerequisite Units: None, but 4B and 4E recommended.
Overview: This unit discusses the general makeup of the U.S. federal budget, the federal debt, and the future of Social Security.
Specific Comments:
- The see-sawing of federal budgets is usually quite interesting (and disconcerting) to students, making it a great quantitative reasoning topic.

- The section on the future of Social Security is likely to be especially surprising to your students — and perhaps to you as well — making it a great topic for class discussion.

Chapter 5: Statistical Reasoning

This chapter is the first of two chapters devoted to statistics. In this chapter, we emphasize *interpretation* of statistical studies as they are typically reported in the news, while most statistical *calculation* appears in the next chapter. Please note:

- We consider this chapter to cover statistical issues that are of fundamental importance to everyone; in contrast, Chapter 6 covers somewhat more advanced issues, and can be skipped if you do not want to spend too much time on statistics.
- There are no explicit prerequisites for this chapter, so you can cover it at any point in your course. However, we recommend covering Chapters 1–3 prior to this chapter, in order to help prepare students with critical thinking skills that they can apply to their study of statistics.

Unit 5A: Fundamentals of Statistics

Prerequisite Units: None.
Overview: The primary purpose of this unit is to introduce basic ideas of statistics including: the relationship between a sample and a population; methods of choosing a sample; and difference between an observational study and an experiment.
Specific Comments:

- This unit moves quickly and covers a lot of ground, but all of the material is fairly easy for students to understand. Nevertheless, it may take some time for the terminology to sink in, so you might want to continue reminding students of the meaning of the terminology throughout your class segment on statistics.
- Note that we introduce the margin of error in this unit without giving much explanation of how it is derived. This is because virtually all statistical reports in the news quote a margin of error, so we feel it is important for students to be able to interpret it even if they don't know where it comes from. We discuss the margin of error in greater depth in Unit 6D.

Unit 5B: Should You Believe a Statistical Study?

Prerequisite Units: 5A.
Overview: This unit offers eight guidelines for deciding whether to believe the results of a statistical study, with each guideline illustrated by examples.
Specific Comments:

- This unit offers a great opportunity to bring in a recent news report of statistical research, which you and your students can then analyze in class according to the eight guidelines.

Unit 5C: Statistical Tables and Graphs

Prerequisite Units: None.
Overview: This unit shows students how to create and interpret frequency tables and basic statistical graphs.
Specific Comments:

- This material is extremely important as tables and graphs are so commonplace, but most students find it fairly easy. Thus, you should be able to cover this unit quickly, and move on to the more advanced graphics in Unit 5D.
- If your students have access to spreadsheet software, you may wish to supplement this unit with some computer-based graphing.

Unit 5D: Graphics in the Media

Prerequisite Units: 5C.
Overview: The purpose of this unit is to show students how to interpret some of the many more complex graphs they are likely to encounter in the media.
Specific Comments:
- Note the emphasis in this unit is on interpreting graphics, as opposed to creating them.
- This unit also offers a great opportunity to bring in examples of media graphics from recent newspapers or magazines. *USA Today* can be a particularly good source of examples.

Unit 5E: Correlation and Causality

Prerequisite Units: None, though 5A through 5C are very useful.
Overview: This unit focuses on the distinction between correlation and causality, and on methods of establishing causality; as part of the discussion, the unit introduces scatter diagrams and types of correlation.
Specific Comments:
- Mistaking correlation for causality is one of the most common errors made by lay people considering statistical data. This unit should help ensure that your students will no longer make this common error.
- The case studies in this unit should be of particular interest to students, especially the one on global warming.

Chapter 6: Putting Statistics to Work

This chapter continues the discussion of statistics at a slightly higher level, showing students the difference between various measures of central tendency (e.g., mean, median, mode), the meaning of variation, the importance of the normal distribution, and basic ideas of statistical inference.

Unit 6A: Characterizing a Data Distribution

Prerequisite Units: 5A–5C.
Overview: This unit covers several basic ways of characterizing data sets, including measures of central tendency (mean, median, mode), shapes of distributions (number of peaks; symmetry or skewness), and a qualitative introduction to variation (dispersion).
Specific Comments:
- Note that we do *not* use summation notation in this unit, as it is not necessary for understanding the concepts. However, you may wish to introduce this notation, particularly if your students are comfortable with symbolic manipulation.
- If your students have graphing calculators or spreadsheets, you may also wish to supplement this unit by showing students how to enter data and compute means and medians.

Unit 6B: Measures of Variation

Prerequisite Units: 6A.

Overview: This unit discusses the importance of variation and several measures of variation including range, quartiles and the five-number summary, and standard deviation.

Specific Comments:
- The Big Bank/Best Bank example of different queuing strategies can make for an interesting class discussion about lines at grocery stores, theatres, and etc.
- Note that while we show students how to calculate the standard deviation for a small data set, this method becomes tedious with larger data sets. Thus, the emphasis is on *interpreting* the standard deviation, which is why we include the "range rule of thumb."
- As with Unit 6A, if your students have graphing calculators or spreadsheets you may wish to show your students how to use them for variation calculations.

Unit 6C: The Normal Distribution

Prerequisite Units: 6A, 6B.

Overview: This unit focuses on the normal distribution and its interpretation.

Specific Comments:
- If you wish to cover the normal distribution in less depth, cover the unit through the 68–95–99.7 Rule and Example 5, but skip the material beginning with Standard Scores.

Unit 6D: Statistical Inference

Prerequisite Units: 6A–6C.

Overview: This unit focuses on three important ideas of statistical inference: statistical significance, the margin of error, and hypothesis testing.

Specific Comments:
- Each of the three major sections of this unit (statistical significance, the margin of error, and hypothesis testing) is essentially independent of the others, so you may choose to cover only particular topics within the unit.
- We are sometimes asked why this unit precedes the chapter on probability (chapter 7), even though the idea of probability is important to statistical inference. The answer is that at the level of detail to which we go in this unit, we use the idea of probability only in its everyday sense. That is, none of the computational skills covered in Chapter 7 are needed here, so it makes sense to keep this unit with the other material on statistics.

Chapter 7: Probability — Living With the Odds

Thanks in part to the rising popularity of legal gambling and lotteries, probability is now a favorite topic for many students. This chapter covers the fundamental ideas of probability. Although we place a fair amount of emphasis on applications to gambling, we also show students some of the many other uses of probability theory, including its use in assessing risk.

Unit 7A: Fundamentals of Probability

Prerequisite Units: None.

Overview: This unit describes three basic ways of finding probabilities: theoretically, empirically, and subjectively. It also develops basic techniques for calculating theoretical probabilities, with emphasis on simple examples involving coins and dice.

Specific Comments:
- Most students need to be led carefully through the step-by-step process of making a probability distribution, but aside from that, most students find the material in this unit fairly easy to grasp.

Unit 7B: Combining Probabilities

Prerequisite Units: 7A.

Overview: This unit focuses on methods for combining probabilities multiplicatively or additively.

Specific Comments:
- Students generally learn the separate methods for *and* probabilities (independent and dependent events) and either/or probabilities (mutually exclusive and non-mutually exclusive events) without too much difficulty, but it takes them a lot of practice to know *when* to apply the appropriate method. Thus, it's useful to cover many examples to help the students gain experience with this issue.
- Note that we introduce what we call the "at least once rule" to cover the case where we seek a probability of an event happening at least once in a set of *n* trials. We do so because this case is so common in real-life situations, and have found this rule to be very useful to students.

Unit 7C: The Law of Large Numbers

Prerequisite Units: 7A, 7B.

Overview: This unit turns to the ideas of the law of averages and expected values, covering some of their many applications.

Specific Comments:
- For the general public, the law of averages and the related "gambler's fallacy" are among the most misunderstood ideas of probability. Thus, this unit may save your students from some very bad days in casinos!
- The concept of an "expected value" is particularly difficult for many students, largely because of the poorly chosen name: it is *not* to be expected *except* as the average of a large number of trials. You'll need to emphasize this point in class.

Unit 7D: Assessing Risk

Prerequisite Units: 7A.

Overview: This unit covers ways in which probabilities are assigned to various risks from empirical data. Emphasis is on risks of travel (air versus car), vital statistics, and life expectancy.

Specific Comments:
- With regard to the issue of acceptable risk (as discussed in the opening parable of the salesman), you may wish to discuss smoking: it is another known risk that many people take anyway.
- Like "expected value" (Unit 7C), the term life expectancy is frequently misunderstood. In particular, students often assume that it tells them how long they can expect to live, when in fact it is based on current demographics and may change in the future with changes in the economy or in medical technology. We have tried to be clear on this point, but it should be emphasized in class.

Unit 7E: Counting and Probability

Prerequisite Units: 7A, 7B.
Overview: This unit focuses on three counting techniques —arrangements with repetition, permutations, and combinations — and their applications to probability.
Specific Comments:
- Although the mathematics in this unit is really nothing more than simple arithmetic, this material can be difficult for many students. If your students have weak mathematical background, you may wish to skip this unit.
- The birthday coincidence examples (Example 8) take some effort to work through but will surprise and delight students.

Chapter 8: Exponential Astonishment

This chapter covers the difference between linear and exponential growth, with emphasis on the astonishing character of the latter. It includes discussion of doubling time and half-life, of real population growth, and of the use of logarithmic scales. Note that:
- This chapter does not include the general exponential equation; that comes in Unit 9C, after we discuss functions and modeling.
- This chapter can be covered without prerequisites; however, for reasons discussed above (in the notes for Chapter 4), we feel it is pedagogically advantageous to cover Chapter 4 first.

Unit 8A: Growth: Linear Versus Exponential

Prerequisite Units: None.
Overview: This short unit introduces the difference between linear and exponential growth, then discusses the impact of doubling with three parables designed to show students the surprising properties of exponential growth.
Specific Comments:
- Students generally enjoy all three parables; the latter one on bacteria in the bottle can be especially thought-provoking.

Unit 8B: Doubling Time and Half-Life

Prerequisite Units: 8A.
Overview: This unit introduces the ideas of doubling times and half-lives, showing how to work with them in calculations and how to find them from percentage growth or decay rates.
Specific Comments:
- Most of this unit is mathematically simple, including the approximate formulas given for doubling time and half-life. If you wish to avoid discussing logarithms, simply skip the last section on exact formulas.
- The exact formulas at the end of the unit involve logarithms, but no algebraic manipulation is required. Thus, you could choose to have your students use the formulas by learning to use the log key on their calculators, even if they still don't really understand logarithms; if you want them to understand logarithms, cover the Brief Review box that goes over their definition and meaning. The derivations of the exact formulas come in Unit 9C.
- If you wish to go deeper into exponential growth immediately, you can cover Unit 9C after 8B.

Unit 8C: Real Population Growth

Prerequisite Units: 8A, 8B.
Overview: This unit talks about issues of future growth of world population, including the questions of how we might try to determine the Earth's carrying capacity and whether population will continue to grow, level out, or decline.
Specific Comments:
- This unit is mostly qualitative, but generally of great interest to students. You can supplement this topic with population issues from the news, which seem to come up quite regularly.

Unit 8D: Logarithmic Scales — Earthquakes, Sounds, and Acids

Prerequisite Units: 8A, 8B.
Overview: This unit covers three commonly used logarithmic scales: the magnitude scale for earthquakes; the decibel scale for sound; and the pH scale for acidity
Specific Comments:
- This unit is especially useful as preparation for core natural science classes, since the scales used here all come up in those classes. It should also be of more general interest since most students have some familiarity with the covered topics.
- Note that, as discussed in the text, the magnitude scale for earthquakes is *not* the original Richter scale, which is no longer in use.

Chapter 9: Modeling Our World

The purpose of this chapter is to introduce students to important ideas in mathematical modeling, but it also serves as a good review of some key ideas from algebra. A few notes:
- Although we have used functions many times earlier in the book, this is the chapter in which we formally define the term. We've waited until now because many students get hung up on the jargon, and the jargon wasn't necessary until this point where we discuss modeling.
- If your students have a reasonably strong background in algebra, you may be able to skip Units 9A and 9B and move directly to Unit 9C on exponential modeling. The advantage of this strategy is that the examples in exponential modeling tend to be more interesting to students than the linear examples covered earlier.

Unit 9A: Functions: The Building Blocks of Mathematical Models

Prerequisite Units: None.
Overview: This unit serves primarily to explain the concepts of functions, graphs, independent and dependent variables, and domain and range. It also introduces the important idea of using functions to model real phenomena.
Specific Comments:
- We urge you to pay particular attention to helping students think about whether a particular function is a valid model for a particular situation.
- Please note that Example 3 on hours of daylight is actually a discrete function, since each day has a particular numbers of daylight. However, we have not called attention to this point, using the example only to show what we mean by a periodic function.

Unit 9B: Linear Modeling

Prerequisite Units: Unit 9A.

Overview: This unit shows students how models are created by focusing on the simplest types of models: those that use *linear* equations.
Specific Comments:
- This unit in essence develops the equation of a line, but tries to do so in a motivating way. We've found this technique effective for students with weak algebraic skills. For those with stronger algebraic skills, the pace may seem slow and you may wish to go directly to the examples and exercises.

Unit 9C: Exponential Modeling

Prerequisite Units: 8A, 8B.
Overview: This unit introduces the exponential function and some of its many applications.
Specific Comments:
- We have placed this unit in the chapter on modeling, which allows us to use the term function as defined in Unit 9A. However, if your students already know what a function is, you can cover this unit as part of your coverage of exponential growth; in fact, it can be covered any time after you have covered Unit 8B.
- The algebraic manipulation of exponential equations, which is covered in this unit, is also useful for manipulating the financial formulas in Chapter 4.
- As a result, some instructors may wish to devote a block of classes to exponential growth, covering in order: Chapter 4, Chapter 8, Unit 9C.

Chapter 10: Modeling with Geometry

This new chapter was partly compiled from two sections on geometry from the previous edition. New material is in 10B and includes concepts in angular versus physical distance, working with latitude and longitude, and how tall to make your house.

Unit 10A: Fundamentals of Geometry

Prerequisite Units: None.
Overview: This unit provides a quick overview of important concepts of geometry that are used in the rest of the chapter.
Specific Comments:
- For students with stronger mathematical backgrounds, much of this unit will be review. However, few students have studied the material that comes under the sections on "Scaling Laws" and the "Surface Area to Volume Ratio."

Unit 10B: Problem Solving with Geometry

Prerequisite Units: Unit 10A.
Overview: This unit offers some interesting applications for basic geometry.
Specific Comments:
- This unit covers topics and examples rarely covered in other math courses. Most of the applications require little more than high school geometry.

Unit 10C: Fractal Geometry

Prerequisite Units: Unit 10A.
Overview: This unit offers a brief introduction to the subject of fractal geometry.
Specific Comments:

- This unit is somewhat more mathematically sophisticated than most other units in the book, and we recommend it only for students with a reasonably strong background in algebra and geometry.

Chapter 11: Mathematics and the Arts

Chapter 10 is the first of three "further applications" chapters that are designed to show students some of the breadth of applications of mathematics. This chapter focuses on connections between mathematics and the arts, while the next two chapters focus on politics (voting and apportionment) and business (network theory), respectively. You can cover these chapters in any order. A few notes:

- Many students find this chapter interesting, but it is especially designed to appeal to art-oriented students who might not otherwise appreciate the relevance of mathematics to their lives.
- Note that this chapter also includes an introduction to geometry (Unit 10A) that can be of more general benefit and an introduction to fractal geometry (Unit 10E) that may appeal to students with an interest in natural sciences as well as to art students.

Unit 11A: Mathematics and Music

Prerequisite Units: None.
Overview: This unit explains the basic mathematical ideas underlying music and harmony.
Specific Comments:
- Although it can be used with any students, this unit is aimed at students with some understanding of music. We particularly recommend it if you are dealing with music majors.
- Note that Example 2 uses the exponential function introduced in Unit 9C, so you may wish to skip this example if you have not covered that unit.

Unit 11B: Perspective and Symmetry

Prerequisite Units: Unit 10A.
Overview: This unit covers the ideas of perspective and symmetry in art, with many examples from famous paintings.
Specific Comments:
- Be sure that your students carefully study the paintings shown in this unit, so that they appreciate the mathematical ideas contained within them.
- You can do many activities with art-oriented students, such as analyzing other paintings or having them make their own sketches with perspective and symmetry.

Unit 11C: Proportion and the Golden Ratio

Prerequisite Units: Unit 10A.
Overview: This unit covers the idea of proportion in art, with special attention to the golden ratio.
Specific Comments:
- The golden ratio makes a good topic for discussion, particularly with regard to whether it truly has greater aesthetic appeal than other ratios.

Chapter 12: Mathematics and Politics

This chapter presents an introduction to the mathematics of voting, apportionment, and redistricting. It should be of general interest to nearly all students, especially given recent controversies over voting systems and the ongoing debate over methods of Congressional redistricting, which should be in the news more and more as the 2010 Census appoaches. A few general notes:

- This is the second of three "further applications" chapters, which can be covered in any order.
- We have found these topics to be fairly easy on a conceptual level, but often difficult for students because they are laden with jargon. As a result, we have worked to reduce the standard jargon that accompanies these topics; hopefully, this jargon reduction will prove beneficial to your students.

Unit 12A: Voting — Does the Majority Always Rule?

Prerequisite Units: None.
Overview: This unit begins by exploring issues that arise in elections with two candidates, then discusses several methods for choosing a winner in an election with three or more candidates: plurality; top-two runoff; sequential runoffs; point system (Borda count); and pairwise comparisons (Condorcet method).
Specific Comments:

- You may wish to start your class presentation of this topic with a discussion of students' memories (at least for older students) and feelings about the 2000 Presidential election.
- Please note that we have worked to minimize the use of jargon that usually accompanies this topic; e.g., we usually refer to a "Borda count" as a "point system" (except when precision demands otherwise) and of "pairwise comparisons" rather than a "Condorcet method."

Unit 12B: Theory of Voting

Prerequisite Units: 11A.
Overview: This unit builds on the previous unit's discussion to cover the theory of voting and Arrow's Impossibility Theorem, along with a brief discussion of voting power.
Specific Comments:

- Again, we have tried to limit jargon; e.g., we list the four standard fairness criteria simply as criteria 1, 2, 3, and 4 — rather than by standard names.

Unit 12C: Apportionment

Prerequisite Units: 11A, 11B.
Overview: This unit introduces basic ideas of apportionment, focusing on apportionment for the U.S. House of Representatives.
Specific Comments:

- This topic is often presented in a strictly chronological order, but we have instead used a presentation that we think will make the topic easier for your students. Namely, we begin by explaining why apportionment is a problem at all, then discuss various apportionment methods and the fairness issues associated with them.

Unit 12D: Dividing the Political Pie

Prerequisite Units: None.
Overview: This unit discusses the ideas that underlie Congressional redistricting, and shows examples of how the drawing of districts can be politically manipulated.
Specific Comments:
- This unit is new to the fourth edition.
- Although this topic has not traditionally been covered in introductory level mathematics courses, it is arguably more relevant than any of the other topics covered in Chapter 12. For example, while voting theory is important and interesting, it is unlikely that our voting systems will change in any major way. Similarly, apportionment, once a huge political issue, is now largely settled, with the exception of no more than a couple of House seats subject to controversy. In contrast, redistricting is almost constantly in the news, and redistricting controversies may affect outcomes for a huge proportion of the seats in Congress.

Chapter 13: Mathematics and Business

This final chapter focuses on network theory (graph theory), and in particular on its applications to business.

Unit 13A: Network Analysis

Prerequisite Units: None.
Overview: This unit introduces basic ideas of network theory, starting with the famous bridges of Königsberg problem and showing many business applications of networks.
Specific Comments:
- Although the material in this unit is quite visual and requires only arithmetic, it is unfamiliar to most students and can therefore be challenging to them, at least at first. It is also heavy with jargon, which is unfortunately unavoidable in this case.

Unit 13B: The Traveling Salesman Problem

Prerequisite Units: 13A.
Overview: This unit introduces the traveling salesman problem and some of its many variations and applications.
Specific Comments:
- It should be emphasized that while the Traveling Salesman Problem is easy to state and has many applications, there are no known efficient methods that can solve it in general.

Unit 13C: Scheduling Problems

Prerequisite Units: 13A, 13B.
Overview: This unit focuses entirely on the use of networks for mapping the flow of a project with many steps, which has important applications to business and management efficiency.
Specific Comments:
- The house building example is somewhat idealized, but should appear in particular to students interested in architecture or construction.

Time Out to Think

Below we offer answers and/or discussion points for the Time Out to Think questions in the book. The Time Out to Think questions are not numbered in the book, so we list them in order within each unit.

Unit 1A

- Not guilty does not mean innocent; it means not enough evidence to prove guilt. If defendants were required to prove innocence, there would be many cases where they would be unable to provide such proof even though they were, in fact, innocent. This relates to the fallacy of appeal to ignorance in the sense that lack of proof of guilt does not mean innocence, and lack of proof of innocence does not mean guilt.
- Students should discuss the circumstances under which character questions should be allowed in court.

Unit 1B

- We needed 8 rows for 3 propositions; adding a fourth proposition means two possible truth values for each of those 8 rows, or 16 rows total. The conjunction is true only if all four propositions are true.
- The purpose of this question is to get students thinking about how the precise definitions of logic sometimes differ from our "everyday" intuition. There is no possible way that Jones could personally eliminate all poverty on Earth, regardless of whether she is elected. Thus, at the time you heard her make this promise, you would certainly conclude that she was being less than truthful. Nevertheless, according to the rules of logic, the only way her statement can be false is if she *is* elected, in which case she would be unable to follow through on the promise. If she is not elected, her claim is true (at least according to the laws of logic).

Unit 1C

- The set of students in the mathematics class could be described by writing each student's name within the braces, separated by commas. The set of countries you have visited would be written with the names of the countries within the braces. The purpose of finding one more example is to get students to think further about the idea of sets.
- This question offers a quick check as to whether students understand the Venn diagram in Figure 1.18. They should see that the statement *some teachers are not men* leaves both questions posed in the time-out unanswered. Thus, from the statement given, it is not possible to know whether some teachers are men. From this, it also follows that we cannot be sure that none of the teachers are men.
- Changing the circle for boys to girls is fine, since a teenager is either one or the other. It would also be fine to change the circle for *employed* to *unemployed*. But the set *girls*, *boys*, and *unemployed* does not work because it offers no place to record whether the teenager is an honor student.
- The purpose of this question is for students to convince themselves that the variety of colors on TVs and monitors is made from just red, green, and blue. Higher-resolution monitors use smaller or more densely packed pixels (or both).
- The two sets in this case are the opposites of the two sets chosen for Figure 1.24, so they work equally well.

Unit 1D

- Clear market research would be the best evidence on which to build the case. For example, use focus groups to react to the story, or show sample movie clips to groups of typical viewers.
- Students should discuss recent examples in which they've made decisions either deductively or inductively.
- Changing from heroin to aspirin does not affect the argument's structure, so it is still valid. It is now also sound, because this change makes both premises true.

Unit 1E

- The pre-election polls suggest that the confusion affected the two sides differently, since the outcome was different from what polls suggested. Of course, the polls may not have been valid.
- Selling tickets in advance guarantees the airline that the seats are sold, so it is worthwhile to provide an incentive for advance sales. The cancellation penalty helps prevent the airline from losing what it thought were sold seats.
- This is a subjective question designed to spur debate.

Unit 2A

- This question should help students think about the units associated with everyday numbers. Some might even pick a page number from the newspaper or magazine, but point out that this has units of "pages." Use this question to probe whether you students really understand what we mean by units.
- This question should help students understand why the two columns must be reciprocals of one another (at least approximately).
- The main point of this question is to make sure your students can get the right value for the peso from a currency table. However, particularly if the value has changed from that listed in Table 2.1, you can use this question to start an interesting discussion of economic factors that might have affected the peso's value. Some factors to consider: inflation rate of Mexican and U.S. economies; growth rates of the economies; political stability; trade between the two countries.
- Such a rise in sea level would inundate many low-lying but heavily populated regions, including much of Florida, the Netherlands, Bangladesh, and inhabited coral islands in the South Pacific. Beyond this type of basic fact, a class discussion might probe secondary effects on the economy and the environment (including damage to river deltas), as well as the social consequences of the changes.

Unit 2B

- The purpose of this question is to make sure students make the connection between abstract ideas of measurement and the ancient origin of units as body measures. In class, you might have everyone do this exercise, and check whether 12 thumb-widths is a reasonable average for adult foot lengths.
- Literally, a megabuck is a million dollars. But it is used colloquially to mean "a lot of money." Student can have fun thinking of other examples of the use of metric prefixes, such as "nanotechnology" for very small machines.
- Even without carrying out the conversions, it should be obvious that this is a Fahrenheit temperature; 59°C is more than halfway between the freezing and boiling points of water, which means it is well over 100°F (a precise conversion shows it is 138.2°F).

No populated place on Earth gets this hot, so the forecast of 59° must refer to a Fahrenheit temperature.
- This question should help students see the relevance of energy units to their lives. Note: many utility bills do not give the price per kilowatt-hour explicitly, but it can be calculated by dividing the total price charged for electricity by the metered usage in kilowatt-hours, both of which are almost always shown clearly.
- You have a greater total volume but essentially the same mass (except for the weight of air) when your lungs are filled with air, so your density is lower and you float better.
- The two beers contain enough alcohol to put you at 12 times the legal limit if it were all in your bloodstream at once. Given the metabolic absorption rate, you should wait at least 3 hours before driving.

Unit 2C

- It should be straightforward for students to see the 4 steps in any of the examples, but will reinforce the idea of how the Polya problem solving process works.
- This question simply checks that students followed Example 1.
- This question simply checks that students followed Example 4.
- This question simply checks that students followed Example 6.

This is a subjective question designed to spur debate.

Unit 3A

- This question reinforces an idea that, while simple, often gives students trouble. Once they can explain it clearly in their own words, they should be ready to move on through the rest of the material in this unit.
- Students simply need to recognize that 200 is the reference value and 600 is the new value. Substituting into the relative change formula then gives:

  [(600 – 200)/200] × 100% = 200%
- The "30% off" sale means that prices are (100 – 30) = 70% of their original values — not nearly as good as a sale where prices are 30% of their original values.
- For the first question, it depends on how we define "effort." If we mean an athlete's personal effort, it is impossible to give 110% because a 100% effort already means the athlete is giving it everything he or she has. But if we define it as past performance efforts, then athletes might well exceed their best previous effort by 10%. For the second question, the answer is clearly yes, since it just means 1.1 times the *minimum* requirement.

Unit 3B

- 5% of $15 billion is $75 million — fifteen times the cost of the advertising campaign. The campaign is probably worth it, although it also depends on your profit margin for the ice cream. E.g., if you can expect a profit of $5 million or more from the additional $75 million in sales, then you'll make money by spending on the advertising. Of course, it's important to keep the uncertainty of the estimate in mind.
- The purpose of this question is to challenge students to think about the enormous implications of being able to replace ALL current energy sources with (in an ideal sense) a single fusion reactor on a small creek. A good offshoot to this question is to ask how much taxpayer money it would be worth spending on the effort to achieve sustained nuclear fusion. FYI: nuclear fusion plants do not have nearly the same waste disposal problem as current fission plants. The product of fusion is helium, which is a harmless gas. The only nuclear waste from fusion plants would arise because neutrons

from the fusion reactions would strike the reactor walls, gradually making the walls themselves radioactive. Not only does this mean far less nuclear waste than from fission plants, but most of the radioactive isotopes produced this way have far shorter half-lives than do uranium and plutonium, so the material does not require the same long-term disposal as fission waste.
- This question is designed only to get students to try out their own simple model.
- Detecting an Earth-like planet around a nearby star is like trying to see a pinhead orbiting a grapefruit — from a distance equivalent to that across the United States.
- Not possible. To meet 600,000 people during a yearlong campaign, the Congressman would have to visit more than 1600 people each day. Going door-to-door, there's just not enough time.

Unit 3C

- Random errors might occur by setting the time incorrectly or if your clock fluctuates in a random way. Systematic errors might occur if you deliberately set your clock a few minutes ahead or behind, or if your clock consistently runs slightly fast or slow.
- With regard to the constitutional issue, there is no correct answer and courts have been divided on the issue when it has come before them. Thus this question can generate a lively political debate. With regard to the political issue, people who are missed in the census tend to be poorer people who reside in regions typically represented by Democratic Congress members. Thus, statistical sampling is likely to increase the number of Democrats in Congress at the expense of the Republicans.
- To know your true weight, we would have to have measured it on a very carefully calibrated scale. Even in that case, it would be difficult to be sure that it is your true weight, since there are always random errors that can occur in measurement.

Unit 3D

- This question is designed to make sure that students understand index number calculations by asking them to calculate the price index using today's price.
- This question is designed to make sure that students understand how index numbers are calculated by asking them to confirm the table values.
- The two curves would cross in 1982, but the general trends would look the same.

Unit 3E

- Although women were admitted at a significantly higher rate than men in Department A, the total number of men admitted is more than five times the total number of women admitted in the department. Thus it would be difficult to say that the department favors women overall. However, it is conceivable that women gained some preference in admissions, perhaps in an effort to increase the low female enrollment. Alternatively, it may simply be that because the department is more popular among men, the relatively few female applicants tended to be more qualified (i.e., women applied only if they were very confident of their abilities). Without investigating the applicant pools in more depth, we cannot draw any conclusion about discrimination.
- This question can be used to spur student discussion of various factors that should play into decisions about biopsies. Shades of gray should emerge, as students realize that an all or none answer is not really appropriate for either question. Some discussion points that might arise: if a woman has previously had breast cancer, a biopsy might seem like a particularly good idea. Similarly, if there is a strong family history of breast cancer,

the biopsy might also be recommended. The question might also spur students to discuss whether or how much of a factor *cost* should play in the decision.

• This question should spur discussion about how people view polygraph results. There is a 90% chance that you'll pass the test, in which case the police would presumably begin to believe in your innocence. However, there is a 10% chance that you'll fail. If the police are aware that most people who fail are still actually innocent, then this might not hurt you. However, most people assume the tests are very reliable, and the police are therefore likely to be even more adamant about your guilt if you fail the test.

Unit 4A

• This question is designed to get students thinking about how they might categorize their own expenses for a budget.
• This subjective question should help students think about short-term versus long-term financial priorities.

Unit 4B

• Doubling the interest rate from 2% to 4% changes the total amount after 535 years from about $9 million to $290 billion — more than 30,000 times as much money in the end.
• With $n = 1$, we get back the formula for compounding once a year. This should be the case because annual compounding means $n = 1$.
• This time out is designed to make sure that students find the e key on their calculator and become acquainted with its value.
• You may have a choice of investments with different expected average returns (and different levels of risk). The comparison may therefore still help you decide which type of investment is best for you, given the amount you have to deposit. For example, suppose you have a choice between a high risk mutual fund that historically averages 10% return and a low risk CD that offers 7% return. If you have $30,000 to deposit in the college fund now, the low-risk investment may be the best bet because you'll be assured of reaching your $100,000 goal. But if you have only $16,000 available now, you might choose the higher risk in hopes that the higher return will get you to your goal. FYI: the specific calculations are still valid if the APY at the assumed interest rate turns out to be the average annual interest rate; we cover this in more detail in Unit 4B.

Unit 4C

• Your best choice in any particular situation will depend on your financial circumstances. Most people don't have nearly $30,000 to put into a savings account, and therefore would opt for the regular payments of a savings plan. However, if you are lucky enough to get a sudden windfall of at least $30,000, such as an inheritance, you might decide to use it as a lump sum for the college fund.
• The highest average return comes from small company stocks, but the worst year for these stocks is much worse than the worst year for any other category, confirming their high risk. The worst year for cash involved virtually no loss, showing the low risk. But cash also generates the lowest average return.
• Of course, there is no correct answer to this question. But it should get students thinking about the factors that determine the future direction of the market, and can stimulate an interesting class discussion about whether the historical gains can be sustained.

Unit 4D

- This question should help students realize how installment loans work. More than half the payment goes to interest because it is early in the loan term when the balance is high, and the 9% interest rate is calculated on this entire balance. Late in the term, when the balance is low, interest will make only a small portion of the payments. For example, when the balance is down to $500, the monthly interest is only $0.0075 \times \$500 = \$3.75$, so almost all of the $95.01 monthly payment will be going to principal at that point.
- Answers will vary, but in general: the shorter term loan is better if you can afford the higher monthly payments; the longer term loan is better if you need to minimize your monthly payments.
- As long as there are no hidden fees, yes! The lower interest rate will save in total interest during the year. And the bank will require monthly payments, which should help enforce your discipline in paying off the loan. (Since the credit card requires only relatively small minimum payments, you must be self-disciplined to pay it off in a year.) Of course, all this assumes that you don't simply go deeper into debt as a result of having lower payments.
- The 15-year loan is better if you are sure you can afford the higher monthly payments; for example, if you have a stable, long-term job and plenty of savings just in case you are laid off or quit. Otherwise, the 30-year loan may be safer. For example, if you have a new job and little savings, you may not want the added risk that comes with *required* high monthly payments.

Unit 4E

- They pay different taxes because of their different filing statuses, which determine the amounts of their deductions and their tax rates. In Robert's case, he also has extra exemptions for is two children. The question of whether the outcome is fair should generate plenty of debate among your students.
- Among the many factors are maintenance cost of the house versus the apartment; utilities cost; whether you have the savings necessary for the home down payment; whether you plan to live in the house short or long-term; whether you think the house is a good investment; etc.
- There's no correct answer, but this question should generate plenty of debate about tax fairness issues.
- Serena pays more tax, but her tax rate is lower. With this example in mind, students can have fun debating the fairness of the capital gains tax rates.

Unit 4F

- For most people, the answer depends on whether they own a home. For homeowners, who generally owe most of the value of their home to a bank, $30,000 is usually small in comparison. For others, including students, their share of the national debt generally is larger than personal debts.
- Students should realize that the rising debt means a greater likelihood that the company won't succeed, and that getting further loans will depend on convincing lenders that the company will eventually become profitable and be able to pay back the loans.
- This is a political question, but clearly Example 4 shows that the projections must be taken with a large grain of salt. Moreover, remember that if other economic

assumptions hold true while taxes are cut or spending is increased, then the surplus will be reduced by the amount of the tax cut or spending.

- Again, this is a political question for which students should draw on their quantitative understanding of investments and the budget.

Unit 5A

- The networks would be biased toward high ratings for their own shows, so no one would believe their own studies even if they did them carefully. Nielsen is an independent company, so in principle is not biased and is more likely to deliver fair ratings.
- In this case the confidence interval is all above 50%, so she can be (at least) 95% confident of winning.

Unit 5B

- The primary difficulties involve what constitutes "resting." Does it mean sleeping? If so, does it depend on whether you are dreaming when heart rate is measured? And so on…

Unit 5C

- The relative frequency for each category represents its fraction of the total. Thus, when all categories are included, the total relative frequency must be the whole of 1.
- Star ratings at restaurants, numbers on player uniforms, social security numbers, telephone numbers, etc. .
- China is the world's most populous country (though India is quite close), so its per capita emissions are much lower than those of the US and other more developed countries. India's per capita emissions are even lower. On a graph of per capita emissions, the U.S. still ranks first, but Canada is very close. China and India are the lowest in per capita emissions. This has important implications to efforts to slow global warming: the less developed countries have an economic interest in development, but if their per capita emissions rise to the level of current developed countries the world will have far more carbon dioxide going into the atmosphere.
- One possible advantage is the pie chart makes it obvious that the total of all the listed categories is 100%, whereas the bar graph does not. Generally, however, most people find it easier to interpret bar graphs than pie charts.

Unit 5D

- Answers will vary depending on the map chosen, but this question should help students understand the meaning of the contours.
- The large rise in recent times has been bringing women toward parity (50% of the competitors). It certainly seems reasonable to think that this parity will be achieved within a few years. However, since it is unlikely that the percentage of men will ever fall much below 50%, the upward trend should slow as parity is approached.
- The graph shows the speed increasing by a factor of 10 every 5 years, which means a factor of 100 in 10 years. Thus speed is predicted to increase from 10^{11} calculations per second to about 10^{13} calculations per second. The steep slope of Figure 5.24b makes it very difficult to make the same prediction with this graph.

Unit 5E

- If a gene makes people prone to both smoking and lung cancer, then this gene would cause them to smoke and also cause them to get lung cancer. In that case, it is the gene, not the smoking, that caused the lung cancer. Note that this question foreshadows the later discussion of possible explanations for correlations by asking students to see how a common underlying cause (the gene) might have led to the observed correlation between smoking and lung cancer.
- This question checks whether students understand how a scatter plot is constructed.
- This is a subjective question that calls on students' ability to argue clearly.
- This question asks students to check the global warming discussion against the principles for establishing causality, which should help them understand why the scientific consensus strongly supports the idea that this is a serious issue for humanity.
- This is a somewhat subjective question, but be aware the scientific consensus is now clearly in the category of "beyond reasonable doubt."

Unit 6A

- In this case, saying that the average contract offer is zero also seems a bit misleading (just as did saying it is $750,000 if we used the mean). Thus, this question asks students to think about the everyday meaning of average in more precise terms..
- Assuming the administration uses 12 faculty members to teach the 12 classes, they could simply redistribute assignments so that each of the 3 courses uses 4 faculty teaching sections of 25 students each. The advantages and disadvantages of such a change are a matter of opinion, but a few factors to consider: redistributing means students will have fairly small classes all around, which is generally a good thing, but will not have the benefit of the extra small class that they now have in one case. Other factors may also be involved, such as having only one qualified faculty member for one of the courses.
- In either a right-skewed or left-skewed distribution, the mean is further away from the mode (center) than the median, which shows that the mean is affected by outliers and the median is not.
- In statistics, it refers to a distortion away from symmetry.

Unit 6B

- This question asks students to think about how the single line helps keep the variation small, then asks them to consider places they frequent where the two different line approaches are used.
- This question just asks students to notice the sense in which the standard deviation is an average of the individual deviations. Astute students may recognize that the larger deviations are more heavily weighted in the calculation as a result of taking the squares.

Unit 6C

- No; the 100th percentile is defined as a score for which 100% of the data values are less than or equal to it. Thus it must be the highest score, so no one can score ABOVE the 100th percentile.
- The most likely explanation is that a minimum height is thought necessary for the army. If there is any maximum height, it must be taller than most men (since men make up

much of the army), which means it is much taller than most women. The issue of fairness is subjective.

Unit 6D

- This is a quick check on student understanding of the concept. The probability is 0.01, or 1 in 100, that results occurred by chance. This is certainly strong evidence in support of the herbal remedy, but by no means does it constitute proof.
- This question is somewhat subjective, but 95% confidence seems reasonable for most surveys, which have no need to be perfect. However, for something of great importance, such as deciding an election, it is far too low. That is why elections must be decided by letting everyone vote, not through statistical sampling.
- The null hypothesis is "the suspect is innocent." A guilty verdict means rejecting the null hypothesis, concluding that the suspect is NOT innocent. A "not guilty" verdict means not rejecting the null hypothesis, in which case we continue to assume that the suspect is innocent.

Unit 7A

- Birth orders of BBG, BGB, and GBB are the outcomes that produce the event of two boys in a family of 3. We can represent the probability of two boys as P(2 boys). This problem is covered later in Example 2.
- The only change from the Example 1 solution is that the event of a July 4 birthday is only 1 of the 365 possible outcomes, so the probability is 1/365.
- (Should be covered only if you covered Unit 6D). The experiment is essentially a hypothesis test. The null hypothesis is that the coins are fair, in which case we should observe the theoretical probabilities. The alternative hypothesis is that the coins are unfair. The results in this case do not differ significantly from the results expected under the null hypothesis. Therefore we do NOT reject the null hypothesis, so we lack sufficient evidence for claiming that the coins are unfair.
- Four coins have $2^4 = 16$ possible outcomes, but only five possible events: 0 heads, 1 head, 2 heads, 3 heads, and 4 heads.

Unit 7B

- the same reasoning suggests that the probability of rolling a 6 in 6 rolls is 6/6, or 1. But you're certainly not guaranteed getting a 6 in 6 rolls of a die, any more than you are guaranteed to get heads if you toss a coin twice. Thus the Chevalier's method for combined probability must be incorrect.
- Replacing the candy makes the events independent, so the probability is the same on each draw. In contrast, eating a chocolate on the first draw lowers the probability of chocolate on the second draw because there are (proportionally) fewer chocolates left in the box. Therefore the probability is greater when you replace the candy.
- Based on Example 7, there is more than a 1 in 3 chance that a 100-year flood will not occur during any 100-year period — a result that surprises many people. But given this substantial probability of no flood in 100 years, you should not be surprised if a 100-year flood has not occurred in the past century. And you certainly should not use this fact to become complacent about the prospect of a flood in future years.
- The small change in probability has a big effect if the game is played often enough. Casinos can count on many games by many people. Therefore they can set the odds only slightly below even, which means almost half the people will feel "lucky" because they won, while still being assured of a tidy profit.

Unit 7C

- This question should help students understand how expected values depend on large enough numbers for the law of averages to be relevant. On a single policy, we can only state a probability, not an expectation. For a probability of 1/500, even 1,000 policies is too small to count on the law of averages. But by a million policies, the expected value ought to be a good approximation of reality.
- This question should make a good starting point for a debate over the impact of lotteries on citizens.
- No. This is the gambler's fallacy in action. As long as the chance of rain on one day is independent of the chance on another, the prior drought has no effect on the probability of rain the next day. Some students will point out that the climate is complex, and one day's weather is not fully independent of prior days weather. However, for the purposes of this question, this subtlety can be ignored…
- The casino can lose money on gambling only if the number of bets placed is too small for the law of averages to come into play. For popular casinos, this is a near-impossibility; that is, the casino is virtually guaranteed to win overall — and win by almost precisely the house edge — on the thousands or millions bets made daily. Of course, a casino can still lose money on other operations, such as its overhead expenses, restaurant operations, and so on.

Unit 7D

- Among many other common measures are fatalities per person, fatalities per trip, and fatalities per hour traveled. Because there are so many fewer airline fatalities per year, flying would appear safer in terms of fatalities per person (in the overall population). The overall question is subject to great debate, and this question simply aims to make sure students argue their points well.
- For the young, stroke is very rare, and the risk from accidents is much higher. For the old, stroke is indeed a greater risk than accidents.
- Women tend to have lower death rates at every age, which may be partly due to biological factors and partly due to environmental factors such as stress. Social policy is affected because we must recognize that women outnumber men in old age. Medical and life insurance rates, if they are adjusted by sex, should be lower for women since they tend to live longer.
- Clearly, longer life spans increase the problem for social security. Beyond that, this question is subjective and students should argue logically.

Unit 7E

- Human population is about 6 billion, so both answers in Example 1 are larger by more than a factor of 10. For license plates, this effectively means the state will never run out of choices. For the passwords, the more relevant question is how long it would take a hacker to run through all 75 billion possibilities to get your password. With high-speed computers, this would not take that long, and 6-character passwords are considered inadequate for high-security applications.
- Instead of 15 players being selected 9 at a time, we have 25 players being selected 9 at a time. Therefore all the instances of "15" in the formula become 25 instead.
- This question helps get students thinking about the final topic coming up ahead, of probability and coincidence. All of the 2,598,960 possible five-card hands have precisely the same probability of 1 in 2,598,960. Thus, the probability of the particular hand described is the same as the probability of the royal flush of spades. The only

difference is that the royal flush is defined to be "special" in the game of poker, whereas most hands are considered quite ordinary. But it's interesting to note that whatever hand you are dealt, you had only a 1 in 2.5 million probability of getting that *particular* hand. Of course, you were bound to get something.

Unit 8A

- As with the bacteria, colonization of other worlds cannot keep up with continued exponential growth. There may be good reasons why we should put colonies on other planets, but solving the population problem is not one of them.

Unit 8B

- The formula tells us that the population after t = 30 years is

  $$\text{new value} = 10,000 \times 2^{\frac{30 \text{ yr}}{10 \text{ yr}}} = 10,000 \times 2^3 = 80,000,$$ agreeing with our earlier result. After 50

  years, the population is $\text{new value} = 10,000 \times 2^{\frac{50 \text{ yr}}{10 \text{ yr}}} = 10,000 \times 2^5 = 320,000.$
- This is a subjective question, but it is difficult to imagine how we could feed, clothe, and house so many people. Fortunately, the population growth rate is already declining.
- Because of its 24,000-year half-life, substantial amounts of Pu–239 will remain radioactive even after 100,000 years. Thus, safe disposal requires putting the plutonium somewhere we can be sure that no one will touch it for hundreds of thousands of years — no easy task.

Unit 8C

- Longer lifespans would mean a dramatic drop in the death rate. Unless the birth rate dropped equally dramatically, the growth rate would rise.
- This is basically a subjective question for which students must call on their knowledge of history. But many historians believe that overshoot and collapse affected many past civilizations. For example the decline of the Anasazi may have occurred, at least in part, because they overstressed their local environment, causing their agricultural production to fall.
- Food production has managed to keep up with population growth so far, so the argument comes down to faith in future technology. If we can keep up and follow a logistic model, everything will be fine. If we cannot keep up with food production, then we face overshoot and collapse, in which case Mathus's nightmare may come true.

Unit 8D

- The building should be designed so that it can roll with the ground, including being able to flex joints within it. No one has yet figured out how to make a building that can withstand any earthquake. Even well-designed buildings sometimes fail due to construction flaws.
- This question should get students to realize that pH shows up on many common products.

Unit 9A

- Students should be able to invent many variable pairs that are plausibly related.
- Dependence does not necessarily imply causality. Time moving ahead does not cause the temperature to change. The sale of snow shovels does not cause the sale of snow tires, although both variables vary together.

- Answers will vary depending on when you cover this chapter, but you'll find that many students have never paid much attention to the simple annual pattern in daylight. The fall equinox occurs near the beginning of most fall semesters; spring semesters typically begin within a few weeks after the winter solstice.

Unit 9B

- With $t = 4$, we see that $N = 41$, which is the value from the graph.

Unit 10A

- Answers will vary, but should be straightforward.
- Acute means sharp in the context of both angles and illness. Obtuse means dull, or less sharp.
- Polytheism and polyester may come up. Polyester is a synthetic made from polymer resins which are made from two or more compounds. In most cases, the suffix *poly-* means "two or more."

Unit 10B

- Quicker students will see almost at once that any route from the library to the subway that moves only east and north will have the same length. If you have covered 7A, some students will be able to get the correct answer to the "how many" question using the multiplication principle or with a tree. There are no shorter routes *along the streets*.

Unit 10C

- This question helps students to check that they understand the pattern. The L_2 segments are 1/9 the length of the L_0 segments because we have twice divided by 3. The L_3 segments are 1/27 the length of the L_0 segments.

Unit 11A

- The frequency an octave higher is 880, and an octave lower is 220.

Unit 11B

- The vanishing point goes at the place where the parallel lines appear to converge.
- Go over the painting with your students to identify the vanishing points; this can be a good class activity.
- This can be answered by going over the tiling patterns in class; also can make a good class activity.

Unit 11C

- You can find numerous other golden ratios in the pentagram; this question is designed mainly as a check that students know what they are looking for.
- This is a subjective question that should engender some interesting debate.
- The numbers are straightforward to confirm, so this question just gives students some practice.

Unit 12A

- Yes. Continuing the given example, if a vote for Sharon changes to a vote for Robert, then Robert wins by 10 to 9 instead of Sharon winning by 10 to 9.

- This is a subjective question that should spur plenty of debate in the aftermath of the 2000 Presidential election.
- This is a subjective question that should engender interesting debate. You might discuss whether your local elections (e.g., mayor) use runoff or plurality.
- There are many possible examples; college football polls are among the easiest and most interesting to study.
- Candidate A is the winner by plurality, with the most first-place votes. By a Borda count, Candidate A gets $3 \times 14 + 2 \times 12 + 1 \times 10 = 76$ points, which is the highest point total of the 3 candidates, so A is again the winner.

Unit 12B

- In general, an election in which one candidate receives a majority will meet the fairness criteria.
- This is a subjective question.
- This is a subjective question. See if they can identify a situation in which it would be appropriate or acceptable to use an approval system.
- Many people consider this to be a serious drawback to approval voting, but others do not. Student opinions will vary.

Unit 12C

- This is a straightforward calculation designed to check that students are understanding which numbers to work with when finding standard quotas. If they can't confirm the quotas quickly, you may need to spend more time in class going over the ideas of the standard divisor and standard quota.
- The Constitution does not clearly specify whether the 1 per 30,000 limit applies only to the total population and total number of representatives, or to the populations and numbers of representatives within each individual state. Washington's second point was basing his veto on the fact that 8 states had allotments of more than 1 per 30,000, but the allotment was less than this for the United States as a whole. Therefore his veto on this ground made sense only if he *assumed* the Constitution meant for this limit to apply to individual states. His wording about context was his way of justifying this assumption.
- Yes: students should verify it state-by-state.
- State C gets an extra seat by the HH method and therefore prefers this method. State D prefers Webster's method.

Unit 12D

- The 2006 elections, in which control of Congress changed from the Republicans to the Democrats, were generally more competitive than in other recent years. Still, the vast majority of Congressmen held their seats.
- Answers will vary depending on how students draw the districts, providing a good opportunity for class discussion.

Unit 13A

- Cross first to the east island over bridge e, then to the north over bridge f.
- This time out simply requires drawing Euler circuits on the given figure.
- No. Every vertex is on the Euler circuit, so you can start at any vertex.
- It should be easy to identify other circuits. There is no Euler circuit because not all vertices have an even number of edges.

Unit 13B

- This question encourages students to proceed by trial and error in search of other Hamiltonian circuits.
- Checks whether students understand how to use the formula. Very straightforward calculation.

Unit 13C

- The time along this path is 10 months. It is not the completion time because from B to C there is a longer time required along the finance edge and finance is a limiting task.

UNIT 1A

QUICK QUIZ

1. **a**. By the definition used in this book, an argument always contains at least one premise and a conclusion.
2. **c**. By definition, a fallacy is a deceptive argument.
3. **b**. An argument must contain a conclusion.
4. **a**. Circular reasoning is an argument where the premise and the conclusion say essentially the same thing.
5. **b**. Using the fact that a statement is unproved to imply that it is false is appeal to ignorance.
6. **b**. "I don't support the President's tax plan" is the conclusion because the premise "I don't trust his motives" supports that conclusion.
7. **b**. This is a personal attack because the premise (I don't trust his motives) attacks the character of the President, and says nothing about the substance of his tax plan.
8. **c**. This is limited choice because the argument does not allow for the possibility that you are a fan of, say, boxing.
9. **b**. Just because *A* preceded *B* does not necessarily imply that *A* caused *B*.
10. **a**. By definition, a straw man is an argument that distorts (or misrepresents) the real issue.

DOES IT MAKE SENSE?

15. Does not make sense. Raising one's voice has nothing to do with logical arguments.
16. Does not make sense. Logical arguments always contain at least one premise and a conclusion.
17. Makes sense. A logical person would not put much faith in an argument that uses premises he believes to be false to support a conclusion.
18. Makes sense. There's nothing wrong with stating the conclusion of an argument before laying out the premises.
19. Does not make sense. One can disagree with the conclusion of a well-stated argument regardless of whether it is fallacious.
20. Makes sense. Despite the fact that an argument may be poorly constructed and fallacious, it still may have a believable conclusion.

BASIC SKILLS AND CONCEPTS

21. a. *Premise*: 70% of the TV audience watched the last round of *American Idol*. *Conclusion*: It must be worth watching.
    b. The fact that a lot of people watched *American Idol* does not imply it is worthwhile viewing.

22. a. *Premise*: The President raised taxes last year. *Conclusion*: This year's increase in revenue is a result of the tax increase.
    b. The fact that the revenue increase followed a tax increase does not prove that it was caused by the tax increase. (Note that this argument also suffers from limited choice – other factors may be responsible for the increase in revenue – but we are focusing on the false cause aspect of the argument in this exercise.)
23. a. *Premise*: No proof exists that global warming will have bad consequences. *Conclusion*: There's no reason to be concerned about global warming.
    b. The fact that something is not proven does not imply it is untrue.
24. a. *Premise*: After a good night's rest, I swam a great race. *Conclusion*: Whenever I get a good night's rest, I'll swim a great race.
    b. The conclusion is reached on the basis of a single incident, which is an unwarranted generalization.
25. a. *Premise*: He refused to testify. *Conclusion*: He must be guilty.
    b. There are many reasons that someone might have for refusing to testify (being guilty is only one of them), and thus this is the fallacy of limited choice.
26. a. *Premise*: Millions of children have been killed or left homeless. *Conclusion*: It is imperative to contribute to relief funds.
    b. This argument compels us to contribute to relief funds based only on the emotionally charged premise that people are being killed and displaced.
27. a. *Premise*: He has an alleged history of borrowing others' work. *Conclusion*: I doubt he wrote that poem.
    b. The speaker is attacking the author's character to reach his conclusion, rather than providing evidence about the poem in question.
28. a. *Premise*: Tolerance of drugs is unacceptable. *Conclusion*: Schools must implement a zero tolerance policy toward drug use.
    b. Both the premise and the conclusion say the same thing: tolerating drugs is a bad idea.
29. a. *Premise*: Crime has been decreasing in New York City. *Conclusion*: We should not build more prisons.
    b. Attention from the real issue of building prisons (presumably in areas that could be far removed from New York) is being diverted by noting that crime in New York City is decreasing. Also, crime rates might not have much to do with the need for more prisons – there may be more important factors, such as the willingness of law enforcement to carry out its job.

30. a. *Premise*: Our Senator is proposing a bill that would increase support for single-parent families. *Conclusion*: She wants to turn this country into a welfare state.
    b. Based on our limited knowledge of the senator, we cannot conclude that she wants to turn the country into a welfare state simply because she supports support for single-parent families. The speaker has distorted the senator's position to suit her conclusion.

31. *Premises*: President Reagan built up the defense system. Afterward, the Soviet Union began to break up. *Conclusion*: Reagan is responsible for the changes leading to the demise of the Soviet Union. This argument suffers from the **false cause** fallacy. It's true that Reagan's defense buildup preceded the demise of the Soviet Union, but we cannot conclude that the former caused the latter simply because it happened first.

32. *Premise*: The Golden Rule is basic to every system of ethics in every culture. *Conclusion*: The Golden Rule is a sound ethical principle. Both the premise and conclusion say essentially the same thing; this is **circular reasoning**.

33. The question asked by the lawyer assumes this *premise*: The mother is now using or has used drugs in the past. *Conclusion*: She should not be granted custody of her children. **Limited choice** is used in this argument, as the question does not allow for the possibility that the mother does not use drugs.

34. *Premise*: Everyone is signing the petition. *Conclusion*: You should sign the petition. This is a blatant **appeal to popularity**. No argument concerning the contents of the petition is given.

35. *Premises*: My mom smoked when she was my age. *Conclusion*: I'm not going to pay attention to her request that I not smoke. This is a **personal attack** on the mother's past transgressions, which should play little part in the child's logical decision about whether to smoke.

36. *Premise*: Most of the great composers of classical music have been men. *Conclusion*: Men are better musicians than women. The conclusion has been reached with a **hasty generalization**, because a small number of male composers were used as evidence to support a claim about all men and women.

37. *Premise*: The ivory-billed woodpecker hasn't been seen in 50 years. *Conclusion*: It is extinct. **Appeal to ignorance** is used here – the lack of proof of the existence of the woodpecker does not imply it is extinct.

38. *Premise*: Both of my best teachers were women. *Conclusion*: Women make better teachers than men. Using a sample of two to make a conclusion about an entire class of people is a **hasty generalization**.

39. *Premise*: Gonzales belongs to the Sierra Club. *Conclusion*: He will not support additional logging in the national forests. This is a **personal attack**, on both Gonzales' membership in the Sierra Club, and the policies of the club, neither of which will necessarily compel Gonzales to vote one way or the other.

40. *Premises*: Violent crime among the youth is on the rise. Violence on television is concurrently on the rise. *Conclusion*: Television violence leads to real violence. **False cause** is at play here, as the existence of violence on television may have nothing to do with the rise of real violence, even though both are occurring at the same time. One could also argue for **limited choice** (there are many other factors that influence a rise in real violence).

41. *Premises*: The percentage of those over 18 who smoke has decreased from 40% of the population to 20%. During the same time, the percentage of those who are overweight has increased from 25% to 35%. *Conclusion*: Quitting smoking leads to overeating. This is **false cause**: the fact that the percentage of smokers has decreased while the percentage of overweight people has increased does not prove the conclusion. (Furthermore, we are not told whether the overweight people are in the group of smokers).

42. There are two arguments presented. *Premise*: Boys score higher on standardized math tests than girls. *Conclusion*: Boys are better at math than girls. *Premise*: Girls score higher on verbal tests than boys. *Conclusion*: Girls have better verbal skills than boys. Both arguments suffer from **hasty generalization** (using limited information about performance on tests to come to an all-sweeping conclusion) and **limited choice** (there may be reasons besides relative skills at math and language that could explain the difference in test scores).

43. *Premise*: My boy loves dolls, and my girl loves trucks. *Conclusion*: There's no truth to the claim that boys prefer mechanical toys while girls prefer maternal toys. Using one child of each gender to come up with a conclusion about all children is **hasty generalization**. It can also be seen as an **appeal to ignorance**: the lack of examples of boys enjoying mechanical toys (and girls maternal toys) does not mean that they don't enjoy these toys.

44. *Premises*: The Social Security system will be bankrupt in as few as 15 years. Senator Jacobs supports Social Security reform. *Conclusion*: Seniors who want to avoid poverty should vote for

Jacobs. An **appeal to emotion** (seniors will become poverty stricken) avoids the real issues.

45. *Premise*: The Republicans favor repealing the estate tax, which falls most heavily on the wealthy. *Conclusion*: Republicans think the wealthy aren't rich enough. (Implied here is that you should vote for Democrats). The argument distorts the position of the Republicans (none of whom would say the rich need to be richer); this is a **straw man**.

46. *Premise*: The Democrats want to raise gas mileage requirements on new vehicles. *Conclusion*: Democrats think the government is the solution to all of our problems. The argument distorts the position of the Democrats (none of whom would claim government is the solution to all of our problems); this is a **straw man**.

UNIT 1B

QUICK QUIZ

1. **c.** This is a proposition because it is a complete sentence making a claim, which could be true or false.
2. **a.** The truth value of a proposition's negation (*not p*) can always be determined by the truth value of the proposition.
3. **c.** Conditional statements are, by definition, in the form of *if p, then q*.
4. **c.** The table will require eight rows because there are two possible truth values for each of the propositions *x, y*, and *z*.
5. **c.** Because it is not stated otherwise, we are dealing with the inclusive *or* (and thus either *p* is true, or *q* is true, or both are true).
6. **a.** The conjunction *p and q* is true only when both are true, and since *p* is false, *p and q* must also be false.
7. **c.** The inclusive disjunction *Calcutta or Bombay* allows for either or both (i.e. at least one) of these words to appear in the article.
8. **a.** In this case, all of the words means both of them (as there are just two), and the conjunction *Calcutta and Bombay* means you want both of the words to appear in the article.
9. **b.** Statements are logically equivalent only when they have the same truth values.
10. **a.** Rewriting the statement in *if p, then q* form gives, "if you want to win, then you've got to play."

DOES IT MAKE SENSE?

17. Does not make sense. Propositions are never questions.
18. Does not make sense. The professor's stance on torture may not have much to do with his level of compassion.
19. Makes sense. If restated in *if p, then q* form, this statement would read, "If we catch him, then he will be dead or alive." Clearly this is true, as it covers all the possibilities. (One could argue semantics, and say that a dead person is not caught, but rather discovered. Splitting hairs like this might lead one to claim the statement does not make sense).
20. Does not make sense. The first statement is in the *if p, then q* form, and the second is the converse (i.e. *if q, then p*). Since the converse of an *if...then* statement is not logically equivalent to the original statement, this doesn't make sense.
21. Does not make sense. Not all statements fall under the purview of logical analysis.
22. Does not make sense. The converse of higher taxes lead to lower revenues is lower revenues lead to higher taxes.

BASIC SKILLS AND CONCEPTS

23. This is not a proposition because it is not a complete sentence, nor does it make a claim to which one could assign a truth value.
24. Since it's a complete sentence that makes a claim (whether true or false is immaterial), it's a proposition.
25. This is a proposition as we can assign a truth value to it, and it's a complete sentence.
26. Questions are never propositions.
27. This is a complete sentence that makes a claim (a false one in this case), so it's a proposition.
28. No claim is made with this statement, so it's not a proposition.
29. Paris is not the capital of Maine. The original statement is false, so its negation is true.
30. There has been one or less U.S. President named Bush. The original proposition is true, so its negation is false.
31. The Nile River is in Africa. The original proposition is false, so its negation is true.
32. Most years do not have 365 days. The original proposition is true, so its negation is false.
33. The city council supports the police chief.
34. The Senator is comfortable with demonstrations. Whether he approves of them is debatable, given the limited information.
35. Congress decided to honor the veto of the tax increase bill, which means Congress did not approve the bill.

36. The Senate voted to push the disaster relief bill through (over the President's objections), so the Senate supports the bill.
37. The Constitution allows for the anti-discrimination policy.
38. New treaties are allowed.
39. This is the truth table for the conjunction *q and r*.

q	*r*	*q and r*
T	T	T
T	F	F
F	T	F
F	F	F

40. This is the truth table for the conjunction *p and s*.

p	*s*	*p and s*
T	T	T
T	F	F
F	T	F
F	F	F

41. "Boston is the capital of Massachusetts" is false. "Moscow is the capital of Russia" is true. The conjunction is false because both propositions in a conjunction must be true for the entire statement to be true.
42. "Sean Penn is an American actor" is true. "Vladimir Putin is a Russian president" is true. Since both propositions are true, the conjunction is true.
43. The two propositions are "Ben is married," and "Ben is a bachelor." We can't determine the truth value for either statement, but the conjunction must be false, because both statements can't be true at the same time.
44. "12 + 6 = 18" is true, but "6 × 4 = 18" is false. Thus the conjunction is false.
45. "Cats have four legs" is true (in general), as is "Whales have no legs," so the conjunction is true.
46. "Some people are tall" is true. "Some people are short" is also true, so the conjunction is true.
47. This is the truth table for *q and r and s*.

q	*r*	*s*	*q and r and s*
T	T	T	T
T	T	F	F
T	F	T	F
T	F	F	F
F	T	T	F
F	T	F	F
F	F	T	F
F	F	F	F

48. This is the truth table for *p and q and r and s*.

p	*q*	*r*	*s*	*p and q and r and s*
T	T	T	T	T
T	T	T	F	F
T	T	F	T	F
T	T	F	F	F
T	F	T	T	F
T	F	T	F	F
T	F	F	T	F
T	F	F	F	F
F	T	T	T	F
F	T	T	F	F
F	T	F	T	F
F	T	F	F	F
F	F	T	T	F
F	F	T	F	F
F	F	F	T	F
F	F	F	F	F

49. *Or* is used in the exclusive sense because you probably can't have both the salad and dessert.
50. With most car warranties, the parts are guaranteed for either 3 years or 36,000 miles, whichever comes first, so this is the exclusive use of *or*.
51. The exclusive *or* is used here as it is unlikely that the statement means you might do both tonight.
52. This is the exclusive *or*, as you won't wear both boots and shoes at the same time.
53. This could be thought of in both ways. If the exclusive *or* is used, the shorts will be made purely of cotton or wool. The inclusive *or* allows for a cotton/wool blend.
54. Most insurance policies that cover "fire or theft" allow for the coverage of both at the same time, so this is the inclusive *or*.
55. This is the truth table for the disjunction *r or s*.

r	*s*	*r or s*
T	T	T
T	F	T
F	T	T
F	F	F

56. This is the truth table for the disjunction *p or r*.

p	*r*	*p or r*
T	T	T
T	F	T
F	T	T
F	F	F

57. This is the truth table for *p and (not p)*.

p	*not p*	*p and (not p)*
T	F	F
F	T	F

58. This is the truth table for *q or (not q)*.

q	*not q*	*q or (not q)*
T	F	T
F	T	T

59. This is the truth table for *p or q or r*.

p	*q*	*r*	*p or q or r*
T	T	T	T
T	T	F	T
T	F	T	T
T	F	F	T
F	T	T	T
F	T	F	T
F	F	T	T
F	F	F	F

60. This is the truth table for *p or (not p) or q*.

p	*(not p)*	*q*	*p or (not p) or q*
T	F	T	T
T	F	F	T
F	T	T	T
F	T	F	T

61. "The Amazon River is in South America" is true. "Beijing is in Germany" is false. The disjunction is true because a disjunction is true when at least one of its propositions is true.

62. Both "$2 \times 5 = 10$" and "$23 + 8 = 31$" are true, and thus the disjunction is true, as all you need is one proposition or the other to be true for the statement to be true.

63. The two propositions are "The light is on" and "The light is off." We can't determine the truth value for either proposition, though one of them must be true, so the disjunction is true.

64. "Sean Penn was an American president" is false. "Abraham Lincoln was an American president" is true. The disjunction is true because at least one of the propositions is true.

65. "Beethoven was a professional ball player" is false. "Gandhi was a professional ball player" is also false. Since both are false, the disjunction is false.

66. "Denver is in Colorado" is true. "Seattle is in Washington" is true. The disjunction is true,

because only one proposition need be true for a disjunction to be true.

67. Use option **a**, and search for *poverty* AND *Miami*.

68. Use options **a** and **c**, and search for (*tsunamis* OR *volcanic eruptions*) AND *Japan*.

69. Use options **a** and **c**, and search for (*museums* OR *concerts*) AND *San Francisco*.

70. Use options **a** and **c**, and search for *unemployment* AND (*Idaho* OR *Montana*).

71. This is the truth table for *if p, then r*.

p	*r*	*if p, then r*
T	T	T
T	F	F
F	T	T
F	F	T

72. This is the truth table for *if r, then s*.

r	*s*	*if r, then s*
T	T	T
T	F	F
F	T	T
F	F	T

73. *Hypothesis*: Trout can swim. *Conclusion*: Trout are fish. Since both are true, the implication is true, because implications are always true except in the case where the hypothesis is true and the conclusion is false.

74. *Hypothesis*: Italy is in Europe. *Conclusion*: China is in Asia. Since both are true, the implication is true.

75. *Hypothesis*: Italy is in Europe. *Conclusion*: China is in Africa. Since the hypothesis is true, and the conclusion is false, the implication is false (this is the only instance when a simple *if p, then q* statement is false).

76. *Hypothesis*: Italy is in Asia. *Conclusion*: China ia in Asia. Since the hypothesis is false, the implication is true, no matter the truth value of the conclusion (which, in this case, is true).

77. *Hypothesis*: $4 \times 4 = 10$. *Conclusion*: America has a queen. Since the hypothesis is false, the implication is true, no matter the truth value of the conclusion (which, in this case, is false).

78. *Hypothesis*: Hemingway was a writer. *Conclusion*: Eminem is a singer. Since both are true, the implication is true.

79. *Hypothesis*: $2 + 2 = 5$. *Conclusion*: Automobiles can swim. Since the hypothesis is false, the implication is true, no matter the truth value of the conclusion (which, in this case, is false).

80. *Hypothesis*: Bees can fly. *Conclusion*: Bees are birds. Since the hypothesis is true, but the conclusion is false, the implication is false.
81. If a person is a resident of St. Paul (*p*), then that person is a resident of Minnesota (*q*).
82. If she's in Congress (*p*), then she is a lawyer (*q*).
83. If you are considered a writer (*p*), then you are a novelist (*q*).
84. If you pass a biology course (*p*), then you meet a one-course science requirement (*q*).
85. If a person has prostate cancer (*p*), then that person is a male (*q*).
86. If you are walking (*p*), then you are living (*q*).
87. *Converse*: If Anne lives in New Orleans, then she lives in Louisiana. *Inverse*: If Anne doesn't live in Louisiana, then she doesn't live in New Orleans. *Contrapositive*: If Anne doesn't live in New Orleans, then she doesn't live in Louisiana. The converse and inverse are always logically equivalent, and the contrapositive is always logically equivalent to the original statement.
88. *Converse*: If the patient is sleeping, then the patient is alive. *Inverse*: If the patient isn't alive, then the patient isn't sleeping. *Contrapositive*: If the patient isn't sleeping, then the patient isn't alive. The converse and inverse are always logically equivalent, and the contrapositive is always logically equivalent to the original statement.
89. *Converse*: If my heart rate increases, then I am running. *Inverse*: If I don't run, then my heart rate won't increase. *Contrapositive*: If my heart rate does not increase, then I am not running. The converse and inverse are always logically equivalent, and the contrapositive is always logically equivalent to the original statement.
90. *Converse*: If it can fly, then it is a penguin. *Inverse*: If it's not a penguin, then it can't fly. *Contrapositive*: If it can't fly, then it isn't a penguin. The converse and inverse are always logically equivalent, and the contrapositive is always logically equivalent to the original statement.
91. *Converse*: If there's gas in the tank, the car's engine is running. *Inverse*: If the car's engine isn't running, then there is no gas in the tank. *Contrapositive*: If there is no gas in the tank, then the car's engine isn't running. The converse and inverse are always logically equivalent, and the contrapositive is always logically equivalent to the original statement.
92. *Converse*: If you live in Hawaii, then you live near the ocean. *Inverse*: If you don't live near the ocean, then you don't live in Hawaii. *Contrapositive*: If you don't live in Hawaii, then you don't live near to the ocean. The converse and inverse are always logically equivalent, and the contrapositive is always logically equivalent to the original statement.
93. If a young man has not wept, then he is a savage. If an old man will not laugh, then he is a fool. Opinions will vary on whether these are true.
94. If you laugh, then the world laughs with you. Opinions will vary on whether this is true.
95. If a person has no vices, then that person has very few virtues. Opinions will vary on whether this is true.
96. If a person reads nothing at all, then that person is better educated than one who reads nothing but newspapers. Opinions will vary on whether this is true.
97. "If Sue lives in Cleveland, then she lives in Ohio," where it is assumed that Sue lives in Cincinnati. (Answers will vary). Because Sue lives in Cincinnati, the hypothesis is false, while the conclusion is true, and this means the implication is true. The converse, "If Sue lives in Ohio, then she lives in Cleveland," is false, because the hypothesis is true, but the conclusion is false.
98. If 2 + 2 = 4, then 3 + 3 = 6. (Answers will vary).
99. If Washington, D.C. is the capital of the United States, then Germany is in Asia. (Answers will vary). The proposition is false, because the hypothesis is true while the conclusion is false. The converse, "If Germany is in Asia, then Washington, D.C. is the capital of the United States," is true, as is any conditional proposition with false hypothesis.
100. It is not possible to write such a proposition. The conditional proposition *if p, then q* is false only when *p* is true and *q* is false. But then its converse *if q, then p* would be true, because any conditional proposition with a false hypothesis is true.
101. a. The book would be on the list because the search finds all entries with either *Steinbeck* or *grapes* (or both).
   b. The book would be on the list because the search finds all entries with *Grapes of Wrath*.
   c. The book would be on the list because the search finds all entries with both *grapes* and *Steinbeck*.
   d. The book would be on the list because the search would find all entries with *Steinbeck* (it would also find entries with *Hemingway*).
   e. The book would not be on the list because the search would find only those items that have both *Hemingway* and *grapes*.
   f. The book would be on the list because the search would find all entries with *Steinbeck* and *grapes* (it would also find all items with *Hemingway* and *grapes*).

102. (1) If the payer does not know that you remarried, then alimony you receive is taxable.
(2) If the payer knows that you remarried, then alimony you receive is not taxable.
(3) If you pay alimony to another party, then it is not deductible on your return.

103. "If a computer exhibits human-level intelligence, then it is capable of massive processing power, around 20 million billion calculations per second." The above statement converts the *necessary* part of the quote into an *if...then* statement. Kurzweil is claiming that any computer capable of mimicking human intelligence must also be capable of performing 20 million billion calculations per second (presumably because our brains possess such processing power). Note that Kurzweil states that massive processing power is not a *sufficient* condition. If it were, he'd be claiming, "If a computer is capable of massive processing power, then it exhibits human-level intelligence." Thus Kurzweil recognizes that even if a computer could be designed to perform 20 million billion calculations per second, it may not be capable of exhibiting human-level intelligence.

104. Following is a truth table for both *not (p and q)* and *(not p) or (not q)*.

p	q	p and q	not (p and q)	(not p) or (not q)
T	T	T	F	F
T	F	F	T	T
F	T	F	T	T
F	F	F	T	T

Since both statements have the same truth values (compare the last two columns of the table), they are logically equivalent.

105. Following is a truth table for both *not (p or q)* and *(not p) and (not q)*.

p	q	p or q	not (p or q)	(not p) and (not q)
T	T	T	F	F
T	F	T	F	F
F	T	T	F	F
F	F	F	T	T

Since both statements have the same truth values (compare the last two columns in the table), they are logically equivalent.

106. Following is a truth table for both *not (p and q)* and *(not p) and (not q)*.

p	q	p and q	not (p and q)	(not p) and (not q)
T	T	T	F	F
T	F	F	T	F
F	T	F	T	F
F	F	F	T	T

Note that the last two columns in the truth table don't agree, and thus the statements are not logically equivalent.

107. Following is a truth table for *not (p or q)* and *(not p) or (not q)*.

p	q	p or q	not (p or q)	(not p) or (not q)
T	T	T	F	F
T	F	T	F	T
F	T	T	F	T
F	F	F	T	T

Note that the last two columns in the truth table don't agree, and thus the statements are not logically equivalent.

108. Following is a truth table for *(p and q) or r* and *(p or r) and (p or q)*.

p	q	r	p and q	(p and q) or r	p or r	p or q	(p or r) and (p or q)
T	T	T	T	T	T	T	T
T	T	F	T	T	T	T	T
T	F	T	F	T	T	T	T
T	F	F	F	F	T	T	T
F	T	T	F	T	T	T	T
F	T	F	F	F	F	T	F
F	F	T	F	T	T	F	F
F	F	F	F	F	F	F	F

Since the fifth and eighth column of the table don't agree, these two statements are not logically equivalent.

109. Following is a truth table for *(p or q) and r* and *(p and r) or (q and r)*.

p	q	r	p or q	(p or q) and r	p and r	q and r	(p and r) or (q and r)
T	T	T	T	T	T	T	T
T	T	F	T	F	F	F	F
T	F	T	T	T	T	F	T
T	F	F	T	F	F	F	F
F	T	T	T	T	F	T	T
F	T	F	T	F	F	F	F
F	F	T	F	F	F	F	F
F	F	F	F	F	F	F	F

Since the fifth and eighth columns agree, the statements are logically equivalent.

UNIT 1C

QUICK QUIZ

1. **b.** The ellipsis is a convenient way to represent all the other states in the U.S. without having to write them all down.

2. **c.** 3.5 is a rational number (a ratio of two integers), but it is not an integer.

3. **a.** When the circle labeled C is contained within the circle labeled D, it indicates that C is a subset of D.

4. **b.** Since the set of boys is disjoint from the set of girls, the two circles should be drawn as non-overlapping circles.

5. **a.** Because all apples are fruit, the set A should be drawn within the set B (the set of apples is a subset of the set of fruits).

6. **c.** Some cross country runners may also be swimmers, so their sets should be overlapping.

7. **a.** The X is placed in the region where *business executives* and *working mothers* overlap to indicate that there is at least one member in that region.

8. **c.** The region X is within both *males* and *athletes*, but not within *Republicans*.

9. **a.** The central region is common to all three sets, and so represents those who are male, Republican, and an athlete.

10. **c.** The sum of the entries in the column labeled Low Birth Weight is 32.

DOES IT MAKE SENSE?

17. Does not make sense. More likely than not, the payments go to two separate companies.

18. Makes sense. A Venn diagram displays the relationship between two sets, and we don't need to comprehend the labels used for the sets to understand the relationship between their members.

19. Does not make sense. The number of students in a class is a whole number, and whole numbers are not in the set of irrational numbers.

20. Makes sense. The number of students in a class is a whole number, and whole numbers are a subset of the real numbers.

21. Does not make sense. A Venn diagram shows only the relationship between members of sets, but does not have much to say about the truth value of a categorical proposition.

22. Does not make sense. A Venn diagram is used to show the relationship between members of sets, but it is not used to determine the truth value for an opinion.

BASIC SKILLS & CONCEPTS

23. 23 is a natural number.
24. −45 is an integer.
25. 2/3 is a rational number.
26. −5/2 is a rational number.
27. 1.2345 is a rational number.
28. 0 is a whole number.
29. π is a real number.
30. $\sqrt{8}$ is a real number.
31. −34.45 is a rational number.
32. $\sqrt{98}$ is a real number.
33. π/4 is a real number.
34. 123/456 is a rational number.
35. −13/3 is a rational number.
36. −145.01 is a rational number.
37. π/129 is a real number.
38. 13,579,023 is a natural number.
39. {1900s, 1910s, 1920s,…, 1990s}.
40. {10, 11, 12,…, 50}.
41. {Washington, Adams, Jefferson}.
42. {Rhode Island}.
43. {California, Colorado, Connecticut}.
44. {Z, Y, X, W, V, U}.
45. {50, 51, 52,…,400}.
46. {Alaska, Washington, Oregon, California, Hawaii}.
47. Because some women are veterinarians, the circles should overlap.

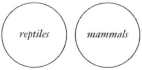

48. No reptile is a mammal, so these sets are disjoint, and the circles should not overlap.

49. All verbs are words, and thus the set of verbs is a subset of the set of words. This means one circle should be contained within the other.

50. Because some lawyers are scuba divers, the circles should overlap.

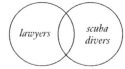

51. Some painters are also musicians, so the circles should overlap.

52. All biochemistry courses are science courses, so one circle should be contained within the other.

53. No negative integer is a natural number, so these sets are disjoint, and the circles should not overlap.

54. All positive integers are whole numbers, so one circle should be placed within the other.

55. The subject is *widows*, and the predicate is *women*.

56. The subject is *pilots*, and the predicate is *women*.

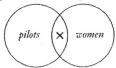

57. All U.S. presidents are people over 30 years old. The subject is *U.S. presidents*, and the predicate is *people over 30 years old*.

58. Some mammals are animals that swim. The subject is *mammals*, and the predicate is *animals that swim*.

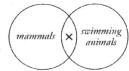

59. No monkey is a gambling animal. The subject is *monkeys*, and the predicate is *gambling animals*.

60. No dog is an animal with a tail. The subject is *dogs*, and the predicate is *animals with tails*.

61. All nurses are people who know CPR. The subject is *nurses*, and the predicate is *people who know CPR*.

62. All taxi cab drivers are highly educated people. The subject is *taxi cab drivers*, and the predicate is *highly educated people*.

63.

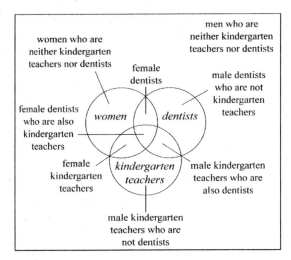

64.

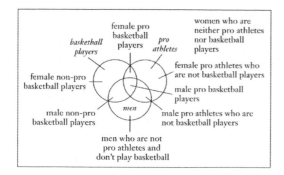

65.

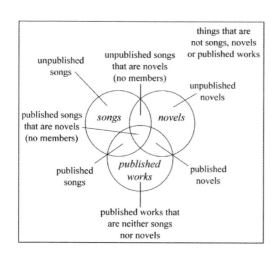

66.

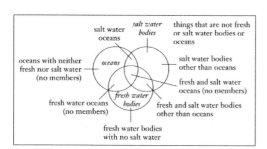

67.

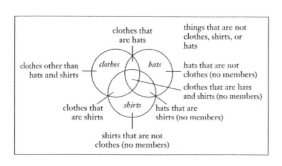

68.

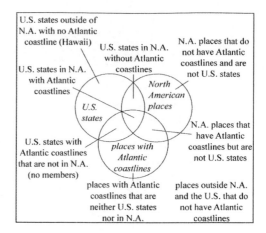

69. a. There are 17 men in the room.
b. There are 19 non-Republicans in the room.
c. There are 6 Republican women in the room.
d. There are 32 people in the room.

70. a. There are 10 non-Republican men.
b. There are 7 men who are Republicans.
c. There are 9 women who are non-Republican.
d. There are 13 Republicans.

71.

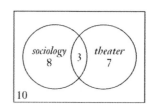

72.

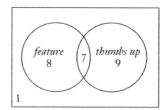

73.

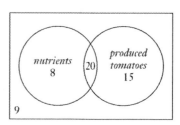

74.

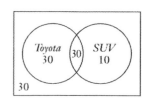

FURTHER APPLICATIONS

75. 26 non-attorneys attended, and 17 of the non-Americans were not attorneys.

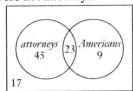

76. 3 students own both types of bike.

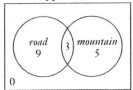

77.

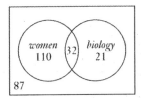

78.

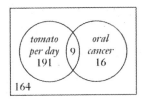

79.

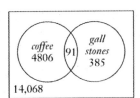

80. a.

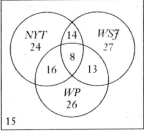

b. The region common to both *WP* and *WSJ* shows that 21 people read both papers (some of these also read *NYT*).

c. The central region shows those who read all three papers, and there are 8 people who do that.

d. All of the regions contained within the three circles correspond to those who read at least one of the papers (which is how one can interpret *NYT* or *WSJ* or *WP*). There are 128 such people.

e. Count the number of people that are in the *NYT* circle, but outside of the *WP* circle, and add them together to arrive at 38 people.

81. a.

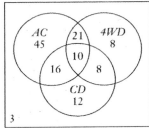

b. The region common to both AC and 4WD shows that 31 people chose both features (this includes those who also chose a CD player).

c. Count the number of people that are in the AC circle, but outside the 4WD circle, and add them together to arrive at 61 people.

d. All of the regions contained within the three circles correspond to those who chose at least one feature (which is how one can interpret AC or 4WD or CD). There are 120 such people.

e. Add the regions that are common to two circles, but not all three, to find that 45 people chose exactly two options.

82.

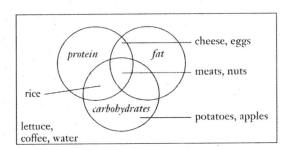

83.

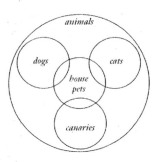

84.

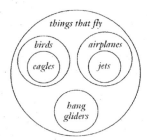

85.

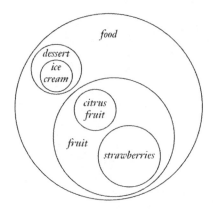

86.

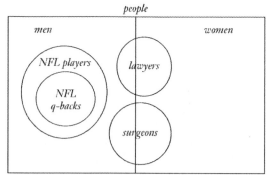

87. The two-way table should look like this:

	Showed improvement	No improvement	Total
New Drug	20	15	35
Placebo	25	40	65
Total	45	55	100

This is one possible Venn diagram.

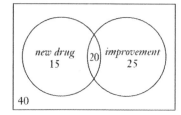

88. The two-way table should look like this:

	U.S. Citizens	Non-U.S. Citizens	Total
Attorneys	100	150	250
Doctors	150	250	400
Total	250	400	650

This is one possible Venn diagram.

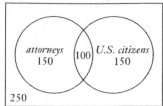

89. Two dogs are purebreds with long tails.
90. The two regions in the Venn diagram that have no members are the men and women with majors other than biology or psychology.

	Men	Women	Total
Biology	25	22	47
Psychology	15	20	35
Double major	12	16	28
Total	52	58	110

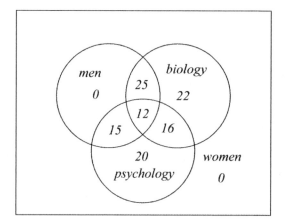

91. As shown in the diagram, the sets *hairy animals* and *fish* do not overlap (because all hairy animals are mammals, and no mammal is a fish). Since some mammals can swim, and hairy animals are mammals, there may be hairy animals that swim. There is nothing in the propositions that excludes the possibility of walking mammals, and thus there may be walking mammals, and for the same reason, there may be hairy animals that walk on land.

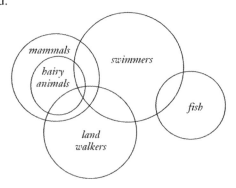

92. Since beans are contained within the set of plants, and meat and dairy products are outside of the set of plants, beans and dairy products are disjoint sets, and thus no bean is a dairy product. There is nothing in the propositions that prohibits the overlap of meat and dairy products, so there could be a meat that is a dairy product. No dairy product is a plant, because it is disjoint from that set. There could be plants that contain protein.

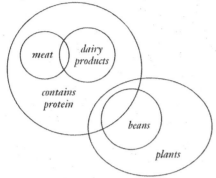

93. There could be conservative Democrats, and there could be liberal Green Party members, because there is nothing in the propositions to prohibit this. No liberal is a Republican, because the set of Republicans is a subset of the set of conservatives, and no liberal is a conservative (which means those sets are disjoint).

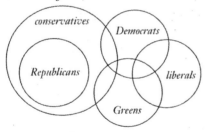

94. a. It is implied here that no Democrat is a Republican, and thus those sets are disjoint, as shown in the diagram.

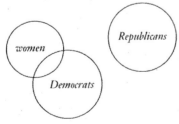

b. Yes, it is possible to meet such a woman, as there is nothing in the propositions to exclude that possibility.

c. Yes, there may be men who are Republicans (if there are any Republicans in attendance, they must be men).

95. a.

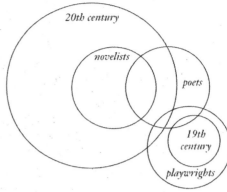

b. No, all of the novelists were born in the 20th century.

c. There is nothing in the facts you noticed that excludes the possibility of a poet born in the 19th century, so, yes, you may have studied such a poet.

d. Yes, there's nothing stated that excludes this possibility.

96. No, it is not possible to draw a Venn diagram with two circles (even when a square around them is included). The three brands are all disjoint sets, so two non-overlapping circles and a square surrounding them would be necessary to depict all the brands, but the information about approval or disapproval could not be shown. If you decided to label one of the circles "Approved," there would be no room left for one of the brands.

97. a. There are 16 different sets of options: choose nothing, A, B, C, D, AB, AC, AD, BC, BD, CD, ABC, ABD, ACD, BCD, and ABCD.

b. No, it is not possible (not with circles, in any case – one can draw three interlocking circles followed by a spiral-shaped tube that snakes through the requisite regions to show all the choices, but the diagram begins to get complicated to the point where it becomes less useful).

c. There are 32 different sets of options: choose nothing, A, B, C, D, E, AB, AC, AD, AE, BC, BD, BE, CD, CE, DE, ABC, ABD, ABE, ACD, ACE, ADE, BCD, BCE, BDE, CDE, ABCD, ABCE, ABDE, ACDE, BCDE, and ABCDE.

d. Notice that with four options, there are $2^4 = 16$ different sets of options, and that with five options, there are $2^5 = 32$ different sets of options. It turns out that this pattern continues so that with n options, there are 2^n different sets of options.

UNIT 1D

QUICK QUIZ

1. **b**. The only way to prove a statement true beyond all doubt is with a valid and sound deductive argument.
2. **c**. A deductive argument that is valid has a logical structure that implies its conclusion from its premises.
3. **c**. If a deductive argument is not valid, it cannot be sound.
4. **a**. Premise 1 claims the set of *knights* is a subset of the set of *heroes*, and Premise 2 claims Paul is a hero, which means the X must reside within the *hero* circle. However, we cannot be sure whether the X should fall within or outside the *knights* circle, so it belongs on the border.
5. **c**. Diagram *a* in question 4 is the correct diagram for its argument, and since X lies on the border of the *knights* circle, Paul may or may not be a knight.
6. **b**. The argument is of the form *denying the conclusion*, and one can always conclude *p* is not true in such arguments. (Whether the argument is sound is another question).
7. **c**. This argument is of the form *affirming the conclusion*, and it is always invalid, which means we can conclude nothing about *p*.
8. **c**. A chain of conditionals from *a* to *d* is necessary before we can claim the argument is valid.
9. **b**. The side opposite the right angle in a right triangle is always the longest, and it's called the hypotenuse.
10. **b**. The Pythagorean theorem states that $c^2 = 4^2 + 5^2 = 16 + 25 = 41$.

DOES IT MAKE SENSE?

19. Does not make sense. One cannot prove a conclusion beyond all doubt with an inductive argument.
20. Makes sense. An inductive argument is judged on its strength.
21. Makes sense. As long as the logic of a deductive argument is valid, if one accepts the truth (or soundness) of the premises, the conclusion necessarily follows.
22. Does not make sense. A deductive argument which is valid is not necessarily sound, and therefore the conclusion may not be true.
23. Does not make sense. This argument is of the form *affirming the conclusion*, and it is always invalid.

24. Does not make sense. Mathematicians generally do not claim a theorem to be true until it is proved with a valid and sound deductive argument.

BASIC SKILLS & CONCEPTS

25. This is an inductive argument because it makes the case for a general conclusion based on many specific observations.
26. This is a deductive argument because a specific conclusion is deduced from more general premises.
27. This is an inductive argument because it makes the case for a general conclusion based on many specific observations.
28. This is an inductive argument because it makes the case for a general conclusion based on many specific observations.
29. This is a deductive argument because a specific conclusion is deduced from more general premises.
30. This is a deductive argument because a specific conclusion is deduced from more general premises.
31. This is an inductive argument because it makes the case for a general conclusion based on several specific observations.
32. This is an inductive argument because it makes the case for a general conclusion based on several specific observations.
33. It is difficult to assert whether the premises are true because there are so many car models made by each of the manufacturers listed, with widely varying gas mileage, and the concept of good gas mileage is not well defined. If the premises are accepted to be true, the argument is moderately strong, and the conclusion may be true (especially when comparing Japanese made cars to American made cars).
34. The premises are true, and the argument is moderately strong (it suffers from the fact that only negative integers are used in the premises, whereas the conclusion speaks to all numbers). The conclusion is true.
35. The premises may be true (they likely all wear expensive basketball shoes, in any case), but the argument is weak, and the conclusion is false.
36. Most music critics would agree that the premise is true (though assessing the truth of any premise is often an exercise in judgment). The argument is weak, and the conclusion is false.
37. The premises are true, and the argument is moderately strong. The conclusion could be true.
38. The premises are true, though the argument is weak (it speaks to only four of many bird species). The conclusion is false.

39. Premise: All islands are tropical lands. The diagram shows the argument is valid. However, it is not sound as the first premise is false.

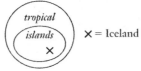

X = Iceland

40. Premise: All dairy products are foods containing protein. The diagram shows the argument is invalid, even though the premises are true. Because it is invalid, the argument cannot be sound.

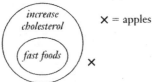

X = soybeans

41. Premise: Fast foods are foods that increase cholesterol. The argument is valid, and the premises are true, so the argument is also sound.

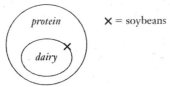

X = apples

42. As shown in the diagram, the argument is not valid because we cannot place the X within the *presidents* circle based on the second premise alone. Though the premises are true, the argument is not sound.

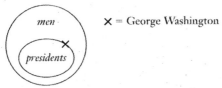

X = George Washington

43. Premise: All states north of the Mason Dixon line are states that get snow. The argument is valid, and the premises are true, so the argument is also sound.

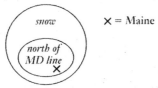

X = Maine

44. Premise: All doctors are people who know anatomy. As the diagram shows, the argument is not valid. If the term "doctor" is defined in its traditional sense, the premises are true, though the argument is not sound.

44. Continued

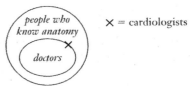

X = cardiologists

45. Premise: All opera singers are people who can whistle a Mozart tune. The diagram shows the argument is valid, and it is sound if we believe the premises to be true (there's room for disagreement on that count as we can't be sure all opera singers can whistle, nor can we be sure they know Mozart).

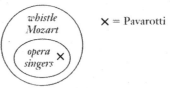

X = Pavarotti

46. No movie star is a person who does his laundry. The argument is valid. The premises could be true, in which case the argument is sound.

X = Jack Applebee

47. Affirming the hypothesis – this form is always valid, as confirmed by the diagram. The premises are true, and thus the argument sound.

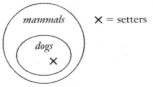

X = setters

48. If you are in the United States and have anything to say, then you have a right to say it at any time. Affirming the hypothesis – this form is always valid, as confirmed by the diagram. The first premise is false, and the argument is not sound.

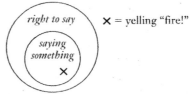

X = yelling "fire!"

49. Affirming the hypothesis – this form is always valid, as confirmed by the diagram. As long as the premises are true, the argument is sound.

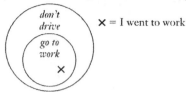

50. Affirming the conclusion – this form is always invalid, as confirmed by the diagram. Since it is invalid, it cannot be sound.

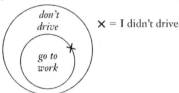

51. Denying the hypothesis – this form is always invalid, as confirmed by the diagram. Since it is invalid, it cannot be sound.

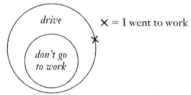

52. If you are a nurse, then you must know CPR. Affirming the hypothesis – this form is always valid, as confirmed by the diagram. To the extent that the premises are true, the argument is sound.

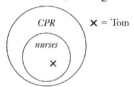

53. Affirming the conclusion – this form is always invalid, as confirmed by the diagram. Since it is invalid, it cannot be sound.

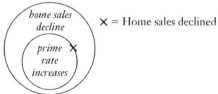

54. Affirming the conclusion – this form is always invalid, as confirmed by the diagram. Since it is invalid, it cannot be sound.

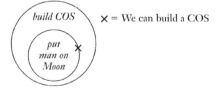

55. The argument is in standard form, and it is valid as there is a clear chain of implications from the first premise to the conclusion.

56. The argument is in standard form, but it is invalid as there is no chain of implications from the premises to the conclusion.

57. The second premise and conclusion should be written as follows to put the argument in standard form. Premise: If taxpayers have less disposable income, the economy will slow down. Conclusion: If taxes are increased, then the economy will slow down. The argument is valid as there is a clear chain of implications from premises to conclusion.

58. The conclusion should be written as: "If taxes are cut, then the deficit will increase." The argument is valid as there is a clear chain of conditionals from premises to conclusion.

59. The statement is true.

60. The statement is not true (consider $c = 0$).

61. The statement is not true (consider negative numbers, or just about any other pair of numbers).

62. The statement is true.

FURTHER APPLICATIONS

63. Answers will vary. An example:
Premise: All living mammals breathe.
Premise: All monkeys are mammals.
Conclusion: All living monkeys breathe.

64. A sound argument must be valid, so this combination is impossible.

65. Answers will vary. An example:
Premise: All mammals fly. (false)
Premise: All monkeys are mammals. (true)
Conclusion: All monkeys fly. (false)

66. Answers will vary. An example:
Premise: All mammals swim. (false)
Premise: All fish are mammals. (false)
Conclusion: All fish swim. (true)

67. Answers will vary. An example:
Premise: All mammals breathe. (true)
Premise: All mammals have hair. (true)
Conclusion: All hairy animals breathe. (true)

68. An example of *affirming the hypothesis* (valid):
Premise: If I am in Phoenix, then I am in Arizona.
Premise: I am in Phoenix.
Conclusion: I am in Arizona.

69. An example of *affirming the conclusion* (invalid):
Premise: If I am in Phoenix, then I am in Arizona.
Premise: I am in Arizona.
Conclusion: I am in Phoenix.

70. An example of *denying the hypothesis* (invalid):
Premise: If I am in Phoenix, then I am in Arizona.
Premise: I am not in Phoenix.
Conclusion: I am not in Arizona.

71. An example of *denying the conclusion* (valid):
    Premise: If I am in Phoenix, then I am in Arizona.
    Premise: I am not in Arizona.
    Conclusion: I am not in Phoenix.
72. Answers will vary, though it's unlikely you'll discover any counter-examples, and thus a strong inductive argument can be made.

UNIT 1E

QUICK QUIZ

1. **b**. A vote for C implies a property tax reduction.
2. **c**. An argument that doesn't clearly spell out all of its premises is weak in logical structure.
3. **c**. With unknown application fees, it's not clear which bank has the better offer.
4. **b**. It's a good deal if you get six haircuts at this shop (and that you remember to get your card punched), but it's a bad deal otherwise.
5. **c**. $20/100 min = 20¢/min.
6. **a**. As long as you remember to get the 50% refund coming to you, you'll spend $200.
7. **c**. Both Jack's argument and this one make a huge leap from premises to conclusion: here's a few examples when *A* happened, so *A* must happen all the time.
8. **b**. You can't compute how much you'll spend with each policy without knowing the number and cost of collisions over the span of a year.
9. **a**. The teacher is assuming that students will do fine without spell checkers, which implies that traditional methods of teaching spelling are effective.
10. **c**. If it did not rain, and today is a Saturday, the Smiths would have a picnic. Since they did not, it must not be a Saturday.

DOES IT MAKE SENSE?

15. Makes sense. The double negative means the insurance company accepted his claim.
16. Does not make sense. Survivors are not typically buried after plane crashes.
17. Does not make sense. If Sue wants to save time, she should take the Blue Shuttle, and save ten minutes.
18. Does not make sense. With a 10% surcharge, Alan will spend $36.30 through Ticketmaster, which is a worse deal than $35 through the box office.
19. Makes sense. Both the duration and mileage of the first warranty is the better deal.
20. Does not make sense. There are other factors besides collision insurance that one must consider when purchasing auto insurance.

BASIC SKILLS & CONCEPTS

21. He has $2 left as he gave away the rest.
22. There are 12 of anything in a dozen.
23. No, it's not possible, as a man who has a widow is dead.
24. No we cannot be sure – she may have been walking.
25. You must meet eight people, as the first six might be Democrats.
26. You must meet seven people, as the first six might all be from the same party.
27. You must meet three people. The first and second might be from different parties, in which case by the third person, you will have met two from the same party.
28. The surgeon is the boy's mother.
29. Jane might go to the movies 2, 3, 4, 5, or 6 days per week.
30. Rita might go swimming 3, 4, or 5 days per week.
31. No it does not follow. Some of the communications majors may be men.
32. Yes, it does follow that one quarter of the exports consist of corn from Caldonia.
33. a. The state constitution is less strict, as the initiative seeks to prevent state courts from interpreting the right of free expression more broadly under the state constitution than under the First Amendment.
    b. A *yes* vote would allow for stronger laws against obscenity.
    c. False. If the initiative passed, then state laws could be as strict as the First Amendment calls for, but not more strict.
34. a. Yes, term limits in the state are currently mandatory.
    b. No, a candidate could voluntarily withdraw from the restrictions of term limits.
    c. Candidates must decide whether to accept term limits (and publicly declare such decision), or run without term limits, giving them the chance of being re-elected to more terms than current term limit regulations dictate.
35. (1) We have enough money to afford a house. (2) We will be staying in the same place long enough to make buying a house sensible. (Answers will vary).
36. (1) Jenny paid for the limousine. (2) anyone who can afford a limousine must be rich. (Answers will vary).
37. (1) Not all countries get along well at present. (2) The United Nations can help nations learn to get along. (Answers will vary).
38. (1) America needs a stronger military. (2) More military spending will mean a stronger military. (Answers will vary).

39. We are looking for possible unstated motives that may be the unstated "real reason" for opposition to the tax cuts. Among the possibilities: (1) a desire to maintain or increase government spending programs, which are more likely to be cut if revenues fall; (2) a belief that the tax system should redistribute wealth from the wealthy to the poor, which is less likely to occur with tax cuts.

40. We are looking for possible unstated motives that may be the unstated "real reason" for support of school vouchers. In this case, the fact that "fixing" the public schools is not discussed as an option suggests a possible hidden motive. Among the possibilities: (1) a desire to send their own children to a private school; (2) a belief that government is inherently incapable of "fixing" the public schools; (3) a desire to allow parochial schools to receive public funding.

41. In all of these problems, the key is to understand situation (iii). Focusing on Monica from part **c**, notice that her earned income plus $250 is $4150, and that number is "the greater of $700 or earned income plus $250" (i.e. $4150 > $700). Since her total of earned and unearned income is $4200, and this is more than the number arrived at using (iii) (i.e. $4200 > $4150), she must file a return. The other situations are similar: compute earned income (up to $4050) plus $250, compare it to $700, take the greater of those two numbers, and compare that result to earned plus unearned income to decide whether the person needs to file a return.
    a. Trent does not need to file a return.
    b. Sally does not need to file a return.
    c. Monica must file a return.
    d. Horace does not need to file a return.
    e. Delila must file a return.

42. a. Estimated tax payments do not need to be made.
    b. Estimated tax payments must be made.
    c. Estimated tax payments do not need to be made.
    d. Estimated tax payments do not need to be made (note that 110% of last year's tax < withholdings < 90% of next year's tax).
    e. Estimated tax payments do not need to be made (note that 90% of next year's tax < withholdings < last year's tax).

43. a. The landlord has one month after June 5 to return the deposit, so the terms have been met.
    b. The landlord has one month after June 5 to return the deposit, so the terms have been met.
    c. The landlord has one month after June 5 to return the deposit, so the terms have not been met.

44. Plan A: If you go, it costs $1600; if you cancel, it costs $400. Plan B: If you go, it costs $2900; if you cancel, it costs nothing. If you go, Plan B costs $1300 more. If you cancel, Plan A costs $400 more.

45. You need estimates of the number of minutes you spend calling during weekday daytime, and during the weekend (the weekday nighttime minutes cost the same under both plans, and thus don't affect the comparison). If the number of weekday daytime minutes is less than one-third the number of weekend minutes, then the new plan is better.

46. A legitimate sweepstakes would not ask you to pay a processing fee in order to claim your prize. Note also that the notice never says your vacation will be fully paid for. In addition, the notice is asking for your credit card number, which should raise a "red flag" that should cause you to delete the message as spam.

FURTHER APPLICATIONS

47. Were there more than 350 people on each jet, or both jets combined? Was there any damage or injuries?

48. In which year were there 2.9 million incidents?

49. Is $83 billion the gross domestic product, or 6% of the gross domestic product?

50. The word "regularly" does not describe the seriousness of the charge; it could mean once every day, or once every month. Also, the term "abuses" is not well defined.

51. a. They could be consistent, because Alice does not specify the time period for her 253 cases, and it's possible Zack is being selective about the cases he chooses to discuss (that is, he may not be talking about all the cases Alice tried).
    b. They could be consistent if Alice obtained many convictions through plea agreements without going to trial.

52. If the estimate of the computer's resale value is accurate, the purchase option costs $900, while the lease option costs $1050. All facts are "hard" except for the resale value.

53. Alicia is a biology major from Alabama. Bob is a communications major from Connecticut. Carla is an art major from Arkansas.

54. The package of four sticks is a better deal (about 31¢ per stick compared to 40¢ per stick), so as long as you anticipate needing an extra stick of butter in the near future, buy the package.

55. Under your current policy (and over the span of a nine-month pregnancy), you'll spend $115 per month, plus $4000 for prenatal care and delivery, for a total of $5035. Under the upgraded policy, you'll spend $275 per month, for a total of $2475. Thus, considering only these costs (we aren't told, for example, what happens if the mother requires an extensive hospital stay due to a C-section or other complications arising from delivery, or what

happens if the baby is born prematurely and requires neo-natal care), the upgraded policy is best.

56. If you go and return on Monday, you'll spend $750 plus $55 on meals, for a total of $805. If you fly out Saturday evening (with no cost in meals for that day), stay in a hotel both Saturday and Sunday night, and eat out on Sunday and Monday, you'll spend $335 + $210 + $110 = $655. As long as you don't mind being away from home a little longer, the weekend trip is the better deal.

57. If you fly nine times with Airline A, at a cost of $3150, your tenth flight will be free (because you will have flown 27,000 miles at that point). If you fly ten times with Airline B, your cost will be $3250. Thus if you plan to fly ten times (or a multiple of ten times), Airline A is cheaper than Airline B.

58. Assuming your accident rate (and the costs of those accidents) remains the same for the next ten years, you should choose the policy with the lower premium of $200 per year. Under that plan, you'll spend $2900 over the next decade ($2000 for the premiums, and $900 for claims, as your $1000 deductible will not come into effect for any of the claims). Under the other plan, you'll spend $5000 ($4500 for premiums, and $500 for claims -- the $200 deductible would save you $400 on a $600 claim).

59. The pitching has been getting worse (answers will vary).

60. The team had better players in the championship year (answers will vary).

61. The soil or watering was different in the two flowerbeds (answers will vary).

62. The volunteers hoped to improve, and their hopes had an effect on their responses (answers will vary).

63. The number of students increased each year.

64. The total amount eaten over a month is less in February because it has fewest days, whereas the amount eaten per day is less in July.

65. Country Y has a high gun suicide rate.

66. The birth rate may be high enough that even after a decrease, it still leads to increased population. Immigration and a lower death rate could also increase the population despite the fact that birth rates are declining.

76. One interpretation of the poem is that the poet was 20 years old when he wrote the poem, and he expects to live to age 70.

UNIT 2A

QUICK QUIZ

1. **a.** Think of the unit *miles per hour*; the unit of *mile* is divided by the unit of *hour*.

2. **b.** The area of a square is its length multiplied by its width (these are, of course, equal for squares), and thus a square of side length 2 mi has area of $2 \text{ mi} \times 2 \text{ mi} = 4 \text{ mi}^2$.

3. **c.** When multiplying quantities that have units, the units are also multiplied, so $\text{ft}^2 \times \text{ft} = \text{ft}^3$.

4. **b.** $1 \text{ mi}^3 = (1760 \text{ yd})^3 = 1760^3 \text{ yd}^3$.

5. **a.** Divide both sides of $1 \text{ L} = 1.06 \text{ qt}$ by 1 L.

6. **b.** Gas mileage is described by distance per unit of gas, and km per L fits this rule.

7. **b.** \$1.20 per euro means 1 euro = \$1.20, which is more than \$1.

8. **c.** $1 \text{ ft}^2 = 12 \text{ in} \times 12 \text{ in} = 144 \text{ in}^2$.

9. **b.** Intuitively, it makes sense to divide a volume (with units of, say, ft^3) by a depth (with units of ft) to arrive at surface area (which has units of ft^2).

10. **a.** Take dollars per gallon and divide it by miles per gallon, and you get

$$\frac{\$}{\text{gal}} \div \frac{\text{mi}}{\text{gal}} = \frac{\$}{\text{gal}} \times \frac{\text{gal}}{\text{mi}} = \frac{\$}{\text{mi}}.$$

DOES IT MAKE SENSE?

17. Does not make sense. 35 miles is a distance, not a speed.

18. Makes sense. Area is often measured in ft^2.

19. Does not make sense. Two ft^2 describes an area, not a volume.

20. Does not make sense. Five acres describes an area, not a volume.

21. Does not make sense. Using the familiar formula *distance = rate × time*, one can see that it would be necessary to divide the distance by the rate (or speed) in order to compute the time, not the other way around.

22. Makes sense. Using the familiar formula *distance = rate × time*, one can see that dividing the distance by the rate (or speed) will result in time.

BASIC SKILLS & CONCEPTS

23. a. $\dfrac{3}{4} \times \dfrac{1}{2} = \dfrac{3 \cdot 1}{4 \cdot 2} = \dfrac{3}{8}$.

   b. $\dfrac{2}{3} \times \dfrac{3}{5} = \dfrac{2 \cdot 3}{3 \cdot 5} = \dfrac{2}{5}$.

c. $\dfrac{1}{2} + \dfrac{3}{2} = \dfrac{1+3}{2} = \dfrac{4}{2} = 2$.

d. $\dfrac{2}{3} + \dfrac{1}{6} = \dfrac{4}{6} + \dfrac{1}{6} = \dfrac{4+1}{6} = \dfrac{5}{6}$.

e. $\dfrac{2}{3} \times \dfrac{1}{4} = \dfrac{2 \cdot 1}{3 \cdot 4} = \dfrac{2}{12} = \dfrac{1}{6}$.

f. $\dfrac{1}{4} + \dfrac{3}{8} = \dfrac{2}{8} + \dfrac{3}{8} = \dfrac{2+3}{8} = \dfrac{5}{8}$.

g. $\dfrac{5}{8} - \dfrac{1}{4} = \dfrac{5}{8} - \dfrac{2}{8} = \dfrac{5-2}{8} = \dfrac{3}{8}$.

h. $\dfrac{3}{2} \times \dfrac{2}{3} = \dfrac{3 \cdot 2}{3 \cdot 2} = 1$.

24. a. $\dfrac{1}{3} + \dfrac{1}{5} = \dfrac{5}{15} + \dfrac{3}{15} = \dfrac{8}{15}$.

   b. $\dfrac{10}{3} \times \dfrac{3}{7} = \dfrac{10 \cdot 3}{3 \cdot 7} = \dfrac{10}{7} = 1\dfrac{3}{7}$.

   c. $\dfrac{3}{4} - \dfrac{1}{8} = \dfrac{6}{8} - \dfrac{1}{8} = \dfrac{5}{8}$.

   d. $\dfrac{1}{2} + \dfrac{2}{3} + \dfrac{3}{4} = \dfrac{6}{12} + \dfrac{8}{12} + \dfrac{9}{12} = \dfrac{23}{12} = 1\dfrac{11}{12}$.

   e. $\dfrac{6}{5} + \dfrac{4}{15} = \dfrac{18}{15} + \dfrac{4}{15} = \dfrac{22}{15}$.

   f. $\dfrac{3}{5} \times \dfrac{2}{7} = \dfrac{3 \cdot 2}{5 \cdot 7} = \dfrac{6}{35}$.

   g. $\dfrac{1}{3} + \dfrac{13}{6} = \dfrac{2}{6} + \dfrac{13}{6} = \dfrac{15}{6} = \dfrac{5}{2} = 2\dfrac{1}{2}$.

   h. $\dfrac{3}{5} \times \dfrac{10}{3} \times \dfrac{3}{2} = \dfrac{3 \cdot 10 \cdot 3}{5 \cdot 3 \cdot 2} = 3$.

25. Answers may vary depending on whether fractions are reduced.

   a. $3.5 = \dfrac{35}{10} = \dfrac{7}{2}$.   b. $0.3 = \dfrac{3}{10}$.

   c. $0.05 = \dfrac{5}{100} = \dfrac{1}{20}$.   d. $4.1 = \dfrac{41}{10}$.

   e. $2.15 = \dfrac{215}{100} = \dfrac{43}{20}$.   f. $0.35 = \dfrac{35}{100} = \dfrac{7}{20}$.

   g. $0.98 = \dfrac{98}{100} = \dfrac{49}{50}$.   h. $4.01 = \dfrac{401}{100}$.

26. Answers may vary depending on whether fractions are reduced.

   a. $2.75 = \dfrac{275}{100} = \dfrac{11}{4}$.   b. $0.45 = \dfrac{45}{100} = \dfrac{9}{20}$.

   c. $0.005 = \dfrac{5}{1000} = \dfrac{1}{200}$.   d. $1.16 = \frac{116}{100} = \frac{29}{25}$.

   e. $6.5 = \dfrac{65}{10} = \dfrac{13}{2}$.   f. $4.123 = \dfrac{4123}{1000}$.

   g. $0.0003 = \dfrac{3}{10,000}$ h. $0.034 = \dfrac{34}{1000} = \dfrac{17}{500}$.

27. a. $1/4 = 0.25$. b. $3/8 = 0.375$.
    c. $2/3 = 0.667$. d. $3/5 = 0.6$.
    e. $13/2 = 6.5$. f. $23/6 = 3.833$.
    g. $103/50 = 2.06$. h. $42/26 = 1.615$.
28. a. $1/5 = 0.2$. b. $4/9 = 0.444$.
    c. $4/11 = 0.364$. d. $12/7 = 1.714$.
    e. $28/9 = 3.111$. f. $56/11 = 5.091$.
    g. $102/49 = 2.082$. h. $15/4 = 3.75$.
29. The price of apple juice has units of dollars per ounces, or $/oz.
30. Speed has units of kilometers per second, or km/s.
31. The cost of carpet has units of dollars per square yard, or $/$yd^2$.
32. The flow rate has units of 5000 cubic feet per second, or 5000 cfs (or ft^3/s).
33. The price of eggplants has units of euros per kilogram, or euro/kg.
34. The price of fabric has units of dollars per square foot, or $/$ft^2$.
35. The gas mileage has units of miles per gallon, or mpg (or mi/gal).
36. The density of rock has units of grams per cubic centimeter, or g/cm^3.
37. $3.5 \text{ mi} \times \dfrac{5280 \text{ ft}}{1 \text{ mi}} = 18,480 \text{ ft}$.
38. $10 \text{ ft} \times \dfrac{12 \text{ in.}}{1 \text{ ft}} = 120 \text{ in}$.
39. $3.5 \text{ hr} \times \dfrac{60 \text{ min}}{1 \text{ hr}} = 210 \text{ min}$.
40. $6 \text{ hr} \times \dfrac{60 \text{ min}}{1 \text{ hr}} \times \dfrac{60 \text{ s}}{1 \text{ min}} = 21,600 \text{ s}$.
41. $3 \text{ lb} \times \dfrac{16 \text{ oz}}{1 \text{ lb}} = 48 \text{ oz}$.
42. $4 \text{ acre} \times \dfrac{43,560 \text{ ft}^2}{1 \text{ acre}} = 174,240 \text{ ft}^2$.
43. $2 \text{ wk} \times \dfrac{7 \text{ day}}{1 \text{ wk}} \times \dfrac{24 \text{ hr}}{1 \text{ day}} \times \dfrac{60 \text{ min}}{1 \text{ hr}} = 20,160 \text{ min}$.
44. $60 \dfrac{\text{mi}}{\text{hr}} \times \dfrac{1 \text{ hr}}{60 \text{ min}} = 1 \dfrac{\text{mi}}{\text{min}}$.
45. $35 \text{ gal} \times \dfrac{4 \text{ qt}}{1 \text{ gal}} = 140 \text{ qt}$.
46. $12 \text{ yr} \times \dfrac{365 \text{ day}}{1 \text{ yr}} \times \dfrac{24 \text{ hr}}{1 \text{ day}} = 105,120 \text{ hr}$.
47. a. The area of the reservoir's base is 120 ft × 40 ft = 4800 ft^2, and the amount of water the reservoir can hold is 120 ft × 40 ft × 9 ft = 43,200 ft^3.
    b. The area of the soccer field is 110 yd × 55 yd = 6050 yd^2, and the volume of the snow is 110 yd × 55 yd × 3 ft = 110 yd × 55 yd × 1 yd = 6050

yd^3 (note that 3 ft was converted to 1 yd before computing the volume).
    c. The area of the base is 120 ft × 120 ft = 14,400 ft^2, and the volume of the building is 120 ft × 120 ft × 330 ft = 4,752,000 ft^3.
48. a. The area of the warehouse floor is 40 yd × 25 yd = 1000 yd^2, and the volume of the cartons is 40 yd × 25 yd × 3 yd = 3000 yd^3.
    b. The area of the bed's floor is 12 ft × 5 ft = 60 ft^2, and the volume of the bed is 12 ft × 5 ft × 3.5 ft = 210 ft^3.
    c. The volume of the can is the area of its base multiplied by its height, which is 6 $in.^2$ × 4 in. = 24 $in.^3$.
49. Note that 1 ft = 12 in., and thus $(1 \text{ ft})^2 = (12 \text{ in.})^2$, which means 1 ft^2 = 144 $in.^2$. This can also be written as $\dfrac{1 \text{ ft}^2}{1728 \text{ in.}^3} = 1$, or $\dfrac{144 \text{ in}^3}{1 \text{ ft}^3} = 1$.
50. Note that 1 ft = 12 in, and thus $(1 \text{ ft})^3 = (12 \text{ in.})^3$, which means 1 ft^3 = 1728 $in.^3$. This can also be written as $\dfrac{1 \text{ ft}^3}{1728 \text{ in.}^3} = 1$, or $\dfrac{1728 \text{ in}^3}{1 \text{ ft}^3} = 1$.
51. Since 1 m = 100 cm, we have $(1 \text{ m})^2 = (100 \text{ cm})^2$, which means 1 m^2 = 10,000 cm^2. This can also be written as $\dfrac{1 \text{ m}^2}{10,000 \text{ cm}^2} = 1$, or $\dfrac{10,000 \text{ cm}^2}{1 \text{ m}^2} = 1$.
52. The area of the room is 16 ft × 22 ft = 352 ft^2. Since 1 yd = 3 ft, we know 1 yd^2 = 9 ft^2, and this can be used to convert to square yards.
$$352 \text{ ft}^2 \times \dfrac{1 \text{ yd}^2}{9 \text{ ft}^2} = 39.1 \text{ yd}^2.$$
53. The volume of the box is 12 ft × 8 ft × 4 ft = 384 ft^3. Since 1 yd = 3 ft, we know 1 yd^3 = 27 ft^3, and this can be used to convert to cubic yards.
$$384 \text{ ft}^3 \times \dfrac{1 \text{ yd}^3}{27 \text{ ft}^3} = 14.2 \text{ yd}^3.$$
54. A conversion factor between cubic feet and cubic inches will be necessary (see exercise 50).
$$4.5 \text{ ft}^3 \times \dfrac{1728 \text{ in.}^3}{1 \text{ ft}^3} = 7776 \text{ in.}^3.$$
55. Use the fact that 1 yd^3 = 27 ft^3 (see exercise 53).
$$320 \text{ ft}^3 \times \dfrac{1 \text{ yd}^3}{27 \text{ ft}^3} = 11.9 \text{ yd}^3.$$
56. Use the fact that 1 ft^3 = 1728 $in.^3$ (exercise 50).
$$4 \text{ ft}^3 \times \dfrac{1728 \text{ in.}^3}{1 \text{ ft}^3} = 6912 \text{ in.}^3.$$

57. Since $1 U.S. is worth 10.95 pesos, the dollar is worth more than the peso (which is about 9¢).

58. One euro is worth $1.272 U.S., whereas one Canadian dollar is worth only $0.8996 U.S. (about 90¢), so the euro is worth more.

59. $2500 \text{ peso} \times \dfrac{\$1}{10.95 \text{ peso}} = \$228.31$, so 2500 pesos is worth 228.31 U.S. dollars. Note that if you use the conversion 1 peso = $0.09136, you'll get an answer of $228.40 U.S. (this is due to errors in rounding).

60. $\$120 \times \dfrac{1 \text{ euro}}{\$1.272} = 94.34 \text{ euros}$, so you can buy 94.34 euros with $120 U.S.

61. $12{,}000 \text{ yen} \times \dfrac{\$1}{111.5 \text{ yen}} = \$107.62$, so you can buy 107.62 U.S. dollars with 12,000 yen. Note that if you use the conversion 1 yen = $0.008965, you'll get an answer of $107.58 U.S. (this is due to errors in rounding).

62. $\dfrac{0.75 \text{ euro}}{1 \text{ L}} \times \dfrac{\$1.272}{1 \text{ euro}} \times \dfrac{0.9464 \text{ L}}{1 \text{ qt}} = \dfrac{\$0.90}{\text{qt}}$, so the price is about 90¢ per quart.

63. $\dfrac{11 \text{ peso}}{1 \text{ L}} \times \dfrac{\$0.09136}{1 \text{ peso}} \times \dfrac{3.785 \text{ L}}{1 \text{ gal}} = \dfrac{\$3.80}{\text{gal}}$, so the price is $3.80 per gallon.

64. $\dfrac{1.80 \text{ euro}}{1 \text{ kg}} \times \dfrac{\$1.272}{1 \text{ euro}} \times \dfrac{1 \text{ kg}}{2.205 \text{ lb}} = \dfrac{\$1.04}{\text{lb}}$, so the price is $1.04 per pound.

65. The car is traveling with speed $\dfrac{13 \text{ mi}}{15 \text{ min}}$, and this needs to be converted to mi/hr.
$$\dfrac{13 \text{ mi}}{15 \text{ min}} \times \dfrac{60 \text{ min}}{1 \text{ hr}} = 52 \dfrac{\text{mi}}{\text{hr}}.$$

66. The plane is traveling with speed $\dfrac{95 \text{ mi}}{10 \text{ min}}$, and this needs to be converted to mi/hr.
$$\dfrac{95 \text{ mi}}{10 \text{ min}} \times \dfrac{60 \text{ min}}{1 \text{ hr}} = 570 \dfrac{\text{mi}}{\text{hr}}.$$

67. Convert $436 million to people using the conversion 1 person = $8.
$$\$436{,}000{,}000 \times \dfrac{1 \text{ person}}{\$8} = 54{,}500{,}000 \text{ people},$$
so 54.5 million people saw the film.

68. Take 54 hits and divide by 152 at-bats to get the batting average in units of hits/at-bats.
$$\dfrac{54 \text{ hits}}{152 \text{ at-bats}} = 0.355 \dfrac{\text{hits}}{\text{at-bats}}.$$
It is customary to report batting averages rounded to the nearest thousandth, as such: .355.

69. Convert 4.7 pounds to dollars by using the conversion 1 lb = $1.29.
$$4.7 \text{ lb} \times \dfrac{\$1.29}{\text{lb}} = \$6.06.$$

70. Convert 2.8 kilograms to dollars by using the conversion 1 kg = $3.50.
$$2.8 \text{ kg} \times \dfrac{\$3.50}{\text{kg}} = \$9.80.$$

71. First, note that 300 million people is 3000 groups of 100,000 people each. The mortality rate is
$$\dfrac{555{,}000 \text{ deaths}}{300{,}000{,}000 \text{ people}} \times \dfrac{300{,}000{,}000 \text{ people}}{3000 \text{ groups of } 100{,}000} = 185 \dfrac{\text{deaths}}{100{,}000}.$$

72. First, note that 300 million people is 3000 groups of 100,000 people each. The mortality rate is
$$\dfrac{695{,}000 \text{ deaths}}{300{,}000{,}000 \text{ people}} \times \dfrac{300{,}000{,}000 \text{ people}}{3000 \text{ groups of } 100{,}000} = 232 \dfrac{\text{deaths}}{100{,}000}.$$

73. Convert 3 million births per year into births per minute.
$$\dfrac{3{,}000{,}000 \text{ births}}{\text{yr}} \times \dfrac{1 \text{ yr}}{365 \text{ d}} \times \dfrac{1 \text{ d}}{24 \text{ hr}} \times \dfrac{1 \text{ hr}}{60 \text{ min}} = 5.7 \dfrac{\text{births}}{\text{deaths}}.$$

74. Divide the total spent by the number of pupils to find the expenditure per pupil.
$$\dfrac{\$371{,}000{,}000}{148{,}000 \text{ pupils}} = \$2507 \text{ per pupil}.$$

75. The average speed in miles per hour is
$$\dfrac{1200 \text{ mi}}{24 \text{ hr}} = 50 \dfrac{\text{mi}}{\text{hr}}.$$

76. Convert one year into dollars:
$$1 \text{ yr} \times \dfrac{52 \text{ wk}}{\text{yr}} \times \dfrac{40 \text{ hr}}{\text{wk}} \times \dfrac{\$13.50}{\text{hr}} = \$28{,}080.$$

77. Convert one year into hours of sleep.
$$1 \text{ yr} \times \dfrac{365 \text{ d}}{\text{yr}} \times \dfrac{7 \text{ hr (of sleep)}}{\text{d}} = 2555 \text{ hr}.$$

78. Convert one lifetime into heart beats.
$$1 \text{ lifetime} \times \dfrac{75 \text{ yr}}{\text{lifetime}} \times \dfrac{365 \text{ d}}{\text{yr}} \times \dfrac{24 \text{ hr}}{1 \text{ d}} \times \dfrac{60 \text{ min}}{1 \text{ hr}} \times \dfrac{60 \text{ beats}}{1 \text{ min}}$$
$$= 2{,}365{,}200{,}000 \text{ beats}.$$

79. The solution is wrong. It's helpful to include units on your numerical values. This would have signaled your error, as witness:
$$(incorrect) \; 0.11 \text{ lb} \div \dfrac{\$7.70}{\text{lb}} = \dfrac{0.11 \text{ lb}^2}{\$7.70} = 0.014 \dfrac{\text{lb}^2}{\$}.$$
Notice that your solution, when the correct units are added, produces units of square pounds per dollar, which isn't very helpful, and doesn't answer the question. The correct solution is
$$0.11 \text{ lb} \times \dfrac{\$7.70}{\text{lb}} = \$0.85.$$

80. The solution is wrong. Attach units to your numerical quantities so that you can determine whether the answer has correct units. When it doesn't, this is an indication there's an error. Here's your incorrect solution with units attached:

$$\frac{5 \text{ mi}}{\text{hr}} \div 3 \text{ hr} = \frac{5 \text{ mi}}{\text{hr}} \times \frac{1}{3 \text{ hr}} = 1.7 \frac{\text{mi}}{\text{hr}^2} \, .$$

It's clear this is incorrect as the question asked how far did you go, and thus you should expect an answer with units of miles. The correct solution is

$$3 \text{ hr} \times \frac{5 \text{ mi}}{\text{hr}} = 15 \text{ mi} \, .$$

81. The solution is wrong. Units should be included with all quantities. When dividing by $11, the unit of dollars goes with the 11 into the denominator (as shown below). Also, while it's reasonable to round an answer to the nearest tenth, it's more useful to round to the nearest hundredth in a problem like this, as you'll be comparing the price per pound of the large bag to the price per pound of the small bag, which is 39¢ per pound. Here's your solution with all units attached, division treated as it should be, and rounded to the hundredth-place:

$$50 \text{ lb} \div \$11 = \frac{50 \text{ lb}}{\$11} = 4.55 \frac{\text{lb}}{\$} \, .$$

This actually produces some useful information, as you can see a dollar buys 4.55 pounds of potatoes. If you're good with numbers, you can already see this is a better buy than 39¢ per pound, which is roughly 3 pounds for a dollar. But it's better to find the price per pound for the large bag:

$$\$11 \div 50 \text{ lb} = \frac{\$11}{50 \text{ lb}} = 0.22 \frac{\$}{\text{lb}} = 22¢ \text{ per pound} \, .$$

Now you can compare it to the price per pound of the small bag (39¢/lb) and tell which is the better buy.

82. The solution is wrong. Always include units with numerical quantities; this helps in deciding whether the correct procedure was followed. Here's your solution with units attached:

$$\frac{1500 \text{ Cal}}{\text{d}} \times \frac{140 \text{ Cal}}{\text{Coke}} = 210,000 \frac{\text{Cal}^2}{\text{d-Coke}} \, .$$

It's clear this calculation won't answer the question (note that as shown, there's nothing mathematically incorrect about the above calculation – it just doesn't provide useful information). The correct solution looks like this:

$$\frac{1500 \text{ Cal}}{\text{d}} \times \frac{1 \text{ Coke}}{140 \text{ Cal}} = 10.7 \frac{\text{Cokes}}{\text{d}} \, .$$

Thus you would need about 11 Cokes per day to meet your caloric needs.

83. Convert 2500 miles into gallons by using the conversion 28 miles = 1 gallon.

$$2500 \text{ mi} \times \frac{1 \text{ gal}}{28 \text{ mi}} = 89.3 \text{ gal} \, .$$

84. Convert 2500 miles into gallons (using 35 miles = 1 gallon), and then gallons into dollars (using 1 gallon = $3.25).

$$2500 \text{ mi} \times \frac{1 \text{ gal}}{35 \text{ mi}} \times \frac{\$3.25}{\text{gal}} = \$232.14 \, .$$

85. a. The driving time when traveling at 55 miles per hour is $2000 \text{ mi} \times \frac{1 \text{ hr}}{55 \text{ mi}} = 36.4 \text{ hr}$, while the time at 70 miles per hour is $2000 \text{ mi} \times \frac{1 \text{ hr}}{70 \text{ mi}} = 28.6 \text{ hr}$.

b. Your car gets 38 miles to the gallon when driving at 55 mph, so the cost is

$$2000 \text{ mi} \times \frac{1 \text{ gal}}{38 \text{ mi}} \times \frac{\$3.25}{\text{gal}} = \$171.05 \, .$$

Your car gets 32 miles to the gallon when driving at 70 mph, so the cost is

$$2000 \text{ mi} \times \frac{1 \text{ gal}}{32 \text{ mi}} \times \frac{\$3.25}{\text{gal}} = \$203.13 \, .$$

86. a. The driving time when traveling at 60 miles per hour is $1500 \text{ mi} \times \frac{1 \text{ hr}}{60 \text{ mi}} = 25 \text{ hr}$, while the time at 75 miles per hour is $1500 \text{ mi} \times \frac{1 \text{ hr}}{75 \text{ mi}} = 20 \text{ hr}$.

b. Your car gets 32 miles to the gallon when driving at 60 mph, so the cost is

$$1500 \text{ mi} \times \frac{1 \text{ gal}}{32 \text{ mi}} \times \frac{\$3.25}{\text{gal}} = \$152.34 \, .$$

Your car gets 25 miles to the gallon when driving at 75 mph, so the cost is

$$1500 \text{ mi} \times \frac{1 \text{ gal}}{25 \text{ mi}} \times \frac{\$3.25}{\text{gal}} = \$195 \, .$$

87. Visualize a rectangular slab of water, 75 feet long, 54 feet wide, and 6 inches high – this is the amount of water that needs to be added to the pool to raise the water level 6 inches. Since 6 in. = 0.5 ft, the volume of this slab is

$$75 \text{ ft} \times 54 \text{ ft} \times 0.5 \text{ ft} = 2025 \text{ ft}^3 \, .$$

88. Buy 36 feet of the 12-ft wide roll, and cut off an 18-ft long piece to be laid along the edge with that dimension. Take the remaining piece (also 18 feet long) and cut off a 2-ft wide strip (which will be waste) – this will cover the remaining portion of the room. The cost is

$$36 \text{ ft} \times 12 \text{ ft} \times \frac{1 \text{ yd}^2}{9 \text{ ft}^2} \times \frac{\$28.50}{\text{yd}^2} = \$1358 \, .$$

A cheaper method ($1254) can be found with two seams.

FURTHER APPLICATIONS

89. The maximum house footprint allowed is 1/4 of a 1/4–acre lot, which is 1/16 of an acre. Convert this to square feet:

$$\frac{1}{16}\text{acre} \times \frac{43,560\,\text{ft}^2}{1\,\text{acre}} = 2722.5\,\text{ft}^2 .$$

90. Convert one day into liters of warmed air using 1 minute = 6 breaths, and 1 breath = 0.5 L.

$$1\,\text{d} \times \frac{24\,\text{hr}}{1\,\text{d}} \times \frac{60\,\text{min}}{1\,\text{hr}} \times \frac{6\,\text{breaths}}{1\,\text{min}} \times \frac{0.5\,\text{L}}{1\,\text{breath}} = 4320\,\text{L} .$$

91. Convert 2 gigabytes into pages, using 2000 bytes = 1 page.

$$2\,\text{Gbyte} \times \frac{1\,\text{billion bytes}}{\text{Gbyte}} \times \frac{1\,\text{page}}{2000\,\text{bytes}} = 1\,\text{million pages}$$

92. a. Convert 15 years into dog years, using 1 year = 7 dog years.

$$15\,\text{yr} \times \frac{7\,\text{dog years}}{\text{yr}} = 105\,\text{dog years} .$$

b. The "terrible twos" stage in humans occurs between year 2 and 3, so the "terrible twos" stage in a dog's life occurs between dog year 2 and dog year 3. Convert each of these into years, and then, since each is a fraction of a year, convert into weeks for better understanding.

$$2\,\text{dog years} \times \frac{1\,\text{yr}}{7\,\text{dog years}} \times \frac{52\,\text{wk}}{1\,\text{yr}} = 15\,\text{weeks} .$$

$$3\,\text{dog years} \times \frac{1\,\text{yr}}{7\,\text{dog years}} \times \frac{52\,\text{wk}}{1\,\text{yr}} = 22\,\text{weeks} .$$

So a dog is between 15 and 22 weeks old when it experiences its "terrible twos" stage.

93. a. The volume of the bath is 6 ft × 3 ft × 2.5 ft = 45 ft³. Fill it to the halfway point, and you'll use 22.5 ft³ of water (half of 45 is 22.5). (Interesting side note: it doesn't matter which of the bathtub's three dimensions you regard as the height – fill it halfway, and it's always 22.5 ft³ of water). When you take a shower, you use

$$1\,\text{shower} \times \frac{10\,\text{min}}{\text{shower}} \times \frac{1.75\,\text{gal}}{\text{min}} \times \frac{1\,\text{ft}^3}{7.5\,\text{gal}} = 2.33\,\text{ft}^3$$

of water, and thus you use considerably more water when taking a bath.

b. Convert 22.5 ft³ of water (the water used in a bath) into minutes.

$$22.5\,\text{ft}^3 \times \frac{7.5\,\text{gal}}{1\,\text{ft}^3} \times \frac{1\,\text{min}}{1.75\,\text{gal}} = 96\,\text{min} .$$

c. Plug the drain in the bathtub, and mark the depth to which you would normally fill the tub when taking a bath. Take a shower, and note how long your shower lasts. Step out and towel off, but keep the shower running. When the water reaches

your mark (you used a crayon, and not a pencil, right?), note the time it took to get there. You now have a sense of how many showers it takes to use the same amount of water as a bath. For example, suppose your shower took 12 minutes, and it takes a full hour (60 minutes) for the water to reach your mark. That would mean every bath uses as much water as five showers.

94. a. Convert 9 billion gallons per day into cfs.

$$\frac{9,000,000,000\,\text{gal}}{\text{d}} \times \frac{1\,\text{ft}^3}{7.5\,\text{gal}} \times \frac{1\,\text{d}}{24\,\text{hr}} \times \frac{1\,\text{hr}}{60\,\text{min}} \times \frac{1\,\text{min}}{60\,\text{s}}$$

$$= 13,889\,\frac{\text{ft}^3}{\text{s}}, \text{ or } 13,889\,\text{cfs} ,$$

which is about 46% of the flow rate of the Colorado River.

b. The volume of water entering the city over the course of a day, in cubic feet, was

$$9,000,000,000\,\text{gal} \times \frac{1\,\text{ft}^3}{7.5\,\text{gal}} = 1,200,000,000\,\text{ft}^3 .$$

The area of the flooded portion of the city, in square feet, was

$$6\,\text{mi}^2 \times \left(\frac{5280\,\text{ft}}{1\,\text{mi}}\right)^2 = 167,270,400\,\text{ft}^2 .$$

If the volume of water is divided by the area it covers, you'll get the average depth of the water (this is similar to exercise 9):

$$\text{average depth} = \frac{\text{volume}}{\text{area}} = \frac{1,200,000,000\,\text{ft}^3}{167,270,400\,\text{ft}^2} = 7.2\,\text{ft} .$$

Thus the water level rose about 7 feet in one day, assuming the entire 6 square miles was covered in that day.

95. Convert 1 week into cubic feet of water.

$$1\,\text{wk} \times \frac{7\,\text{d}}{1\,\text{wk}} \times \frac{24\,\text{hr}}{1\,\text{d}} \times \frac{60\,\text{min}}{1\,\text{hr}} \times \frac{60\,\text{s}}{1\,\text{min}} \times \frac{25,800\,\text{ft}^3}{\text{s}}$$

$$= 15,603,840,000\,\text{ft}^3 ,$$

which is about 15.6 billion cubic feet. Since

$$\frac{15,603,840,000}{1,200,000,000,000} = 0.013 , \text{ about 1.3\% of the water}$$

in the reservoir was released.

UNIT 2B

QUICK QUIZ

1. **c.** The metric prefix *kilo* means 1000, so a kilometer is 1000 meters.

2. **c.** The metric prefix *mega* means 1,000,000, so a megaton is one million tons.

3. **a.** A millimeter is one-thousandth of a meter (or 0.001 meter), which is about the size of the point on a pen.

4. **a.** Apples are most likely to be sold by units of weight (or more accurately, mass), and thus euros per kilogram is the best answer.

5. **c.** One liter is equal to 1.057 quart, which is about one quart.

6. **c.** Water boils at 100°C (at sea level), so 105°C is boiling hot.

7. **b.** A watt is defined to be one joule per second, which is a unit of power, not energy.

8. **c.** Energy used by an appliance is computed by multiplying the power rating by the amount of time the appliance is used, so you need to know how long the light bulb is on in order to compute the energy it uses in that time span.

9. **a.** Multiplying the population density, which has units of $\frac{\text{people}}{\text{mi}^2}$, by the area, which has units of mi^2, will result in an answer with units of people.

10. **b.** Concentrations of gases are often stated in parts per million (and the other two answers make no sense).

DOES IT MAKE SENSE?

18. Makes sense. Liquids are measured in liters, and since one liter is about a quart, drinking two liters is a reasonable amount.

19. Does not make sense. First of all, we use the unit of kilogram to measure mass, not weight, though mass and weight are often used interchangeably in everyday conversation. Even so, a bicyclist with mass of 300 kg would weigh more than 650 pounds (on the surface of the earth), which is an unheard of weight for a professional cyclist.

20. Makes sense. 100 km/hr is roughly 60 mi/hr, which is a reasonable speed on an interstate.

21. Does not make sense. The units of liters per second might be used to measure the flow rate of a faucet, but not the speed at which someone runs (meters per second would make more sense for that).

22. Does not make sense. The world record for the high jump is around 8 feet (about 2.4 meters), and no one can high jump 7 meters.

23. Makes sense. 10,000 meters is 10 kilometers, which is about 6.2 miles, a common length for foot races. Anyone who can run six back-to-back 9-minute miles has no trouble running 10,000 meters in less than an hour.

24. Does not make sense. A milligram is a thousandth of a gram, and there are about 450 grams in a pound. Thus 3 milligrams is a very small weight compared to the weight of a book.

25. Does not make sense. The unit of meter measures length, not volume.

26. Makes sense. There are 4184 joules in a Calorie, and when 10,000,000 joules is converted into Calories, the result is about 2400 Calories, which is a typical caloric intake for an active person.

27. Does not make sense. Utility companies bill you for energy use (typically in units of kW-hr), not power ratings (recall that the watt is a unit of power).

28. Does not make sense. The volume of a sphere is $V = \frac{4}{3}\pi r^3$, so the volume of a beach ball with a radius of 20 cm (about 8 inches) would be more than 32,000 cm^3. This translates into a mass of 320,000 grams if the density is 10 grams per cm^3, which is 320 kg. The mass of a beach ball isn't anywhere near that large.

BASIC SKILLS & CONCEPTS

29. $10^4 \times 10^7 = 10^{4+7} = 10^{11}$.

30. $10^5 \times 10^{-3} = 10^{5-3} = 10^2$.

31. $10^6 \div 10^2 = 10^{6-2} = 10^4$.

32. $10^8 \div 10^{-4} = 10^{8-(-4)} = 10^{12}$.

33. $10^{-2} \times 10^{-6} = 10^{-2+(-6)} = 10^{-8}$.

34. $10^{-6} \div 10^{-8} = 10^{-6-(-8)} = 10^2$.

35. $10^{12} \times 10^{23} = 10^{12+23} = 10^{35}$.

36. $10^{-4} \div 10^5 = 10^{-4-5} = 10^{-9}$.

37. $10^{25} \div 10^{15} = 10^{25-15} = 10^{10}$.

38. $10^1 + 10^0 = 10 + 1 = 11$.

39. $10^2 + 10^{-1} = 100 + 0.1 = 100.1$.

40. $10^2 - 10^1 = 100 - 10 = 90$.

41. $10^{12} \div 10^{-4} = 10^{12-(-4)} = 10^{16}$.

42. $10^{23} \times 10^{-23} = 10^{23-23} = 10^0 = 1$.

43. $10^4 + 10^2 = 10,000 + 100 = 10,100$.

44. $10^{15} \div 10^{-5} = 10^{15-(-5)} = 10^{20}$.

45. Answers will vary. Consider a person who is 5 ft 10 in. tall. Since 5 ft $= 5 \text{ ft} \times \frac{12 \text{ in.}}{1 \text{ ft}} = 60 \text{ in.}$, that person is 60 in. + 10 in. = 70 in. tall.

46. Answers will vary. Consider a person who weighs 150 lb. That person will weigh

$$150 \text{ lb} \times \frac{16 \text{ oz}}{1 \text{ lb}} = 2400 \text{ oz}, \text{ which is}$$

$$150 \text{ lb} \times \frac{1 \text{ ton}}{2000 \text{ lb}} = 0.075 \text{ ton}.$$

47. Convert a cubic foot of water into pounds.

$$1 \text{ ft}^3 \text{ (of water)} \times \frac{7.48 \text{ gal}}{1 \text{ ft}^3} \times \frac{8.33 \text{ lb}}{1 \text{ gal}} = 62.3 \text{ lb} \ .$$

Now convert that answer into ounces.

$$62.3 \text{ lb} \times \frac{16 \text{ oz}}{1 \text{ lb}} = 997 \text{ oz} \ .$$

48. Use the fact that 1 nautical mile = 6076.1 feet to convert knots into mph.

$$30 \text{ knots} = \frac{30 \text{ naut. mi}}{\text{hr}} \times \frac{6076.1 \text{ ft}}{1 \text{ naut. mi}} \times \frac{1 \text{ mi}}{5280 \text{ ft}} = 34.5 \frac{\text{mi}}{\text{hr}}$$

49. Convert 2 gallons to pints, and then into cubic inches.

$$2 \text{ gal} \times \frac{4 \text{ qt}}{1 \text{ gal}} \times \frac{2 \text{ pt}}{1 \text{ qt}} = 16 \text{ pt};$$

$$16 \text{ pt} \times \frac{28.88 \text{ in.}^3}{1 \text{ pt}} = 462 \text{ in.}^3.$$

50. Convert fluid ounces into cubic inches.

$$12 \text{ oz} \times \frac{1 \text{ pt}}{16 \text{ oz}} \times \frac{28.88 \text{ in.}^3}{1 \text{ pt}} = 21.66 \text{ in.}^3 \ .$$

51. Convert bushels to cubic feet.

$$100,000 \text{ bushels} \times \frac{4 \text{ pecks}}{1 \text{ bushel}} \times \frac{8 \text{ qt}}{1 \text{ peck}} \times \frac{67.2 \text{ in.}^3}{1 \text{ qt}} \times \frac{1 \text{ ft}^3}{1728 \text{ in.}^3}$$
$$= 124,444 \text{ ft}^3 \ .$$

52. Divide the volume by the area it covers to find the depth of the garbage pile. Since the volume is reported in cubic feet, and the dimensions of the football field are given in yards, it is best to convert the football field's dimensions into feet before finding its area.

$$100 \text{ yd} \times \tfrac{3 \text{ ft}}{1 \text{ yd}} = 300 \text{ ft}; \ 60 \text{ yd} \times \tfrac{3 \text{ ft}}{1 \text{ yd}} = 180 \text{ ft}$$

So the area is $300 \text{ ft} \times 180 \text{ ft} = 54,000 \text{ ft}^2$, and the depth is $\frac{500,000 \text{ ft}^3}{54,000 \text{ ft}^2} = 9.26 \text{ ft}$.

53. You can tell the factor by which the first unit is larger (or smaller) than the second by dividing one into the other. Rewrite metric prefixes as powers of 10, and then simplify, as shown below.

$$\frac{1 \text{ cm}}{1 \text{ km}} = \frac{10^{-2} \text{ m}}{10^3 \text{ m}} = \frac{10^{-2}}{10^3} = 10^{-2-3} = 10^{-5} \ ,$$

which is one hundred-thousandth. This means a centimeter is 100,000 times smaller than a kilometer.

54. See exercise 53.

$$\frac{1 \text{ mL}}{1 \text{ L}} = \frac{10^{-3} \text{ L}}{1 \text{ L}} = 10^{-3} \ .$$ This is a thousandth, so a milliliter is 1000 times smaller than a liter.

55. See exercise 53.

$$\frac{1 \text{ L}}{1 \text{ mL}} = \frac{1 \text{ L}}{10^{-3} \text{ L}} = \frac{1}{10^{-3}} = 10^3 = 1000 \ ,$$ so a liter is 1000 times larger than a milliliter.

56. See exercise 53.

$$\frac{1 \ \mu m}{1 \text{ cm}} = \frac{10^{-6} \text{ m}}{10^{-2} \text{ m}} = 10^{-6-(-2)} = 10^{-4} \ ,$$ which is one ten-thousandth, so a micrometer is 10,000 times smaller than a centimeter.

57. See exercise 53.

$$\frac{1 \text{ m}^2}{1 \text{ km}^2} = \frac{1 \text{ m}^2}{(10^3 \text{ m})^2} = \frac{1 \text{ m}^2}{10^6 \text{ m}^2} = \frac{1}{10^6} = 10^{-6} \ ,$$ which is one millionth, so a square meter is one million times smaller than a square kilometer.

58. See exercise 53.

$$\frac{1 \text{ cm}^3}{1 \text{ m}^3} = \frac{(10^{-2} \text{ m})^3}{1 \text{ m}^3} = \frac{10^{-6} \text{ m}^3}{1 \text{ m}^3} = 10^{-6} \ ,$$ which is one millionth, so a cubic centimeter is one million times smaller than a cubic meter.

59. $8 \text{ m} \times \dfrac{3.28 \text{ m}}{1 \text{ ft}} = 26.2 \text{ ft}$.

60. $125 \text{ cm} \times \dfrac{1 \text{ m}}{100 \text{ cm}} \times \dfrac{1 \text{ yd}}{0.9144 \text{ m}} = 1.37 \text{ yd}$.

61. $10 \text{ lb} \times \dfrac{1 \text{ kg}}{2.205 \text{ lb}} = 4.54 \text{ kg}$.

62. $84 \text{ qt} \times \dfrac{1 \text{ L}}{1.057 \text{ qt}} = 79.47 \text{ L}$. (Note: you'll get an answer of 79.50 L if you use the conversion 0.9464 liter = 1 quart).

63. $45 \text{ L} \times \dfrac{1 \text{ gal}}{3.785 \text{ L}} = 11.89 \text{ gal}$.

64. Square both sides of the conversion 1 mi = 1.6093 km to find the conversion between square miles and square kilometers.

$$(1 \text{ mi})^2 = (1.6093 \text{ km})^2 \Rightarrow 1 \text{ mi}^2 = 2.59 \text{ km}^2 \ .$$

Now use this to complete the problem.

$$10 \text{ mi}^2 \times \frac{2.59 \text{ km}^2}{1 \text{ mi}^2} = 25.9 \text{ km}^2 \ .$$

65. Cube both sides of the conversion 2.54 cm = 1 in. to find the conversion between cubic centimeters and cubic inches.

$$(2.54 \text{ cm})^3 = (1 \text{ in.})^3 \Rightarrow 16.387 \text{ cm}^3 = 1 \text{ in.}^3 \ .$$

Now use this to complete the problem.

$$5 \text{ cm}^3 \times \frac{1 \text{ in.}^3}{16.387 \text{ cm}^3} = 0.31 \text{ in.}^3 \ .$$

66. Square both sides of the conversion 1 m = 3.28 ft to find the conversion between square meters and square feet.

$$(1 \text{ m})^2 = (3.28 \text{ ft})^2 \Rightarrow 1 \text{ m}^2 = 10.7584 \text{ ft}^2 \ .$$

Now use this to complete the problem.

$$8550 \text{ ft}^2 \times \frac{1 \text{ m}^2}{10.7584 \text{ ft}^2} = 794.73 \text{ m}^2 .$$

67. $\dfrac{10 \text{ kg}}{1 \text{ m}^3} \times \dfrac{2.205 \text{ lb}}{1 \text{ kg}} \times \left(\dfrac{1 \text{ m}}{3.28 \text{ ft}}\right)^3 = 0.62 \dfrac{\text{lb}}{\text{ft}^3} .$

68. $\dfrac{25 \text{ mi}}{\text{hr}} \times \dfrac{1 \text{ hr}}{60 \text{ min}} \times \dfrac{1 \text{ min}}{60 \text{ s}} \times \dfrac{1.6093 \text{ km}}{1 \text{ mi}} \times \dfrac{1000 \text{ m}}{1 \text{ km}} = 11.2 \dfrac{\text{m}}{\text{s}} .$

69. a. Use C = (F – 32)/1.8. C = (45 – 32)/1.8
   = 7.2°C.
   b. Use F = 1.8C + 32. F = 1.8(20) + 32 = 68°F.
   c. F = 1.8(-15) + 32 = 5°F.
   d. F = 1.8(-30) + 32 = -22°F.
   e. C = (70 – 32)/1.8 = 21.1°C.

70. a. Use F = 1.8C + 32. F = 1.8(-8) +32 = 17.6°F.
   b. Use C = (F – 32)/1.8. C = (15 – 32)/1.8
   = -9.4°C.
   c. F = 1.8(15) + 32 = 59°F.
   d. C = (75 – 32)/1.8 = 23.9°C.
   e. C = (20 – 32)/1.8 = -6.7°C.

71. a. Use C = K – 273.15. C = 50 – 273.15
   = -223.15°C.
   b. C = 240 – 273.15 = -33.15°C.
   c. Use K = C + 273.15. K = 10 + 273.15
   = 283.15 K.

72. a. Use K = C + 273.15. K = -40 + 273.15
   = 233.15 K.
   b. Use C = K – 273.15. C = 400 – 273.15
   = 126.85°C.
   c. K = 125 + 273.15 = 398.15 K.

73. Power is the rate at which energy is used, so the power is 1000 Calories per hour. Convert this to joules per second, or watts.

$$\frac{1000 \text{ Cal}}{1 \text{ hr}} \times \frac{1 \text{ hr}}{60 \text{ min}} \times \frac{1 \text{ min}}{60 \text{ s}} \times \frac{4184 \text{ j}}{1 \text{ Cal}} = \frac{1162 \text{ j}}{\text{s}} = 1162 \text{ W} .$$

Yes, this is plenty to keep a 100-watt bulb shining, assuming the energy generated playing basketball can be converted to electrical energy without too much loss.

74. Power is the rate at which energy is used, so the power is 300 Calories per 45 minutes. Convert this to joules per second, or watts.

$$\frac{300 \text{ Cal}}{45 \text{ min}} \times \frac{1 \text{ min}}{60 \text{ s}} \times \frac{4184 \text{ j}}{1 \text{ Cal}} = \frac{465 \text{ j}}{\text{s}} = 465 \text{ W} .$$

Yes, this is plenty to keep a 100-watt bulb shining, assuming the energy generated doing aerobics can be converted to electrical energy without too much loss.

75. a. Convert kilowatt-hours into joules.

$$1000 \text{ kW-hr} \times \frac{3,600,000 \text{ j}}{1 \text{ kW-hr}} = 3.6 \times 10^9 \text{ j} .$$

b. June has 30 days, so the average power is

$$\frac{3,600,000,000 \text{ j}}{30 \text{ d}} \times \frac{1 \text{ d}}{24 \text{ hr}} \times \frac{1 \text{ hr}}{60 \text{ min}} \times \frac{1 \text{ min}}{60 \text{ s}} = \frac{1389 \text{ j}}{\text{s}} = 1389 \text{ W} .$$

One could also begin with 1000 kW-hr per 30 days, and convert that into watts, using 1 watt = 1 joule per second.

c. First, convert joules into liters.

$$3.6 \times 10^9 \text{ j} \times \frac{1 \text{ L}}{12,000,000 \text{ j}} = 300 \text{ L} .$$

Now convert liters into gallons.

$$300 \text{ L} \times \frac{1 \text{ gal}}{3.785 \text{ L}} = 79 \text{ gal} .$$

Thus it would take 300 liters = 79 gallons of oil to provide the energy shown on the bill (assuming all the energy released by the burning oil could be captured and delivered to your home with no loss).

76. a. Convert kilowatt-hours into joules.

$$970 \text{ kW-hr} \times \frac{3,600,000 \text{ j}}{1 \text{ kW-hr}} = 3,492,000,000 \text{ j} .$$

b. September has 30 days, so the average power is

$$\frac{3,492,000,000 \text{ j}}{30 \text{ d}} \times \frac{1 \text{ d}}{24 \text{ hr}} \times \frac{1 \text{ hr}}{60 \text{ min}} \times \frac{1 \text{ min}}{60 \text{ s}} = \frac{1347 \text{ j}}{\text{s}} = 1347 \text{ W} .$$

One could also begin with 970 kW-hr per 30 days, and convert that into watts, using 1 watt = 1 joule per second.

c. First, convert joules into liters.

$$3,492,000,000 \text{ j} \times \frac{1 \text{ L}}{12,000,000 \text{ j}} = 291 \text{ L} .$$

Now convert liters into gallons.

$$291 \text{ L} \times \frac{1 \text{ gal}}{3.785 \text{ L}} = 77 \text{ gal} .$$

Thus it would take 291 liters = 77 gallons of oil to provide the energy shown on the bill (assuming all the energy released by the burning oil could be captured and delivered to your home with no loss).

77. Density is mass per unit volume, so the density of the pebble is $\dfrac{40 \text{ g}}{10 \text{ cm}^3} = 4 \dfrac{\text{g}}{\text{cm}^3}$. It will sink in water because the density of water is $1 \dfrac{\text{g}}{\text{cm}^3}$.

78. Density is mass per unit volume, so the density of the jug is $\dfrac{6 \text{ kg}}{8 \text{ L}} \times \dfrac{1000 \text{ g}}{1 \text{ kg}} \times \dfrac{1 \text{ L}}{1000 \text{ cm}^3} = 0.75 \dfrac{\text{g}}{\text{cm}^3}$. It will float in water because the density of water is $1 \dfrac{\text{g}}{\text{cm}^3}$.

79. Population density is people per unit area, so the average population density of the U.S. is

$$\frac{300,000,000 \text{ people}}{3,500,000 \text{ mi}^2} = 85.7 \frac{\text{people}}{\text{mi}^2} .$$

80. The population density for Hawaii is

$$\frac{1,300,000 \text{ people}}{6425 \text{ mi}^2} = 202 \ \frac{\text{people}}{\text{mi}^2}.$$

The population density for Arizona is

$$\frac{5,200,000 \text{ people}}{113,609 \text{ mi}^2} = 46 \ \frac{\text{people}}{\text{mi}^2},$$

which is smaller than Hawaii's population density.

81. The population density for New Jersey is

$$\frac{8,400,000 \text{ people}}{7419 \text{ mi}^2} = 1132 \ \frac{\text{people}}{\text{mi}^2}.$$

The population density for Wyoming is

$$\frac{490,000 \text{ people}}{97,105 \text{ mi}^2} = 5 \ \frac{\text{people}}{\text{mi}^2},$$

which is smaller than New Jersey's population density.

82. Information density is bytes per unit area, so the disk's information density is

$$\frac{250 \text{ Gbyte}}{40 \text{ cm}^2} = 6.25 \ \frac{\text{Gbyte}}{\text{cm}^2}.$$

83. a. BAC is usually measured in units of grams of alcohol per 100 milliliters of blood. A woman who drinks two glasses of wine, each with 20 grams of alcohol, has consumed 40 grams of alcohol. If she has 4000 milliliters of blood, her BAC is

$$\frac{40 \text{ g}}{4000 \text{ mL}} = \frac{0.01 \text{ g}}{\text{mL}} \times \frac{100}{100} = \frac{1 \text{ g}}{100 \text{ mL}}.$$

It is fortunate that alcohol is not absorbed immediately, because if it were, the woman would most likely die – a BAC above 0.4 g/mL is typically enough to induce coma or death.

b. If alcohol is eliminated from the body at a rate of 10 grams per hour, then after 3 hours, 30 grams would have been eliminated. This leaves 10 grams in the woman's system, which means her BAC is $\frac{10 \text{ g}}{4000 \text{ mL}} = \frac{0.0025 \text{ g}}{\text{mL}} \times \frac{100}{100} = \frac{0.25 \text{ g}}{100 \text{ mL}}$. This is well above the legal limit for driving, so it is not safe to drive. Of course this solution assumes the woman survives 3 hours of lethal levels of alcohol in her body, because we have assumed all the alcohol is absorbed immediately. In reality, the situation is somewhat more complicated.

84. a. BAC is usually measured in units of grams of alcohol per 100 milliliters of blood. A man who drinks 8 ounces of hard liquor has consumed 70 grams of alcohol, and with 6000 milliliters of blood, his BAC is

$$\frac{70 \text{ g}}{6000 \text{ mL}} = \frac{0.0117 \text{ g}}{\text{mL}} \times \frac{100}{100} = \frac{1.17 \text{ g}}{100 \text{ mL}}.$$

It is fortunate that alcohol is not absorbed immediately, because if it were, the man would be dead – a BAC above 0.4g/mL is typically enough to induce coma or death.

b. If alcohol is eliminated from the body at a rate of 15 grams per hour, then after 4 hours, 60 grams would have been eliminated. This leaves 10 grams of alcohol in the man's system, which means his BAC is $\frac{10 \text{ g}}{6000 \text{ mL}} = \frac{0.0017 \text{ g}}{\text{mL}} \times \frac{100}{100} = \frac{0.17 \text{ g}}{100 \text{ mL}}$. This is well above the legal limit for driving, so it is not safe to drive. Of course this solution assumes the man survives 4 hours of lethal levels of alcohol in his body, because we have assumed all the alcohol is absorbed immediately. In reality, the situation is somewhat more complicated.

85. a. A metric mile is $1500 \text{ m} \times \frac{3.28 \text{ ft}}{1 \text{ m}} = 4290$ ft. A USCS mile is 5280 ft. Since 4290/5280 = 0.932, the metric mile is 93.2% of the USCS mile.

86. Convert 1/16 inch into millimeters.

$$\frac{1}{16} \text{ in.} \times \frac{2.54 \text{ cm}}{1 \text{ in.}} \times \frac{10 \text{ mm}}{1 \text{ cm}} = 1.59 \text{ mm}.$$

Since the metric socket set uses subdivisions of 0.5 mm, the tools are not interchangeable, because 1.59 is not an integer multiple of 0.5, and there are more metric sockets for a given range of values than there are USCS sockets.

87. Mauna Kea is 18,200 ft + 13,796 ft = 31,996 ft when measured from its base on the ocean floor to its peak. This is $31,996 \text{ ft} \times \frac{1 \text{ mi}}{5280 \text{ ft}} = 6.06$ mi, and $31,996 \text{ ft} \times \frac{1 \text{ m}}{3.28 \text{ ft}} \times \frac{1 \text{ km}}{1000 \text{ m}} = 9.75$ km. When measured this way, Mauna Kea is higher than Mt. Everest, but, in the opinion of this author, it would be silly to claim Mauna Kea as the highest mountain in the world. The altitude of a mountain is its distance above sea level, and it's hardly fair to use one definition of altitude for one mountain, and another definition for an island mountain. After all, one could argue that Mt. Everest rises from the Bay of Bengal in India, and since the bay extends deep into the Indian Ocean, Mt. Everest is significantly "taller" than the 29,035 ft used here.

88. The Cullinan diamond weighs 3106 carats, which is $3106 \text{ carats} \times \frac{0.2 \text{ g}}{1 \text{ carat}} \times \frac{1000 \text{ mg}}{1 \text{ g}} = 621,200 \text{ mg}$, and

$$3106 \text{ carats} \times \frac{0.2 \text{ g}}{1 \text{ carat}} \times \frac{1 \text{ kg}}{1000 \text{ g}} \times \frac{2.205 \text{ lb}}{1 \text{ kg}} = 1.37 \text{ lb}.$$

The Star of Africa weighs 530.2 carats, which is 106,040 mg, and 0.23 lb (the conversions being identical to those shown above).

89. 24-karat gold is 100% pure, and since 25% of 24 is $0.25 \times 24 = 6$, a nugget that is 25% pure is 6-karat gold.

90. 15 grams of 14-karat gold is $\frac{14}{24} \times 15\,\text{g} = 8.75\,\text{g}$ of pure gold.

91. $2.5\,\text{carats} \times \frac{0.2\,\text{g}}{1\,\text{carat}} = 0.5\,\text{g}$.

92. No, 30-karat gold is not possible, because 24-karat gold is 100% pure, and one cannot exceed 100% purity.

93. In order to compute the cost, we need to find the energy used by the refrigerator in kW-hr, and then convert to cents (after which it may make sense to convert to dollars). This can be done in a single chain of unit conversions, beginning with the idea that energy = power × time (this is true because power is the rate at which energy is consumed; that is, power = energy/time).

$$350\,\text{W} \times 1\,\text{yr} \times \frac{1\,\text{kW}}{1000\,\text{W}} \times \frac{365\,\text{d}}{1\,\text{yr}} \times \frac{24\,\text{hr}}{1\,\text{d}} \times \frac{10¢}{1\,\text{kW-hr}} \times \frac{\$1}{100¢}$$

$= \$306.60$, or about $307.

94. In order to compute the cost, we need to find the energy used by the hair dryer in kW-hr, and then convert to cents. This can be done in a single chain of unit conversions, beginning with the idea that energy = power × time.

$$1800\,\text{W} \times 10\,\text{min} \times \frac{1\,\text{kW}}{1000\,\text{W}} \times \frac{1\,\text{hr}}{60\,\text{min}} \times \frac{11¢}{1\,\text{kW-hr}} = 3.3¢ \,.$$

This is the cost to run the hair dryer each day, because you use it for only 10 minutes per day. To find the cost per year, multiply 3.3¢ by 365 (1 year = 365 days) to get 1204.5¢, or about $12.05 per year.

95. Compute the energy used by a 75-watt bulb in 10,000 hours. This will be the energy saved when replacing a 100-watt bulb with a 25-watt bulb.

$$75\,\text{W} \times 10,000\,\text{hr} \times \frac{1\,\text{kW}}{1000\,\text{W}} = 750\,\text{kW-hr} \,.$$

Convert 750 kW-hr into cents (and then dollars) to find out how much money is saved.

$$750\,\text{kW-hr} \times \frac{10¢}{1\,\text{kW-hr}} \times \frac{\$1}{100¢} = \$75 \,.$$

96. a. Your power is the rate at which you use energy, and thus your average power is 2500 Calories per day. Convert this to watts.

$$\frac{2500\,\text{Cal}}{\text{d}} \times \frac{1\,\text{d}}{24\,\text{hr}} \times \frac{1\,\text{hr}}{60\,\text{min}} \times \frac{1\,\text{min}}{60\,\text{s}} \times \frac{4184\,\text{j}}{1\,\text{Cal}} = 121\frac{\text{j}}{\text{s}} \,.$$

Since 1 W = 1 j/s, this is 121 watts.

b. $\dfrac{2500\,\text{Cal}}{\text{d}} \times \dfrac{365\,\text{d}}{\text{yr}} \times \dfrac{4184\,\text{j}}{1\,\text{Cal}} = 3,817,900,000\,\text{j}$, so you need about 3.8 billion joules each year from food, which is very close to 1% of your total energy consumption (3.8 billion/400 billion = 0.0095).

97. Since energy = power × time, the power plant can produce (assuming a 30-day month)

$$1.5 \times 10^9\,\text{W} \times 1\,\text{month} \times \frac{30\,\text{d}}{\text{month}} \times \frac{24\,\text{hr}}{\text{d}} \times \frac{1\,\text{kW}}{1000\,\text{W}}$$

$= 1.08 \times 10^9\,\text{kW-hr} = 1.08$ billion kW-hr

of energy every month. The plant needs

$$1.08 \times 10^9\,\tfrac{\text{kW-hr}}{1\,\text{month}} \times \tfrac{1\,\text{kg}}{450\,\text{kW-hr}} = 2.4 \times 10^6\,\tfrac{\text{kg}}{\text{month}} \,,$$

or 2.4 million kg of coal every month. Because

$$1.08 \times 10^9\,\text{kW-hr} \times \frac{1\,\text{home}}{1000\,\text{kW-hr}} = 1.08 \times 10^6\,\text{homes} \,,$$

the plant can serve 1.08 million homes.

98. Since energy = power × time, the power plant can produce (assuming a 30-day month)

$$740\,\text{MW} \times 1\,\text{month} \times \frac{30\,\text{d}}{1\,\text{month}} \times \frac{24\,\text{hr}}{1\,\text{d}} \times \frac{1000\,\text{kW}}{1\,\text{MW}}$$

$$= 5.328 \times 10^8\,\text{kW-hr}$$

of energy each month. The amount of uranium used each month is given by

$$5.328 \times 10^8\,\frac{\text{kW-hr}}{\text{month}} \times \frac{1\,\text{kg}}{16 \times 10^6\,\text{kW-hr}} = 33.3\,\frac{\text{kg}}{\text{month}} \,.$$

The plant can serve 532,800 homes, because

$$5.328 \times 10^8\,\text{kW-hr} \times \frac{1\,\text{home}}{1000\,\text{kW-hr}} = 532,800\,\text{homes} \,.$$

99. At 20% efficiency, this solar panel can generate 200 watts of power when exposed to direct sunlight. Since energy = power × time, and because the panel receives the equivalent of 6 hours of direct sunlight, the panel can produce

$$200\,\text{W} \times 6\,\text{hr} \times \frac{1\,\text{kW}}{1000\,\text{W}} \times \frac{3,600,000\,\text{j}}{\text{kW-hr}} = 4,320,000\,\text{j} \,.$$

This occurs over the span on one day, so the panel produces an average power of

$$\frac{4,320,000\,\text{j}}{\text{d}} \times \frac{1\,\text{d}}{24\,\text{hr}} \times \frac{1\,\text{hr}}{60\,\text{min}} \times \frac{1\,\text{min}}{60\,\text{s}} = 50\,\frac{\text{j}}{\text{s}} = 50\,\text{W} \,.$$

100. In exercise 99, each solar panel covers one square meter. You would need

$$1\,\text{kW} \times \frac{1000\,\text{W}}{1\,\text{kW}} \times \frac{1\,\text{panel}}{50\,\text{W}} = 20\,\text{panels} \,,$$

which is 20 square meters of solar panels.

101. Energy = power × time, so the energy produced by a wind turbine over the course of a year is

$$200\,\text{kW} \times 1\,\text{yr} \times \frac{365\,\text{d}}{1\,\text{yr}} \times \frac{24\,\text{hr}}{1\,\text{d}} = 1,752,000\,\text{kW-hr} \,.$$

This is enough energy to serve

$$1,752,000\,\text{kW-hr} \times \frac{1\,\text{home}}{10,000\,\text{kW-hr}} = 175\,\text{homes} \,.$$

102. a. Energy = power × time, so the energy produced by the wind farms over the span of a year is

$$4.3 \times 10^9 \text{ W} \times 1 \text{ yr} \times \frac{365 \text{ d}}{1 \text{ yr}} \times \frac{24 \text{ hr}}{1 \text{ d}} \times \frac{1 \text{ kW}}{1000 \text{ W}}$$

$$= 3.7688 \times 10^{10} \text{ kW-hr} .$$

This is enough energy to serve

$$3.7688 \times 10^{10} \text{ kW-hr} \times \frac{1 \text{ home}}{10,000 \text{ kW-hr}}$$

$$= 3,768,800 \text{ homes} .$$

b. If the 3.7688×10^{10} kW-hr of energy produced by wind farms were instead produced from fossil fuels, there would be

$$3.7688 \times 10^{10} \text{ kW-hr} \times \frac{1.5 \text{ lb}}{1 \text{ kw-hr}} = 5.6532 \times 10^{10} \text{ lb} ,$$

or about 56.5 billion pounds of carbon dioxide entering the atmosphere each year.

UNIT 2C

QUICK QUIZ

1. **c**. Look at example 1 (*Box Office Receipts*) in this unit.

2. **a**. You must have done something wrong as gas mileage is reported in units of miles per gallon.

3. **b**. Common experience tells us that batteries can power a flashlight for many hours, not just a few minutes nor several years.

4. **b**. An elevator that carried only 10 kg couldn't accommodate even one person (a 150 lb person weighs about 75 kg), and hotel elevators aren't designed to carry hundreds of people (you'd need at least 100 people to reach 10,000 kg).

5. **b**. Refer to the discussion of Zeno's paradox in the text. There, it was shown that the sum of an infinite number of ever-smaller fraction is equal to 2, and thus we can eliminate answers **a** and **c**. This leaves **b**.

6. **a**. If you cut the cylinder along its length, and lay it flat, it will form a rectangle with width equal to the circumference of the cylinder (i.e. 10 in.), and with length equal to the length of the cylinder.

7. **c**. A widow is a woman who survives the death of her husband, and thus the man is dead, making it impossible for him to marry anyone.

8. **c**. It could happen that the first 20 balls selected are odd, in which case the next two would have to be even, and this is the first time one can be certain of selecting two even balls.

9. **b**. The most likely explanation is that the A train always arrives 10 minutes after the B train. Suppose the A train arrives on the hour (12:00, 1:00, 2:00,...), while the B train arrives ten minutes before the hour (11:50, 12:50, 1:50,...). If Karen gets to the station in the first 50 minutes of the hour, she'll take the B train; otherwise she'll take the A train. Since an hour is 60 minutes long, 5/6 of the time, Karen will take the B train to the beach. Note that 5/6 of 30 days is 25 days, which is the number of times Karen went to the beach. The other scenarios *could* happen, but they aren't nearly as likely as the scenario in answer **b**.

10. **b**. Label the hamburgers as A, B, and C. Put burgers A and B on the grill. After 5 minutes, turn burger A, take burger B and put it on a plate, and put burger C on the grill. After 10 minutes, burger A is cooked, while burgers B and C are half-cooked. Finish off burgers B and C in the final 5 minutes, and you've cooked all three in 15 minutes.

DOES IT MAKE SENSE?

13. Does not make sense. There is no problem-solving recipe that can be applied to all problems.

14. Makes sense. It's generally a waste of time to blindly dive into the solution of a problem if you don't take the time to understand its nature.

15. Does not make sense. The four-step method is applicable to a wide variety of problems, and is not limited to mathematical problems. (It's not a cure-all, either, but it's quite useful, and worth learning).

16. Does not make sense. Pictures can be extremely beneficial in the problem solving process as they allow young and old alike to visualize the problem.

BASIC SKILLS & CONCEPTS

17. You won't be able to determine the exact number of child and adult tickets sold, but the method of trial-and-error leads to the following possible solutions: (1 child, 6 adult), (4 child, 4 adult), (7 child, 2 adult), (10 child, 0 adult). Along the way, you may have noticed that the number of adult tickets must be an even number, because when it is odd, the remaining money cannot be divided evenly into $20 (child) tickets.

18. The method of trial-and-error produces the following possible recipes: (12 cranberry, 0 ginger ale), (11 c, 2 g), (10 c, 4 g), (9 c, 6 g), (8 c, 8 g), (7 c, 10 g), (6 c, 12 g), (5 c, 14 g), (4 c, 16 g), (3 c, 18 g), (2 c, 20 g), (1 c, 22 g), (0 c, 24 g). You probably won't be able to find the exact recipe for the punch except in the first and last cases. In the first, there's no ginger ale, and thus a quick taste test will reveal no carbonation, and nothing but

cranberry flavor. In the last, there's no need for a taste test as the color of the punch will tell you there's nothing but ginger ale in the bowl. If you really needed to find the recipe you used, check the garbage can.

19. Jill runs 100 meters in 15 seconds, so she'll run 105 meters in 15.75 seconds. To see why this is so, treat her rate of 100 m/15 s as a unit conversion factor (the reciprocal of which can also be used): $105 \text{ m} \times \frac{15 \text{ s}}{100 \text{ m}} = 15.75 \text{ s}$. In the first race, Jack runs 95 meters in 15 seconds, so his time to the finish line (at 100 meters) in the second race is $100 \text{ m} \times \frac{15 \text{ s}}{95 \text{ m}} = 15.7895 \text{ s}$. The difference of these times, 15.7895 s – 15.75 s = 0.0395 s, is the amount of time by which Jill beats Jack.

20. Based on the first race data, Hack runs 200 meters in the time it takes Quill to run 190 meters. In the second race, Hack will catch up to Quill 10 meters from the finish line (because Hack has covered 200 meters at that point, and Quill has covered 190 meters). Hack will win the race in the last ten meters, because Hack runs faster than Quill.

21. Note that after two hours, the cars collide, because the first travels at 80 km/hr, and thus covers 160 km, while the second travels at 100 km/hr, and covers 200 km. The canary is flying at 120 km/hr for the entire 2 hours, so it has flown 240 km.

22. At 250 ft/s, it will take the skydiver 16 seconds to reach the ground $\left(4000 \text{ ft} \times \frac{1 \text{ s}}{250 \text{ ft}} = 16 \text{ s} \right)$. In the same time, the falcon will have flown 8000 feet $\left(500 \frac{\text{ft}}{\text{s}} \times 16 \text{ s} = 8000 \text{ ft} \right)$.

23. On the second transfer, there are four possibilities to consider. A) All three marbles are black. B) Two are black, one is white. C) One is black, two are white. D) All three are white. In case A), after the transfer, there are no black marbles in the white pile, and no white marbles in the black pile. In case B), one white marble is transferred to the black pile, and one black marble is left in the white pile. In case C), two white marbles are transferred to the black pile, and two black marbles are left in the white pile. In case D), three white marbles are transferred to the black pile, and three black marbles are left in the white pile. In all four cases, there are as many white marbles in the black pile as there are black marbles in the white pile after the second transfer.

24. The method of solution is identical to exercise 23, except that there are five cases to consider.

25. Cut one of the columns lengthwise, and press it flat – this results in a rectangle with height = 12 feet, and width = circumference of column = 3 feet. As shown in example 5, a wrap of ribbon becomes the hypotenuse of a right triangle. The base of the triangle is 3 feet. Because there are ten wraps per column, its height is one-tenth the height of the column, which is 12/10 = 6/5 ft. By the Pythagorean theorem, the length of one wrap of ribbon is $h = \sqrt{3^2 + \left(\frac{6}{5} \right)^2} = 3.231 \text{ ft}$, and thus 32.31 feet of ribbon are required for one column (ten wraps, each of length 3.231 ft). To wrap all 40 columns, multiply 32.31 by 40 to arrive at 1292.4 feet.

26. Cut the pipe along its length, and press it flat – this results in a rectangle with height = 20 cm, and width = circumference of pipe = 6 cm. As shown in example 5, a wrap of wire becomes the hypotenuse of a right triangle, whose base is 6 cm, and whose height, because there are 8 turns of wire, is 1/8 of 20 cm = 2.5 cm. By the Pythagorean theorem, the length of one turn of the wire is $h = \sqrt{6^2 + 2.5^2} = 6.5 \text{ cm}$, and thus the total length of wire required is 52 cm (8 turns of wire, each 6.5 cm long).

27. If the rail forms a circular arc, as stated in the problem, the radius of this circle would be quite large, and the curvature of the arc would be very small. Thus a straight line is a reasonable approximation to the slowly-turning curve of the circular arc. A circle of radius 1/2-mile would not make a good approximation, because the length of the semi-circular arc so formed would be half the circumference of a circle of radius 1/2-mile. This comes out to 8294 ft, which is more than 3000 feet longer than the straight rail. However, we are told the straight rail only increases in length by one foot.

28. Proceeding as in example 6, the circular arc formed by the bowed track can be approximated by two congruent right triangles. Since 1 km is 100,000 cm, the base of one of the triangles is 50,000 cm, and its hypotenuse is 50,005 cm. The height of the triangle can be computed as
$$h = \sqrt{50,005^2 - 50,000^2} = 707 \text{ cm},$$
which is about 7.1 meters.

30. For every 220 people, 120 are male, and 100 are female. Thus 120/220 = 54.55% of the population is male, and 100/220 = 45.45% of the population is female. The difference in these percents (9.1%) represents the percent of men who will not be able to find a spouse. 9.1% of 450 million is 0.091×450 million = 40,950,000, or about 41 million. This of course assumes one female for every male – the reality is somewhat different

when things like divorce and second marriages are factored into the equation.

FURTHER APPLICATIONS

31. This problem can be solved by trial and error. Using one bag of topsoil, for example, leaves 22 cubic feet, which would require 11 bags of fertilizer. Thus one solution is (1 topsoil, 11 fertilizer). The others are found in a similar fashion: (3 topsoil, 8 fertilizer), (5 topsoil, 5 fertilizer), (7 topsoil, 2 fertilizer). You may have noticed along the way that there must be an odd number of bags of topsoil so that the remaining volume to be filled by fertilizer is divisible by two.

32. Note that at least one truck must have passed over the counter as there are an odd number of counts, and we must have an odd number of trucks for the same reason. Beginning with one truck, followed by 3, 5, 7, etc. trucks, and computing the number of cars that go along with these possible truck solutions, we arrive at the following answers: (1 truck, 16 cars), (3 t, 13 c), (5 t, 10 c), (7 t, 7 c), (9 t, 4 c), and (11 t, 1 c).

33. Following the hint given in the problem, the best place to start is with a drawing that shows the room cut along its vertical corners and laid flat. Figure 33a shows the room and the configuration of the amplifier and speaker before the cuts are made, and Figure 33b shows the room in "flat mode." Note that there are at least two solutions to consider (a third will be presented in Figure 33c).

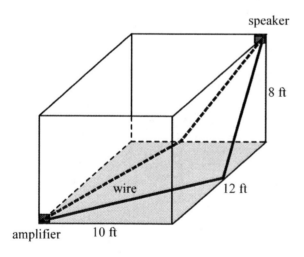

FIGURE 33a

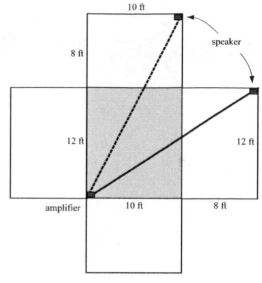

FIGURE 33b

In flat mode, it is clear that the shortest distance between the amplifier and the speaker is a straight line, though there are two possible paths (the upper right hand corner of the room, where the speaker is situated, must be represented twice, as shown in Figure 33b). In both cases, the distance from the amplifier to the speaker can be computed using the Pythagorean theorem.

Case 1 (lower triangle): the length of the wire is

$$\sqrt{18^2 + 12^2} = \sqrt{468} = 21.6 \text{ ft} .$$

Case 2 (upper triangle): the length of the wire is

$$\sqrt{20^2 + 10^2} = \sqrt{500} = 22.4 \text{ ft} .$$

Based on these calculations, the shortest length of wire needed to connect the amplifier to the speaker is 21.6 ft. However, there's a third possibility that is not evident when looking at Figure 33b. In order to see it, the room must be cut and laid flat in a different configuration, shown here.

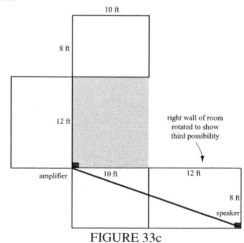

FIGURE 33c

This solution has the wire traveling along the walls of the room for its entire length, which is

$$\sqrt{22^2 + 8^2} = \sqrt{548} = 23.4 \text{ ft}.$$

Since this does not produce a shorter length of wire than the previous solution, the answer remains 21.6 ft (different room dimensions might reveal that Figure 33c is the best choice). There are other ways to run the wire not shown here, such as rotating the back wall in a manner similar to Figure 33c (this gives an equivalent solution of 23.4 ft), or running the wire along the ceiling. However, the problem states the wire is to run along the floor and walls, so the ceiling solutions need not be considered. Try some solutions along the ceiling if you're curious – you'll find they are equivalent to running the wire along the floor.

34. Refer to Figure 33a. If the wire must run along the edges of the room, the shortest distance is 10 ft + 12 ft + 8 ft = 30 ft. There are six ways to produce this minimum length, depending on which direction one chooses at each corner.

35. Assuming the endpoints of the bridge are at the level of the river, and that the length of the curved bridge can be reasonably approximated by two straight lines (as shown in Figure 35), the height of the bridge can be determined by the Pythagorean theorem.

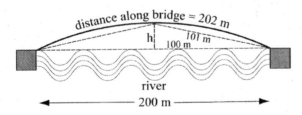

FIGURE 35

$$h = \sqrt{101^2 - 100^2} = \sqrt{201} = 14 \text{ m}.$$

36. Assuming the endpoints of the bridge are at the level of the river, and that the walking distance along the bridge can be reasonably approximated by straight lines, the distance is twice the length of the hypotenuse H shown in Figure 36.

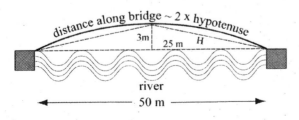

FIGURE 36

H can be computed using the Pythagorean theorem.

$$H = \sqrt{25^2 + 3^2} = \sqrt{634} = 25.2 \text{ m}.$$

Double this answer to find the length along the bridge: 50.4 meters.

37. In going from the first floor to the third floor, you have gone up two floors. Since it takes 30 seconds to do that, your pace is 15 seconds per floor. Walking from the first floor to the sixth floor means walking up five floors, and at 15 seconds per floor, this will take 75 seconds.

38. Reuben's birthday is December 31, and he's talking to you on January 1. Thus two days ago, he was 20 years old on December 30. He turned 21 the next day. "Later *next* year," refers to almost two years later, when he will turn 23 (*this* year on December 31, he will turn 22).

39. You might pick one of each kind of apple on the first three draws. On the fourth draw, you are guaranteed to pick an apple that matches one of the first three, so four draws are required.

40. That man is the son of the person speaking (who, in turn, is the son of his father, and an only child).

41. The blind fiddler is a woman.

42. The woman gained $100 in each transaction, so she gained $200 overall.

43. Select a fruit from the box labeled *Apples and Oranges*. If it's an apple, that box must be the *Apple* box (because its original label is incorrect, leaving only *Apples* or *Oranges* as its correct label). The correct label for the box labeled *Oranges* is either *Apples* or *Apples and Oranges*, but we just determined the box containing apples, so the correct label for this box is *Apples and Oranges*. There's only one choice left for the box labeled *Apples*, and that's *Oranges*. A similar argument allows one to determine the correct labeling for each box if an orange is selected first.

44. Select one ball from the first barrel, two balls from the second barrel, three from the third, and so on, ending with ten balls chosen from the tenth barrel. Find the weight of all 55 balls thus chosen. If all the balls weighed one ounce, the weight would be 55 ounces. But we know one of the barrels contains two-ounce balls. Suppose the first barrel contained the two-ounce balls – then the weighing would reveal a result of 56 ounces, and we'd know the first barrel was the one that contains two-ounce balls. If, in fact, the second barrel contained the two-ounce balls, the combined weight would be 57 ounces. A combined weight of 58 ounces means the third barrel contained the heavy balls. Continuing in this fashion, we see that a combined weight of *n* ounces more than 55 ounces

corresponds to the *nth* barrel containing the two-ounce balls.

45. Seven crossings are required. Trip 1: the woman crosses with the goose. Trip 2: the woman returns to the other shore by herself. Trip 3: the woman takes the mouse across. Trip 4: the woman returns with the goose. Trip 5: the woman brings the wolf across. Trip 6: the woman returns to the other shore by herself. Trip 7: the woman brings the goose over. In this way, the goose is never left alone with the wolf, nor the mouse with the goose. The foursome could get to the other side of the river in five crossings if you give rowing abilities to the animals, but the statement of the problem (and common sense) probably forbids it (the boat "…will hold only herself and one other animal"). Try it anyway for an interesting twist to the problem.

46. Turn both the 7-minute and 4-minute hourglasses over to begin timing. At 4 minutes, turn the 4-minute hourglass over again. At 7 minutes, turn the 7-minute hourglass over; there will be one minute of sand left in the 4-minute hourglass. At 8 minutes, the upper chamber of the 4-minute hourglass will be empty, and one minute of sand will have drained into the lower chamber of the 7-minute hourglass. Turn the 7-minute hourglass over to time the last minute. This is only one solution of many. Another: Turn both hourglasses over whenever their upper chambers are empty. After 12 minutes (three cycles of the 4-minute hourglass), there will be 5 minutes of sand in the bottom chamber of the 7-minute hourglass. Turn that hourglass on its side. Now you are prepared to measure a 9-minute interval whenever you please (use the 5 minutes of sand in the 7-minute hourglass, followed by one cycle of the 4-minute hourglass).

47. Ten rungs will be showing – the boat rises with the tide.

48. A balance scale is one that displays a needle in the middle when both sides of the scale are loaded with equal weights. Put six coins on each side of the scale. The side with the heavy coin will be lower, so discard the other six. Now put three coins of the remaining six on each side of the scale, and as before, discard the three that are in the light group. Finally, select two of the remaining three coins, and put one on each side of the scale. The scale will be even if the heavy coin is not on the scale. The scale will tip to one side if the heavy coin was in the final selection. This is just one solution – another begins by dividing the 12 coins into three groups of four coins. See if you can supply the logic necessary to find the heavy coin in that scenario.

49. It's possible you'll pick a sock of each color on the first two draws, but on the third draw, you are assured of making a match.

50. Cleo visited Elf last. The second clue tells us Alma and Bess could not visit in consecutive hours, which means one must have visited in the morning, and the other in the evening. The third clue tells us Alma could not visit at 8:00 am, because then she would have gone before both Cleo and Dina. So at this stage we know Alma visited at 8 p.m., and Bess at 9 a.m., and the second clue also tells us at least one of Cleo or Dina visited in the morning. This leaves three possibilities to consider: Cleo and Dina both visited in the morning, Cleo visited in the morning while Dina came at night, or Dina came in the morning while Cleo showed up at night. Of these, only the last satisfies clue four, so Dina must have visited at 11 a.m., and Cleo at 10 p.m. (which means Cleo visited Elf last).

51. The first prisoner would know he had a white hat if he saw red hats on prisoners 2 and 3. Since he doesn't know the color of his hat, prisoners 2 and 3 are both wearing white hats, or one has a white hat while the other has a red hat. If prisoner 2 saw a red hat on prisoner 3, he would know that he must have a white hat (he can't have a red hat while seeing red on prisoner 3, because then prisoner 1 would know his color). But he doesn't know, which means prisoner 3 must have a white hat. Prisoner 3 doesn't need to see the hats of the other prisoners; he can deduce that his hat is white simply by hearing the other two prisoners confess they don't know what hats they are wearing.

52. The visitor should patronize the barber with unkempt hair, because he's the barber that cuts the hair of the other barber (who has a splendid hair cut). Of course we are assuming that these barbers don't travel out of town to get their hair done.

53. The coin has revolved twice (720° of revolution). The best way to see this is to duplicate the experiment. Another way to think about it: consider two circular clocks (instead of coins), nestled side by side, both in the same position, with 12-o'clock pointing straight ahead (see Figure 53). Roll the right clock around the left clock until the 12's are touching. The right clock has rotated 180°, but it's made only 1/4 of its journey around the left clock. By the time it makes the full journey around, it will have rotated 720°.

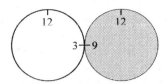

initial position of clocks

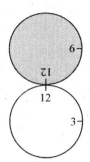

right clock has rotated 180°
(it's upside down), yet it has
made only 1/4 of its journey
around the left clock

FIGURE 53

54. When a clock chimes five times, there are four pauses between each chime. Since it takes five seconds to chime five times, each pause lasts 1.25 seconds. There are nine pauses that need to be accounted for when the clock chimes 10 times, and thus it takes $9 \times 1.25 = 11.25$ seconds to chime 10 times. This solution assumes it takes no time for the clock to chime once (we'd need to know the duration of the chime to solve it otherwise).

55. a. Assume the babies are named A, B, C, and D. If two babies are correctly tagged, the other two labels must be switched for their labels to be incorrect. Thus the problem boils down to counting the number of ways two of the babies can be correctly tagged. Listing all the options is the easiest way to count them. Babies AB could be correctly labeled (leaving babies C and D labeled incorrectly), and the other options for correct labels are AC, AD, BC, BD, and CD. This makes six different ways.

b. If three of the babies have correct labels, the other baby must also have a correct label, which means there is no way to label three of the babies correctly while the fourth is labeled incorrectly.

56. Each guest has, in fact, spent $9. But not all of the $27 spent is resting in the cash register at the front desk. The front desk has $25, the bellhop has $2 (this adds up to the $27 spent), and each guest has $1, for a total of $30. The reason the problem is perplexing is that we think of the $2 held by the bellhop as a *positive* $2, and so it should be added to the $27 spent by the guests to somehow produce the original $30. But from the perspective of the desk clerk running the cash register, the $2 is a *negative* value – it represents money out of the till. $30 (*positive*) came into the till, $2 (*negative*) went to the bellhop, and $1 (*negative*) went to each of the guests. Thus the equation we should be looking at is 30 – 2 – 1 – 1 – 1 = $25 in the cash register (which is correct), or $27 - $2 = $25 (also correct), but *not* $27 + $2 (which is just silly).

UNIT 3A

QUICK QUIZ

1. **b**. A quantity triples when it is increased by 200%.
2. **b**. The absolute change is 75,000 – 50,000 = 25,000, and the relative change is $\frac{75,000-50,000}{50,000} = 0.5 = 50\%$.
3. **c**. A negative relative change corresponds to a decreasing quantity.
4. **c**. Suppose Joshua scored 1000 on the SAT. Then Emily would have scored 1500 (50% more than 1000), and Joshua's score is clearly two-thirds of Emily's score (1000/1500 = 2/3).
5. **c**. 120% of $10 is $12.
6. **c**. Multiplying a pre-tax price by 1.09 is equivalent to adding 9% tax to the price, and thus dividing a post-tax price by 1.09 will result in the original price. To find out how much tax was paid, take the post-tax price, and subtract the original price: $47.96 $- \frac{\$47.96}{1.09}$.
7. **a**. The relative change in interest rates that go from 6% to 9% is $\frac{9\%-6\%}{6\%} = 0.5 = 50\%$.
8. **c**. When a price is decreased by 100%, it drops to zero, as the entire amount of the price is deducted from the original price.
9. **c**. 10% of $1000 is $100, so your monthly earnings after one year will be $1100. Each year thereafter, your earnings will increase by more than $100 per year (because 10% of $1100 is more than $100), and the end result will be more than $1500.
10. **b**. The only thing we can conclude with certainty is that she won between 20% and 30% of her races. To prove this rigorously, one could detour into an algebra calculation (let x = number of races entered in high school, let y = number of races entered in college, and show that $\frac{0.3x + 0.2y}{x + y}$ is between 20% and 30%). Try different values for x and y, and compute the win percentage of all the races Emily entered to see that answers **a** and **c** are not correct.

DOES IT MAKE SENSE?

17. Makes sense. If a country's population is declining, then the percent change will be negative (and several of Europe's countries have, indeed, experienced recent declines in population).
18. Makes sense. As a 100% increase corresponds with a doubling, a 200% increase corresponds with a tripling.
19. Makes sense. An older child could easily weigh 25% more than a younger child (think of 100-pound and 125-pound children).
20. Does not make sense. You cannot decrease your caloric intake by more than 100% (and you wouldn't want to do that for too long).
21. Does not make sense. Consider the case where I earn $100, and you earn $120. You earn $20 more than I do, which corresponds to 20% more than me (because 20% of $100 is $20). Even though I earn $20 less than you, I do not earn 20% less than you (because 20% of $120 is not $20). In fact, I earn 1/6 less than you do, which is about 16.7% less.
22. Does not make sense. Decreasing a quantity by several successive percent changes is not equivalent to a one-time percent decrease that is the sum of the successive changes. This can be seen with a simple example: take $100 and decrease it by 10% to $90, followed by another 10% decrease to $81. Now take the same $100 and decrease it by 20% to $80. Two successive 10% changes is not equivalent to a single 20% change, just like ten successive 10% changes is not equivalent to a 100% change.
23. Makes sense. This just means that the incidence of cancer for children living near toxic landfills was seven times larger than the incidence of cancer among other children.
24. Does not make sense. In a weighted average like this, the course average is computed by taking 75% of the pre-final work, and adding it to 25% of the final exam score. The student in this scenario would end up with a 65% course average, because $0.75 \times 60\% + 0.25 \times 80\% = 65\%$.
25. Makes sense. If the rate of return on the fund used to be 10%, then a 50% increase would result in a rate of return of 15%.
26. Makes sense. A 100% increase is the same as a doubling, and twice 2% is 4%.

BASIC SKILLS AND CONCEPTS

27. 2/5 = 0.4 = 40%.
28. 30% = 0.3 = 3/10.
29. 0.20 = 1/5 = 20%.
30. 0.85 = 85% = 17/20.
31. 150% = 1.5 = 3/2.
32. 2/3 = 0.666… = 66.66…%.
33. 4/9 = 0.444… = 44.44…%.
34. 1.25 = 125% = 5/4.
35. 5/8 = 0.625 = 62.5%.
36. 44% = 0.44 = 11/25.
37. 69% = 0.69 = 69/100.

38. $4.25 = 425\% = 17/4$.
39. $7/5 = 1.4 = 140\%$.
40. $121\% = 1.21 = 121/100$.
41. $4/3 = 1.333\ldots = 133.33\ldots\%$.
42. $0.666\ldots = 2/3 = 66.66\ldots\%$.
43. 9 to 3 = 3. 3 to 9 = 1/3. 9 is 300% of 3. Note that the ratio of B to A is just the reciprocal of the ratio of A to B, and that 300% is simply the ratio of A to B expressed as a percent.
44. 125 to 5 = 25. 5 to 125 = 1/25. 125 is 2500% of 5. Note that the ratio of B to A is just the reciprocal of the ratio of A to B, and that 2500% is simply the ratio of A to B expressed as a percent.
45. 16 to 48 = 1/3. 48 to 16 = 3. 16 is 33.33...% of 48.
46. 23 to 8 = 2.875. 8 to 23 = 0.348. 23 is 287.5% of 8.
47. 440 to 8 = 55. 8 to 440 = 1/55. 440 is 5500% of 8.
48. 75 to 325 = 3/13. 325 to 75 = 13/3. 75 is 23.1% of 325.
49. 8.1 million to 21 million = 0.386. 21 million to 8.1 million = 2.593. 8.1 million is 38.6% of 21 million.
50. 3.0 million to 0.65 million = 4.62. 0.65 million to 3.0 million = 0.217. 3.0 million is 462% of 0.65 million.
51. 4.1 million to 2.4 million = 1.71. 2.4 million to 4.1 million = 0.59. 4.1 million is 171% of 2.4 million.
52. 3.1 people to 2.6 people = 1.19. 2.6 people to 3.1 people = 0.84. 3.1 people is 119% of 2.6 people.
53. 1500 square feet to 2300 square feet = 0.65. 2300 square feet to 1500 square feet = 1.53. 1500 square feet is 65% of 2300 square feet.
54. $23,000 to $214,000 = 0.11. $214,000 to $23,000 = 9.3. $23,000 is 11% of $214,000.
55. 220 is 51.2 % of 430 because 220/430 = 0.512.
56. 123 is 21.6% of 569 because 123/569 = 0.216.
57. 145 is 33.3% of 436 because 145/436 = 0.333.
58. 190,000 is 23.5% of 807,000 because 190,000/807,000 = 0.235.
59. 2.8 million is 16.8% of 16.7 million because 2.8/16.7 = 0.168.
60. 100,500 is 15.6% of 643,800 because 100,500/643,800 = 0.156.
61. John's absolute change in salary was $28,000 – $20,000 = $8000, and the relative change was $\dfrac{\$28,000 - \$20,000}{\$20,000} = 0.4 = 40\%$. Mary's absolute change was $35,000 – $25,000 = $10,000, and the relative change was $\dfrac{\$35,000 - \$25,000}{\$25,000} = 0.4 = 40\%$.

Thus Mary's salary grew more in absolute terms, but the relative change was the same. This happened because we are comparing Mary's larger absolute change to her also larger initial salary.

62. The absolute change in Clarkville's population was 2200 people – 1400 people = 800 people, and the relative change was $\dfrac{2200-1400}{1400} = 0.57 = 57\%$. The absolute change in Centerville's population was 29,000 people – 27,000 people = 2000 people, and the relative change was $\dfrac{29,000-27,000}{27,000} = 0.07 = 7\%$. Thus Centerville experienced a larger absolute change, while Clarkville experienced a larger relative change. This happened because Clarkville's absolute change, though small when compared to Centerville's absolute change, is much larger in comparison to its original population.
63. The absolute change is 300 million – 76 million = 224 million people. The relative change is $\dfrac{300,000,000-76,000,000}{76,000,000} = 2.95 = 295\%$.
64. The absolute change is $2150 billion – $130 billion = $2020 billion (or just over $2 trillion). The relative change is $\dfrac{2150-130}{130} = 15.54 = 1554\%$.
65. The absolute change is 1450 papers – 2226 papers = –776 papers. The relative change is $\dfrac{1450-2226}{2226} = -0.349 = -34.9\%$.
66. The absolute change is 910,600 deaths – 1,008,000 deaths = – 97,400 deaths. The relative change is $\dfrac{910,600-1,008,000}{1,008,000} = -0.097 = -9.7\%$.
67. The absolute difference is 2.20 million papers – 1.12 million papers = 1.08 million papers. The relative difference is $\dfrac{2,200,000-1,120,000}{1,120,000} = 0.964 = 96.4\%$, which means *USA Today*'s circulation is 96.4% more than the circulation of the *New York Times*.
68. The absolute difference is $12.1 billion – $5.8 billion = $6.3 billion. The relative difference is $\dfrac{12.1-5.8}{5.8} = 1.09 = 109\%$, which means the arms sales in the United States was 109% more than the sales in Russia.
69. The absolute difference is 77 million arrivals – 50 million arrivals = 27 million arrivals. The relative difference is $\dfrac{77-50}{50} = 0.54 = 54\%$, which means there were 54% more arrivals in France than in Spain.
70. The absolute difference is 8.8 million barrels – 5.7 million barrels = 3.1 million barrels. The relative difference is $\dfrac{8.8-5.7}{5.7} = 0.544 = 54.4\%$, which

means Saudi Arabia produced 54.4% more barrels than the United States.

71. The relative difference is 593,700 injuries – 535,100 injuries = 58,600 injuries. The relative difference is $\frac{593,700 - 535,100}{535,100} = 0.11 = 11\%$, which means there were 11% more basketball related injuries than bicycle related injuries.

72. The absolute difference is 80.1 years – 77.4 years = 2.7 years. The relative difference is $\frac{80.1 - 77.4}{77.4} = 0.035 = 3.5\%$, which means the life expectancy in Canada is 3.5% longer than the life expectancy in the United States.

73. Will's height is 122% of Wanda's height because 22% *more than* expresses a relative difference in heights, and this is equivalent to 100% + 22% *of* the reference height (i.e. Wanda's height).

74. Norway's area is 124% of Colorado's area because 24% *more than* expresses a relative difference in area, and this is equivalent to 100% + 24% *of* the reference area (i.e. Colorado's area).

75. Minnesota's population is 91% of Maryland's population because 9% *less than* expresses a relative difference in population, and this is equivalent to 100% – 9% *of* the reference population (i.e. Maryland's population).

76. Henry's salary is 55% of Ingrid's salary because 45% *less than* expresses a relative difference in salary, and this is equivalent to 100% – 45% *of* the reference salary (i.e. Ingrid's salary).

77. Since the wholesale price is 40% *less than* the retail price, it is 60% *of* the retail price, which means it is 0.6 times the retail price.

78. The original price is 2 times as much of the sale price, because 100% (original price) is twice as large as 50% (sale price).

79. Since the retail cost is 30% *more than* the wholesale cost, it is 130% *of* the wholesale cost, which means it is 1.3 times the wholesale cost.

80. A 40% off sale means prices are discounted 40%. Since 40% of $80 is 0.4 × $80 = $32, the sale price is $80 – $32 = $48.

81. The absolute change is 13.2% – 9.2% = 4 percentage points. The relative change is $\frac{13.2 - 9.2}{9.2} = 0.435 = 43.5\%$.

82. The absolute change is 20% – 27% = –7 percentage points. The relative change is $\frac{20 - 27}{27} = -0.259 = -25.9\%$.

83. The absolute change is 60% – 39% = 21 percentage points. The relative change is $\frac{60 - 39}{39} = 0.538 = 53.8\%$.

84. The absolute change is 85% – 25% = 60 percentage points. The relative change is $\frac{85 - 25}{25} = 2.4 = 240\%$.

85. In the first case, 33% of city employees in Freetown ride the bus to work because 10% *more than* 30% is 33%. In the second case, 40% of the city employees in Freetown ride the bus, because 40% is 10 percentage points more than 30%.

86. The first statement implies that the precipitation is 180 inches, because 200% *of* 90 is two times as large as 90. The second statement means that the relative difference between the average and this year's precipitation is 200%, which is three times the average amount, or 270 inches.

87. The final cost is $760 + 0.076 × $760 = $817.76.

88. The pre-tax price is $107.69/1.062 = $101.40.

89. The final cost is $19,200 × 1.072 = $20,582.40.

90. The pre-tax price is $3706.31/1.081 = $3428.59.

91. The cost for the dinner before the tip was $76.40/1.20 = $63.67.

92. If you leave $50 for a bill of $42.50, you left a $7.50 tip, which is 17.6% of $42.50 (because 7.50/42.50 = 0.176 = 17.6%).

93. The glass holds 4.17 ounces of wine, because 12% of 4.17 is 0.5 ounce. One can arrive at this answer by noting that 12% of the volume (call it V) is 0.5 ounce, which translates to $0.12V = 0.5$. Divide 0.5 by 0.12 to find V.

94. The current rate of smoking among twelfth-graders (22%) is 20% *more than* the previous rate (label it R), which means it's 120% *of* R. This translates into $1.20R = 22\%$. Divide 22% by 1.20 to find R: 22%/1.2 = 18.3%.

95. False. If Sue's weight began at W pounds, and she lost 15% of that weight, she would weigh $0.85W$ pounds. If she now gains 15%, her new weight would be $1.15 \times 0.85W = 0.9775W$ pounds. This is 2.25% less than her original weight.

96. False. Assign an arbitrary number to your salary, such as $100. A pay raise of 5% results in a new salary of $105. A 5% cut in the new salary yields $0.95 \times \$105 = \$99.75$. Thus your salary has changed (it's dropped 0.25% over the two changes in pay).

97. False. Assign an arbitrary number to your property taxes before the increases, such as $100. If taxes increase by 6% in the first year, you'll pay $106. If they increase again by 7% in the next year, you'll pay $1.07 \times \$106 = \$113.42$. This is an increase of 13.42%, not 13%.

98. False. Assign an arbitrary number to the original SAT scores, such as 1000. If the scores fell 20% one year, they would be at 800, and if they rose 30% the next year, they would be at $1.3 \times 800 = 1040$. This is an overall improvement of 4%, not 10%.

99. Not possible. A price can decrease at most by 100%. Once you've deducted 100% from a price, it's free.

100. Not possible. Mary would have to have no height at all to be 100% shorter than Vivian.

101. Possible. An increase of 400% means the price of real estate is five times what it used to be.

102. Possible. This means Super Oats has twice the amount of calcium found in Regular Oats.

103. Possible. This means your computer is five times faster than my computer.

104. Not possible. At a maximum, your computer could be 100% slower than mine (in which case your computer doesn't work at all).

105. No, the mean score for both classes is not 85%. Assuming a 100-point exam, the first class scored a total of $25 \times 86 = 2150$ points, and the second class scored a total of $30 \times 84 = 2520$ points. Thus the combined number of points scored by 55 students is $2150 + 2520 = 4670$, and the mean score for both classes is $4670/55 = 84.9\%$.

106. No, his new batting average is not .450. As in exercise 105, one can't average averages. In this exercise, we can't compute his new average as we don't know how many at-bats he's had in the previous games, but it can't be 4 at-bats (because there's no way he'd be batting .400 in that scenario), and this would be the only case where averaging averages would produce the correct result.

FURTHER APPLICATIONS

107. True. 10% of 60% is 1/10 of 60%, which is 6%.

108. False. 20% of 40% is $0.2 \times 40\% = 8\%$, not 80%.

109. False. Some of the hotels may have both a pool and a restaurant, and those would be counted twice if the percentages were just added together.

110. This is true as long as those who drive to school are not bus drivers who park the bus at school and attend classes there.

111. An increase of 466% means Internet use in 2004 was 566% *of* the level in 2001 (call it *x*). This translates into $5.66x = 7.23\%$. Divide by 5.66 to find *x*: $x = 7.23\%/5.66 = 1.28\%$.

112. Since $\$37,729/\$20,718 = 1.821$, the annual income for adults with bachelor degrees is 182.1% *of* the income for those with a high school diploma, which means the bachelor degree income is 82.1% *more than* the high school income.

113. Add 20% of $3 billion to $3 billion to get $3.6 billion ($3 \times 1.2 = 3.6$).

114. The statement means 3.4% *of* the profits at the beginning of the year (call it *P*) is equal to $1.1 billion. This translates into $0.034P = \$1.1$ billion. Divide $1.1 billion by 0.034 to find *P*. $P = \$1.1$ billion/$0.034 = \$32.4$ billion.

115. The percent of people worried last winter (call it *W*) is up 16%, which means 116% *of W* is the new level of 80%. This translates to $1.16W = 80\%$. Divide by 1.16 to find *W*. $W = 80\%/1.16 = 69\%$.

116. Iraq produces 5% *of* 3.5 million barrels per day today, which is 0.05×3.5 million $= 0.175$ million, or 175,000 barrels per day.

117. Within three years, 60% *of* the 625,000 released prisoners will have been rearrested, which amounts to $0.60 \times 625,000 = 375,000$ rearrested.

118. The sales in the previous year (call it *S*) experienced a relative change of 54%, which means 154% *of S* is equal to $450 million. This translates to $1.54S = \$450$ million. Divide by 1.54 to find *S*. $S = \$450$ million/$1.54 = \$292$ million.

119. The price of Oracle's stock in the previous week (call it *P*) increased by 3%, which means 103% *of P* is equal to $13.48. This translates to $1.03P = \$13.48$, and thus $P = \$13.09$ (divide by 1.03).

120. Because $\$1 \div \$2.50 = 0.4$, the cost in Iraq is 40% *of* the cost in Saudi Arabia, which implies the cost in Iraq is 60% *less than* the cost in Saudi Arabia. Since $10 is 400% *of* $2.50, the cost in the United States is 300% *more than* the cost in Saudi Arabia.

UNIT 3B

QUICK QUIZ

1. **a.** The decimal point must move seven places to the left to transform 70,000,000 into scientific notation, and thus its value is 7×10^7.

2. **c.** 1277 is roughly 10^3, and 14,385 is of order 10^4, so their product is around 10^7.

3. **c.** 10^9 is larger than 10^5 by a factor of 10^4, which is ten thousand.

4. **c.** One person, who drives 15,000 miles in a year in a vehicle that gets 25 mpg, uses 600 gallons of gas per year. There are 300 million Americans, and if each used this much gas, the total would be

$$3 \times 10^8 \text{ people} \times \frac{6 \times 10^2 \text{ gal}}{\text{person}} = 18 \times 10^{10} \text{ gal} = 1.8 \times 10^{11}$$

gallons of gasoline, which is 180 billion gallons. Of course, not everyone drives 15,000 miles every year (children, the elderly, and urban dwellers come to mind). On the other hand, this estimate doesn't even consider all the gas used by trucking, airlines, and other industries. Certainly the answer can't be **a** or **b**, as these estimates are much too small. 100 billion gallons is probably a conservative estimate.

5. **c.** A dollar bill is about 6 inches long, or about 15 cm long, and thus 8 million of them amounts to

$$8 \times 10^6 \text{ bills} \times \frac{1.5 \times 10^1 \text{ cm}}{\text{bill}} \times \frac{1 \text{ km}}{10^5 \text{ cm}} = 12 \times 10^2 \text{ km},$$

which is 1200 kilometers. This is enough to get into outer space, but not near enough to reach the moon.

6. **c.** If you know the song from the Broadway musical *Rent*, you may recall that there are 525,600 minutes in a year. 1.2×10^{-10} year is just over one ten-billionth of a year, which isn't even close to a minute (it's a small fraction of a second). Clearly the sun won't burn out in the next fraction of a second, nor in the next minute.

7. **b.** If 1 inch = 20 miles, then 6 inches is $6 \times 20 = 120$ miles.

8. **b.** $1 billion is $1000 million, so at $10 million per year, it will take 100 years to earn $1 billion.

9. **c.** Assuming you're willing to campaign for eight hours per day (which is roughly 500 minutes), and that you'll limit yourself to 10 minutes of talking at each house (including travel time between houses), you'll be able to visit 50 households per day, or 100 houses in two days. This translates into 500 houses in two weeks (campaigning five days per week), or 1000 households in a month, or 12,000 households in a year-long campaign, where you do nothing but campaigning. Clearly it would be impossible to carry out your plan before the election – pay for some TV advertisements instead.

10. **a.** The largest Division 1 college football stadiums hold about 100,000 fans. In a lottery with the stated odds, there's only one winning ticket for every 1,000,000 printed, which means there are 999,999 losing tickets. More likely than not, the fans in the stadium will be disappointed (and it's more likely still they will be disappointed in a smaller stadium).

DOES IT MAKE SENSE?

19. Makes sense. The page you are reading right now has two columns, each of which has about 50 lines, and there are roughly 10 words per line, for a total of 1000 words per page. A book with $10^5 = 100,000$ words would have 100 pages. A paperback with pages about half the size of this solutions manual would be two-hundred pages long.

20. Does not make sense. A very rough estimate for the number of minutes in a lifetime might use 100 years per life, 400 days per year, 20 hours per day, and 60 minutes per hour. This means somewhere between 10^7 and 10^8 minutes in a lifetime. Even if you could view several commercials each minute, you couldn't come anywhere close to 10^{50} commercials over a lifetime of continuous TV viewing.

21. Makes sense. At ten feet per floor, an apartment building with 20 floors would be 200 feet tall.

22. Does not make sense. With 300 million Americans, each would have to spend roughly $3 per year to reach $1 billon. Housing costs far exceed $3 per person per year.

23. Does not make sense. A typical NFL stadium holds 70,000 fans. At an unrealistic speed of 10 signatures per minute, it would take the football star 7000 minutes (roughly 100 hours) to provide signatures for all the fans (who would grow restless waiting in line for a signature after about 15 minutes).

24. Makes sense. This is a large company if it has more than 500 employees, and the salaries for the low-skilled jobs might be around $20,000 per year (about $10 per hour). $(5 \times 10^2) \times (2 \times 10^4) = 10^7$, so the sum of all these salaries is $10 million, which is on the order of what a CEO of a large company earns.

BASIC SKILLS AND CONCEPTS

25. a. $3 \times 10^3 = 3000 = $ three thousand .

 b. $6 \times 10^6 = 6,000,000 = $ six million .

 c. $3.4 \times 10^5 = 340,000 = $ three hundred forty thousand.

 d. $2 \times 10^{-2} = 0.02 = $ two hundredths .

 e. $2.1 \times 10^{-4} = 0.00021 = $ twenty-one hundred-thousandths.

 f. $4 \times 10^{-5} = 0.00004 = $ four hundred - thousandths.

26. a. $8 \times 10^2 = 800 = $ eight hundred .

 b. $5 \times 10^3 = 5000 = $ five thousand .

 c. $9.6 \times 10^4 = 96,000 = $ ninety-six thousand .

 d. $2 \times 10^{-3} = 0.002 = $ two thousandths .

 e. $3.3 \times 10^{-5} = 0.000033 = $ thirty-three millionths.

 f. $7.66 \times 10^{-2} = 0.0766 = $ seven hundred sixty - six ten-thousandths.

27. a. $233 = 2.33 \times 10^2$.

 b. $126,547 = 1.26547 \times 10^5$.

 c. $0.11 = 1.1 \times 10^{-1}$.

 d. $9736.23 = 9.73623 \times 10^3$.

e. $124.58 = 1.2458 \times 10^2$.

f. $0.8642 = 8.642 \times 10^{-1}$.

28. a. $4327 = 4.327 \times 10^3$.

b. $984.35 = 9.8435 \times 10^2$.

c. $0.0045 = 4.5 \times 10^{-3}$.

d. $624.87 = 6.2487 \times 10^2$.

e. $0.1357 = 1.357 \times 10^{-1}$.

f. $98.180004 = 9.8180004 \times 10^1$.

29. a. $(3 \times 10^3) \times (2 \times 10^2) = 6 \times 10^5$.

b. $(4 \times 10^2) \times (3 \times 10^8) = 12 \times 10^{10} = 1.2 \times 10^{11}$.

c. $(3 \times 10^3) + (2 \times 10^2) = 3000 + 200 = 3200$
$= 3.2 \times 10^3$.

d. $(8 \times 10^{12}) \div (4 \times 10^4) = 2 \times 10^8$.

30. a. $(4 \times 10^7) \times (2 \times 10^8) = 8 \times 10^{15}$.

b. $(3.2 \times 10^5) \times (2 \times 10^4) = 6.4 \times 10^9$.

c. $(4 \times 10^3) + (5 \times 10^2) = 4000 + 500 = 4500$
$= 4.5 \times 10^3$.

d. $(9 \times 10^{13}) \div (3 \times 10^{10}) = 3 \times 10^3$.

31. a. 10^{35} is 10^9 (1 billion) times as large as 10^{26}.

b. 10^{27} is 10^{10} (10 billion) times as large as 10^{17}.

c. 1 billion is 10^3 (1000) times as large as 1 million.

d. 7 trillion is 10^9 (1 billion) times as large as 7 thousand.

e. 2×10^{-6} is 10^3 (1000) times as large as 2×10^{-9}.

f. 6.1×10^{29} is 10^2 (100) times as large as 6.1×10^{27}.

32. a. 5 billion (5×10^9) is 20 times as large as 250 million (2.5×10^8).

b. 9.3×10^2 is 3×10^4 (30,000) times as large as 3.1×10^{-2}.

c. 1×10^{-8} is 5×10^4 (50,000) times as large as 2×10^{-13}.

d. 3.5×10^{-2} is 5×10^5 (500,000) times as large as 7×10^{-8}.

e. 1 thousand (10^3) is 10^6 (1 million) times as large as 1 thousandth (10^{-3}).

f. 10^{12} is 10^{21} times as large as 10^{-9}.

33. Total energy consumption in the United States is about 1×10^{20} joules.

34. The coal extracted in the United States in 2005 produced 2.3×10^{16} Btu of energy.

35. The hard drive on my computer has a capacity of 1.2×10^{10} bytes.

36. U.S. emissions of carbon dioxide in 2005 totaled about 6×10^9 metric tons.

37. The diameter of a typical bacterium is about 1×10^{-6} meter.

38. A beam of light can travel the length of a football field in 3×10^{-8} seconds.

39. a. 300,000 is 3×10^5, and 100 is 1×10^2, so their product is 3×10^7, or 30,000,000. This is an exact answer as no estimation was necessary.

b. 5.1 million is about 5×10^6, and 1.9 thousand is about 2×10^3, so their product is about 1×10^{10}, which is 10 billion. The exact answer (computed with a calculator) is 9.69 billion.

c. Since 2.1×10^6 is about 2 million, $4 \times 10^9 \div 2.1 \times 10^6$ is about 2×10^3, or 2000. The exact answer is nearer to 1.9×10^3 (1904.76 is a rounded answer).

d. 33 multiplied by 3.1 is very close to 100, so $(33 \times 10^6) \times (3.1 \times 10^3)$ is about 100×10^9, which is 1×10^{11}. The exact answer is 1.023×10^{11}.

e. 4,288,364 is about 4×10^6, and 2132 is about 2×10^3, so their quotient is about 2×10^3, or 2000. The exact answer is 2011 (rounded).

f. $(6.129845 \times 10^6) \div (2.198 \times 10^4)$ is about $(6 \times 10^6) \div (2 \times 10^4) = 3 \times 10^2$, or 300. The exact answer is 279 (rounded).

40. a. $(5.6 \times 10^9) \div (2 \times 10^2) = 2.8 \times 10^7$. This is an exact answer as no estimation is necessary (provided you can divide 5.6 by 2 in your head – estimate 5.6 billion as 6 billion if not, to arrive at an approximate answer of 3×10^7).

b. Since 4 divided by 2.6 is about 2, 4 trillion ÷ 260 million = $(4 \times 10^{12}) \div (2.6 \times 10^8)$ is about 2×10^4 = 20,000. The exact answer is 15385 (rounded).

c. $9000 \times 54,986$ is close to $(1 \times 10^4) \times (5 \times 10^4)$, which is 5×10^8. The exact answer is 4.95×10^8 (rounded).

d. 3 billion ÷ 25,000 is close to $(3 \times 10^9) \div (3 \times 10^4)$, which is 10^5. The exact answer is 1.2×10^5.

e. 5987×341 is about $(6 \times 10^3) \times (3 \times 10^2)$, which is 1.8×10^6. Because we rounded 341 all the way down to 300, a better approximation is 2×10^6. The exact answer is 2,041,567, or 2.04×10^6 (rounded).

f. $43 \div 765$ is about $(4 \times 10^1) \div (8 \times 10^2)$, which is 5×10^{-2}, or 0.05. The exact answer is 0.056 (rounded).

41. Answers will vary regarding the estimates made, but most people spend more money on gas each year than on movies. If you see two movies per month, spending \$10 per movie, that's \$20 per month, which amounts to \$240 per year. On the other hand, if you fill up your gas tank twice per month, spending \$30 to fill a tank, that's \$60 per month, which amounts to \$720 per year.

42. Answers will vary regarding the estimates made, but it's certainly possible to walk across the United States in a year. If you walked at a modest rate of 2 miles per hour, for 8 hours each day, you would walk 16 miles per day. Over the course of one year (365 days), you'd end up walking 5840 miles, which is almost enough to go there and back again (it's about 3000 miles from New York to California). Thus even with rest days scheduled, you'd have no trouble walking the distance in a year.

43. Assuming you sleep 7 hours per day, and that you study less than 7 hours per day, you'll sleep more than you study. In particular, if you sleep 7 hours each night, you'll sleep 2555 hours over the course of a year. If you study 6 hours per day over the course of a school year (30 weeks, or two semesters), you'll study 1260 hours per year.

44. A typical professional football stadium holds 70,000 people, while a typical movie theater has about 300 seats. Ten movie theaters would hold only 3000 people, so a stadium holds many more people.

45. Answers will vary, but if one-third of the population (100 million people) each spend \$100 per year on movies, that would produce \$10 billion in revenue.

46. Assuming 10 breaths per minute, one can estimate the number of breaths taken in a week with a unit conversion: $1 \text{ wk} \times \dfrac{7 \text{ d}}{\text{wk}} \times \dfrac{24 \text{ hr}}{\text{d}} \times \dfrac{60 \text{ min}}{\text{hr}} \times \dfrac{10 \text{ breaths}}{\text{min}}$, which is about 100,000 breaths per week (answers will vary).

47. Answers will vary, but assuming a daily water intake of 2 pints, one can estimate the annual water consumption with a unit conversion: $1 \text{ yr} \times \dfrac{365 \text{ d}}{\text{yr}} \times \dfrac{2 \text{ pt}}{\text{d}} \times \dfrac{1 \text{ qt}}{2 \text{ pt}} \times \dfrac{1 \text{ gal}}{4 \text{ qt}}$, which is about 90 gallons per year.

48. Answers will vary. Page 157 of the text has two columns, each with about 40 lines, and each line has about 10 words. Thus there are approximately 800 words on that page. If we treat that page as representative of the entire book, which has about 800 pages, there are about 640,000 words in the book.

49. Insurance companies use the figure of 15,000 miles per year for the average distance driven by an adult. If your car gets 25 miles to the gallon, you'll use about 600 gallons each year. Answers will vary, of course.

50. Money spent on food varies widely from person to person, depending on frequency of restaurant visits, food preferences, caloric intake, and locale.

51. Table 3.1 states that 4 million joules are required for one hour of running, and that an average candy bar supplies 1 million joules of energy. Thus four candy bars would be needed for each hour of running, which means you'd need to eat 24 candy bars to supply the energy for six hours of running.

52. The average home uses 50 million joules per day, which amounts to 1.5 billion joules per month (assuming a 30-day month). Divide 1.5 billion joules per month by 12 million joules per liter of oil to arrive at 125 liters per month.

53. One kilogram of uranium-235 releases 5.6×10^{13} joules, which is 35,000 times as much as the energy released by one kilogram of coal (1.6×10^9 joules): $\dfrac{5.6 \times 10^{13}}{1.6 \times 10^9} = 35,000$.

54. One liter of water supplies enough hydrogen to produce 7×10^{13} joules of energy through fusion, and this is almost 6 million times as much energy released by burning a liter of oil (1.2×10^7 joules): $\dfrac{7 \times 10^{13}}{1.2 \times 10^7} = 5,833,333$.

55. $\dfrac{5 \times 10^7 \text{ joules}}{\text{home}} \times \dfrac{1 \text{ liter H}_2\text{O}}{7 \times 10^{13} \text{ joules}} = 7 \times 10^{-7} \dfrac{\text{liters}}{\text{home}}$. This is just a little less than one millionth of a liter.

56. $\dfrac{5 \times 10^{20} \text{ joules}}{\text{world}} \times \dfrac{1 \text{ liter H}_2\text{O}}{7 \times 10^{13} \text{ joules}} = 7.14 \times 10^6 \dfrac{\text{liters}}{\text{world}}$. This is about 7 million liters.

57. $\dfrac{1 \times 10^{20} \text{ joules}}{\text{yr}} \times \dfrac{1 \text{ kg uranium}}{5.6 \times 10^{13} \text{ joules}} = 1.8 \times 10^6 \dfrac{\text{kg}}{\text{yr}}$. Thus 1.8 million kg of uranium would be needed to supply the annual energy needs of the United States.

58. The sun generates 1×10^{34} joules each year. A simple unit conversion tells us how much energy is generated by the sun in a second: $\dfrac{1 \times 10^{34} \text{ j}}{\text{yr}} \times \dfrac{1 \text{ yr}}{365 \text{ d}} \times \dfrac{1 \text{ d}}{24 \text{ hr}} \times \dfrac{1 \text{ hr}}{60 \text{ min}} \times \dfrac{1 \text{ min}}{60 \text{ sec}} = \dfrac{3.2 \times 10^{26} \text{ j}}{\text{sec}}$. This is more than enough to supply U.S. energy needs for a year (about 3 million times as much as is needed, in fact).

59. Since there are 100,000 cm in 1 km, the scale is 100,000 to 1.

60. There are 253,400 inches in 4 miles, as shown here: $4 \text{ mi} \times \frac{5280 \text{ ft}}{1 \text{ mi}} \times \frac{12 \text{ in.}}{1 \text{ ft}} = 253,440$ inches, and thus the scale is 253,440 to 1.

61. Since 2 inches represents 2 miles, 1 inch represents one mile, and as there are 63,360 inches in one mile $(1 \text{ mi} \times \frac{5280 \text{ ft}}{1 \text{ mi}} \times \frac{12 \text{ in.}}{1 \text{ ft}} = 63,360 \text{ in.} .)$, the scale is 63,360 to 1.

62. There are 126,720 inches in two miles (see exercise 61), and thus the scale is 126,720 to 3, or 42,240 to 1.

63. Since there are 20,000,000 cm in 200 km, the scale is 20,000,000 to 5, or 4,000,000 to 1.

64. 10 cm for every 10 km is equivalent to 1 cm for every 1 km, and thus the scale is 100,000 to 1 (see exercise 59).

65. There are about 820 ft in 250 meters (see below), so the scale is 820 to 1.
$$250 \text{ m} \times \frac{100 \text{ cm}}{\text{m}} \times \frac{1 \text{ ft}}{30.48 \text{ cm}} = 820 \text{ ft} .$$

66. There are about 3281 ft in 1 km (see below), so the scale is 3281 to 1.
$$1 \text{ km} \times \frac{1000 \text{ m}}{\text{km}} \times \frac{100 \text{ cm}}{\text{m}} \times \frac{1 \text{ ft}}{30.48 \text{ cm}} = 3281 \text{ ft} .$$

67. In order to scale down each of the actual diameters and distances listed in the table, begin by dividing by 10,000,000,000 (10 billion). Since this produces tiny answers when units of kilometers are used, it is best to convert to a more convenient unit. The table below shows diameters listed in millimeters (rounded to the nearest tenth of a millimeter), and distances listed in meters (rounded to the nearest meter).

Planet	Model Diameter	Model distance from Sun
Mercury	0.5 mm	6 m
Venus	1.2 mm	11 m
Earth	1.3 mm	15 m
Mars	0.7 mm	23 m
Jupiter	14.3 mm	78 m
Saturn	12.0 mm	143 m
Uranus	5.2 mm	287 m
Neptune	4.8 mm	450 m

68. As noted in Example 8, *Alpha Centauri* is about 4.1×10^{13} km from Earth. The amount of time needed to reach *Alpha Centauri* traveling at 50,000 km/hr can be found by dividing the distance by the rate of speed:
$$\text{time} = \frac{4.1 \times 10^{13} \text{ km}}{50,000 \text{ km/hr}} = 8.2 \times 10^8 \text{ hr} ,$$

which is 820 million hours. A quick conversion shows that this is nearly 100,000 years. Thus interstellar travel is beyond our means until we design a ship that will last 100,000 years, and that will support many generations of the crew, or until we build a ship that travels much faster than 50,000 km/hr.

69. The scale on this timeline would be 14 billion years to 100 meters, and thus 1 billion years is equivalent to 1/14 of 100 meters, which amounts to 7.1 meters. Since 10,000 years is 1/100,000 of one billion years, we only need to divide 7.1 meters by 100,000 to find the distance that goes with 10,000 years. This gives 0.000071 meters, or 0.071 millimeters.

FURTHER APPLICATIONS

70. $\frac{4.1 \times 10^6 \text{ births}}{\text{yr}} \times \frac{1 \text{ yr}}{365 \text{ d}} \times \frac{1 \text{ d}}{24 \text{ hr}} \times \frac{1 \text{ hr}}{60 \text{ min}} = 7.8 \frac{\text{births}}{\text{min}}$.

71. $\frac{1.4 \times 10^6 \text{ crimes}}{\text{yr}} \times \frac{1 \text{ yr}}{365 \text{ d}} \times \frac{1 \text{ d}}{24 \text{ hr}} = 160 \frac{\text{crimes}}{\text{hr}}$.

72. $\frac{1.3 \times 10^8 \text{ births}}{\text{yr}} \times \frac{1 \text{ yr}}{365 \text{ d}} \times \frac{1 \text{ d}}{24 \text{ hr}} \times \frac{1 \text{ hr}}{60 \text{ min}} = 247 \frac{\text{births}}{\text{min}}$.

73. There are roughly 300 million Americans, and since 300 million metric tons of corn are produced, there's one metric ton per person.

74. The thickness of a stack of ten $1 bills is about one millimeter, and this can be used to convert $264 billion into a height.
$$\$2.64 \times 10^{11} \times \frac{1 \text{ mm}}{\$10} \times \frac{1 \text{ km}}{10^6 \text{ mm}} = 2.64 \times 10^4 \text{ km} .$$

75. The thickness of a stack of ten $1 bills is about one millimeter, and this can be used to convert $8.5 trillion into a height.
$$\$8.5 \times 10^{12} \times \frac{1 \text{ mm}}{\$10} \times \frac{1 \text{ km}}{10^6 \text{ mm}} = 8.5 \times 10^5 \text{ km} .$$

76. There are about 300 million Americans, so the amount spent per person is $4 billion/300 million people = $13.33 per person.

77. $1.35 \times 10^6 \text{ students} \times \frac{1 \text{ stadium}}{70,000 \text{ students}} = 19 \text{ stadiums}$.

78. a. $1 \text{ cm}^3 \times \left(\frac{10^4 \ \mu\text{m}}{1 \text{ cm}}\right)^3 \times \frac{1 \text{ cell}}{100 \ \mu\text{m}^3} = 1 \times 10^{10} \text{ cells}$, or 10 billion cells.

b. One liter is 1000 milliliters, or 1000 cubic centimeters, so there are 1000 times as many cells in a liter as there are in a cubic centimeter, which comes to 1×10^{13} cells (see part a).

c. If one liter of water weighs 1 kilogram, then a person who weighs 70 kg has a volume of 70 liters. From part b, we know each liter contains 1×10^{13} cells, and thus we need only multiply that result by 70 to find the number of cells in a human body. This results in 7×10^{14} cells.

79. Answers will vary, but if you assume there are 200 million drivers in the U.S. (2/3 of the population), and each uses 1000 gallons of gas per year, then roughly 2 trillion kg of carbon dioxide was added to the atmosphere over the past year:

$$2 \times 10^8 \text{ drivers} \times \frac{1000 \text{ gal}}{\text{driver}} \times \frac{10 \text{ kg}}{\text{gal}} = 2 \times 10^{12} \text{ kg}.$$

80. If we assume an average of three people per household, there are 100 million households in the U.S. (because there are 300 million people). If 4.5 trillion gallons is enough to supply all households for five months, then 4.5/5 trillion (9×10^{11}) gallons is sufficient for one month. Thus each household uses $\dfrac{9 \times 10^{11} \text{ gal}}{1 \times 10^8 \text{ households}} = 9,000$ gallons per month. Answers will vary regarding whether this is reasonable, but considering water used for bathing, washing, drinking, cooking, cleaning, and upkeep of the lawn/garden, this is within the ballpark.

81. a. Energy = power × time, so we need to multiply the solar power by one second, and then take 0.06% of the result, followed by 1% of that result to account for the fact that not all solar power is converted into plant matter.

$$180,000 \times 10^{12} \text{ W} = 1.8 \times 10^{17} \frac{\text{j}}{\text{s}} \times 1 \text{ s} = 1.8 \times 10^{17} \text{ j}.$$ This is the amount of energy that reaches the earth each second. Multiply by 0.0006, and then by 0.01 (the decimal equivalent of 0.06% and 1%) to find the amount of energy stored in plant matter each second – this results in 1.08×10^{12} joules.

b. If 1.08×10^{12} joules of energy are used every second, that's the same as 1.08×10^{12} watts, or about 1 terawatt. This is only 10% of the world's electricity demand, so it would not be enough.

c. To avoid depleting plant life, it's necessary to use fossil fuels, which provide the energy stored by plants over thousands of years.

82. a. The volume of a sphere is $V = \frac{4}{3}\pi r^3$, and thus the volume of the white dwarf will be $\frac{4}{3}\pi (6400 \text{ km})^3$.

Density is mass per unit volume, so the density of the white dwarf will be

$$\frac{2 \times 10^{30} \text{ kg}}{\frac{4}{3}\pi (6400 \text{ km})^3} \times \left(\frac{1 \text{ km}}{10^5 \text{ cm}} \right)^3 = 1821 \frac{\text{kg}}{\text{cm}^3}.$$

b. Since a teaspoon is about 4 cubic centimeters, and each cubic centimeter has mass of 1821 kg (part a), a teaspoon will have a mass of 7300 kg, which is about the mass of a tank.

c. Following the calculations in part a, the density is $\dfrac{2.8 \times 10^{30} \text{ kg}}{\frac{4}{3}\pi (10 \text{ km})^3} \times \left(\dfrac{1 \text{ km}}{10^5 \text{ cm}} \right)^3 = 7 \times 10^{11} \dfrac{\text{kg}}{\text{cm}^3}$, which means one cubic centimeter of this material is more than ten times the mass of Mount Everest.

83. Answers will vary, but if a ream of paper (500 sheets) weighs 8 pounds, then each sheet will weigh 1/500 of 8 pounds, which is 0.016 lb.

84. Careful measurements show that a penny is about 1.5 mm thick, a nickel 1.8 mm, a dime 1.3 mm, and a quarter 1.7 mm thick. The easiest way to make these measurements is to measure a stack of ten coins, and divide the answer by ten. Although a quarter is almost the thickest coin (among these), its value is 2.5 times as much as the thinnest coin, the dime, and yet it's thickness is not anywhere near 2.5 times as thick as a dime (it's about 1.3 times as thick). So while you'll get more dimes in a stack that is as tall as you are, the value of that stack won't be as much as the value of the stack of quarters – take the quarters.

85. Answers will vary considerably, depending upon the sand that is used to make the estimate.

86. Answers will vary considerably, depending on the amount of light pollution in the area where one might make an estimate.

UNIT 3C

QUICK QUIZ

1. **b**. The best economists can do when making projections into the future is to base their estimates on current trends, but when these trends change, it often proves the predictions wrong.

2. **a**. There are two significant digits in 5.0×10^{-1}, while the other answers have only one.

3. **b**. 1.020 has four significant digits, 1.02 has three, and 0.000020 has only two.

4. **a**. Random errors can either be too high or too low, and averaging three readings is likely to reduce random errors because the high readings typically cancel the low readings.

5. **b**. If you place the thermometers in sunlight, this is a problem with your system of measurement, and the readings will all be too high, which is a systematic error.

6. **c**. Since all the scores are affected the same way (50 points too low), this is an example of a systematic error.

7. **b**. The absolute error in all cases was -50 points, but unless all students had the same score (very unlikely), the relative errors will be different.

8. **a**. Because the scale is able to report your weight to the nearest 1/10 of a pound, it is fairly precise (in comparison to standard bathroom scales), but its accuracy is lacking as it is off by more than 30 pounds (in 146 pounds).

9. **a**. Reporting the debt to the nearest penny is very precise, though the debt is so large that we really don't know it to that level of precision, and thus it is not likely to be very accurate.

10. **a**. Multiplying the gas mileage by the tank capacity will produce the number of miles the car can go on a full tank (290 miles), so the question boils down to this: "How many significant digits should be used when reporting the answer?" Since there are two significant digits in 29 mpg, and three in 10.0 gallons, we should use two significant digits in the answer (use the rounding rule for multiplication), and thus the answer is 290 miles.

DOES IT MAKE SENSE?

17. Does not make sense. Predicting the federal deficit for the next year to the nearest million dollars is nearly impossible.

18. Makes sense. It is difficult to estimate the population (in both developing and developed countries), and it is reasonable to claim the error in these estimates may be 10% or more.

19. Does not make sense. Unless you have access to an exceptionally precise scale, you could never measure your weight to that level of precision (and even with an excellent scale, your weight changes at the level reported when you sweat, breath, lose a few hairs, etc.).

20. Does not make sense. It is very unlikely that anyone could count the number of people attending a rally to the nearest person when the number of attendees is in the thousands.

21. Does not make sense. A typical yard stick may be precise to the nearest 1/16 of an inch, but certainly not to the nearest micrometer.

22. Makes sense. Suppose you measure your weight with a scale that is precise to the nearest 1/10 of a pound, but you fail to take your shoes and clothes off before stepping on the scale. The reading will not be very accurate (off by a pound or more), and increasing the level of precision to, say, 1/100 of a pound won't help matters.

23. Makes sense. Provided the company's revenue is $1 billion, $1 million would be only 0.1% of revenue, and it wouldn't be considered a large error.

24. Does not make sense. Random errors can also affect accuracy (and in just about every measurement made, the measuring device has a finite level of precision that prevents perfect accuracy).

BASIC SKILLS & CONCEPTS

25. a. 3.   b. 88.   c. 0.
    d. 185.   e. 1945.   f. 3.
    g. 6.   h. 1500.   i. −14.

26. a. 567.5; 570.   b. 23.5; 20.
    c. 34.5; 30.   d. 123.5; 120.
    e. −34.8; −30.   f. 45.5; 50.
    g. −76.3; −80.   h. 32.5; 30.
    i. 0.0; 0.

27. There are four significant digits, and it is precise to the nearest dollar.

28. There are five significant digits, and it is precise to the nearest 0.001 mph.

29. There is one significant digit, and it is precise to the nearest 10 mph.

30. There is one significant digit, and it is precise to the nearest 0.01 centimeter.

31. There are six significant digits, and it is precise to the nearest 0.00001 mile.

32. There are two significant digits, and it is precise to the nearest 10,000 years.

33. There are two significant digits, and it is precise to the nearest 1000 seconds.

34. There are 3 significant digits, and it is precise to the nearest 0.000001 meter.

35. There are seven significant digits, and it is precise to the nearest 0.0001 pound.

36. There is one significant digit, and it is precise to the nearest 0.00001 liter.

37. There are four significant digits, and it is precise to the nearest 0.1 km/s.

38. There are four significant digits, and it is precise to the nearest one billion kg.

39. $45 \times 32.1 = 1440$.

40. $45 \times 32.1 = 1444.5$.

41. $231.89 \div 0.034 = 6800$.

42. $231.89 \div 0.034 = 6820$ (the ones place is significant).

43. $(2.3 \times 10^5) \times (7.963 \times 10^3) = 1.83149 \times 10^3$.

44. $(6.667 \times 10^3) \times (8.9421 \times 10^{-2}) = 5.962 \times 10^2$.

45. Random errors may be introduced when the cars are not counted properly, and systematic errors could occur due to interpretation of what constitutes a sport utility vehicle.

46. Random errors may occur when people are miscounted, and systematic errors may happen when homeless people are not counted, or when college students are counted twice.

47. Random errors could occur if the average is calculated incorrectly. Systematic errors might occur if people repeatedly understate their incomes to avoid higher taxes.

48. Random errors could occur if the average is calculated incorrectly. Systematic errors might occur if people overstate their incomes.

49. Random errors could occur by misreading the scale. A minor systematic error could occur if deli employees routinely measured the weight with the meat already in the deli bag.

50. Random errors may be introduced if the scale is read incorrectly, and systematic errors occur due to clothes, and may occur due to a poorly calibrated scale.

51. Random errors may occur due to miscounting of kernels, and a systematic error could occur if the clerk overfills the box for friends.

52. Random errors could occur if the stopwatch used to measure the times is read incorrectly, while systematic errors may occur if a stopwatch is not calibrated correctly.

53. Problem (1) is a random error because the mistakes may be too high or two low. Problem (2) is a systematic error, because the tax payer likely underreported his income.

54. Problem (1) is a random error because the number of people with AIDS is either too high or too low, depending on the incorrect diagnosis. Problem (2) is a systematic error as those who never seek help result in an undercounting of the number of people with AIDS.

55. This is a systematic error that results in all altitude readings being 2780 lower than they should be.

56. Random errors are involved here, most likely due to hurried measurements or cutting, which leads to lengths that are sometimes too long, and sometimes too short.

57. The absolute error is measured value − true value, or $19.00 − $18.50 = $0.50. The relative error is
$$\frac{\text{measured value} - \text{true value}}{\text{true value}} = \frac{\$19 - \$18.50}{\$18.50} = 0.027 = 2.7\%$$

.

58. The absolute error is measured value − true value, or 30 lb − 29 lb = 1 lb. The relative error is
$$\frac{\text{measured value} - \text{true value}}{\text{true value}} = \frac{30 \text{ lb} - 29 \text{ lb}}{29 \text{ lb}} = 3.4\% \ .$$

59. The absolute error is $39.20 − $43.24 = −$4.04. The relative error is ($39.20 − $43.24)/$43.24 = −0.093 = −9.3%.

60. Regarding 48 inches as the true value (because you measured the other value), the absolute error is 47.5 in. − 48 in. = −0.5 in. The relative error is (47.5 in. − 48 in.)/48 in. = −0.01 = −1%.

61. Regarding 6 cups as the true value (because you measured 6.25 cups), the absolute error is 6.25 cups − 6 cups = 0.25 cup. The relative error is (6.25 cups − 6 cups)/6 cups = 0.042 = 4.2%.

62. The absolute error is 13 mi − 13.34 mi = −0.34 mi. The relative error is −0.34 mi/13.34 mi = −0.025 = −2.5%.

63. The absolute error is 9 hr − 10 hr = −1 hr. The relative error is −1 hr/10 hr = −0.1 = −10%.

64. The absolute error is 0.1 cm − 0.13 cm = −0.03 cm. The relative error is −0.03 cm/0.13 cm = −0.23 = −23%.

65. The measurement obtained by the tape measure is more accurate because the value is closer to your true height than the value obtained at the doctor's office (1/8 inch versus 0.4 inch). However, the laser at the doctor's office is more precise as it measures to the nearest 0.05 (or 1/20) inch, while the tape measure measures to the nearest 1/8 inch.

66. The laser at the doctor's office is both more precise and more accurate, as it measures your height exactly (while the tape measure is off by 1/8 inch), and it measures to the nearest 0.05 (or 1/20) inch compared to the nearest 1/8 inch.

67. The digital scale at the gym is both more precise and more accurate. It is more precise because it measures to the nearest 0.01 kg, while the health clinic's scale measures to the nearest 0.5 kg, and it is more accurate because its reported weight is nearer to your true weight than the scale at the health clinic.

68. The scale at the health clinic is more accurate because the error in measuring your true weight is only 0.05 kg, while the error of the digital scale is 0.07 kg. The digital scale is more accurate, because it gives readings to the nearest 0.01 kg compared to the clinic's scale, which gives readings to the nearest 0.5 kg.

69. A calculator gives 60 hr − 1.45 hr = 58.55 hr. This should be rounded to the nearest 10 hr because that's the level of precision of 60 hr (we can't be sure whether the 0 in 60 is a significant digit, so we must assume that it is not). The final answer is 60 hr.

70. The first measurement is precise to the nearest minute, so the answer should be reported to the nearest minute. 2 hr 37 min + 1 hr 22 min 15 s = 3 hr 59 min 15 s, which rounds to 3 hr 59 min.

71. A calculator gives 62.5 km/hr × 2.4 hr = 150 km. The second measurement has two significant digits, and so does our final answer, so it needn't be changed.

72. Each number has two significant digits, so the answer should be reported with two significant digits. 110 km/55 min = 2 km/min. Using two significant digits, we should write 2.0 km/min.

73. The least precise measurement is 36 miles, which is precise to the nearest mile, so the answer should be rounded to the nearest mile. 36 mi + 2.2 mi =

73. 38.2 mi, which is 38 mi when rounded to the correct level of precision.

74. 50 kg + 1.25 kg = 51.25 kg, but the answer must be reported to the nearest 10 kg, as that's the level of precision of the first weight. Thus the final answer is 50 kg.

75. The cost is $2.1 million/120,345 people = $17.45 per person. However, as the first measurement has only two significant digits, so must the answer, so we round to $17 per person.

76. A calculator gives 630,000 constituents × $4.25/constituent = $2,677,500. However, as the first number has only two significant digits, we must use only two in the final answer: $2.7 million.

FURTHER APPLICATIONS

77. This measurement could have many sources of errors, both random and systematic (for example, transient people might get counted twice, and people on the frontier – remember, this is 1820 – might be undercounted). The measurement is not believable as the level of precision (to the nearest person) is unattainable. In the time it would take to conduct the survey, many people would have been born and died, and people immigrating to the country change its population on a daily basis.

78. Both measurements could be affected by random and systematic errors (for example, the definition of what constitutes a farm could affect the count, the selling of farm property to developers could affect the acreage, the merging of two farms into one would affect the count, and errors in recording the data could occur). The number of farms is not believable to the level of precision given (see discussion above), though it's reasonable to expect that the total acreage is known to the nearest 100,000 acres.

79. Systematic errors could arise depending on how the length of a river is defined and how it is measured (should we measure along the banks, or right down the middle?), and random errors could easily arise due to changes in the course of the river over time, or errors in recording the data. The fact is not believable because (as explained above), it is rather difficult to define how the length of a river should be measured, let alone measure such a long river to the nearest mile.

80. Systematic errors could be present if the equipment (such as a transit) used to measure the height is faulty, and random errors could occur in several ways (e.g. if a transit is used, and it wasn't aimed precisely at the top of the building). The fact is believable as long as precise instruments are used to measure the height.

81. Random and systematic errors could be present in the temperature readings that lead to the average high of 88 degrees. The fact is believable to the level of precision given.

82. Random and systematic errors may occur in the lab where tests are conducted to determine whether a patient has AIDS. The number is not believable to the level of precision reported – it's doubtful any researcher has access to all the medical records necessary to attain that level of precision.

83. The mathematical models used to estimate the mass of the earth could introduce systematic errors, and random errors could be introduced in the experiments conducted to find the mass. The mass is believable to the level of precision given.

84. A species is a declared endangered species based on whether it appears on a list maintained by the government, and thus as long as the number of entries is counted correctly, there isn't much room for error in the number, and it is believable to the precision given.

UNIT 3D

QUICK QUIZ

1. **b.** The 1985 index of 210.9 is a little more than twice as large as the 1975 index of 100, so the price of gas in 1985 is roughly twice as much as the price in 1975.

2. **c.** If you know the price of gas in 1970, you can divide today's price by the 1970 price to get the index number for the current year.

3. **b.** Like most indexes, the CPI is designed to allow one to compare prices from one year to another.

4. **c.** To compare prices in one year to prices in another, one can just divide the CPI from one year by the other – this tells you the factor by which prices in one year differ from prices in another.

5. **c.** The CPI in 2005 was 195.3, and it was 152.4 in 1995. Thus prices in 2005 are 28% more than prices in 1995 (because 195.3/152.4 = 1.28). If the CPI were recalibrated so that 1995 = 100, the new CPI in 2005 would be 128, which is lower than 195.3.

6. **b.** As long as the computers being compared are of comparable power, since the prices have declined, the index would decrease.

7. **a.** If the cost of college has increased faster than the CPI, but one's salary has only kept pace with the CPI, then the cost of college as a percentage of salary has increased, making it more difficult to afford.

8. **a**. If your salary increases faster than the CPI, then it has more purchasing power than in previous years.

9. **c**. Measured in 2006 dollars, gas was less than $1.50 per gallon in 1998–1999, and this is lower than any other time shown on the chart.

10. **c**. In order to reflect the fact that housing prices have tripled from 1985 to 2005, the index would also triple, from 100 to 300.

DOES IT MAKE SENSE?

15. Does not make sense. One must consider the affect of inflation on the price of gas, and compare the prices in, say, 2006 dollars in order to make a valid comparison.

16. Makes sense. As long as the speaker of the statement lives in a country where the CPI has increased over the past seven years (i.e. where there has been inflation), a stable salary would lose purchasing power over time.

17. Makes sense. A penny in Franklin's day would be worth something on the order of a dollar today.

18. Makes sense. As long as the price of a car has increased at a rate lower than the CPI over the last couple decades, a car would be cheaper when compared to prices (in today's dollars) of twenty years ago.

19. Does not make sense. The reference year that is chosen for an index number does not affect the trends of inflation, so if milk is more expensive in 1995 dollars, it should also be more expensive in 1975 dollars.

20. Does not make sense. Students on financial aid rely on government programs for funding, and the money spent on these programs is directly tied to the CPI.

BASIC SKILLS & CONCEPTS

21. To find the index number, take the current price and divide it by the 1975 price: $2.80/$0.567 = 4.938 = 493.8\%$. The price index number is 493.8 (the percentage sign is dropped).

22. To find the index number, take the current price and divide it by the 1975 price: $2.45/$0.567 = 4.321 = 432.1\%$. The price index number is 432.1 (the percentage sign is dropped).

23. The price index number in 1995 is 212.5, which means prices in 1995 were 212.5% of the prices in 1975. Thus $10 spent on gas in 1975 is equivalent to $10 \times 212.5\% = \$10 \times 2.125 = \$21.25$.

24. To find the factor by which 1965 prices were smaller than 1985 prices, divide their index numbers: $55/210.9 = 0.2608$. This means prices in 1965 were 26.08% of prices in 1985, and thus $15

spent in 1985 is equivalent to $15 \times 0.2608 = \$3.91$ in 1965 dollars.

25. With 1965 as the reference value, the price index number for that year is 100. To find the index for 1955, divide the 1955 price by the 1965 price, convert to a percent, and drop the percent sign:

$$\frac{29.1¢}{31.2¢} = 0.933 = 93.3\%, \text{ so the index is } 93.3.$$

Follow the same procedure to find the index for 1975: $\frac{56.7¢}{31.2¢} = 1.817 = 181.7\%$, so the index is 181.7. Do the same thing for the remaining years to arrive at the following index numbers. 1985 = 383.3. 1995 = 386.2. 2000 = 496.8. 2005 = 740.4.

26. With 2000 as the reference value, the price index number for that year is 100. To find the index for 1955, divide the 1955 price by the 2000 price, convert to a percent, and drop the percent sign:

$$\frac{29.1¢}{155.0¢} = 0.188 = 18.8\%, \text{ so the index is } 18.8.$$

Follow the same procedure to find the index for 1965: $\frac{31.2¢}{155.0¢} = 0.201 = 20.1\%$, so the index is 20.1.

Do the same thing for the remaining years to arrive at the following index numbers. 1975 = 36.6. 1985 = 77.2. 1995 = 77.7. 2005 = 149.0.

27. Divide the 2005 CPI by the 1975 CPI to find the factor by which prices in 2005 were larger than prices in 1975: $\frac{\text{CPI}_{2005}}{\text{CPI}_{1975}} = \frac{195.3}{53.8} = 3.63$. This means prices in 2005 were 3.63 times larger than prices in 1975, so $20,000 in 1975 is equivalent to $20,000 \times 3.63 = \$72,600$ in 2005.

28. Divide the 2005 CPI by the 1981 CPI to find the factor by which prices in 2005 were larger than prices in 1981: $\frac{\text{CPI}_{2005}}{\text{CPI}_{1981}} = \frac{195.3}{90.9} = 2.149$. This means prices in 2005 were 2.149 times larger than prices in 1981, so $45,000 in 1981 is equivalent to $45,000 \times 2.149 = \$96,705$ in 2005, which is about $96,700.

29. Inflation is the relative change in the CPI, which is $\frac{\text{CPI}_{1978} - \text{CPI}_{1977}}{\text{CPI}_{1977}} = \frac{65.2 - 60.6}{60.6} = 0.076 = 7.6\%$.

30. Inflation is the relative change in the CPI, which is $\frac{\text{CPI}_{2005} - \text{CPI}_{2002}}{\text{CPI}_{2002}} = \frac{195.3 - 179.9}{179.9} = 0.086 = 8.6\%$. Note that this is inflation over the span of three years (that is, it is not an annual rate of inflation).

31. Because $\frac{\text{CPI}_{2004}}{\text{CPI}_{1979}} = \frac{188.9}{72.6} = 2.6$, prices in 2004 were 2.6 times as large as prices in 1979. Thus a 75¢

loaf of bread would be $\$0.75 \times 2.6 = \$1.95$ in 2004 dollars.

32. Because $\dfrac{CPI_{2005}}{CPI_{1975}} = \dfrac{195.3}{53.8} = 3.63$, prices in 2005 were 3.63 times as large as prices in 1975. Thus a $\$4500$ car would be $\$4500 \times 3.63 = \$16,335$ in 2005 dollars.

33. Because $\dfrac{CPI_{1975}}{CPI_{2000}} = \dfrac{53.8}{172.2} = 0.3124$, prices in 1975 were 0.3124 times those in 2000. Thus a $\$7.00$ movie would be $\$7.00 \times 0.3124 = \$2.19$ in 1975 dollars.

34. The price in 1980 dollars is
$$\$15 \times \frac{CPI_{1980}}{CPI_{2000}} = \$15 \times \frac{82.4}{172.2} = \$7.18.$$

35. The purchasing power of a 1973 dollar in terms of 2002 dollars is $\$1 \times \dfrac{CPI_{2002}}{CPI_{1973}} = \$1 \times \dfrac{179.9}{44.4} = \$4.05$.

36. The purchasing power of a 1976 dollar in terms of 1996 dollars is $\$1 \times \dfrac{CPI_{1996}}{CPI_{1976}} = \$1 \times \dfrac{156.9}{56.9} = \$2.76$.

37. In Palo Alto, the price would be $\$300,000 \times \dfrac{365}{87}$, which is $\$1.26$ million. In Sioux City, the price would be $\$300,000 \times \dfrac{47}{87} = \$162,000$. In Boston, the price would be $\$300,000 \times \dfrac{182}{87} = \$627,600$.

38. In Juneau, the price would be $\$570,000 \times \dfrac{100}{182}$, which is $\$313,000$. In Manhattan, the price would be $\$570,000 \times \dfrac{495}{182} = \$1.55$ million. In Tulsa, the price would be $\$570,000 \times \dfrac{52}{182} = \$163,000$.

39. In Spokane, the price would be $\$250,000 \times \dfrac{78}{75}$, which is $\$260,000$. In Denver, the price would be $\$250,000 \times \dfrac{87}{75} = \$290,000$. In Juneau, the price would be $\$250,000 \times \dfrac{100}{75} = \$333,000$.

40. In Providence, the price would be $\$1$ million $\times \dfrac{91}{495} = \$184,000$. In Spokane, the price would be $\$1$ million $\times \dfrac{78}{495} = \$158,000$. In Tulsa, it would be $\$1$ million $\times \dfrac{52}{495} = \$105,000$.

41. Health care spending increased by a percent of $\dfrac{\$1.8 \times 10^{12} - \$80 \times 10^{9}}{\$80 \times 10^{9}} = 21.5 = 2150\%$, whereas the overall rate of inflation was $\dfrac{CPI_{2004} - CPI_{1973}}{CPI_{1973}} = \dfrac{188.9 - 44.4}{44.4} = 3.25 = 325\%$.

42. The relative change in cost for an airline ticket was $\frac{\$360 - \$230}{\$230} = 0.565$, or a 56.5% increase. The overall rate of inflation was $\dfrac{CPI_{2005} - CPI_{1980}}{CPI_{1980}}$
$= \dfrac{195.3 - 82.4}{82.4} = 1.37 = 137\%$.

43. The relative change in the cost of college was $\dfrac{\$27,516 - \$5900}{\$5900} = 3.66 = 366\%$. The rate of inflation was $\dfrac{CPI_{2004} - CPI_{1980}}{CPI_{1980}} = \dfrac{188.9 - 82.4}{82.4} = 1.29$, which is an increase of 129%.

44. The relative change in the cost of college was $\dfrac{\$11,354 - \$2490}{\$2490} = 3.56 = 356\%$. The rate of inflation was $\dfrac{CPI_{2004} - CPI_{1980}}{CPI_{1980}} = \dfrac{188.9 - 82.4}{82.4} = 1.29$, which is an increase of 129%.

45. The relative change in the price of a home was $\dfrac{\$155,500 - \$75,300}{\$75,300} = 1.07 = 107\%$. The rate of inflation was $\dfrac{CPI_{2004} - CPI_{1990}}{CPI_{1990}} = \dfrac{188.9 - 130.7}{130.7} = 0.45$, which is an increase of 45%.

46. The relative change in the price of a home was $\dfrac{\$241,300 - \$129,600}{\$129,600} = 0.86 = 86\%$. The rate of inflation was $\dfrac{CPI_{2004} - CPI_{1990}}{CPI_{1990}} = \dfrac{188.9 - 130.7}{130.7}$
$= 0.45 = 45\%$.

47. As shown in the first line of the table, $\$0.25$ in 1938 dollars is worth $\$2.78$ in 1996 dollars.

48. As shown in the table, $\$1.00$ in 1956 dollars is worth $\$5.77$ in 1996 dollars.

49. In 1996, actual dollars are 1996 dollars.

50. 2005 dollars are worth less than 1996 dollars due to inflation.

51. The 1979 minimum wage, measured in 1979 dollars, was $\$2.90$. To convert this to 1996 dollars, use the CPI from 1996 and 1979.
$$\$2.90 \times \frac{CPI_{1996}}{CPI_{1979}} = \$2.90 \times \frac{156.9}{72.6} = \$6.27.$$
This agrees with the entry in the table.

52. The 1981 minimum wage, measured in 1981 dollars, was $\$3.35$. To convert this to 1996 dollars, use the CPI from 1996 and 1981.
$$\$3.35 \times \frac{CPI_{1996}}{CPI_{1981}} = \$3.35 \times \frac{156.9}{90.9} = \$5.78.$$
This agrees with the entry in the table.

53. The purchasing power of the minimum wage was highest in 1968, when its value in 1996 dollars was highest ($7.21). Since all entries in the last column are listed in 1996 dollars, we can make valid comparisons between values in the column.

UNIT 3E

QUICK QUIZ

1. **a**. As stated in the text surrounding the table, the old treatment had a better overall treatment rate, even though the new treatment performed better in each category.

2. **a**. 63% refers to the percent of men admitted to Department B.

3. **b**. Even though Derek had a higher GPA in each of the two years, we can't be sure his overall GPA was higher than Terry's – Simpson's paradox may be at play.

4. **a**. A *false negative* means the test detected no cancer (that's the *negative* part) even though the person has it (the *false* part).

5. **c**. A *false positive* means the test detected steroids (that's the *positive* part), but the person never used steroids (that's the *false* part).

6. **c**. The last row in the column labeled *Tumor is benign* shows the total of those who did not have malignant tumors.

7. **b**. Those who had false negatives (15) and false positives (1485) make up the group who had incorrect test results.

8. **c**. Imagine a test group of 1000 women, where 900 are actually pregnant, and 100 are not. Of those who are pregnant, 1% (that is, 9 women) will test negative. Of those who aren't pregnant, 99% (that is, 99 women) will test negative. Thus 108 women test negative, and 99 of them actually aren't pregnant. Since 99/108 is not 99% (it's closer to 92%), statement **c** is not true (it may be true in other scenarios, but in general, it is not).

9. **b**. A person earning $200,000 will save 2.9% of his income, which is $5800. A person earning $50,000 will save 4.4% of his income, which is $2200. Thus the person earning $200,000 or more will save more total tax dollars than someone earning between $40,000 and $50,000.

10. **c**. A person earning more than $200,000 will see his tax bill fall by 2.9% (see Republican table).

DOES IT MAKE SENSE?

15. Makes sense. If Simpson's paradox is at work, both categories could show an improvement with the new drug even though overall, the old drug may have done a better job.

16. Does not make sense. It is not clear who played the better game – one would have to look at the actual baskets made to determine who scored more points.

17. Does not make sense. There are scenarios (see discussion in text concerning mammograms and drug tests, for example) where a positive test may not correlate well with the probability that a bag contains banned materials, even though the test is 98% accurate.

18. Does not make sense. See discussion in text concerning polygraph tests.

19. Does not make sense. Both sides can make a valid argument for their position (see discussion in text about tax cuts).

20. Makes sense. If the percent increase in the annual budget was less than the CPI, the purchasing power of dollars received is lower this year than last, which amounts to a cut in the budget.

BASIC SKILLS & CONCEPTS

21. As shown in the tables, Josh had a higher batting average in both the first and second half of the season. Jude had the higher overall batting average (80/200 = .400 versus 85/220 = .386). This illustrates Simpson's paradox because it's a case where one person (Josh) performed better in two of two categories (the first and second halves of the season), and yet Jude outperformed Josh over the course of the entire season.

22. As shown in the tables, Allen had a higher completion percentage in both the first and second half of the game. Abner had the higher overall completion percentage (14/31 = 45% versus 11/26 = 42%). This illustrates Simpson's paradox because it's a case where one person (Allen) performed better in two out of two categories (the first and second halves of the game), and yet Abner outperformed Allen over the course of the entire game.

23. a. New Jersey had higher scores in both categories (283 versus 281, and 252 versus 250), but Nebraska had the higher overall average (277 versus 272).

b. The explanation lies in Simpson's paradox: it's possible for one state (Nebraska) to score lower in both categories, and yet have a higher overall percentage. This is due to the different racial makeup of the two state's populations. The white students are scoring better than the nonwhite students in both states, and Nebraska has a larger percentage of white students than New Jersey, so they influence the overall scores more heavily than the white students in New Jersey.

c. The verification is an exercise in a weighted average. 87% of the population had an average of 281, and 13% of the population had an average of 250, so the overall average is 0.87(281) + 0.13(250) = 277.

d. As in part **c**, we only have to compute a weighted average: 0.66(283) + 0.34(252) = 272.

e. See part **b**.

24. a. The SAT scores all decreased by about 3 points in each of the grade categories.

b. The overall SAT scores increased by 10 points between 1988 and 1998.

c. This is an illustration of Simpson's paradox because SAT scores went down in each of the five grade categories, and yet in the overall picture, they increased.

25. a. The death rate for whites was 8400/4,675,000 = 0.0018 = 0.18%. For nonwhites, it was 500/92,000 = 0.0054 = 0.54%. Overall, the death rate was 8900/4,767,000 = 0.0019 = 0.19%.

b. The death rate for whites was 130/81,000 = 0.0016 = 0.16%. For nonwhites, it was 160/47,000 = 0.0034 = 0.34%. Overall, the death rate was 290/128,000 = 0.0023 = 0.23%.

c. Simpson's paradox is at work here because the death rates for TB in each category (white and nonwhite) were higher in New York City than in Richmond, and yet the overall death rate due to TB was higher in Richmond. The paradox arises because Richmond had a different racial makeup than New York City: it had a much higher percentage of nonwhite residents than New York, and as the death rate for TB was much higher among nonwhites than whites in both cities, the higher percentage of nonwhites in Richmond has a more pronounced influence on the death rate.

26. Simpson's paradox is at work here because the Gazelles saw a larger time improvement than the Cheetahs in each category (10s versus 9s among those who weight trained, and 2s versus 1s among those who did not), and yet the Cheetahs realized a larger time improvement across the entire team. To determine the percentage of each team that used weight training, we need to use the idea of a weighted average. Suppose the ratio of Gazelles who used weight training is represented by x. Then the ratio of those who did not use weight training is $1 - x$. The weighted average across the entire team is 6.0 s, so we must solve $10x + 2(1 - x) = 6$ for x. This results in $x = 0.5$, so 50% of the Gazelles used weight training. In a similar fashion, the percent of Cheetahs who used weight training can be determined: $9x + 1(1 - x) = 6.2$, which results in a solution of $x = 0.65$. Thus 65% of the Cheetahs used weight training. As the table shows, weight training improves race times on both teams

much more dramatically than using no weight training, and since the Cheetahs had a higher percentage of runners who used weight training, it makes sense they had a better overall improvement in times.

27. a. There are 10,000 total participants with tumors in the study (lower right hand entry), and 1% of them (100) have malignant tumors. Since the test is 90% accurate, 90 of those with malignant tumors will be true positives, while the other 10 will be false negatives. 99% of the women (9900) will have benign tumors. 90% of these (8910) will be true negatives, while 10% of these (990) will be false positives. The only numbers in the table not yet verified are the first two entries in the Total column; these are simply the sum of the rows in which they lie.

b. Of the 1080 who have positive mammograms, only 90 are true positives, so only 90/1080 = 8.3% of them actually have cancer.

c. 100 of the women have cancer (malignant tumors), and 90 of those will have a true positive test result, which is 90%. Thus if you really have cancer, the test will detect it 90% of the time.

d. Of the 8920 who have a negative mammogram, only 10 of them are false negatives, which translates to a probability of 10/8920 = 0.11%.

28. a. Beginning with the last row, there are 2000 employees, and 1% of them (20) use drugs, while the other 99% (1980) do not. The first column shows the 20 drug users, and 85% of them (17) will be detected when they lie about their drug use, while 3 of them will avoid detection. The second column shows the 1980 non-users, and 85% of them (1683) will pass the polygraph when they tell the truth that they don't use drugs. The other 297 of them will be falsely accused of using drugs, because they will fail the test. The entries in last column are simply the sum of the rows in which they lie.

b. 314 are accused of lying, but only 17 of them are actually lying; the remaining 297 (the falsely accused) are telling the truth. 297/314 = 94.6% are falsely accused.

c. 1686 are found to be truthful, and 1683 of them actually are telling the truth, and thus 1683/1686 = 99.8% of those found truthful really were telling the truth.

29. a. Beginning with the last row, the sample size is 4000, and 1.5% of them (60) have the disease, while the remaining 3940 do not. The first column shows the 60 with the disease, and the test detects 90% of them (54), but misses 6 of them. The second column shows the 3940 who do not have the disease, and the test says 90% of them (3546) do not have the disease (a negative test), but it

says 10% of them (394) do have the disease. The entries in the last column are simply the sum of the rows in which they lie.

b. 54 of the 60 (90%) who have the disease test positive.

c. 54 of the 448 (12%) who test positive actually have the disease. In part **b**, the answer of 90% is the ratio of those who test positive out of those who have the disease, while the answer of 12% here is the ratio of those who have the disease among those that test positive.

d. As shown in part **c**, if you test positive, you have a 12% chance of actually having the disease. This is 8 times the overall incidence rate (1.5%), which means there is reason for concern, and yet it's still a fairly low chance that you actually have the disease.

30. One can argue that funding for the program is being cut because there was a 1% rise in the budget, and yet the CPI is 3%, which means the purchasing power of the new budget has decreased. On the other hand, the funding has certainly increased from $1 billion to $1.01 billion.

FURTHER APPLICATIONS

31. a. Spelman won 10/29 = 34% of its home games and 12/16 = 75% of its away games, while Morehouse won 9/28 = 32% of its home games and 56/76 = 74% of its away games. Since Spelman is better than Morehouse in each category, it's the better team.

b. Morehouse won 65/104 = 62.5% of all the games they played, while Spelman won 22/45 = 49% of all the games they played. Based on these figures, Morehouse is the better team.

c. Disregarding the strength of the opponents each college played, it's universally accepted that the team with a higher percentage of wins is the better team, and thus the claim in part **b** makes more sense. Additionally, it's more difficult to win away games than home games, and while both teams have an impressive away-game win percentage, Morehouse complied its overall record of 62.5% with many more away games.

32. a. Drug B cured 101/900 = 11.2% of female patients and 196/200 = 98% of male patients, while Drug A cured 5/100 = 5% of female patients and 400/800 = 50% of male patients. Since Drug B outperformed drug A in both categories, it's the more effective drug.

b. Drug A cured 405/900 = 45% of all patients, while Drug B cured 297/1100 = 27% of all patients, so Drug A is more effective than Drug B.

c. Because the drugs had such different effects on men and women, the individual cure rates should

be cited and used for evaluating the drugs (that is, the claim in part **a** makes more sense).

33. a. Note that 10% of the 5000 at risk people is 500, and this is the sum of the first row in the first table. For the 20,000 people in the general population, note that 0.3% of 20,000 is 60, and this is the sum of the first row in the second table. 95% of the 500 infected people in the at risk group should test positive, and 5% should test negative – take 95% and 5% of 500 to verify the first row entries in the first table. 95% of the 4500 at risk people who aren't infected should test negative, while 5% should test positive – take 95% and 5% of 4500 to verify the second row in the first table. A similar process will show that the numbers in the second table are also correct.

b. 475/500 = 95% of those with HIV test positive. 475/700 = 67.9% of those who test positive have HIV. The percentages are different because the number of people in each group (those who have HIV and those who test positive) is different.

c. As shown in part **b**, if you test positive, and you are in the at risk group, you have a 67.9% chance of carrying the disease. This is much greater than the overall percentage of those who have the disease (10%), which means if you test positive, you should be concerned.

d. 57/60 = 95% of those with HIV test positive. 57/1054 = 5.4% of those who test positive have HIV. The two percentages are different because the number of people in each group (those who have HIV and those who test positive) is different.

e. As shown in part **d**, if you test positive, and you are in the general population, you have a 5.4% chance of carrying the disease. This is larger than the overall percentage of those who have the disease (0.3%), but it's still small enough that it's best to wait for more tests before becoming alarmed.

34. a. Excelsior Airlines has a higher percentage of on-time flights in each of the five cities shown in the table.

b. First, compute the number of overall on-time arrivals for Excelsior by multiplying the percents in each row by the number of arrivals for each city, and adding these together:
0.889(559) + 0.948(233) + 0.914(232) + 0.831(605) + 0.858(2146) = 3274 on-time flights. Divide this by the total number of flights (3775) to find the overall on-time percentage: 3274/3775 = 86.7%.

Next, do the same thing for Paradise:
0.856(811) + 0.921(5255) + 0.855(448) + 0.713(449) + 0.767(262) = 6438 on-time flights, which means an overall on-time percentage of 6438/7225 = 89.1%.

c. Simpson's paradox is evident here because Excelsior had a higher percentage of on-time flights in each of the five cities, yet Paradise had the higher overall percentage of on-time flights.

35. The data suggest a hiring preference for women because a higher percentage of women were hired in each of the two categories (white-collar and blue-collar jobs). On the other hand, if one looks at the overall picture, it turns out a higher percentage of male applicants was hired. (There were 20% of 200 applicants = 40 female workers hired for white-collar jobs, and 85% of 100 applicants = 85 female workers hired for blue-collar jobs. Thus there were 125 workers hired from a pool of 300 applicants, which is 125/300 = 41.7%. There were 15% of 200 applicants = 30 male workers hired for white-collar jobs, and 75% of 400 applicants = 300 male workers hired for blue-collar jobs. Thus there were 330 workers hired from a pool of 600 applicants, which is 330/600 = 55%.) This is an example of Simpson's paradox because females were hired at a greater rate in both categories of workers, and yet males were hired at a greater rate overall. The paradox can be resolved by realizing that there were many more males hired for the blue-collar jobs, which are more abundant than the white-collar jobs, and thus the male-dominated blue-collar jobs have a greater influence on the overall hiring rate.

36. Treatment A had a better cure rate in each of the two trials (20% versus 15% in the first trial, and 85% versus 75% in the second trial). The overall cure rate for Treatment A was 125/300 = 41.7%, while the overall cure rate for Treatment B was 330/600 = 55%, and thus Treatment B had the better overall cure rate. This is an example of Simpson's paradox because Treatment A performed better in each of the trials, and yet Treatment B performed better overall. The paradox can be resolved by realizing that there were more people in the second trial who received Treatment B.

41. a. The absolute difference in savings is $12,838 − $211 = $12,627. A single person earning $41,000 will save $211/$41,000 = 0.5% of income. A single person earning $530,000 will save $12,838/$530,000 = 2.4% of income.
b. The absolute difference in savings is $13,442 − $1208 = $12,234. A married couple earning $41,000 will save $1208/$41,000 = 2.9% of income. A married couple earning $530,000 will save $13,442/$530,000 = 2.5% of income.

UNIT 4A

QUICK QUIZ

1. **a**. Evaluating your budget allows you to look critically at your cash flow, which affects personal spending.
2. **a**. Your cash flow is determined by the amount of money you earn (income), and the amount you spend.
3. **b**. If your cash flow is negative, you are spending more than you take in.
4. **c**. You should prorate all once-per-year expenses and include them in your monthly budget.
5. **b**. Housing typically costs about one-third of your income.
6. **c**. As a percentage of income, health care expenses are not too alarming, though they grow rapidly as one ages.
7. **a**. You can't save without money left over at the end of the month, which corresponds to a positive cash flow.
8. **c**. Trey spends about $5 per day on cigarettes, which comes to $150 per month.
9. **c**. Kira spends $7.50 per day on soda, so over the course of a year, she spends nearly $3000.
10. **b**. Each week, you use about 22 gallons of gas, because (400 mi)/(18 mi/gal) = 22.2 gal. With gas at $3/gal, this comes to $66/week, or $3432/year. A car that gets 50 mi/gal will use about one-third of the gas used by your old car (because 50 is almost three times as large as 18), which means it will cost about $1100/year for gas. The difference between these two values is the amount you save, around $2200.

DOES IT MAKE SENSE?

17. Does not make sense. All the smaller expenses do add up, and they have a significant influence on your budget.
18. Makes sense. If you have a negative monthly cash flow, your debt will rise.
19. Makes sense. When prorated as a per-month expense, an $1800 vacation costs $150 per month.
20. Makes sense. Cash flow is determined by income and spending, and one way to turn a negative cash flow into a positive cash flow (other factors being equal) is to earn more money.
21. Does not make sense. Divide $15,000 by 365 (days per year) to find that an annual expense of $15,000 comes to $41 per day. Pizza and a soda do not cost that much.

22. Does not make sense. You generally get what you pay for, and cheap insurance usually goes hand-in-hand with minimal benefits and hidden costs.

BASIC SKILLS & CONCEPTS

23. Natasha spends $5 each week on lottery tickets, and using 52 weeks per year, this comes to $260 per year. She spends $120 each month on food, which is $1440 per year. The amount she spends on lottery tickets is $260/$1440 = 18% of the amount she spends on food.
24. Jeremy spends $6 each week on the newspaper, which comes to $312 per year. He spends $20 per week, or $1040 per year on gas. The amount he spends on the *New York Times* is $312/$1040 = 30% of the amount he spends on gas.
25. Suzanne spends $85 per month for her cell phone usage, which is $1020 per year. This is $1020/$200 = 510% of the amount she spends on health insurance.
26. Marcus spends $4 per day on *iTunes*, which comes to $1460 per year. He spends $350 each month on rent, or $4200 per year. The amount he spends on *iTunes* is $1460/$4200 = 35% of the amount he spends on rent.
27. Sheryl spends $9 each week on cigarettes, which comes to $468 per year. She spends $30 each month on dry cleaning, or $360 per year. The amount she spends on cigarettes is $468/$360 = 130% of the amount she spends on dry cleaning.
28. Ted spends $60 every two weeks on concert tickets, which is $30 per week. Using 52 weeks per year, he spends $1560 per year on tickets, which is $1560/$500 = 312% of the amount he spends on car insurance.
29. Vern spends $21 per week on beer, which amounts to $1092 per year. This is $1092/$700 = 156% of the amount he spends on textbooks.
30. Sandy spends $35 every two weeks, which is $17.50 every week on gas. This comes to $910 per year. She spends $60 per month, or $720 per year for her TV/Internet services. The amount she spends on gas is $910/$720 = 126% of the amount she spends on TV/Internet services.
31. Since 18%/12 = 1.5%, you spend 1.5% of $650 on interest each month, which is $0.015 \times \$650 = \$9.75$. Over the span of a year, you'll spend $117 on interest.
32. Since 21%/12 = 1.75%, Brooke spends 1.75% of $900, or $0.0175 \times \$900 = \$15.75$ on interest each month. Over the course of a year, she'll spend $189 on interest.
33. Vic's balance is $2200 – $300 = $1900. He spends 3% of $1900, or $0.03 \times \$1900 = \$57$ each month on interest. This comes to $684 per year.

34. Deanna pays 9% of $700, or $0.09 \times \$700 = \$63.00$ on interest each month. Over the course of a year, she'll spend $756 on interest.

35. Sara spends $4800 per semester, or $9600 per year, which is $9600/12 = \$800$ per month.

36. Jake spends $550 \times 15 = \$8250$ for 15 credit-hours each semester, and $400 for books, which comes to $8650 each semester, or $17,300 per year. Thus his monthly cost is $17,300/12 = \$1442$.

37. At $280/credit, Moriah spends $280 \times 15 = \$4200$ per quarter on tuition. Add this to her quarterly fees ($190), and her dorm room charge ($2300), with the result that she spends $6690 per quarter. Over the span of a year, she spends $6690 \times 3 = \$20,070$, which means she spends $20,070/12 = \$1673$ per month.

38. Each year, Juan spends $500 \times 12 = \$6000$ on rent, $800 \times 2 = \$1600$ on insurance, and $900 at the health club, for a total of $8500 per year. His monthly cost is $8500/12 = \$708$.

39. Nguyen spends $200 + \$400 \times 2 = \$1000$ each year on these expenses, or $1000/12 = \$83$ per month.

40. Using 52 weeks per year, Randy spends $25 \times 52 + \$45 \times 4 = \$1480$ on these expenses each year. That's $1480/12 = \$123$ per month.

41. Income $= \$600 \times 12 + \$400 \times 12 + \$5000 = \$17,000$ per year. Expenses $= \$450 \times 12 + \$50 \times 48 + \$3000 \times 2 + \$100 \times 48 = \$18,600$ per year. Thus annual cash flow is $17,000 - \$18,600 = -\$1600$, and monthly cash flow is $-\$1600/12 = -\$133$.

42. Income $= \$1200 \times 12 + \$7000 + \$8000 = \$29,400$ per year. Expenses $= \$600 \times 12 + \$70 \times 48 + \$7500 + \$40 \times 12 + \$200 \times 12 + \$65 \times 12 = \$21,720$ per year. Thus annual cash flow is $29,400 - \$21,720 = \$7680$, and monthly cash flow is $7680/12 = \$640$.

43. Income $= \$2300 \times 12 = \$27,600$. Expenses $= \$800 \times 12 + \$90 \times 48 + \$125 \times 12 + \$360 \times 2 + \$400 \times 2 + \$25 \times 48 + \$400 \times 12 + \$85 \times 12 = \$23,960$. Thus annual cash flow is $27,600 - \$23,960 = \$3640$, and monthly cash flow is $3640/12 = \$303$.

44. Income $= \$32,000 + \$200 \times 12 = \$34,400$ per year. Expenses $= \$700 \times 12 + \$150 \times 48 + \$450 \times 12 + \$150 \times 12 + \$500 \times 2 + \$200 \times 12 + \$600 + \$800 \times 12 = \$36,400$. Thus annual cash flow is $34,400 - \$36,400 = -\$2000$, and monthly cash flow is $-\$2000/12 = -\$167$.

45. The woman spends $900/\$3200 = 28\%$ of her income on rent (i.e. housing), which is below average.

46. The couple spends $400/\$3500 = 11\%$ on entertainment, which is above average.

47. The man spends $200/\$3600 = 5.6\%$ on health care, which is about average.

48. The couple earns $45,500/12 = \$3792$ per month, and spends $700/\$3792 = 18\%$ on transportation, which is below average.

49. The couple spends $600/\$4200 = 14\%$ on health care, which is above average.

50. The family earns $48,000/12 = \$4000$ per month, and spends $1500/\$4000 = 37.5\%$ on housing, which is above average.

51. The cost of using the old car for five years is computed below.
Gas:
$$\frac{250 \text{ mi}}{\text{wk}} \times \frac{1 \text{ gal}}{21 \text{ mi}} \times \frac{\$3.50}{1 \text{ gal}} \times \frac{52 \text{ wk}}{\text{yr}} \times 5 \text{ yr} = \$10,833 \,.$$
Insurance: $\dfrac{\$400}{\text{yr}} \times 5 \text{ yr} = \$2000 \,.$

Repairs: $\dfrac{\$1500}{\text{yr}} \times 5 \text{ yr} = \$7500 \,.$

Total: $10,833 + \$2000 + \$7500 = \$20,333$.
The cost for using the new car for five years is computed below.
Gas: $\dfrac{250 \text{ mi}}{\text{wk}} \times \dfrac{1 \text{ gal}}{45 \text{ mi}} \times \dfrac{\$3.50}{1 \text{ gal}} \times \dfrac{52 \text{ wk}}{\text{yr}} \times 5 \text{ yr} = \$5056 \,.$

Insurance: $\dfrac{\$800}{\text{yr}} \times 5 \text{ yr} = \$4000 \,.$

Purchase Price: $16,000.
Total: $5056 + \$4000 + \$16,000 = \$25,056$.
Using the old car is less expensive, but not by a large factor. After five years, if you use the old car, you'll have a junky car, whereas if you bought the new car, you'd have a nice car after five years.

52. Over five years, the old car would cost $18,200 for gas, $3000 for insurance, and $6000 for repairs, for a total of $27,200. The new car would cost $5460 for gas, $4000 for insurance, and $12,000 to buy it, for a total of $21,460. (See details in exercise 51, which is identical except for the numbers used). Using the new car is less expensive over five years.

53. If you buy the car for $22,000, and sell it three years later for $10,000, you will have spent $12,000. If you lease the car for three years (36 months) you will spend $1000 + \$250 \times 36 = \$10,000$. It is cheaper to lease in this case.

54. If you buy the car for $22,000, and sell it four years later for $8000, you will have spent $14,000. If you lease the car for four years ($48 months), you will spend $1000 + \$300 \times 48 = \$15,400$. It is cheaper to buy the car in this case.

55. At the in-state college, you will spend $4000 + \$700 \times 12 = \$12,400$ each year. At the out-of-state college, you will spend $6500 + \$450 \times 12 = \$11,900$. It will cost less out-of-state.

56. If you go to Concord, you will spend $3000 + $800 × 12 = $12,600. If you go to Versalia, you will spend $16,000 – $10,000 + $350 × 12 + $2000 = $12,200. It is cheaper to attend Versalia.

57. If you take the course, you will spend $1500, and use 150 hours of time that could be used to earn money in a job. If you work those 150 hours, you will earn $1500.

58. If you take the part-time job, you will earn $15 × 20 = $300 per week, though you will spend $150 on entertainment, which comes to a net earnings of $150 per week. If you take the full-time job, you will earn $12 × 40 = $480 per week. If finances are the only consideration, the full-time job is the better choice.

FURTHER APPLICATIONS

59. Note that it costs $10 less per month to operate the new dryer, and thus in 62 months, you would have saved $620, which is long enough to pay for the new dryer.

60. The annual cost for using the old car is shown below.

Gas: $\dfrac{300 \text{ mi}}{\text{wk}} \times \dfrac{1 \text{ gal}}{18 \text{ mi}} \times \dfrac{\$3.50}{\text{gal}} \times \dfrac{52 \text{ wk}}{\text{yr}} = \dfrac{\$3033}{\text{yr}}$.

Insurance: $500/yr.
Repairs: $1500/yr.
Total: $3033 + $500 + $1500 = $5033 per year.
The annual cost for using the new car is determined only by the cost of gasoline and insurance, which comes to $1213 per year (the calculation is similar to what's shown above) and $800 per year, respectively. This results in operation costs of $2013 per year. Since you save $5033 – $2013 = $3020 each year by using the new car, it will take about five years to recoup the $15,000 cost of the new car.

61. a. If you didn't have the policy, you'd pay all of the costs of the claims, which is $450 + $925 = $1375. If you did have the policy, you'd pay two years of premiums (2 × $550 = $1100), all of the $450 claim, and $500 of the $925 claim, for a grand total of $2050.
    b. Without the insurance policy, your cost would be $450 + $1200 = $1650. With the policy, you'd pay premiums for two years, and $200 on each claim for a total of 2 × $650 + 2 × $200 = $1700.
    c. Without the policy, your cost would be $200 + $1500 = $1700. With the policy, you'd pay premiums for two years, $200 for the first claim, and $1000 for the second claim, for a total of 2 × $300 + $200 + $1000 = $1800.

62. Under Plan A, you'll pay $1000 for the down payment, $400 for each of 24 months (two years), and $10,000 for the residual, which totals to $1000 + $400 × 24 + $10,000 = $20,600. Under Plan B, the cost will be $500 + $250 × 36 + $9500 = $19,000. Under Plan C, the cost will be $175 × 48 + $8000 = $16,400, and this is the least expensive plan.

63. a. You'll pay $25 for each of the office visits, $200 for each trip to the emergency room, and $1000 for the surgery, plus one year of premiums, for a grand total of $25 × 3 + $200 × 2 + $1000 + $350 × 12 = $5675.
    b. If you did not have the insurance policy, your cost is the total of the numbers in the second column, which is $8220.

64. a. You'll pay $25 for each office visit, $400 for the January 23rd trip to the emergency room, $500 for the September 23rd trip to the emergency room, $1400 for the April 13th surgery, $5000 for the June 14th surgery, and one year of premiums, for a grand total of $25 × 2 + $400 + $500 + $1400 + $5000 + $300 × 12 = $10,950.
    b. You'll pay $25 for each office visit, $200 for each trip to the emergency room, $1400 for the April 13th surgery, $1500 for the June 14th surgery, and one year of premiums, for a grand total of $25 × 2 + $200 × 2 + $1400 + $1500 + $700 × 12 = $11,750.
    c. With no insurance, you would pay all of the costs listed in the table out-of-pocket, for a total of $10,700. This is cheaper than both Plan A and Plan B, though going without health insurance is very risky: if you have a huge expense (such as extensive care while recovering from a car wreck), you have to pay all of it.

UNIT 4B

QUICK QUIZ

1. **b.** Compound interest always yields a greater balance than simple interest when the APR is the same.

2. **a.** If you begin with a principle P, and add 5% to its value after one year, the result is $P + 0.05P = 1.05P$, which means the principle increases by a factor of 1.05 each year.

3. **c.** The compound interest formula states $A = P \times (1 + \text{APR})^Y$. With an APR of 6.6%, the balance after five years would be $A = P \times (1 + 0.066)^5$, which means the account increases in value by a factor of 1.066^5.

4. **a.** The APR of 4% is divided evenly into four parts so that each quarter (three months), the account increases in value by 4%/4 = 1%.

5. **c.** Compounding interest more often always results in a greater annual percentage yield.

6. **b.** The APY is the same as the APR with annual compounding, but it's larger in all other cases.

7. **c.** After 20 years, the account earning 10% APR will have grown by a factor of $1.1^{20} = 6.73$, whereas the account earning 5% APR will have grown by a factor of $1.05^{20} = 2.65$. Thus the 10% APR account will have earned almost three times as much interest.

8. **a.** The continuously compounded interest formula reads $A = P \times e^{(APR \times Y)}$, and thus after two years, the balance is $A = \$500 \times e^{(0.06 \times 2)} = \$500 \times e^{0.12}$.

9. **a.** The compound interest formula assumes a constant APR for as many years as you have your money invested in an account.

10. **c.** Bank accounts that earn compound interest grow by larger amounts as time goes by, and this is a hallmark of exponential growth.

DOES IT MAKE SENSE?

19. Does not make sense. You earn more interest under compound interest when the APR is the same.

20. Makes sense. The APY is a function of both the APR and the number of compounding periods. If one bank had more compounding periods than the other, its APY would be greater.

21. Does not make sense. A bank with an APR of 5.9% compounded daily is a better deal than a bank with 6% APR compounded annually (all other things being equal) because the APY in the first case is greater.

22. Does not make sense. There is a diminishing return when banks offer to compound interest more often, and even under the situation where a bank compounds interest continuously (i.e. more often than every trillionth of a second), the APY has a finite limit.

23. Makes sense. One's bank account grows based on the APY, and an APR of 5% could certainly result in an APY of 5.1% if the number of compounding periods per year was just right.

24. Makes sense. At 4% APR (compounded annually), and over the span of twenty years, the value of an account will grow by a factor of $1.04^{20} = 2.19$, which is more than double the original amount.

BASIC SKILLS & CONCEPTS

25. $x = 12$ (add 3 to both sides).

26. $y = 3$ (subtract 4 from both sides).

27. $z = 16$ (add 10 to both sides).

28. $x = 4$ (divide both sides by 2).

29. $p = 4$ (divide both sides by 3).

30. $y = 4$ (subtract 2, and divide both sides by 4).

31. $z = 4$ (add 1, and divide both sides by 5).

32. $y = -2$ (subtract 1, and divide both sides by -6).

33. $3x - 4 = 2x + 6 \Rightarrow 3x = 2x + 10 \Rightarrow x = 10$.

34. $5 - 4s = 6s - 5 \Rightarrow 10 - 4s = 6s \Rightarrow 10 = 10s \Rightarrow s = 1$.

35. $3a + 4 = 6 + 4a \Rightarrow 3a - 2 = 4a \Rightarrow a = -2$.

36. $3n - 16 = 53 \Rightarrow 3n = 69 \Rightarrow n = 23$.

37. $6q - 20 = 60 + 4q \Rightarrow 6q = 80 + 4q \Rightarrow 2q = 80 \Rightarrow q = 40$.

38. $5w - 5 = 3w - 25 \Rightarrow 5w = 3w - 20 \Rightarrow 2w = -20 \Rightarrow w = -10$.

39. $t/4 + 5 = 25 \Rightarrow t/4 = 20 \Rightarrow t = 80$.

40. $2x/3 + 4 = 2x \Rightarrow 4 = 4x/3 \Rightarrow 4x = 12 \Rightarrow x = 3$.

41. You'll earn 5% of $1000, or $0.05 \times \$1000 = \$50$, each year. After ten years, you will have earned $500 in interest, so that your balance will be $1500.

42. Each year, you'll earn 7% of $1000 $= 0.07 \times \$1000 = \$70$. After five years, you will have earned $350 in interest, and your balance will be $1350.

43. Each year, you'll earn 3% of $3000 $= 0.03 \times \$3000 = \$90$. After 20 years, you will have earned $1800 in interest, and your balance will be $4800.

44. Each year, you'll earn 6.5% of $5000 $= 0.065 \times \$5000 = \$325$. After 20 years, you will have earned $\$325 \times 20 = \$6500$ in interest, and your balance will be $11,500.

45.

	Yancy		Samantha	
Year	Interest	Balance	Interest	Balance
0	-----	$5000	-----	$5000
1	$250	$5250	$250	$5250
2	$250	$5500	$262.50	$5512.50
3	$250	$5750	$275.63	$5788.13
4	$250	$6000	$289.41	$6077.53
5	$250	$6250	$303.88	$6381.41

Yancy's balance increases by $1250, or 25% of its original value. Samantha's increases by $1,381.41, or 27.6% of its original value. (Note on values shown in the table: the balance in one year added to next year's interest does not necessarily produce next year's balance due to rounding errors. Each value shown is rounded correctly to the nearest cent).

46.

	Trevor		Kendra	
Year	Interest	Balance	Interest	Balance
0	-----	$1000	-----	$1000
1	$60	$1060	$60	$1060
2	$60	$1120	$63.60	$1123.60
3	$60	$1180	$67.42	$1191.02
4	$60	$1240	$71.46	$1262.48
5	$60	$1300	$75.75	$1338.23

Trevor's balance increases by $300, or 30% of its original value. Kendra's increases by $338.23, or 33.8% of its original value.

47. $A = \$3000(1 + 0.03)^{10} = \$4031.75$.

48. $A = \$10,000(1 + 0.05)^{20} = \$26,532.98$.

49. $A = \$40,000(1 + 0.07)^{25} = \$217,097.31$.

50. $A = \$3000(1 + 0.04)^{12} = \$4803.10$.

51. $A = \$8000(1 + 0.06)^{25} = \$34,334.97$.

52. $A = \$40,000(1 + 0.085)^{30} = \$462,330.07$.

53. $A = \$4000\left(1 + \dfrac{0.035}{12}\right)^{12 \cdot 10} = \$5673.38$.

54. $A = \$2000\left(1 + \dfrac{0.03}{365}\right)^{365 \cdot 5} = \$2323.65$.

55. $A = \$15,000\left(1 + \dfrac{0.056}{4}\right)^{4 \cdot 20} = \$45,617.10$.

56. $A = \$10,000\left(1 + \dfrac{0.0275}{12}\right)^{12 \cdot 5} = \$11,472.21$.

57. $A = \$2000\left(1 + \dfrac{0.07}{12}\right)^{12 \cdot 15} = \$5697.89$.

58. $A = \$3000\left(1 + \dfrac{0.05}{365}\right)^{365 \cdot 10} = \$4945.99$.

59. $A = \$25,000\left(1 + \dfrac{0.062}{4}\right)^{4 \cdot 30} = \$158,318.38$.

60. $A = \$15,000\left(1 + \dfrac{0.078}{12}\right)^{12 \cdot 15} = \$48,147.25$.

61. The APY is the relative increase in the balance of a bank account over the span of one year. The easiest way to compute it when the APR is known is to find the one-year balance, compute the relative increase, and express the answer as a percent. When the principal is not given, any amount can be used – here, we will use $100.

1-year balance: $A = \$100\left(1 + \dfrac{0.035}{365}\right)^{365 \cdot 1} = \$103.56$.

The relative increase is $3.56/$100 = 3.56%, so the APY is 3.56%.

62. The APY is the relative increase in the balance of a bank account over the span of one year. The easiest way to compute it when the APR is known is to find the one-year balance, compute the relative increase, and express the answer as a percent. When the principal is not given, any amount can be used – here, we will use $100.

1-year balance: $A = \$100\left(1 + \dfrac{0.045}{12}\right)^{12 \cdot 1} = \$104.59$.

The relative increase is $4.59/$100 = 4.59%, so the APY is 4.59%.

63. See #61 for details. The one-year balance is $A = \$100\left(1 + \dfrac{0.0425}{12}\right)^{12 \cdot 1} = \$104.33$. The relative increase (APY) is $4.33/$100 = 4.33%.

64. See #62 for details. The one-year balance is $A = \$100\left(1 + \dfrac{0.0225}{4}\right)^{4 \cdot 1} = \$102.27$. The relative increase (APY) is $2.27/$100 = 2.27%.

65. The one, five, and twenty-year balances are:
One year: $A = \$3000e^{0.04 \times 1} = \$3122.43$.
Five years: $A = \$3000e^{0.04 \times 5} = \$3664.21$.
Twenty years: $A = \$3000e^{0.04 \times 20} = \$6676.62$.
To compute the APY, find the relative increase in the balance of the account after one year.
APY = $122.43/$3000 = 4.08%.

66. The one, five, and twenty-year balances are:
One year: $A = \$2000e^{0.05 \times 1} = \$2102.54$.
Five years: $A = \$2000e^{0.05 \times 5} = \$2568.05$.
Twenty years: $A = \$2000e^{0.05 \times 20} = \$5436.56$.
To compute the APY, find the relative increase in the balance of the account after one year.
APY = $102.54/$2000 = 5.13%.

67. The one, five, and twenty-year balances are:
One year: $A = \$10,000e^{0.08 \times 1} = \$10,832.87$.
Five years: $A = \$10,000e^{0.08 \times 5} = \$14,918.25$.
Twenty years: $A = \$10,000e^{0.08 \times 20} = \$49,530.32$.
To compute the APY, find the relative increase in the balance of the account after one year.
APY = $832.87/$10,000 = 8.33%.

68. The one, five, and twenty-year balances are:
One year: $A = \$3000e^{0.075 \times 1} = \$3233.65$.
Five years: $A = \$3000e^{0.075 \times 5} = \$4364.97$.
Twenty years: $A = \$3000e^{0.075 \times 20} = \$13,445.07$.
To compute the APY, find the relative increase in the balance of the account after one year.
APY = $233.65/$3000 = 7.79%.

69. The one, five, and twenty-year balances are:
One year: $A = \$2500e^{0.065 \times 1} = \$2667.90$.
Five years: $A = \$2500e^{0.065 \times 5} = \$3460.08$.
Twenty years: $A = \$2500e^{0.065 \times 20} = \$9173.24$.
To compute the APY, find the relative increase in the balance of the account after one year.
APY = $167.90/$2500 = 6.72%.

70. The one, five, and twenty-year balances are:
One year: $A = \$500e^{0.07 \times 1} = \$536.25$.
Five years: $A = \$500e^{0.07 \times 5} = \$709.53$.
Twenty years: $A = \$500e^{0.07 \times 20} = \$2027.60$.
To compute the APY, find the relative increase in the balance of the account after one year.
APY = $36.25/$500 = 7.25%.

71. Solve $\$20,000 = P(1+0.05)^{10}$ for P to find

$$P = \frac{\$20,000}{(1+0.05)^{10}} = \$12,278 \ .$$

72. Solve $\$20,000 = P\left(1+\dfrac{0.045}{4}\right)^{4\cdot10}$ for P to find

$$P = \frac{\$20,000}{\left(1+\dfrac{0.045}{4}\right)^{4\cdot10}} = \$12,785 \ .$$

73. Solve $\$20,000 = P\left(1+\dfrac{0.06}{12}\right)^{12\cdot10}$ for P to find

$$P = \frac{\$20,000}{\left(1+\dfrac{0.06}{12}\right)^{12\cdot10}} = \$10,993 \ .$$

74. Solve $\$20,000 = P\left(1+\dfrac{0.04}{365}\right)^{365\cdot10}$ for P to find

$$P = \frac{\$20,000}{\left(1+\dfrac{0.04}{365}\right)^{365\cdot10}} = \$13,407 \ .$$

75. Solve $\$100,000 = P\left(1+\dfrac{0.04}{365}\right)^{365\cdot18}$ for P to find

$$P = \frac{\$100,000}{\left(1+\dfrac{0.04}{365}\right)^{365\cdot18}} = \$48,677 \ .$$

76. Solve $\$100,000 = P\left(1+\dfrac{0.055}{365}\right)^{365\cdot18}$ for P to find

$$P = \frac{\$100,000}{\left(1+\dfrac{0.055}{365}\right)^{365\cdot18}} = \$37,160 \ .$$

77. Solve $\$100,000 = P\left(1+\dfrac{0.09}{12}\right)^{12\cdot18}$ for P to find

$$P = \frac{\$100,000}{\left(1+\dfrac{0.09}{12}\right)^{12\cdot18}} = \$19,910 \ .$$

78. Solve $\$100,000 = P\left(1+\dfrac{0.035}{12}\right)^{12\cdot18}$ for P to find

$$P = \frac{\$100,000}{\left(1+\dfrac{0.035}{12}\right)^{12\cdot18}} = \$53,308 \ .$$

FURTHER APPLICATIONS

79. After 10 years, Chang has $705.30; after 30 years, he has $1403.40. After 10 years, Kio has $722.52; after 30 years, she has $1508.74. Kio has $17.22, or 2.4% more than Chang after 10 years. She has $105.34, or 7.5% more than Chang after 30 years.

80. After 10 years, José has $2586.61; after 30 years, he has $7691.46. After 10 years, Marta has $2611.21; after 30 years, she has $7912.99. Marta has $24.60, or 0.95% more than José after 10

years. She has $221.53, or 2.9% more than José after 30 years.

81. To compute the APY, find the one-year balance in the account, using any principal desired ($100 is used here), and then compute the relative increase in the value of the account over one year.
One-year balance, compounded quarterly:

$$A = \$100\left(1+\frac{0.066}{4}\right)^{4\cdot1} = \$106.77 \ .$$

APY = $6.77/$100 = 6.77%.
One-year balance, compounded monthly:

$$A = \$100\left(1+\frac{0.066}{12}\right)^{12\cdot1} = \$106.80 \ .$$

APY = $6.80/$100 = 6.80%.
One-year balance, compounded daily:

$$A = \$100\left(1+\frac{0.066}{365}\right)^{365\cdot1} = \$106.82 \ .$$

APY = $6.82/$100 = 6.82%.
As the number of compounding periods per year increases, so does the APY, though the rate at which it increases slows down.

82. To compute the APY, find the one-year balance in the account, using any principal desired ($100 is used here), and then compute the relative increase in the value of the account over one year.
One-year balance, compounded quarterly:

$$A = \$100\left(1+\frac{0.05}{4}\right)^{4\cdot1} = \$105.09 \ .$$

APY = $5.09/$100 = 5.09%.
One-year balance, compounded monthly:

$$A = \$100\left(1+\frac{0.05}{12}\right)^{12\cdot1} = \$105.12 \ .$$

APY = $5.12/$100 = 5.12%.
One-year balance, compounded daily:

$$A = \$100\left(1+\frac{0.05}{365}\right)^{365\cdot1} = \$105.13 \ .$$

APY = $5.13/$100 = 5.13%.
As the number of compounding periods per year increases, so does the APY, though the rate at which it increases slows down.

83.

	Account 1		Account 2	
Year	Interest	Balance	Interest	Balance
0	-----	$1000	-----	$1000
1	$55	$1055	$57	$1057
2	$58	$1113	$60	$1116
3	$61	$1174	$63	$1179
4	$65	$1239	$67	$1246
5	$68	$1307	$70	$1317
6	$72	$1379	$74	$1391
7	$76	$1455	$79	$1470
8	$80	$1535	$83	$1553
9	$84	$1619	$88	$1640
10	$89	$1708	$93	$1733

Account 1 has increased in value by $708, or 70.8%. Account 2 has increased by $733, or 73.3%. (Note on values shown in the table: the balance in one year added to next year's interest does not necessarily produce next year's balance due to rounding errors. Each value shown is rounded correctly to the nearest dollar).

84. a. If there is only one compounding period during the year, the balance will increase by the APR in one year. Thus, the APY is the APR.
b. With more than one compounding per year, the APY is always greater than the APR. The APY reflects the cumulative effects of several compounding periods during the year. At the end of the year, the balance will be greater than if there had been only one compounding period.
c. APY does *not* depend on the starting principal. It gives the relative increase (as a percent) in the balance.
d. The more compounding periods per year, the greater the APY.

85. After 5 years, Bernard has $A = \$1600(1.04)^5 = \$1946.64$; after 20 years, he has $A = \$1600(1.04)^{20} = \$3505.80$. After 5 years, Carla has $A = \$1400(1+\frac{0.05}{365})^{365\cdot5} = \$1797.60$; after 20 years, she has $A = \$1400(1+\frac{0.05}{365})^{365\cdot20} = \$3805.33$. Carla has the higher balance after 20 years because her account has a larger APR, and thus the balance catches up to and exceeds Bernard's balance over the long run.

86. After 5 years, Brian has $A = \$1600(1.055)^5 = \$2091.14$; after 20 years, he has $A = \$1600(1.055)^{20} = \$4668.41$. Celeste has $A = \$1400e^{0.052\times5} = \$1815.70$ after 5 years, and she has $A = \$1400e^{0.052\times20} = \$3960.90$ after 20 years. Brian has a larger balance in both cases, and always will as his APY is greater than Celeste's APY, even though she earns interest compounded continuously. He also began with a larger principal.

87. For Plan A, solve $\$75,000 = P(1.05)^{35}$ for P to find $P = \dfrac{\$75,000}{(1.05)^{35}} = \$13,597$. For Plan B, solve $\$75,000 = Pe^{0.045\times35}$ for P to find $P = \dfrac{\$75,000}{e^{0.045\times35}} = \$15,526$.

89. To obtain an exact solution for this problem, one must use logarithms (studied in a later chapter). If your initial investment *P* is to triple, we must solve $3P = P(1.08)^t$ for *t* in order to find out how long it takes. Begin by dividing both sides by *P* (it will cancel from both sides), and then take the

logarithm of both sides: $\log 3 = \log(1.08)^t$. A property of logarithms says the exponent *t* can be moved in front of the logarithm, as such: $\log 3 = t \log(1.08)$. Now divide both sides by log 1.08 to arrive at the answer: $t = (\log 3)/(\log 1.08) = 14.3$ years. Thus it will take about 14.3 years for your investment to triple in value. Another way to come to the solution is to try various values of *t* in $(1.08)^t$ – you will have found a solution when $(1.08)^t$ is about 3.

90. See exercise 89. Solve $1.5P = P(1.07)^t$ for *t* to arrive at $t = (\log 1.5)/(\log 1.07) = 6$ years.

91. See exercise 89. Solve $\$100,000 = \$1000(1.07)^t$ for *t*. Begin by dividing both sides by $1000; this yields $100 = (1.07)^t$. Now take the logarithm of both sides, and apply a property of logarithms to get $\log 100 = t \log 1.07$. Divide both sides by log 1.07 to find $t = (\log 100)/(\log 1.07) = 68.1$ years. Trial and error may also produce the same result if you are patient.

92. a.

n	1	4	12	365	500	1000
APY	12.00	12.55	12.68	12.75	12.75	12.75

b. The one-year balance (using *P* = $100) is $A = \$100e^{0.12\times1} = \$112.75$, and thus the APY is $\$12.75/\$100 = 12.75\%$.

c.

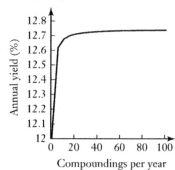

Annual Percentage Yield (APY) with APR = 12%

d. The APY is higher with continuous compounding than with any other periodic compounding.
e. At the end of one year, you will have $A = \$500e^{0.12\times1} = \$563.75$. After five years, you will have $A = \$500e^{0.12\times5} = \$911.06$.

93. The trick to solving this problem is to treat each $500 deposit separately. The first $500 deposit earns 6% interest for 5 full years, so its value is $A = \$500(1.06)^5 = \$669.11$. The $500 deposit made after the first year earns interest for only 4 years, so its value on December 31 of the last year is

$A = \$500(1.06)^4 = \$631.24$. In a similar fashion, one can compute the future value of each \$500 deposit, realizing that the length of time each is in the bank decreases by one year compared to the previous deposit:

3rd deposit: $A = \$500(1.06)^3 = \$595.51$.

4th deposit: $A = \$500(1.06)^2 = \$561.80$.

5th deposit: $A = \$500(1.06)^1 = \$530$.

The sum of all deposits is the value of the account on December 31 of the last year: \$669.11 + \$631.24 + \$595.51 + \$561.80 + \$530 = \$2987.66.

UNIT 4C

QUICK QUIZ

1. **a**. As the number of compounding periods n increases, so does the APY, and a higher APY means a higher accumulated balance.

2. **c**. As long as the savings plan in which you are investing money has a positive rate of return, the balance will increase as time increases.

3. **c**. The total return on a five-year investment is simply the percent change of the balance over five years.

4. **b**. The annual return is the APY that gives the same overall growth in five years as the total return.

5. **a**. If you deposit \$100 per month for ten years (120 months), you have deposited a total of \$12,000 into the savings plan. Since the balance was \$22,200, you earned \$22,200 – \$12,000 = \$10,200 in interest.

6. **a**. If you can find a low risk, high return investment, that's the best of both worlds, and adding high liquidity (where it's easy to access your money) is like icing on the cake. Good luck.

7. **c**. See table 4.6.

8. **a**. The P/E ratio is the share price divided by earnings per share.

9. **b**. If the bond is selling at 103 points, it is selling at 103% of its face value, which is $1.03 \times \$5000 = \$5150$.

10. **c**. The one-year return is simply a measure of how well the mutual fund has done over the last year, and it could be higher or lower than the three-year return (which measures how well the fund has done over the last three years).

DOES IT MAKE SENSE?

19. Does not make sense. With an APR of 4%, the savings plan formula gives a balance of

$$A = \frac{\$25\left[\left(1 + \frac{0.04}{12}\right)^{12 \cdot 30} - 1\right]}{\left(\frac{0.04}{12}\right)} = \$17,351 \text{ after 30 years,}$$

which probably wouldn't cover expenses for even one year of retirement (and certainly interest earned on that balance would not be enough for retirement). You should plan to save considerably more than \$25 per month for a retirement plan.

20. Does not make sense. When you find an investment that guarantees an APR of 15% for the next 30 years, please tell me about it.

21. Does not make sense. Stocks can be a risky investment (you might lose all of your money), and most financial advisors will tell you to diversify your investments.

22. Makes sense. A liquid investment is one where it is easy to access your money.

23. Does not make sense. Stocks are considered a risky investment (especially in the short term). In general, an investment with a greater return is even more risky, and thus the claim that there is no risk at all is dubious, at best.

24. Makes sense. Financial advisors generally tell retired people (who depend on their life savings for income) to invest in low-risk funds, lest they lose a big portion of their nest egg. U.S. Treasury bills, notes and bonds are considered low-risk investments.

BASIC SKILLS & CONCEPTS

25. $2^3 = 2 \times 2 \times 2 = 8$.

26. $3^4 = 3 \times 3 \times 3 \times 3 = 81$.

27. $4^3 = 64$.

28. $3^{-2} = \frac{1}{3^2} = \frac{1}{9}$.

29. $16^{1/2} = \sqrt{16} = 4$.

30. $81^{1/2} = \sqrt{81} = 9$.

31. $64^{-1/3} = \frac{1}{64^{1/3}} = \frac{1}{\sqrt[3]{64}} = \frac{1}{4}$.

32. $2^3 \times 2^5 = 2^{3+5} = 2^8 = 256$.

33. $3^4 \div 3^2 = 3^{4-2} = 3^2 = 9$.

34. $6^2 \times 6^{-2} = 6^{2+(-2)} = 6^0 = 1$.

35. $25^{1/2} \div 25^{-1/2} = 25^{1/2-(-1/2)} = 25^1 = 25$.

36. $3^3 + 2^3 = 27 + 8 = 35$.

37. $x^2 = 25 \Rightarrow (x^2)^{1/2} = 25^{1/2} \Rightarrow x = \sqrt{25} = 5$. Another solution is $x = -5$.

38. $y^3 = 27 \Rightarrow (y^3)^{1/3} = 27^{1/3} \Rightarrow y = \sqrt[3]{27} = 3$.

39. $(x-4)^2 = 36 \Rightarrow ((x-4)^2)^{1/2} = 36^{1/2} \Rightarrow x - 4 = \sqrt{36} \Rightarrow x = 4 + 6 = 10$. Another solution is $x = -2$.

40. $p^{1/3} = 3 \Rightarrow (p^{1/3})^3 = 3^3 \Rightarrow p = 27$.

41. $(t/3)^2 = 16 \Rightarrow ((t/3)^2)^{1/2} = 16^{1/2} \Rightarrow$
$t/3 = \sqrt{16} \Rightarrow t = 3 \times 4 = 12$. Another solution is $x = -12$.

42. $w^2 + 2 = 27 \Rightarrow w^2 = 25 \Rightarrow w = \sqrt{25} = 5$. Another solution is $x = -5$.

43. $u^9 = 512 \Rightarrow (u^9)^{1/9} = 512^{1/9} \Rightarrow u = \sqrt[9]{512} = 2$.

44. $v^3 + 4 = 68 \Rightarrow v^3 = 64 \Rightarrow v = \sqrt[3]{64} = 4$.

45. $A = \dfrac{\$200\left[\left(1+\frac{0.12}{12}\right)^{12\times0.75} - 1\right]}{\left(\frac{0.12}{12}\right)} = \$1873.71$. Note that 9 months is $3/4 = 0.75$ year, which is why we used $Y = 0.75$ in the formula.

46. $A = \dfrac{\$100\left[\left(1+\frac{0.12}{12}\right)^{12\times1} - 1\right]}{\left(\frac{0.12}{12}\right)} = \$1268.25$.

47. $A = \dfrac{\$600\left[\left(1+\frac{0.06}{12}\right)^{12\times1.5} - 1\right]}{\left(\frac{0.06}{12}\right)} = \$11,271.47$. Note that 18 months is 1.5 years.

48. $A = \dfrac{\$250\left[\left(1+\frac{0.05}{12}\right)^{12\times2} - 1\right]}{\left(\frac{0.05}{12}\right)} = \$6296.48$. Note that 24 months is 2 years.

49. You save for 40 years, so the value of the IRA is
$A = \dfrac{\$75\left[\left(1+\frac{0.05}{12}\right)^{12\times40} - 1\right]}{\left(\frac{0.05}{12}\right)} = \$114,451.51$. Since you deposit \$75 each month for 40 years, your total deposits are $\dfrac{\$75}{\text{mo}} \times \dfrac{12 \text{ mo}}{\text{yr}} \times 40 \text{ yr} = \$36,000$. The value of the account is just over three times the amount you deposited.

50. She saves for 40 years, so the value of the IRA is
$A = \dfrac{\$50\left[\left(1+\frac{0.0625}{12}\right)^{12\times40} - 1\right]}{\left(\frac{0.0625}{12}\right)} = \$106,595.63$. Since she deposits \$50 each month for 40 years, her total deposits are $\dfrac{\$50}{\text{mo}} \times \dfrac{12 \text{ mo}}{\text{yr}} \times 40 \text{ yr} = \$24,000$. The value of her account is more than four times the value of the amount invested.

51. $A = \dfrac{\$300\left[\left(1+\frac{0.07}{12}\right)^{12\times18} - 1\right]}{\left(\frac{0.07}{12}\right)} = \$129,216.31$. You have deposited $\dfrac{\$300}{\text{mo}} \times \dfrac{12 \text{ mo}}{\text{yr}} \times 18 \text{ yr} = \$64,800$, which is about one-half of the value of the account.

52. $A = \dfrac{\$200\left[\left(1+\frac{0.045}{12}\right)^{12\times18} - 1\right]}{\left(\frac{0.045}{12}\right)} = \$66,373.60$. You have deposited $\dfrac{\$200}{\text{mo}} \times \dfrac{12 \text{ mo}}{\text{yr}} \times 18 \text{ yr} = \$43,200$, which is about two-thirds of the value of the account.

53. Solve $\$75,000 = \dfrac{PMT\left[\left(1+\frac{0.075}{12}\right)^{12\times18} - 1\right]}{\left(\frac{0.075}{12}\right)}$ for PMT. $PMT = \dfrac{\$75,000\left(\frac{0.075}{12}\right)}{\left[\left(1+\frac{0.075}{12}\right)^{12\times18} - 1\right]} = \$164.98$. You should deposit \$164.98 each month.

54. Solve $\$2,000,000 = \dfrac{PMT\left[\left(1+\frac{0.06}{12}\right)^{12\times30} - 1\right]}{\left(\frac{0.06}{12}\right)}$ for PMT. $PMT = \dfrac{\$2,000,000\left(\frac{0.06}{12}\right)}{\left[\left(1+\frac{0.06}{12}\right)^{12\times30} - 1\right]} = \$1991.01$. You should deposit \$1991.01 each month.

55. Solve $\$15,000 = \dfrac{PMT\left[\left(1+\frac{0.055}{12}\right)^{12\times3} - 1\right]}{\left(\frac{0.055}{12}\right)}$ for PMT. $PMT = \dfrac{\$15,000\left(\frac{0.055}{12}\right)}{\left[\left(1+\frac{0.055}{12}\right)^{12\times3} - 1\right]} = \$384.19$. You should deposit \$384.19 each month.

56. Solve $\$5,000,000 = \dfrac{PMT\left[\left(1+\dfrac{0.08}{12}\right)^{12\times45} - 1\right]}{\left(\dfrac{0.08}{12}\right)}$ for

PMT. $PMT = \dfrac{\$5,000,000\left(\dfrac{0.08}{12}\right)}{\left[\left(1+\dfrac{0.08}{12}\right)^{12\times45} - 1\right]} = \$947.95$. You

should deposit \$947.95 each month.

57. First, find out how large your retirement account needs to be in order to produce \$100,000 in interest (at 6% APR) each year. You want 6% of the total balance to be \$100,000, which means the total balance should be \$100,000/0.06 = \$1,666,667. Now solve

$\$1,666,667 = \dfrac{PMT\left[\left(1+\dfrac{0.06}{12}\right)^{12\times30} - 1\right]}{\left(\dfrac{0.06}{12}\right)}$ for PMT.

$PMT = \dfrac{\$1,666,667\left(\dfrac{0.06}{12}\right)}{\left[\left(1+\dfrac{0.06}{12}\right)^{12\times30} - 1\right]} = \$1659.18$. You should

deposit \$1659.18 each month.

58. First, find out how large your retirement account needs to be in order to produce \$200,000 in interest (at 6% APR) each year. You want 6% of the total balance to be \$200,000, which means the total balance should be \$200,000/0.06 = \$3,333,333. Now solve

$\$3,333,333 = \dfrac{PMT\left[\left(1+\dfrac{0.06}{12}\right)^{12\times40} - 1\right]}{\left(\dfrac{0.06}{12}\right)}$ for PMT.

$PMT = \dfrac{\$3,333,333\left(\dfrac{0.06}{12}\right)}{\left[\left(1+\dfrac{0.06}{12}\right)^{12\times40} - 1\right]} = \$1673.79$. You should

deposit \$1673.79 each month.

59. The total return is the relative change in the investment, and since you invested \$6000 (100 shares at \$60 per share), the total return is $\dfrac{\$9400 - \$6000}{\$6000} = 0.567 = 56.7\%$. The annual return is the APY that would give the same overall growth in five years, and the formula for

computing it is $\left(\dfrac{A}{P}\right)^{(1/Y)} - 1$. Thus the annual return

is $\left(\dfrac{\$9400}{\$6000}\right)^{(1/5)} - 1 = 0.094 = 9.4\%$.

60. The total return is the relative change in the investment, or $\dfrac{\$12,500 - \$8000}{\$8000} = 0.563 = 56.3\%$. The annual return is the APY that would give the same overall growth in 20 years, and the formula for computing it is $\left(\dfrac{A}{P}\right)^{(1/Y)} - 1$. Thus the annual

return is $\left(\dfrac{\$12,500}{\$8000}\right)^{(1/20)} - 1 = 0.023 = 2.3\%$.

61. The total return is $\dfrac{\$11,300 - \$6500}{\$6500} = 73.8\%$. The

annual return is $\left(\dfrac{\$11,300}{\$6500}\right)^{(1/20)} - 1 = 2.8\%$.

62. You invested \$5000 (200 shares at \$25 per share), so the total return is $\dfrac{\$8500 - \$5000}{\$5000} = 70.0\%$. The

annual return is $\left(\dfrac{\$8500}{\$5000}\right)^{(1/3)} - 1 = 19.3\%$.

63. The total return is $\dfrac{\$2000 - \$3500}{\$3500} = -42.9\%$. The

annual return is $\left(\dfrac{\$2000}{\$3500}\right)^{(1/3)} - 1 = -17.0\%$.

64. The total return is $\dfrac{\$3000 - \$5000}{\$5000} = -40.0\%$. The

annual return is $\left(\dfrac{\$3000}{\$5000}\right)^{(1/5)} - 1 = -9.7\%$.

65. The total return is $\dfrac{\$12,600 - \$7500}{\$7500} = 68.0\%$. The

annual return is $\left(\dfrac{\$12,600}{\$7500}\right)^{(1/10)} - 1 = 5.3\%$.

66. The total return is $\dfrac{\$2200 - \$10,000}{\$10,000} = -78.0\%$. The

annual return is $\left(\dfrac{\$2200}{\$10,000}\right)^{(1/10)} - 1 = -14.1\%$.

67. \$500 invested in small-company stocks would be worth $\$500(1+0.126)^{70} = \$2,026,083.50$. \$500 invested in large-company stocks would be worth $\$500(1+0.104)^{70} = \$509,102.40$. For long-term bonds and U.S. Treasury bills, the investment would be worth $\$500(1+0.059)^{70} = \$27,649.50$, and $\$500(1+0.037)^{70} = \$6360.38$, respectively.

68. A \$2000 investment in small-company stocks would be worth $\$2000(1+1.429) = \$4858$ one year later under the best-case scenario. The other

investments (large-company stocks, long-term bonds, and U.S. Treasury bills) would be worth $3080, $2852, and $2294, respectively, under the best-case scenario. If it was the worst of years, the investment in small-company stocks would be worth $2000(1 − 0.58) = $840 one year later, and the other investments would be worth $1134, $1838, and $1999.60, respectively (the calculations are similar).

69. McDonald's (MCD) had the largest price gain at $0.31 per share. Since it closed at $24.42 yesterday, its price two days ago was $24.42 − $0.31 = $24.11.

70. Monsanto (MON) had the largest decline in price at $0.29 per share. Since it closed at $21.64 yesterday, its price two days ago was $21.93.

71. Monsanto is trading at $21.64 at the close of yesterday, and this is about one dollar less than its 52-week high price of $22.60. The other stocks are trading at prices significantly lower than their 52-week high.

72. Motorola is trading at $9.43 at the close of yesterday, and this is about two dollars more than its 52-week low price of $7.30. The other stocks are trading at prices significantly higher than their 52-week low.

73. You can expect a dividend payment of $520, because the stock pays $0.52 per share in dividends.

74. McDonald's has the highest dividend per share at $0.72. Since you own 100 shares, you'll get a dividend payment of $72.

75. McDonald's would be the best investment as it has the highest dividend yield ($0.72 per share).

76. You shouldn't invest in Mueller, as it doesn't offer dividend payments.

77. a. Yes, McDonald's earned a profit because its P/E ratio is 12, which means its share price divided by earnings (or profit) per share was 12. This implies share price = 12 × earnings per share.
b. Since share price = 12 × earnings per share, earnings per share = (share price)/12 = $24.42/12 = $2.04 per share.
c. The stock prices are about right.

79. a. No, Motorola showed a loss last year (the P/E ratio is listed as "dd").
b. The company didn't earn anything per share as it had a loss last year.
c. Given that the stock is losing money, the stock is expensive.

81. a. Yes, Mueller earned a profit because its P/E ration is 16, which means its share price divided by earnings (or profit) per share was 16. This implies share price = 16 × earnings per share.

b. Since share price = 16 × earnings per share, earnings per share = (share price)/16 = $27.11/16 = $1.69 per share.
c. The price is a little expensive (because 16 is larger than the P/E ration of 12 to 14, the historical average).

83. The current yield on a bond is its annual interest payment divided by its current price. A $1000 bond with a coupon rate of 2% pays $1000 × 0.02 = $20 per year in interest, so this bond has a current yield of $20/$950 = 2.11%.

84. The current yield on a bond is its annual interest payment divided by its current price. A $1000 bond with a coupon rate of 2.5% pays $1000 × 0.025 = $25 per year in interest, so this bond has a current yield of $25/$1050 = 2.38%.

85. The annual interest payment on this bond is $1000 × 0.055 = $55, so its current yield is $55/$1100 = 5%.

86. The annual interest payment on this bond is $10,000 × 0.03 = $300, so its current yield is $300/$9500 = 3.16%.

87. The price of this bond is 105% × $1000 = $1050, and it has a current yield of 3.9%, so the annual interest earned is $1050 × 0.039 = $40.95.

88. The price of this bond is 98% × $1000 = $980, and its current yield is 1.5%, which means the annual interest will be $980 × 0.015 = $14.70.

89. The price of this bond is 114.3% × $1000 = $1143, and its current yield is 6.2%, which means the annual interest will be $1143 × 0.062 = $70.87.

90. The price of this bond is 102.5% × $10,000 = $10,250, and it has a current yield of 3.6%, so the annual interest earned is $10,250 × 0.036 = $369.

91. The 3-year return on SocInvBdA is 10%, which means the fund earned an average of 10% each of the last three years. Thus a $500 investment is now worth $500(1 + 0.10)^3 = $665.50.

92. The 3-yr return on SocInvEqA is − 0.9%, which means the fund lost an average of 0.9% per year for each of the last three years. Thus a $500 investment is now worth $500(1 − 0.009)^3 = $486.62.

FURTHER APPLICATIONS

93. After 10 years, the balance in Yolanda's account is
$$A = \frac{\$200\left[\left(1 + \frac{0.05}{12}\right)^{12 \times 10} - 1\right]}{\left(\frac{0.05}{12}\right)} = \$31,056.46.$$ She

deposits $200 per month, so her total deposits are
$$\frac{\$200}{\text{mo}} \times \frac{12 \text{ mo}}{\text{yr}} \times 10 \text{ yr} = \$24,000.$$ Zach's account is

worth $A = \dfrac{\$2400\left[\left(1+\frac{0.05}{1}\right)^{1\times10}-1\right]}{\left(\frac{0.05}{1}\right)} = \$30{,}186.94$.

He deposits $2400 per year, so his total deposits are $\dfrac{\$2400}{yr}\times 10\text{ yr} = \$24{,}000$. Yolanda comes out ahead even though both deposited the same amount of money because the interest in her account is compounded monthly, while Zach's is compounded yearly, which means Yolanda enjoys a higher APY.

94. After 10 years, the balance in Polly's account is

$A = \dfrac{\$50\left[\left(1+\frac{0.06}{12}\right)^{12\times10}-1\right]}{\left(\frac{0.06}{12}\right)} = \$8193.97$. She

deposits $50 per month, so her total deposits are $\dfrac{\$50}{mo}\times\dfrac{12\text{ mo}}{yr}\times 10\text{ yr}=\$6000$. Quint's account is

worth $A = \dfrac{\$40\left[\left(1+\frac{0.065}{12}\right)^{12\times10}-1\right]}{\left(\frac{0.065}{12}\right)} = \$6736.13$. He

deposits $40 per month, so his total deposits are $\dfrac{\$40}{mo}\times\dfrac{12\text{ mo}}{yr}\times 10\text{ yr}=\$4800$. Polly comes out ahead despite the fact that she has the lower APR, because she deposited more each month.

95. After 10 years, the balance in Juan's account is

$A = \dfrac{\$400\left[\left(1+\frac{0.06}{12}\right)^{12\times10}-1\right]}{\left(\frac{0.06}{12}\right)} = \$65{,}551.74$. His total

deposits are $\dfrac{\$400}{mo}\times\dfrac{12\text{ mo}}{yr}\times 10\text{ yr} = \$48{,}000$. The balance in Maria's account is

$A = \dfrac{\$5000\left[\left(1+0.065\right)^{10}-1\right]}{(0.065)} = \$67{,}472.11$. Her total

deposits are $\dfrac{\$5000}{yr}\times 10\text{ yr}=\$50{,}000$. Maria comes out ahead because she has a higher APR (and APY, it turns out), and she deposits more money over the course of the 10 years.

96. After 10 years, the balance in George's account is

$A = \dfrac{\$40\left[\left(1+\frac{0.07}{12}\right)^{12\times10}-1\right]}{\left(\frac{0.07}{12}\right)} = \$6923.39$. His total

deposits are $\dfrac{\$40}{mo}\times\dfrac{12\text{ mo}}{yr}\times 10\text{ yr}=\$4800$. Harvey's

balance is $A = \dfrac{\$150\left[\left(1+\frac{0.075}{4}\right)^{4\times10}-1\right]}{\left(\frac{0.075}{4}\right)} = \$8818.79$.

His total deposits are $\dfrac{\$150}{qtr}\times\dfrac{4\text{ qtr}}{yr}\times 10\text{ yr} = \$6000$.

Harvey comes out ahead because he deposited more money, and had a higher APR (and APY).

97. Your balance will be $A = \dfrac{\$50\left[\left(1+\frac{0.07}{12}\right)^{12\cdot15}-1\right]}{\left(\frac{0.07}{12}\right)} =$

$15,848.11$, so you won't reach your goal.

98. Your balance will be $A = \dfrac{\$75\left[\left(1+\frac{0.07}{12}\right)^{12\cdot15}-1\right]}{\left(\frac{0.07}{12}\right)} =$

$23,772.17$, so you won't reach your goal.

99. Your balance will be $A = \dfrac{\$100\left[\left(1+\frac{0.06}{12}\right)^{12\cdot15}-1\right]}{\left(\frac{0.06}{12}\right)} =$

$29,081.87$, so you won't reach your goal.

100. Your balance will be $A = \dfrac{\$200\left[\left(1+\frac{0.05}{12}\right)^{12\cdot15}-1\right]}{\left(\frac{0.05}{12}\right)} =$

$53,457.79 so you will reach your goal.

101. The total return is $\dfrac{\$8.25-\$6.05}{\$6.05} = 36.4\%$.

Incidentally, this is also the annual return (because you bought the stock a year ago), and it doesn't matter how many shares you bought.

102. The total return is $\dfrac{\$8.25-\$46.25}{\$46.25} = -82.2\%$.

103. The total return was $\dfrac{\$22{,}000{,}000-\$5000}{\$5000} =$

439,900%. The annual return was $\left(\dfrac{\$22{,}000{,}000}{\$5000}\right)^{(1/50)} -1 = 18.3\%$, which is much

higher than the average annual return for large-company stocks.

105. a. At age 35, the balance in Mitch's account is

$A = \dfrac{\$1000\left[\left(1+0.07\right)^{10}-1\right]}{(0.07)} = \$13{,}816.45$. At this

point, it is no longer appropriate to use the savings plan formula as Mitch is not making further deposits into the account. Instead, use this balance as the principal in the compound interest formula, and compute the balance 40 years later. $A = \$13,816.45(1 + 0.07)^{40} = \$206,893.82$. (Note that the rounded balance of $13,816.45 was not used in this computation, but rather the more exact answer stored in a calculator – this is the way it would happen in a banking institution).

b. At age 75, the balance in Bill's account is

$$A = \frac{\$1000\left[(1 + 0.07)^{40} - 1\right]}{(0.07)} = \$199,635.11.$$

c. Mitch deposited $1000 per year for ten years, which is $10,000. Bill deposited $1000 per year for 40 years, which is $40,000, or four times as large as Mitch's total deposits.

UNIT 4D

QUICK QUIZ

1. **a**. Monthly payments go up when the loan principal is larger because you are borrowing more money.
2. **a**. The payment will be higher for a 15-year loan because there is less time to pay off the principal.
3. **b**. A higher APR means more money goes to paying off interest, and this corresponds with a higher payment.
4. **b**. Most of an early payment goes to interest, because the principal is large at the beginning stages of a loan, and thus the interest is also large.
5. **c**. Every year you'll pay $12,000, and thus after ten years, you'll pay $120,000.
6. **c**. Most credit card loans only require that you make a minimum payment each month; there is no specified time in which you must pay off a loan.
7. **c**. A two-point origination fee just means that you must pay 2% of the loan principal in advance, and 2% of $200,000 is $4000.
8. **b**. Add $500 to 1% (one point) of the loan principle of $120,000 to find the advanced payment required.
9. **c**. Refinancing a loan is not a good idea if you've nearly paid the loan off.
10. **a**. A shorter loan always has higher monthly payments (all other things being equal) because there is less time to pay off the principal, and you'll spend less on interest because the principal decreases more quickly.

DOES IT MAKE SENSE?

17. Makes sense. For a typical long-term loan, most of the payments go toward interest for much of the loan term. See Figure 4.8 in the text.
18. Makes sense. This plan is the essence of refinancing a loan.
19. Does not make sense. Making only the minimum required payment on a credit card is asking for financial trouble as the interest rates on credit cards are typically exorbitant. You'll end up spending a lot of your money on interest.
20. Does not make sense. Credit card companies often offer teaser rates to get new customers – after three months, the interest rate will balloon to who knows what level, and that's what matters in the long run.
21. Makes sense. In the worst-case scenario, the ARM loan will be at 6% in the last year you expect to live in the home, so it's certain you'll save money on the first two years, and you may even save during the last year.
22. Does not make sense. While it's true that you'll save money on interest if you take a 15-year loan, there are many scenarios where it's better to take a 30-year loan (for example: you may not be able to afford the higher payments that go with a 15-year loan; if interest rates are low, there are tax benefits and investment strategies that make a 30-year loan a wiser choice).

BASIC SKILLS & CONCEPTS

23. a. The starting principal is $80,000 with an annual interest rate of 7%. You'll make 12 payments each year (one per month) for 20 years, and each payment will be $620.

b. Since you make 12 payments per year for 20 years, you'll make $12 \times 20 = 240$ payments in total, which amounts to $240 \times \$620 = \$148,800$ over the term of the loan.

c. Since the loan principal is $80,000, you'll pay $148,800 – $80,000 = $68,800 in interest, and of course $80,000 of your payments will go toward the principal.

24. a. The starting principal is $15,000 with an annual interest rate of 9%. You'll make 12 payments each year (one per month) for 10 years, and each payment will be $190.

b. Because you make 12 payments per year for 10 years, you'll make $12 \times 10 = 120$ payments in total, which amounts to $120 \times \$190 = \$22,800$ over the term of the loan.

c. Because the loan principal is $15,000, you'll pay $22,800 – $15,000 = $7,800 in interest, and of course $15,000 of your payments will go toward the principal.

25. a. The monthly payment is

$$PMT = \frac{\$50,000\left(\frac{0.10}{12}\right)}{1-\left(1+\frac{0.10}{12}\right)^{-12\times20}} = \$482.51 \,.$$

b. The total payment is $\$482.51 \times 12 \times 20 = \$115,802.40$.

c. The money spent on interest is $\$115,802.40 - \$50,000 = \$65,802.40$, while $\$50,000$ goes toward the principal.

26. a. The monthly payment is

$$PMT = \frac{\$12,000\left(\frac{0.08}{12}\right)}{1-\left(1+\frac{0.08}{12}\right)^{-12\times10}} = \$145.59 \,.$$

b. The total payment is $\$145.59 \times 12 \times 10 = \$17,470.80$.

c. The money spent on interest is $\$17,470.80 - \$12,000 = \$5470.80$, while $\$12,000$ goes toward the principal.

27. a. The monthly payment is

$$PMT = \frac{\$200,000\left(\frac{0.075}{12}\right)}{1-\left(1+\frac{0.075}{12}\right)^{-12\times30}} = \$1398.43 \,.$$

b. The total payment is $\$1398.43 \times 12 \times 30 = \$503,434.80$.

c. The money spent on interest is $\$503,434.80 - \$200,000 = \$303,434.80$, while $\$200,000$ goes toward the principal.

28. a. The monthly payment is

$$PMT = \frac{\$150,000\left(\frac{0.075}{12}\right)}{1-\left(1+\frac{0.075}{12}\right)^{-12\times15}} = \$1390.52 \,.$$

b. The total payment is $\$1390.52 \times 12 \times 15 = \$250,293.60$.

c. The money spent on interest is $\$250,293.60 - \$150,000 = \$100,293.60$, while $\$150,000$ goes toward the principal.

29. a. The monthly payment is

$$PMT = \frac{\$200,000\left(\frac{0.09}{12}\right)}{1-\left(1+\frac{0.09}{12}\right)^{-12\times15}} = \$2028.53 \,.$$

b. The total payment is $\$2028.53 \times 12 \times 15 = \$365,135.40$.

c. The money spent on interest is $\$365,135.40 - \$200,000 = \$165,135.40$, while $\$200,000$ goes toward the principal.

30. a. The monthly payment is

$$PMT = \frac{\$100,000\left(\frac{0.085}{12}\right)}{1-\left(1+\frac{0.085}{12}\right)^{-12\times15}} = \$984.74 \,.$$

b. The total payment is $\$984.74 \times 12 \times 15 = \$177,253.20$.

c. The money spent on interest is $\$177,253.20 - \$100,000 = \$77,253.20$, while $\$100,000$ goes toward the principal.

31. a. The monthly payment is

$$PMT = \frac{\$10,000\left(\frac{0.12}{12}\right)}{1-\left(1+\frac{0.12}{12}\right)^{-12\times3}} = \$332.14 \,.$$

b. The total payment is $\$332.14 \times 12 \times 3 = \$11,957.04$.

c. The money spent on interest is $\$11,957.04 - \$10,000 = \$1957.04$, while $\$10,000$ goes toward the principal.

32. a. The monthly payment is

$$PMT = \frac{\$10,000\left(\frac{0.10}{12}\right)}{1-\left(1+\frac{0.10}{12}\right)^{-12\times5}} = \$212.47 \,.$$

b. The total payment is $\$212.47 \times 12 \times 5 = \$12,748.20$.

c. The money spent on interest is $\$12,748.20 - \$10,000 = \$2748.20$, while $\$10,000$ goes toward the principal.

33. a. The monthly payment is

$$PMT = \frac{\$150,000\left(\frac{0.08}{12}\right)}{1-\left(1+\frac{0.08}{12}\right)^{-12\times15}} = \$1433.48 \,.$$

b. The total payment is $\$1433.48 \times 12 \times 15 = \$258,026.40$.

c. The money spent on interest is $\$258,026.40 - \$150,000 = \$108,026.40$, while $\$150,000$ goes toward the principal.

34. a. The monthly payment is

$$PMT = \frac{\$100,000\left(\frac{0.07}{12}\right)}{1-\left(1+\frac{0.07}{12}\right)^{-12\times30}} = \$665.30 \,.$$

b. The total payment is $\$665.30 \times 12 \times 30 = \$239,508.00$.

c. The money spent on interest is $\$239,508.00 - \$100,000 = \$139,508.00$, while $\$100,000$ goes toward the principal.

35. The monthly payment is

$$PMT = \frac{\$150,000\left(\dfrac{0.085}{12}\right)}{1-\left(1+\dfrac{0.085}{12}\right)^{-12\times30}} = \$1153.37 \ .$$

To compute the interest owed at the end of one month, multiply the beginning principal of $150,000 by the monthly interest rate of 8.5%/12. This gives $150,000(0.085/12) = $1062.50. Because the monthly payment is $1153.37, the amount that goes toward principal is $1153.37 − $1062.50 = $90.87. Subtract this from $150,000 to get a new principal of $150,000 − $90.87 = $149,909.13.

For the second month, repeat this process, but begin with a principal of $149,909.13. The results are shown in the following table through the third month – note that rounding errors at each step propagate through the table, which means that our answers may differ slightly from those that a bank would compute.

End of month	Interest	Payment toward principal	New Principal
1	$1062.50	$90.87	$149,909.13
2	$1061.86	$91.51	$149,817.62
3	$1061.21	$92.16	$149,725.46

36. The monthly payment is

$$PMT = \frac{\$24,000\left(\dfrac{0.08}{12}\right)}{1-\left(1+\dfrac{0.08}{12}\right)^{-12\times15}} = \$229.36 \ .$$

To compute the interest owed at the end of one month, multiply the beginning principal of $24,000 by the monthly interest rate of 8%/12. This gives $24,000(0.08/12) = $160. Because the monthly payment is $229.36, the amount that goes toward principal is $229.36 − $160 = $69.36. Subtract this from $24,000 to get a new principal of $24,000 − $69.36 = $23,930.64.

For the second month, repeat this process, but begin with a principal of $23,930.64. The results are shown in the following table through the third month – note that rounding errors at each step propagate through the table, which means that our answers may differ slightly from those that a bank would compute.

End of month	Interest	Payment toward principal	New Principal
1	$160.00	$69.36	$23,930.64
2	$159.54	$69.82	$23,860.82
3	$159.07	$70.29	$23,790.53

37. For the 3-year loan at 7% APR, the monthly payment is $PMT = \dfrac{\$12,000\left(\dfrac{0.07}{12}\right)}{1-\left(1+\dfrac{0.07}{12}\right)^{-12\times3}} = \$370.53$. The

monthly payment for the 4-year loan is $290.15, and for the 5-year loan, it is $243.32 (the computations being similar to those used for the 3-year loan). Since you can afford only the payments on the 5-year loan, that loan best meets your needs.

38. For the 2-year loan at 8% APR, the monthly

payment is $PMT = \dfrac{\$4000\left(\dfrac{0.08}{12}\right)}{1-\left(1+\dfrac{0.08}{12}\right)^{-12\times2}} = \$180.91$. The

monthly payment for the 3-year loan is $127.20, and for the 4-year loan, it is $101.45 (the computations being similar to those used for the 3-year loan). Since you can afford payments on the 3-year and 4-year loans, either would work for your budget.

39. The monthly payment is

$$PMT = \frac{\$5000\left(\dfrac{0.18}{12}\right)}{1-\left(1+\dfrac{0.18}{12}\right)^{-12\times1}} = \$458.40 \ .$$

Your total payments are $458.40 × 12 = $5500.80.

40. The monthly payment is

$$PMT = \frac{\$5000\left(\dfrac{0.20}{12}\right)}{1-\left(1+\dfrac{0.20}{12}\right)^{-12\times2}} = \$254.48 \ .$$

Your total payments are $254.48 × 24 = $6107.52.

41. The monthly payment is

$$PMT = \frac{\$5000\left(\dfrac{0.21}{12}\right)}{1-\left(1+\dfrac{0.21}{12}\right)^{-12\times3}} = \$188.38 \ .$$

Your total payments are $188.38 × 36 = $6781.68.

42. The monthly payment is

$$PMT = \frac{\$5000\left(\frac{0.22}{12}\right)}{1-\left(1+\frac{0.22}{12}\right)^{-12\times1}} = \$467.97 \ .$$

Your total payments are $\$467.97 \times 12 = \$5615.64$.

43. Complete the table as shown in the first month. To find the interest for the second month, compute $\$1093.00 \times 0.015 = \$16.40$. To find the new balance, compute $\$1093.00 + \$75 + \$16.40 - \$200 = \$984.40$. Continue in this fashion to fill out the rest of the table. Note that rounding errors at each step will propagate through the table: a credit card company computing these balances might show slightly different values.

Month	Pmt	Expenses	Interest	New balance
0				$1200.00
1	$200	$75	$18.00	$1093.00
2	$200	$75	$16.40	$984.40
3	$200	$75	$14.77	$874.17
4	$200	$75	$13.11	$762.28
5	$200	$75	$11.43	$648.71
6	$200	$75	$9.73	$533.44
7	$200	$75	$8.00	$416.44
8	$200	$75	$6.25	$297.69
9	$200	$75	$4.47	$177.16
10	$200	$75	$2.66	$54.82

In the 11th month, a partial payment of $\$54.82 + \$54.82 \times 0.015 + \$75 = \$130.64$ will pay off the loan.

44. To find the interest for the first month, compute $\$1200 \times 0.015 = \$18$. To find the new balance, compute $\$1200 + \$75 + \$18 - \$300 = \$993$. Continue in this fashion to fill out the rest of the table. Note that rounding errors at each step will propagate through the table.

Month	Pmt	Expenses	Interest	New balance
0				$1200.00
1	$300	$75	$18.00	$993.00
2	$300	$75	$14.90	$782.90
3	$300	$75	$11.74	$569.64
4	$300	$75	$8.54	$353.18
5	$300	$75	$5.30	$133.48

In the 6th month, a partial payment of $\$133.48 + \$133.48 \times 0.015 + \$75 = \$210.48$ will pay off the loan.

45. Complete the table as shown in the first month. To find the interest for the second month, compute $\$179.50 \times 0.015 = \$2.69$. To find next month's balance, compute $\$179.50 + \$150 + \$2.69 - \$150 = \$182.19$. Continue in this fashion to fill out the rest of the table. Note that rounding errors at each step will propagate through the table: a credit card company computing these balances might show slightly different values.

Month	Pmt	Expenses	Interest	Balance
0				$300.00
1	$300	$175	$4.50	$179.50
2	$150	$150	$2.69	$182.19
3	$400	$350	$2.73	$134.92
4	$500	$450	$2.02	$86.94
5	$0	$100	$1.30	$188.24
6	$100	$100	$2.82	$191.06
7	$200	$150	$2.87	$143.93
8	$100	$80	$2.16	$126.09

46. a. The monthly interest payment is $\$4000(0.06/12) = \$20$.

b. The monthly interest payment is $\$4000(0.24/12) = \$80$, or four times as much as the teaser rate.

47. Under Option 1, the monthly payment is

$$PMT = \frac{\$200,000\left(\frac{0.08}{12}\right)}{1-\left(1+\frac{0.08}{12}\right)^{-12\times30}} = \$1467.53 \ , \text{ and the total}$$

cost of the loan is $\$1467.53 \times 12 \times 30 = \$528,310.80$. Under Option 2, the monthly

payment is $PMT = \dfrac{\$200,000\left(\frac{0.075}{12}\right)}{1-\left(1+\frac{0.075}{12}\right)^{-12\times15}} = \$1854.02$,

and the total cost of the loan is $\$1854.02 \times 12 \times 15 = \$333,723.60$. You'll pay considerably more interest over the term of the loan in Option 1, but you may be able to afford the payments under that option more easily.

48. Under Option 1, the monthly payment is

$$PMT = \frac{\$75,000\left(\frac{0.08}{12}\right)}{1-\left(1+\frac{0.08}{12}\right)^{-12\times30}} = \$550.32 \ , \text{ and the total}$$

cost of the loan is $\$550.32 \times 12 \times 30 = \$198,115.20$. Under Option 2, the monthly payment is $PMT = \dfrac{\$75{,}000\left(\dfrac{0.07}{12}\right)}{1-\left(1+\dfrac{0.07}{12}\right)^{-12\times15}} = \$674.12$,

and the total cost of the loan is $\$674.12 \times 12 \times 15 = \$121{,}341.60$. You'll pay considerably more interest over the term of the loan in Option 1, but you may be able to afford the payments under that option more easily.

49. Under Option 1, the monthly payment is

$PMT = \dfrac{\$60{,}000\left(\dfrac{0.0715}{12}\right)}{1-\left(1+\dfrac{0.0715}{12}\right)^{-12\times30}} = \$405.24$, and the total

cost of the loan is $\$405.24 \times 12 \times 30 = \$145{,}886.40$. Under Option 2, the monthly

payment is $PMT = \dfrac{\$60{,}000\left(\dfrac{0.0675}{12}\right)}{1-\left(1+\dfrac{0.0675}{12}\right)^{-12\times15}} = \$530.95$,

and the total cost of the loan is $\$530.95 \times 12 \times 15 = \$95{,}571.00$. See #47 for pros and cons.

50. Under Option 1, the monthly payment is

$PMT = \dfrac{\$180{,}000\left(\dfrac{0.0725}{12}\right)}{1-\left(1+\dfrac{0.0725}{12}\right)^{-12\times30}} = \$1227.92$, and the

total cost of the loan is $\$1227.92 \times 12 \times 30 = \$442{,}051.20$. Under Option 2, the monthly

payment is $PMT = \dfrac{\$180{,}000\left(\dfrac{0.068}{12}\right)}{1-\left(1+\dfrac{0.068}{12}\right)^{-12\times15}} = \$1597.83$,

and the total cost of the loan is $\$1597.83 \times 12 \times 15 = \$287{,}609.40$. See #48 for pros and cons.

51. Under Choice 1, your monthly payment is

$PMT = \dfrac{\$120{,}000\left(\dfrac{0.08}{12}\right)}{1-\left(1+\dfrac{0.08}{12}\right)^{-12\times30}} = \$880.52$, and the

closing costs are $1200. For Choice 2, the

payment is $PMT = \dfrac{\$120{,}000\left(\dfrac{0.075}{12}\right)}{1-\left(1+\dfrac{0.075}{12}\right)^{-12\times30}} = \$839.06$,

and the closing costs are $\$1200 + \$120{,}000(0.02) = \$3600$. You'll save $\$880.52 - \$839.06 = \$41.46$ each month with Choice 2, though it will take $\$2400/(\$41.46$ per month$) = 58$ months (about 5 years) to recoup the higher closing costs, and thus Choice 2 is the better option only if you intend to keep the house for at least 5 years.

52. Under Choice 1, your monthly payment is

$PMT = \dfrac{\$120{,}000\left(\dfrac{0.085}{12}\right)}{1-\left(1+\dfrac{0.085}{12}\right)^{-12\times30}} = \$922.70$, with no

closing costs. For Choice 2, the payment is

$PMT = \dfrac{\$120{,}000\left(\dfrac{0.075}{12}\right)}{1-\left(1+\dfrac{0.075}{12}\right)^{-12\times30}} = \$839.06$, and the

closing costs are $\$1200 + \$120{,}000(0.04) = \$6000$. You'll save $\$922.70 - \$839.06 = \$83.64$ each month with Choice 2, though it will take $\$6000/(\$83.64$ per month$) = 72$ months (6 years) to recoup the higher closing costs, and thus Choice 2 is the better option only if you intend to keep the house for at least 6 years.

53. Under Choice 1, your monthly payment is

$PMT = \dfrac{\$120{,}000\left(\dfrac{0.0725}{12}\right)}{1-\left(1+\dfrac{0.0725}{12}\right)^{-12\times30}} = \$818.61$, and the

closing costs are $\$1200 + \$120{,}000(0.01) = \$2400$. For Choice 2, the payment is

$PMT = \dfrac{\$120{,}000\left(\dfrac{0.0675}{12}\right)}{1-\left(1+\dfrac{0.0675}{12}\right)^{-12\times30}} = \$778.32$, and the

closing costs are $\$1200 + \$120{,}000(0.03) = \$4800$. You'll save $\$818.61 - \$778.32 = \$40.29$ each month with Choice 2, though it will take $\$2400/(\$40.29$ per month$) = 60$ months (5 years) to recoup the higher closing costs, and thus Choice 2 is the better option only if you intend to keep the house for at least 5 years.

54. Under Choice 1, your monthly payment is

$PMT = \dfrac{\$120{,}000\left(\dfrac{0.075}{12}\right)}{1-\left(1+\dfrac{0.075}{12}\right)^{-12\times30}} = \$839.06$, and the

closing costs are $1000. For Choice 2, the

payment is $PMT = \dfrac{\$120{,}000\left(\dfrac{0.065}{12}\right)}{1-\left(1+\dfrac{0.065}{12}\right)^{-12\times30}} = \$758.48$,

and the closing costs are $\$1500 + \$120{,}000(0.04) = \$6300$. You'll save $\$839.06 - \$758.48 = \$80.58$ each month with Choice 2, though it will take $\$5300/(\$80.58$ per month$) = 66$ months (5.5 years) to recoup the higher closing costs, and thus Choice 2 is the better option only if you intend to keep the house for at least 5.5 years.

55. a. The monthly payment is

$$PMT = \frac{\$30{,}000\left(\dfrac{0.09}{12}\right)}{1-\left(1+\dfrac{0.09}{12}\right)^{-12\times20}} = \$269.92 \, .$$

b. The monthly payment is

$$PMT = \frac{\$30{,}000\left(\dfrac{0.09}{12}\right)}{1-\left(1+\dfrac{0.09}{12}\right)^{-12\times10}} = \$380.03 \, .$$

c. If you pay the loan off in 20 years, the total payments will be $\$269.92 \times 12 \times 20 = \$64{,}780.80$. If you pay it off in 10 years, the total payments will be $\$380.03 \times 12 \times 10 = \$45{,}603.60$.

56. a. The monthly payment is

$$PMT = \frac{\$60{,}000\left(\dfrac{0.08}{12}\right)}{1-\left(1+\dfrac{0.08}{12}\right)^{-12\times25}} = \$463.09 \, .$$

b. The monthly payment is

$$PMT = \frac{\$60{,}000\dfrac{\left(\dfrac{0.08}{12}\right)}{12}}{1-\left(1+\dfrac{0.08}{12}\right)^{-12\times15}} = \$573.39 \, .$$

c. If you pay the loan off in 25 years, the total payments will be $\$463.09 \times 12 \times 25 = \$138{,}927$. If you pay it off in 15 years, the total payments will be $\$573.39 \times 12 \times 15 = \$103{,}210.20$.

57. Following example 10 in the text, the interest on the $150,000 loan in the first year will be approximately $7\% \times \$150{,}000 = \$10{,}500$, which means the monthly payment will be about $\$10{,}500/12 = \$875$. With the 5% ARM, the interest will be approximately $5\% \times \$150{,}000 = \$7500$, and thus the monthly payment will be about $\$7500/12 = \$625$. You'll save $\$875 - \$625 = \$250$ each month with the ARM. In the third year, the rate on the ARM will be 1.5% higher than the fixed rate loan, and thus the yearly interest payments will differ by $\$150{,}000 \times 0.015 = \$2250$, which amounts to $187.50 per month.

58. Following example 10 in the text, the interest on the $125,000 loan in the first year will be approximately $8.5\% \times \$125{,}000 = \$10{,}625$, which means the monthly payment will be about $\$10{,}625/12 = \$885.42$. With the 5.5% ARM, the interest will be approximately $5.5\% \times \$125{,}000 = \$6875$, and thus the monthly payment will be about $\$6875/12 = \$572.92$. You'll save about $313 each month with the ARM. In the second year, the rate on the ARM will be 1.5% higher than the fixed rate loan, and thus the yearly interest

payments will differ by $\$125{,}000 \times 0.015 = \$1875$, which is about $156 per month.

FURTHER APPLICATIONS

59. Solve

$$\$500 = \frac{P\left(\dfrac{0.09}{12}\right)}{1-\left(1+\dfrac{0.09}{12}\right)^{-12\times30}} = P\frac{\left(\dfrac{0.09}{12}\right)}{1-\left(1+\dfrac{0.09}{12}\right)^{-12\times30}} \quad \text{for}$$

P by computing the fraction on the right, and dividing it into $500. This results in P = $62,141 (rounded to the nearest dollar), and it represents the largest loan you can afford with monthly payments of $500. The loan will pay for 80% of the house you wish to buy (you must come up with a 20% down payment). Thus 80% × (*house price*) = $62,141, which means *house price* = $62,141/0.80 = $77,676. You can afford a house that will cost about $78,000.

60. Solve $\$1200 = \dfrac{P\left(\dfrac{0.075}{12}\right)}{1-\left(1+\dfrac{0.075}{12}\right)^{-12\times30}}$ for P by

computing the fraction on the right, and dividing it into $1200. This results in P = $171,621 (rounded to the nearest dollar), and it represents the largest loan you can afford with monthly payments of $1200. The loan will pay for 80% of the house you wish to buy (you must come up with a 20% down payment). Thus 80% × (*house price*) = $171,621, which means *house price* = $171,621/0.80 = $214,526. You can afford a house that will cost about $215,000.

61. a. The monthly payment for the first loan is

$$PMT = \frac{\$10{,}000\left(\dfrac{0.08}{12}\right)}{1-\left(1+\dfrac{0.08}{12}\right)^{-12\times15}} = \$95.57 \, . \quad \text{The payments}$$

for the other two loans are calculated similarly; you should get $130.17 and $158.34, respectively.
b. For the first loan, you'll pay $\$95.57 \times 12 \times 15 = \$17{,}202.60$ over its term. The total payments for the other loans are computed in a similar fashion – you should get $31,240.80 and $19,000.80, respectively. Add them together to get $67,444.20.
c. The monthly payment for the consolidated loan

will be $PMT = \dfrac{\$37{,}500\left(\dfrac{0.085}{12}\right)}{1-\left(1+\dfrac{0.085}{12}\right)^{-12\times20}} = \$325.43$, and

the total payment over 20 years will be $78,103.20. You'll pay about $11,000 more for the consolidated loan ($78,103.20 – $67,444.20 =

$10,659), but your monthly payments will be lower for the first ten years ($325.43 versus $95.57 + $130.17 + $158.34 = $384.08). If, as a recent graduate, your budget is tight, it may be worth it to consolidate the loans. It also means you'll have to keep track of only one loan instead of three, though with automatic withdrawals offered by most banks, this isn't as much of an issue today as it might have been 15 years ago.

62. a. You'll owe 22% × $2000 = $440.
    b. You'll pay $440 × 12 = $5280.
    c. The monthly payment for the loan would be

$$PMT = \frac{\$2000\left(\frac{0.10}{12}\right)}{1-\left(1+\frac{0.10}{12}\right)^{-12\times3}} = \$64.53 .$$

This is significantly lower than the amount owed to the car-title lender.

63. a. The annual ($n = 1$) payment is $8718.46; the monthly ($n = 12$) payment is $716.43, the bi-monthly ($n = 26$) payment is $330.43, and the weekly ($n = 52$) payment is $165.17. The weekly payment is computed below; the others are done in a similar fashion.

$$PMT = \frac{\$100,000\left(\frac{0.06}{52}\right)}{1-\left(1+\frac{0.06}{52}\right)^{-52\times20}} = \$165.17 .$$

    b. The total payout for each scenario is as follows: $174,369.20 ($n = 1$); $171,943.20 ($n = 12$); $171,823.60 ($n = 26$); and $171,776.80. The total payout when $n = 52$ is shown below; the others are done in a similar fashion.

$$\frac{\$165.17}{\text{week}} \times \frac{52 \text{ weeks}}{\text{year}} \times 20 \text{ years} = \$171,776.80 .$$

    c. The total payout decreases as n increases.

64. a. The monthly payment is $716.43 (see 63a).
    b. If each year you send 13 payments of $716.43 to the bank, you will be making annual payments of $716.43 × 13 = $9313.59. This is equivalent to making monthly payments of $9313.59/12 = $776.13. Using that amount as *PMT* in the loan payment formula yields

$$\$776.13 = \frac{\$100,000\left(\frac{0.06}{12}\right)}{1-\left(1+\frac{0.06}{12}\right)^{-12\times Y}} .$$

To find out how long it will take to pay off the loan, we must solve for Y. The trick is to realize this is an exponential equation, and solving such equations requires the use of logarithms (discussed later in the text). Recall that the exponential expression must be isolated before taking the logarithm of both sides. The steps are shown below (with units of dollars omitted; it is understood that Y is measured in years in the loan payment formula). Begin by cross-multiplying.

$$776.13\left[1-\left(1+\frac{0.06}{12}\right)^{-12Y}\right]=100000\left(\frac{0.06}{12}\right)$$

$$776.13\left[1-(1.005)^{-12Y}\right]=500 \text{ (simplify)}$$

$$1-(1.005)^{-12Y}=\frac{500}{776.13} \text{ (divide by 776.13)}$$

$$-(1.005)^{-12Y}=-0.355... \text{ (subtract 1)}$$

$$(1.005)^{-12Y}=0.355... \text{ (divide by } -1)$$

$$-12Y\log(1.005)=\log(0.355...) \text{ (take logs)}$$

$$Y=\frac{\log(0.355...)}{-12\log(1.005)}=17.3 \text{ years} .$$

Another way to set up the problem is to imagine that the 13 payments are sent to the bank at equal time intervals over the course of the year. As with the savings plan formula, the loan formula used in the text assumes the compounding period is equal to the payment period (that is, if you send payments in 13 times per year, the bank compounds interest 13 times per year). With these assumptions, the problem boils down to solving the following equation for Y:

$$\$716.43 = \frac{\$100,000\left(\frac{0.06}{13}\right)}{1-\left(1+\frac{0.06}{13}\right)^{-13\times Y}} .$$

You can solve it following the same procedure as before, and you should find an answer that is virtually the same (it differs in the thousandths-place).

UNIT 4E

QUICK QUIZ

1. **a.** Gross income is defined as the total of all income you receive.
2. **c.** The first portion of your income is taxed at 10% (the portion being determined by your filing status – see Table 4.10), the next at 15%, and only the last portion is taxed at 25%.
3. **a.** A tax credit reduces your tax bill by the dollar amount of the credit, so your tax bill will be reduced by $1000.
4. **b.** A tax deduction reduces your taxable income, so if you have a deduction of $1000, and you are in the 15% tax bracket, your bill will be reduced by 15% of $1000, or $150. This answer assumes you are far enough into the 15% tax bracket so

that reducing your taxable income by $1000 means you remain in the 15% bracket.

5. **b.** You can claim deductions of $4000 + $2000 = $6000 as long as you itemize deductions.

6. **a.** If you chose to itemize your deductions, the only thing you can claim is the $1000 contribution, and as this is less than your standard deduction of $5150, it won't give relief to your tax bill (in fact, you'd pay more tax it you were to itemize deductions in this situation – take the standard deduction).

7. **c.** FICA taxes are taxes levied on income from wages (and tips) to fund the Social Security and Medicare programs.

8. **a.** Joe will pay 7.65% of his income for FICA taxes. Kim pays 7.65% of only her first $94,200; she pays 1.45% of her remaining salary, for a total FICA tax of 0.0765($94,200) + 0.0145($150,000 – $94,200) = $8015.40, which is 5.3% of her income. David pays nothing at all in FICA taxes because income from capital gains is not subject to FICA taxes.

9. **b.** Assuming all are of the same filing status, Jerome pays the most because his FICA taxes will be highest, followed by Jenny, and then Jacqueline.

10. **c.** Taxes on money deposited into tax-deferred accounts are *deferred* until a later date: you don't have to pay taxes on that money now, but you will when you withdraw the money in later years.

DOES IT MAKE SENSE?

21. Does not make sense. We know nothing of the rest of the picture for these two individuals – they may have very different deductions, and thus different tax bills.

22. Does not make sense. If you care for a dependent child, you earn the child tax credit, whether you itemize deductions or not.

23. Makes sense. You can deduct interest paid on the mortgage of a home if you itemize deductions, and for many people, the mortgage interest deduction is the largest of all deductions.

24. Does not make sense. The $12,000 mortgage interest deduction would be greater than the standard deduction coming to these people (whether they file separately or jointly), and thus there would be a tax benefit.

25. Makes sense (in some scenarios). Bob and Sue might be hit with the "marriage penalty" when they file taxes, and if they postpone their wedding until the new year, they could avoid the penalty for at least the previous tax year.

26. Makes sense. The top rate for dividends is 15%, no matter how much you earn in dividends.

27. Makes sense. Those who are self-employed must pay both the employee and employer ends of the FICA tax, and for any profit up to $94,200, the rate is 7.65%. Self-employed people must pay twice that rate, or 15.3%.

28. Makes sense. The tax break that one enjoys with tax-deferred investments results in a tax savings that ultimately affects take-home pay.

BASIC SKILLS & CONCEPTS

29. Antonio's gross income was $47,200 + $2400 = $49,600. His AGI was $49,600 – $3500 = $46,100. His taxable income was $46,100 – $3300 – $5150 = $37,650.

30. Marie's gross income was $28,400 + $95 = $28,495, and her AGI was the same as she had no adjustments to income. Her taxable income was $28,495 – $3300 – $5150 = $20,045.

31. Isabella's gross income was $88,750 + $4900 = $93,650. Her AGI was $93,650 – $6200 = $87,450. Her taxable income was $87,450 – $3300 – $9050 = $75,100.

32. Lebron's gross income was $3,452,000 + $54,200 = $3,506,200. His AGI was $3,506,200 – $30,000 = $3,476,200. His taxable income was $3,476,200 – $674,500 = $2,801,700. Lebron needs a good tax lawyer.

33. Your itemized deductions total to $8600 + $2700 + $645 = $11,945, and since this is larger than the standard deduction of $10,300, you should itemize your deductions.

34. Your itemized deductions total to $3700 + $760 = $4460, and since this is less than the standard deduction of $5150, you should claim the standard deduction.

35. Suzanne's gross income is $33,200 + $350 = $33,550, her AGI is $33,550 – $500 = $33,050, and her taxable income is $33,050 – $3300 – $5150 = $24,600. She should claim the standard deduction because it is much higher than her itemized deduction of $450.

36. Malcolm's gross income and AGI are both $23,700, and his taxable income is $23,700 – $3300 – $5150 = $15,250. He should claim the standard deduction because it is higher than his itemized deduction of $4500.

37. Wanda's gross income was $35,400 + $500 = $35,900, her AGI was the same, and her taxable income was $35,900 – $3300 × 3 – $5150 = $20,850. She should claim the standard deduction because it is higher than her itemized deduction of $1500.

38. Emily and Juan had a gross income of $75,300 + $2000 + $1650 = $78,950, their AGI was $78,950 – $3240 = $75,710, and their taxable income was $75,710 – $3300 × 4 – $10,300 = $52,210. They

should claim the standard deduction of $10,300 for married couples because it's higher than their itemized deductions.

39. Gene owes 10% × ($7550) + 15% × ($30,650 − $7550) + 25% × ($35,400 − $30,650) = $5408 (taxes are rounded to the nearest dollar).

40. Sarah and Marco owe 10% × ($15,100) + 15% ($61,300 − $15,100) + 25% × ($87,500 − $61,300) = $14,990.

41. Bobbi owes 10% × ($7550) + 15% × ($30,650 − $7550) + 25% × ($61,850 − $30,650) + 28% × ($77,300 − $61,850) = $16,346.

42. Abraham owes 10% × ($7550) + 15% × ($23,800 −$7550) = $3193.

43. Paul owes 10% × ($10,750) + 15% × ($41,050 − $10,750) + 25% × ($89,300 − $41,050) − $1000 = $16,683.

44. Pat owes 10% × ($10,750) + 15% × ($41,050 − $10,750) + 25% × ($57,000 − $41,050) − $1000 = $8608.

45. Winona and Jim owe 10% × ($15,100) + 15% × ($61,300 − $15,100) + 25% × ($105,500 − $61,300) − $2000 = $17,490.

46. Chris owes 10% × ($7550) + 15% × ($30,650 − $7550) + 25% × ($61,850 − $30,650) + 28% × ($94,225 − $61,850) + 33% × ($127,300 − $94,225) = $32,000.

47. Their bill will be reduced by $500.

48. Her bill will be reduced by $500.

49. Her taxes will not be affected because she is claiming the standard deduction, and a $1000 charitable contribution must be itemized.

50. His tax bill will be reduced by 15% of $1000, or $150, provided he is far enough into the 15% tax bracket that his $1000 contribution does not drop him into the lower bracket.

51. His tax bill will be reduced by 28% of $1000, or $280, provided he is far enough into the 28% bracket that his $1000 contribution does not drop him into the lower bracket.

52. Her tax bill will be reduced by 35% of $1000, or $350, provided she is far enough into the 35% bracket that her $1000 contribution does not drop her into the lower bracket.

53. The $1800 per month of your payment that goes toward interest would be deductible, which means you'd save 33% × $1800 = $594 each month in taxes. Thus your $2000 mortgage payment would effectively be only $2000 − $594 = $1406, which is less than your rent payment of $1600. Buying the house is cheaper. This solution assumes that the $1800 × 12 = $21,600 interest deduction would not drop you into the 28% bracket (if it did, the solution would be more complicated).

54. The $600 per month of your payment that goes toward interest would be deductible, which means you'd save 15% × $600 = $90 each month in taxes. Thus your $675 mortgage payment would effectively be only $675 − $90 = $585, which is less than your rent payment of $600. Buying the house is cheaper. This solution assumes that the $600 × 12 = $7200 interest deduction would not drop you into the 10% tax bracket (if it did, the solution would be more complicated).

55. Maria saves 33% of $10,000, or $3300 in taxes, which means the true cost of her mortgage interest is $6700. Steve saves 15% of $10,000, or $1500 in taxes, which means the true cost of his mortgage interest is $8500. This solution assumes their deductions do not drop them into the lower tax bracket.

56. Yolanna saves 35% of $4000, or $1400 in taxes, which means the true cost of her contribution is $2600. Alia saves 10% of $4000, or $400 in taxes, which means the true cost of her contribution is $3600. This solution assumes Yolanna does not drop into the 33% bracket as a result of her contribution.

57. Luis will pay 7.65% × $28,000 = $2142 in FICA taxes. His taxable income is $28,000 − $3300 − $5150 − $2500 = $17,050. He will pay 10% × ($7550) + 15% × ($17,050 − $7550) = $2180 in income taxes, and thus his total tax bill will be $2142 + $2180 = $4322. This is $4322/$28,000 = 15.4% of his gross income, so his effective tax rate is 15.4%.

58. Carla will pay 7.65% × $34,500 = $2639 in FICA taxes. Her gross income is $34,500 + $750 = $35,250, and her taxable income is $35,250 − $3300 − $5150 − $3000 = $23,800. She will pay 10% × ($7550) + 15% × ($23,800 − $7550) = $3193 in income taxes, and thus her total tax bill will be $2639 + $3193 = $5832. This is $5832/$35,250 = 16.5% of her gross income, so her effective tax rate is 16.5%.

59. Jack will pay 7.65% × $44,800 = $3427 in FICA taxes. His gross income is $44,800 + $1250 = $46,050, and his taxable income is $46,050 − $3300 − $5150 − $2000 = $35,600. He will pay 10% × ($7550) + 15% × ($30,650 − $7550) + 25% × ($35,600 − $30,650) = $5458 in income taxes, and thus his total tax bill will be $3427 + $5458 = $8885. This is $8885/$46,050 = 19.3% of his gross income, so his effective tax rate is 19.3%.

60. Alejandro will pay 7.65% × ($94,200) + 1.45% × ($102,400 − $94,200) = $7325 in FICA taxes. His gross income is $102,400 + $4450 = $106,850, and his taxable income is $106,850 − $3300 − $5150 − $9500 = $88,900. He will pay 10% × ($7550) + 15% × ($30,650 − $7550) + 25% × ($74,200 − $30,650) + 28% × ($88,900 −

$74,200) = $19,224 in income taxes, and thus his total tax bill will be $7325 + $19,224 = $26,549. This is $26,549/$106,850 = 24.8% of his gross income, so his effective tax rate is 24.8%.

61. Brittany will pay 7.65% × $48,200 = $3687 in FICA taxes. Her taxable income is $48,200 − $3300 − $5150 = $39,750. She will pay 10% × ($7550) + 15% × ($30,650 − $7550) + 25% × ($39,750 − $30,650) = $6495 in income taxes, and thus her total tax bill will be $3687 + $6495 = $10,182. This is $10,182/$48,200 = 21.1% of her gross income, so her effective tax rate is 21.1%.

62. Larae will pay 7.65% × $21,200 = $1622 in FICA taxes. Her taxable income is $21,200 − $3300 − $5150 = $12,750. She will pay 10% × ($7550) + 15% × ($12,750 − $7550) = $1535 in income taxes, and thus her total tax bill will be $1622 + $1535 = $3157. This is $3157/$21,200 = 14.9% of her gross income, so her effective tax rate is 14.9%.

63. Pierre will pay 7.65% × ($94,200) + 1.45% × ($120,000 − $94,200) = $7580 in FICA taxes, and because his taxable income is $120,000 − $3300 − $5150 = $111,550, he will pay 10% × ($7550) + 15% × ($30,650 − $7550) + 25% × ($74,200 − $30,650) + 28% × ($111,550 − $74,200) = $25,566 in income taxes. His total tax bill is $7580 + $25,566 = $33,146, so his overall tax rate is $33,146/$120,000 = 27.6%. Katarina will pay nothing in FICA taxes, and her income taxes will be 5% × ($30,650) + 15% × ($111,550 − $30,650) = $13,668 − like Pierre, her taxable income is $111,550, but she is taxed at the special rates for dividends and long-term capital gains. Her overall tax rate is $13,668/$120,000 = 11.4%.

64. Deion will pay 7.65% × $60,000 = $4590 in FICA taxes, and because his taxable income is $60,000 − $3300 − $5150 = $51,550, he will pay 10% × ($7550) + 15% × ($30,650 − $7550) + 25% × ($51,550 − $30,650) = $9445 in income taxes. His total tax bill is $4590 + $9445 = $14,035, so his overall tax rate is $14,035/$60,000 = 23.4%. Josephina will pay nothing in FICA taxes, and her income taxes will be 5% × ($30,650) + 15% × ($51,550 − $30,650) = $4668 − like Deion, her taxable income is $51,550, but she is taxed at the special rates for dividends and long-term capital gains. Her overall tax rate is $4668/$60,000 = 7.8%.

65. Because you are in the 15% tax bracket, every time you make a $400 contribution to your tax-deferred savings plan, you save 15% × $400 = $60 in taxes. Thus your take-home pay is reduced not by $400, but by $340.

66. Because you are in the 25% tax bracket, every time you make a $600 contribution to your tax-deferred savings plan, you save 25% × $600 = $150 in taxes. Thus your take-home pay is reduced not by $600, but by $450.

67. Because you are in the 25% tax bracket, every time you make an $800 contribution to your tax-deferred savings plan, you save 25% × $800 = $200 in taxes. Thus your take-home pay is reduced not by $800, but by $600.

68. Because you are in the 33% tax bracket, every time you make an $800 contribution to your tax-deferred savings plan, you save 33% × $800 = $264 in taxes. Thus your take-home pay is reduced not by $800, but by $536.

FURTHER APPLICATIONS

69. Gabriella's taxable income is $44,500 − $3300 − $5150 = $36,050, so her income tax is 10% × ($7550) + 15% × ($30,650 − $7550) + 25% × ($36,050 − $30,650) = $5570. Roberto's taxable income is $33,400 − $3300 − $5150 = $24,950, so his income tax is 10% × ($7550) + 15% × ($24,950 − $7550) = $3365. If they delay their marriage, they will pay $5570 + $3365 = $8935 in taxes. If they marry, their combined AGI will be $44,500 + $33,400 = $77,900, and their taxable income will be $77,900 − $3300 × 2 − $10,300 = $61,000. Their income taxes will be 10% × ($15,100) + 15% × ($61,000 − $15,100) = $8395, which is lower than the taxes they would pay as individuals, and thus they will not face a marriage penalty (in fact, they'll benefit from becoming married).

70. Joan's taxable income is $32,500 − $3300 − $5150 = $24,050, so her income tax is 10% × ($7550) + 15% × ($24,050 − $7550) = $3230. Paul's taxable income is $29,400 − $3300 − $5150 = $20,950, so his income tax is 10% × ($7550) + 15% × ($20,950 − $7550) = $2765. If they delay their marriage, they will pay $3230 + $2765 = $5995 in taxes. If they marry, their combined AGI will be $32,500 + $29,400 = $61,900, and their taxable income will be $61,900 − $3300 × 2 − $10,300 = $45,000. Their income taxes will be 10% × ($15,100) + 15% × ($45,000 − $15,100) = $5995, which is the same amount they would pay as individuals, and thus they will not face a marriage penalty.

71. Steve's taxable income is $185,000 − $3300 − $5150 = $176,550, so his income tax is 10% × ($7550) + 15% × ($30,650 − $7550) + 25% × ($74,200 − $30,650) + 28% × ($154,800 − $74,200) + 33% × ($176,550 − $154,800) = $44,853. Mia's tax is, of course, the same, so if they delay their marriage, they will pay $89,706. If they marry, their combined AGI will be $185,000 × 2 = $370,000, and their taxable income will be

$370,000 - $3300 \times 2 - $10,300 = $353,100. Their income taxes will be 10% × ($15,100) + 15% × (61,300 – 15,100) + 25% × ($123,700 – $61,300) + 28% × ($188,450 – $123,700) + 33% × ($336,550 – $188,450) + 35% × ($353,100 – $336,550) = $96,836, which is more than the taxes they would pay as individuals, and thus they will face a marriage penalty.

72. Lisa's taxable income is $85,000 – $3300 – $5150 = $76,550, so her income tax is 10% × ($7550) + 15% × ($30,650 – $7550) + 25% × ($74,200 – $30,650) + 28% × ($76,550 – $74,200) = $15,766. Patrick pays no income tax, so if they delay their marriage, they will pay $15,766. If they marry, their combined AGI will be $85,000, and their taxable income will be $85,000 – $3300 × 2 – $10,300 = $68,100. Their income taxes will be 10% × ($15,100) + 15% × (61,300 – 15,100) + 25% × ($68,100 – $61,300) = $10,140, which is lower than the taxes they would pay as individuals, and thus they will not face a marriage penalty (in fact, they'll benefit from becoming married).

UNIT 4F

QUICK QUIZ

1. **b**. Bigprofit.com had more outlays (expenses) than receipts (income) by $1 million, so it ran a deficit for 2006 of $1 million. Its debt is the total amount owed to lenders over the years; this is $7 million.

2. **c**. The federal debt is about $9 trillion dollars, and when divided evenly among all 300 million U.S. citizens, it comes to about $30,000 per person.

3. **c**. The error in predicting the budget is around 10%, and 10% of $2.5 trillion is $250 billion. Thus if receipts were 10% below what was predicted, the deficit would be $350 billion, and if receipts were 10% above what was predicted, there would be a surplus of $150 billion.

4. **b**. Discretionary outlays differ from mandatory outlays in that Congress passes a budget every year that spells out where the government will spend its discretionary funds.

5. **a**. Interest on the debt must be paid so that the government does not default on its loans, and Medicare is an entitlement program that is part of mandatory spending. On the other hand, all money spent on defense is considered discretionary spending.

6. **a**. Mandatory expenses include money spent on Social Security, Medicare, interest on the debt, government pensions, and Medicaid, and together these programs constitute almost 60% of the budget (see Figure 4.13).

7. **b**. The $100 billion is supposed to be deposited into an account used to pay off future Social Security recipients, but instead, the government spends the money at hand, and essentially writes IOUs to itself, and places these in the account.

8. **b**. Publicly held debt is the money the government owes to those who have purchased Treasury bills, notes, and bonds.

9. **b**. The gross debt is the sum of all of the money that the government owes to individuals who have purchased bonds, and the money it owes to itself.

10. **c**. The amount of money set aside for education grants is miniscule in comparison to the billions of dollars the government will be required to spend on Social Security in 2030.

DOES IT MAKE SENSE?

19. Makes sense. Each U.S. citizen would have to spend about $30,000 to retire the federal debt, and it's certainly true that this exceeds the personal debt of many people.

20. Does not make sense. In 2006, outlays were about $2.65 trillion (Table 4.12), and 8% of that (Figure 4.13) went toward the government's annual interest payment on the debt, which means around $212 billion was spent on interest for the debt. Divide that by 300 million U.S. citizens, and you get about $700 – this is not enough to buy a new car.

21. Does not make sense. The financial health of the government is very much dependent upon what happens with Social Security and the FICA taxes collected to fund it. The term "off-budget" is nothing more than a label that separates the Social Security program from the rest of the budget.

22. Makes sense. When receipts are more than outlays, the government ran a surplus for that year, but the debt may increase anyway, for a variety of reasons. Among them: the government claims to be running a surplus when the on-budget net income is positive even though it also spends off-budget (i.e. Social Security) funds; and the total debt may increase because of the huge amount of interest owed to holders of Treasury bills.

23. Does not make sense. The government has a difficult time predicting deficits or surpluses even one year out – it cannot predict what will happen with any level of accuracy in ten years.

24. Does not make sense. Despite the fact that the government collects more in FICA taxes than it owes to Social Security recipients (and due to demographics, this trend is expected to continue for some time), it spends all of that money on

other programs even though it is supposed to deposit it into the Social Security trust fund.

BASIC SKILLS & CONCEPTS

25. a. Your receipts are $38,000, and your outlays are $12,000 + $6000 + $1200 + $8500 = $27,700, so you have a surplus.

    b. A 3% raise means your receipts will be $38,000 + 3% × $38,000 = $39,140, and your outlays will be $27,700 + $8500 = $36,200, so you'll still have a surplus, though it will be smaller.

    c. Your receipts will be $39,140 (see part **b**), and your outlays will be $27,700 × 1.01 + $7500 = $35,477, so you will be able to afford it.

26. a. Your receipts are $28,000, and your outlays are $8,000 + $4500 + $1600 + $10,400 = $24,500, so you have a surplus.

    b. A 2% raise means your receipts would be $28,000 + 2% × $28,000 = $28,560, and your outlays would be $24,500 + $5200 = $29,700, so you could not afford to pay off all of the debt.

    c. Your receipts will be $28,560 (see part **b**), and your outlays will be $24,500 × 1.01 + $3500 = $28,245, so you will be able to afford it.

27. $\dfrac{\$9 \times 10^{12}}{170 \times 10^6 \text{ workers}} = \text{about } \dfrac{\$53,000}{\text{worker}}$.

28. $\dfrac{\$9 \times 10^{12}}{120 \times 10^6 \text{ families}} = \dfrac{\$75,000}{\text{family}}$.

29. a. The interest on the debt will be 8.2% × $773,000 = $63,000 (rounded to the nearest thousand dollars).

    b. The total outlays are $600,000 + $200,000 + $250,000 + $63,000 = $1,113,000, so the year-end deficit is $1,050,000 − $1,113,000 = −$63,000, and the year-end accumulated debt is −$773,000 − $63,000 = −$836,000.

    c. The interest on the debt in 2009 will be 8.2% × $836,000 = $69,000 (rounded to the nearest thousand dollars).

    d. The total outlays are $600,000 + $200,000 + $69,000 = $869,000, so the year-end surplus is $1,100,000 − $869,000 = $231,000, and the year-end accumulated debt is −$836,000 + $231,000 = −$605,000, assuming all surplus is devoted to paying down the debt.

30. a. The interest on the debt will be 8.2% × $773,000 = $63,000 (rounded to the nearest thousand dollars).

    b. The total outlays are $850,000 + $290,000 + $210,000 + $63,000 = $1,413,000, so the year-end deficit is $975,000 − $1,413,000 = −$438,000, and the year-end accumulated debt is −$773,000 − $438,000 = −$1,211,000.

    c. The interest on the debt in 2009 will be 8.2% × $1,211,000 = $99,000 (rounded to the nearest thousand dollars).

    d. The total outlays are $850,000 + $290,000 + $99,000 = $1,239,000, so the year-end deficit is $1,050,000 − $1,239,000 = −$189,000, and the year-end accumulated debt is −$1,211,000 − $189,000 = −$1,400,000.

31. With a 1% decrease in total receipts in 2006, total receipts would be 99% × $2407 = $2383, and thus the deficit would be $2383 − $2654 = −$271 (billion). A 0.5% increase in total outlays would result in total outlays of 100.5% × $2654 = $2667, and thus the deficit would be $2407 − $2667 = −$260 (billion).

32. With a 0.5% decrease in total receipts in 2006, receipts would be 99.5% × $2407 = $2395, and thus the deficit would be $2395 − $2654 = −$259 (billion). A 1% increase in total outlays would result in outlays of 101% × $2654 = $2681, and thus the deficit would be $2407 − $2681 = −$274 (billion).

33. Individual income taxes were 44% of $2407 billion = $1059 billion, or just over $1 trillion.

34. Social insurance taxes were 37% of $2407 billion = $891 billion.

35. Excise taxes were 3% of $2407 billion = $72 billion.

36. Social Security expenses were 21% of $2654 = $557 billion.

37. Medicare expenses were 13% of $2654 = $345 billion.

38. Defense and Homeland Security expenses were 20% of $2654 = $531 billion.

39. Because *unified net income − off-budget net income = on-budget net income*, we have $40 billion − $180 billion = −$140 billion. In other words, despite the fact that the government proclaimed a surplus of $40 billion for this year, it actually ran a deficit of $140 billion due to the fact that the money earmarked for the Social Security trust fund was never deposited there (it was spent on other programs).

40. Because *unified net income − off-budget net income = on-budget net income*, we have −$220 billion − $205 billion = −$425 billion. In other words, despite the fact that the government proclaimed a deficit of $220 billion for this year, it actually ran a deficit of $425 billion due to the fact that the money earmarked for the Social Security trust fund was never deposited there (it was spent on other programs).

41. The government could cut discretionary spending, it could borrow money by issuing Treasury notes, or it could raise taxes (of course, a combination of these three would also be an option).

42. The government could cut discretionary spending, it could borrow money by issuing Treasury notes, or it could raise taxes (of course, a combination of these three would also be an option).

FURTHER APPLICATIONS

43. $\$9 \times 10^{12} \times \frac{1 \text{ s}}{\$1} \times \frac{1 \text{ hr}}{3600 \text{ s}} \times \frac{1 \text{ d}}{24 \text{ hr}} \times \frac{1 \text{ yr}}{365 \text{ d}} = 285,388 \text{ yr}$.

It would take about 285,000 years.

44. The dimensions of a dollar bill are about 6.5 cm by 16.5 cm, so its area is around 100 cm^2. Convert $9 trillion into square kilometers:

$$\$9 \times 10^{12} \times \frac{100 \text{ cm}^2}{\$1} \times \left(\frac{1 \text{ km}}{100,000 \text{ cm}} \right)^2 = 90,000 \text{ km}^2.$$

This is $\frac{90,000 \text{ km}^2}{10,000,000 \text{ km}^2} = 0.9\%$ of the area of the United States. A more careful estimate (using $6.5 \text{ cm} \times 16.5 \text{ cm} = 107.25 \text{ cm}^2$) gives an answer closer to 100,000 km^2, or 1% of the land area.

45. In ten years, the debt will be
$$\$9 \times 10^{12} (1 + 0.01)^{10} = \$9.9 \times 10^{12},$$
or about $9.9 trillion. In 50 years, it will be
$$\$9 \times 10^{12} (1 + 0.01)^{50} = \$14.8 \times 10^{12},$$
or about $14.8 trillion.

46. In ten years, the debt will be
$$\$9 \times 10^{12} (1 + 0.02)^{10} = \$11 \times 10^{12},$$
or about $11 trillion. In 50 years, it will be
$$\$9 \times 10^{12} (1 + 0.02)^{50} = \$24.2 \times 10^{12},$$
or about $24.2 trillion.

47. The projected outlays are $2590 billion + $223 billion = $2813 billion. If the outlays were higher by 5%, they would be 105% × $2813 billion = $2954 billion, and if the receipts were lower by 5%, they would be 95% × $2590 billion = $2461 billion. This would result in a deficit of $2461 billion − $2954 billion = −$493 billion.

48. The projected outlays are $2590 billion + $223 billion = $2813 billion. If the outlays were higher by 10%, they would be 110% × $2813 billion = $3094 billion, and if the receipts were lower by 11%, they would be 89% × $2590 billion = $2305 billion. This would result in a deficit of $2305 billion − $3094 billion = −$789 billion.

49. $PMT = \dfrac{\$5 \times 10^{12} \left(\dfrac{0.04}{1} \right)}{1 - \left(1 + \dfrac{0.04}{1} \right)^{-1 \times 10}} = \$6.16 \times 10^{11}$, which is

$616 billion per year.

50. $PMT = \dfrac{\$5 \times 10^{12} \left(\dfrac{0.02}{1} \right)}{1 - \left(1 + \dfrac{0.02}{1} \right)^{-1 \times 15}} = \$3.89 \times 10^{11}$, which is

$389 billion per year.

51. $\$9 \times 10^{12} \times \dfrac{1 \text{ wk}}{\$150 \times 10^{6}} \times \dfrac{1 \text{ yr}}{52 \text{ wk}} = 1154$ years.

52. The annual revenue required from the lottery would be $9 trillion/50 = $180 billion, though this means annual lottery sales would need to be $360 billion (because only half of the proceeds go toward reduction of the debt). Divide $360 billion by 300 million citizens to find that each citizen would need to spend $1200 per year in lottery tickets. An interesting result of such a massive lottery is that there would be a number of very rich people at the end of the 50-year lottery experiment: roughly $9 trillion in prize money would be distributed. In fact, if a random citizen were chosen every day (for 50 years) to be the lottery winner for the day, that person would win about $500 million.

UNIT 5A

QUICK QUIZ

1. **a**. The population is the complete set of people or things that are being studied.
2. **c**. Those who donated money to the governor's campaign are much more likely to approve of his job.
3. **a**. A representative sample is one where the characteristics of the sample match those of the population.
4. **b**. Those who do not receive the treatment (in this case, a cash incentive) are in the control group. Note that the teacher could also randomly select a third group of students who don't even know they are part of the experiment – she could study their attendance rates, and this would be another control group.
5. **c**. The experiment is not blind, because the participants know whether they are receiving money or not, and the teacher knows to which group each student belongs.
6. **a**. The purpose of a placebo is to control for psychological effects that go along with being a participant of the study.
7. **c**. A placebo effect results when participants of the study improve because they think they are receiving the treatment.
8. **c**. A single-blind experiment is one where the participants do not know whether they are part of the treatment group or the control group, but the person conducting the experiment does know.
9. **b**. With a margin of error of 3%, both Poll X and Poll Y have predictions that overlap (in that Poll X predicts Powell will receive 46% to 52% of the vote, and Poll Y predicts he will receive 50% to 56% of the vote), and so they are consistent in their predictions.
10. **b**. The confidence interval is simply the results of the poll plus-or-minus the margin of error.

DOES IT MAKE SENSE?

19. Does not make sense. A sample is a subset of the population, and thus it cannot exceed the size of the population.
20. Makes sense. Due to the random nature of the selection process, it certainly may happen that a sample, though well chosen, does not reflect the characteristics of the population.
21. Does not make sense. The control group should receive the same treatment given to the treatment group.

22. Makes sense. In an experiment where the results are derived from interviews conducted by those running the experiment, a bias may be present if the interviewers know who belongs to the control and treatment groups, and thus it is reasonable to doubt the results.
23. Makes sense. The poll makes a prediction about the outcome of the election, and though we can place a reasonable level of confidence in the results of the poll, it cannot tell the future for us.
24. Makes sense. As long as the sample is chosen carefully, a small sample can often provide good estimates about the population from which it was drawn.

BASIC SKILLS & CONCEPTS

25. The population is all Americans, and the sample was the set of those surveyed. The population parameters are the opinions of Americans on Iran, and the sample statistics consist of the opinions of those who were surveyed.
26. The population is the set of stars in the galaxy, and the sample is the set of stars selected for measurement. The population parameter is the average distance from Earth of all of the stars in the galaxy, whereas the sample statistic is the average distance from Earth of just those stars in the sample.
27. The population is the set of *USA Today* readers (or perhaps just those who read *USA Today* on the Internet), and the sample is the set of people who responded to the survey. The population parameter is the percent of *USA Today* readers who drink at least one caffeinated beverage per day, and the sample statistic is the percent of those who responded to the survey that drink at least one such beverage per day.
28. The population is the set of Americans who intend to take a summer vacation, and the sample is the set of those surveyed. The population parameter is the percent of those who plan to cancel their vacation, while the sample statistic is the percent of those surveyed who plan to cancel their vacation.
29. The population is the set of adult Americans, and the sample is the 2435 adults who were sampled. The population parameters are the opinions of American adults on public schools, whereas the sample statistics are the opinions of those surveyed.
30. The population is the 1.6 million first-year college students, and the sample is the 261,000 students surveyed. The population parameters are the attitudes of all first-year students, and the sample statistics are the attitudes of those surveyed.

31. *Step 1*: The goal is to determine the average time spent per day listening to iPods among a population of students at a middle school. *Step 2*: Randomly select (from a list of all students at the school) a sample from the population. *Step 3*: Determine iPod use from those in the sample, either with an interview, a survey, or a device that measures more precisely when the iPod is in use. *Step 4*: Conclude that the iPod use among all students is similar to iPod use among the sample. *Step 5*: Assess the results and formulate a conclusion.

32. *Step 1:* The goal of the study is to determine the level of frustration with air travel among a population of all business travelers. *Step 2*: Randomly select a representative sample of business travelers to participate in the study. *Step 3*: Interview or survey those in the sample to determine the level of frustration. *Step 4*: Infer that the level of frustration experienced among the sample is the same for all travelers. *Step 5*: Assess the results and draw conclusions from your study.

33. *Step 1*: The population of this study is American male college students, and the goal is to determine the percentage of the population that works at Sudoku puzzles at least once per week. *Step 2*: Choose a representative sample of male college students. *Step 3*: Survey students and determine the percentage of those in the sample who do Sudoku puzzles. *Step 4*: Infer the percentage of the population who do Sudoku puzzles from the results of the study. *Step 5*: Assess the results and draw conclusions.

34. *Step 1*: The goal is to determine the average tip (as a percentage of the total bill) that is left at restaurants among a population of those that go to restaurants. *Step 2*: Select a representative sample of people who go to restaurants. *Step 3*: Determine the average tip among those in the sample. *Step 4*: Conclude that the average tip for those in the sample is the same for those in the population. *Step 5*: Assess the results and formulate a conclusion.

35. *Step 1*: The population in the study is all cars made in Japan, and the goal is to find the average lifetime of windshield wipers on those cars. *Step 2*: Select a representative sample of cars made in Japan. *Step 3*: Formulate a method to determine lifetimes of windshield wipers, and compute the average lifetime. *Step 4*: Infer the average lifetime found in *Step 3* is the same for all cars made in Japan. *Step 5*: Assess the results and formulate a conclusion.

36. *Step 1*: The goal is to determine the percentage of vegetarians among a population of all high school students. *Step 2*: Choose a representative sample

of high school students. *Step 3*: Determine the percentage of students among those in the sample who are vegetarians. *Step 4*: Infer the percentage of vegetarians among all high school students. *Step 5*: Assess the results and formulate a conclusion.

37. The first 50 girls met in the cafeteria is the most representative sample for girls at a particular school because they are a random sample of students at that school. The other groups are not likely to be representative for the following reasons: athletes are generally required to carry a minimum GPA in order to participate in a sports program; those in advanced placement courses are typically good students with above average study habits; and students who participate in theater are more likely to have better time management skills than a random student. All of these would contribute to a bias in the samples regarding study habits.

38. The group of students enrolled in a required class is going to be the most representative group among those at the college because presumably all students must be enrolled in this class, and thus a random sample of students would be found in such a class. Those in a single dormitory will be influenced by the culture at that particular dorm, which may not be representative of the entire student body, (especially if this is a college where upperclassmen move out of the dorms into apartments, and are responsible for cooking their own meals). Students majoring in public health will be more educated about the benefits of a healthy diet, and thus it's likely a bias exists regarding their eating habits. Finally, the students who participate in sports probably eat differently than a random student.

39. This is an example of stratified sampling as the sample of taxpayers is broken in several categories (or strata).

40. This is an example of convenience sampling, because the sample is the set of people who voluntarily respond to a survey.

41. This is an example of stratified sampling as the participants are divided into groups based on age.

42. This is a systematic sampling: a rule (or simple system) is used to select each chip.

43. This is a simple random sampling because the people are selected at random.

44. This is an example of convenience sampling because the sample is made up of those who happen to show up at a particular supermarket.

45. This is an observational study, with a case-control element, where the cases are those who have a tendency to lie, and the controls are those who do not lie.

46. This is an observational study, with a case-control element, where the cases are patients with melanoma, and the controls are cancer-free patients.

47. This is an observational study, with no case-control component.

48. This is an observational study, with a case-control component, where the cases are participants who exercised regularly, and the controls are participants who do not exercise regularly.

49. This is an experiment where the treated group consists of swimmers who included weight training in their workouts, and the control group consists of those who did no weight training. It would be difficult to incorporate the ideas of placebos and blinding in this experiment as there is no way to mask the fact that the subject is weight training.

50. This is an observational study with no case-control.

51. An observational study would be sufficient to determine the average number of hours worked.

52. A simple observational study consisting of a survey would be sufficient to determine the percentage of voters who favor an amendment.

53. Use an observational study with a case-control to find the answer. The cases would be teenagers with a diet high in dairy products, while the control would be those who have a diet not so dependent upon dairy products.

54. To answer this question, an experiment would work best: give 50 people a new car and ask them to use only standard fuel for, say, the next year, and give another group of 50 people the same car, but require them to use only high-ethanol fuel. Carefully record the mileage and fuel use every time the gas tank is filled, and determine which group obtained better mileage.

55. An experiment would answer this question best. Recruit people to participate in the study, and ask one group to take a multi-vitamin every day, while the other group receives a placebo. Observe the rate of strokes among each group to determine the effect of multi-vitamins.

56. To answer this question, one should use an experiment to determine whether the Sunday horoscope is more accurate than the weekday horoscopes.

57. The confidence interval is 50.5% to 55.5%, and because there are only two candidates, it is likely (though not guaranteed) the Republican will win, so a victory party is called for.

58. The confidence interval is 46.5% to 50.5%, and thus it's possible the Democratic candidate could win the election.

59. The confidence interval is 49% to 67%. You cannot be sure a majority of Americans changed vacation plans because it's possible (49%) that a minority changed plans.

60. The confidence interval is 67% to 73%. The fact that the poll does not agree with the voting records percentage of 61% does not necessarily imply people were lying. It may be that the sample was not representative of the population of voters.

FURTHER APPLICATIONS

61. Because a significantly larger percentage of those who received the drug showed improvement compared to those who did not receive the drug, there is good evidence that the treatment is effective (or at least more effective than no treatment at all).

62. There is no difference in rates of improvement between the treatment group and the control group, so there is no evidence that suggests the treatment is effective.

63. Because a significantly larger percentage of those who received the drug showed improvement compared to those who did not receive the drug, there is good evidence that the treatment is effective.

64. There is no evidence that the drug treatment is effective – in fact, it may be harmful, as a larger percentage of those who did not receive treatment showed improvement.

65. a. The population is adults with children (or perhaps people who think they may have children in the future), and the population parameter is the percentage of adults who responded yes.
b. The sample is the 748 adults, and the sample statistic is the percentage of those adults who responded yes.
c. The confidence interval is 59.3% to 66.7%.

66. a. The population is all American adults, and the population parameter is the percentage of adults who believe moral values are worsening.
b. The sample is the 1002 adults surveyed, and the sample statistic is the percentage of these people who believe moral values are worsening.
c. The confidence interval is 77.8% to 84.2%.

67. a. The population is all people of working age, and the population parameter is the percentage of the population that is unemployed.
b. The sample is people of working age in 60,000 households, and the sample statistic is the percentage of those in the sample that are unemployed.
c. The confidence interval is 6.2% to 6.6%.

68. a. The population is the set of American adults, and the population parameter is the percentage of adults who responded yes.

b. The sample is the 1546 adults who were surveyed, and the sample statistic is the percentage of those people who responded yes.

c. The confidence interval is 73.5% to 78.5%.

69. a. The population is registered voters, and the population parameters are the percentage of voters who think the government is listening to your phone conversations (yes), and the percentage who think the government is not listening (no).

b. The sample is the 900 voters surveyed, and the sample statistics are the percentage of those surveyed who think the government is listening to their phone conversations, and the percentage who think the government is not listening.

c. The confidence interval for those responding "no" is 27% to 33%, and for those responding "yes," it is 55% to 61%.

70. a. The population is adults, and the population parameter is the percentage of adults who kept money in a savings account.

b. The sample is the 2000 adults surveyed, and the sample statistic is the percentage of those people who kept money in a savings account.

c. The confidence interval is 61.8% to 66.2%.

UNIT 5B

QUICK QUIZ

1. **c**. When the wrong technique is used in a statistical study, one should put little faith in the results.

2. **b**. While it is possible that an oil company can carry out legitimate and worthy research on an environmental problem it caused, the opportunity (and temptation) for bias to be introduced should make you wary of the results.

3. **a**. The fact that the researchers interviewed only those living in dormitories means the sample chosen may not be representative of the population of all freshmen, some of whom don't live on campus.

4. **b**. The poll that determines the winner suffers from participation bias, as those who vote choose to do so. Also true is that those who vote almost certainly watch the show, while the vast majority of Americans do not watch it, nor do they care who wins.

5. **b**. The quantities that a statistical study attempts to measure are called variables of interest, and this study is measuring the weights of 6-year-olds.

6. **a**. The quantities that a statistical study attempts to measure are called variables of interest, and this survey is measuring the number of visits to the dentist.

7. **c**. It's reasonable to assume that people who use sunscreen do so because they spend time in the sun, and this can lead to sunburns.

8. **c**. The availability error is best avoided by carefully choosing the order in which answers to a survey are presented, and in this case, it's best to switch the order for half of the people being polled.

9. **b**. A self-selected survey suffers from participation bias, where people make the choice to participate (that is, they select themselves, rather than being randomly selected by a polling company).

10. **b**. Carefully conducted statistical studies give us good information about that which is being studied, but it's always possible for unforeseen problems (such as confounding variables) to arise, and the "95% confidence" that was spoken of in Unit 5A (and expanded upon in Unit 6D) can always come into play.

DOES IT MAKE SENSE?

15. Does not make sense. A TV survey with phone-in responses suffers from participation bias, whereas a survey carried out by professional pollsters more likely than not will give better results.

16. Makes sense. A survey about religious beliefs (in general) will suffer from selection bias if the sample consists only of Catholics.

17. Does not make sense. Statistical studies can rarely (if ever) make the claim that the results are proven beyond all doubt.

18. Does not make sense. A careful study that makes the claim "this training regimen will increase your jogging speed by 1%" is essentially meaningless – a very small change in jogging speed may result from any number of factors, and attributing the change to the training regimen is putting too much faith in the study.

BASIC SKILLS & CONCEPTS

19. You should not put much faith in the study because the sample is not likely to be representative of the population.

20. Because the study was double-blind, precautions have been taken to assure quality information, and thus there is no reason to doubt the veracity of the results.

21. A study done by a conservative group to determine opinions about a Democratic tax plan could easily include biases, so you should doubt the results.

22. Because this study found results that negatively impact the company conducting the study, there is no reason to doubt the results. Had the company

found their product was superior, you would do well to think otherwise.

23. You should doubt a poll that suffers from participation bias, as this one does.

24. This study suffers from selection bias, and thus you should put little trust in the results.

25. It is very difficult to quantify or even define a fulfilling life, and thus this study is essentially meaningless (and you should not trust it).

26. There is no reason to doubt the results of this study based on the information given.

27. You should doubt the results of this study because there is no control group to which results might be compared.

28. Based on the information given, this observational study appears to be one that you can trust.

29. There are at least two reasons to doubt the study: it suffers from the availability error, and the sample may not be representative of the population (unless the population is defined to be those who shop at that store).

30. The wording of the question in this study is poorly chosen if its purpose is to determine whether people would support a flag-burning amendment. There is ample reason to doubt the results.

31. There are plenty of reasons to doubt this claim, among them is that the sample (long-distance runners) is not representative of the population (all athletes).

32. Citing statistics about the weights of school children hardly constitutes a proof that new exercise classes should be mandatory (the old exercise classes may do a better job at weight control than the new classes). You should doubt this claim.

33. The Census Bureau is a reputable organization, and there's no reason to doubt the claim (one might argue that a Census statistic which has far reaching political implications could be biased, but this claim is pretty neutral).

34. You should doubt the claim – our ability to measure the duration of a cold is made difficult by how we define the start and finish of a cold. Also, the difference between 6.8 and 7 days is so minimal that any number of variables could have influenced even a carefully controlled study. The shorter duration found by the study may have nothing to do with the cold treatment.

35. There's no reason to doubt this claim.

36. You should doubt this claim because there is no mention of a control group who took fewer than two pills per day.

FURTHER APPLICATIONS

37. People who visit the Web site are more inclined toward saving animals rather then getting rid of

them, and thus the vote on the issue of euthanasia is heavily biased (this is an example of participation bias).

38. Women who stay at home with their children (and to a much lesser extent, men who do the same), and retired people are more likely than the general population to have the time to shop from 10:00 a.m. to noon. The survey will suffer from a selection bias in that this group of shoppers is not representative of the entire population of shoppers.

39. A potential selection bias exists in this survey because the people who vote from 7:00 to 7:30 a.m. may not be a representative sample of the voting population (those in the sample are more likely to be working people who vote on the way to their jobs).

40. The state of New York tends to vote in favor of Democratic candidates (it's more often than not a "blue state" in recent times), and thus the exit poll will suffer from selection bias.

41. This survey will suffer from a selection bias due to the fact that the National Guard is charged with protecting the borders, and thus their views on immigration won't be representative of the entire country.

42. The study will be influenced by a selection bias, as only those who choose to return the survey will be counted in the final tally.

43. Planned Parenthood members have different views on the issue of contraceptives for high school students than the population of American adults (that is, they are not a representative sample), and thus this survey is influenced by the selection bias.

44. This study is likely to be influenced by a conflict of interest – the scientists work for an organization that opposes genetically engineered crops, and yet they are being asked to decide whether such crops pose threats to the environment.

45. Answers will vary.

46. Answers will vary.

47. The stat-byte makes no mention of how "hours of delay are measured," nor are there any comparative values offered that would put the "27,144 hours" into context.

48. We don't know the criteria used to judge restaurants, and we don't know anything about the sample or its size. (Consider, for example, a sample that included only 5 restaurants in New York City).

49. The way in which the question was asked may have influenced responses, and we know nothing of the sample or its size.

50. What question was asked that had 60% of Americans in favor of repealing estate taxes? (In particular, are they made aware that only 2% paid estate taxes, and that this 2% likely constituted

those with large estates?) We don't know how large the sample was, nor whether it was representative of the population.

51. We don't know what question was asked to obtain the responses (was it the same question?), and we don't know the sample or its size.

52. We don't know what conditions qualify for intensive care in the U.S., and we don't know how the information concerning babies in India was obtained.

53. A headline like this implies "illegal drugs" to most readers, and the government study includes smoking and drinking (both of which are legal and largely acceptable practices in many segments of society). The study is based upon top movie rentals, and yet the headline implies all movies. It's a misleading headline.

54. The difference between the percentages (82% versus 79%) is not statistically significant, so the headline may be overstating its case. Also true is that the term "sex" used in the headline has a different connotation to most readers than a "satisfying sex life," which has a more wholesome feel to it.

55. The headline might have some truth to it (and to the credit of the headline writer, the word "may" is included in the claim), but the study is based upon a small sample, and there's a potential conflict of interest as Welch Foods (think Welch Grape Juice) has an interest in a favorable outcome for the study.

56. a. There were 1185 + 158 = 1343 people who completed the study.

b.

	Exercise	No Exercise	Total
Dementia	106	52	158
No Dementia	912	273	1185
Total	1018	325	1343

c. Following is one of four possible Venn diagrams.

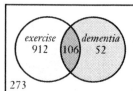

UNIT 5C

QUICK QUIZ

1. **b.** The relative frequency of a category expresses its frequency as a fraction or percentage of the total, and thus is $25/100 = 0.25$.

2. **c.** We would need to know the number of As assigned before being able to compute the cumulative frequency.

3. **b.** Qualitative data describe non-numerical categories.

4. **c.** The sizes of the wedges are determined by the percentage of the data that corresponds to a particular category, and this is the same as the relative frequency for that category.

5. **a.** Depending on how you want to display the data, you could actually use any of the three options listed. However, a line chart is used for numerical data, which means you would have to suppress the names of the tourist attractions (your categories would becomes bins, such as "0-2 million"). For a pie chart, you would need to compute the relative frequencies of the data, and while that's not terribly difficult, it requires an extra step. It would be most appropriate to use a bar graph, with the various tourist attractions as categories (e.g. Disney World, Yosemite National Park, etc.), and the annual number of visitors plotted on the y-axis.

6. **c.** The ten tourist attractions are the categories for a bar graph, and these belong on the horizontal axis.

7. **a.** With 100 data points, each precise to the nearest 0.001, it would be best to bin the data into several categories.

8. **c.** A line chart is often used to represent time-series data.

9. **c.** A histogram is a bar graph for quantitative data categories.

10. **b.** For each dot in a line chart, the horizontal position is the center of the bin it represents.

DOES IT MAKE SENSE?

17. Does not make sense. A frequency table has two columns, one of which lists the frequency of the various categories.

18. Makes sense. A relative frequency of 0.3 means 30% of the grades were Bs, which is reasonable.

19. Does not make sense. The width of the bars in a bar chart is not important (though they should all be of the *same* width in a histogram, and even for those bar charts that are not histograms, even-width bars look better).

20. Makes sense. As long as the teacher's key is correct, the frequencies should be the same in both charts.
21. Does not make sense. The position of the wedges in a pie chart is immaterial.
22. Makes sense. The total of all frequencies in a pie chart should always be 100% (or very near to that – sometimes the total does not add up to 100% due to rounding).
23. Does not make sense. Bar charts can be used for qualitative data: the categories are the qualities of concern, and the vertical axis shows the frequency of each category (or the relative frequencies).
24. Does not make sense. Histograms are used for quantitative data, and they have a natural order imposed by the numbers used (usually these are listed smallest-to-largest, corresponding to left-to-right).

BASIC SKILLS & CONCEPTS

25.

Grade	Freq.	Rel. freq.	Cum. freq.
A	2	0.10	2
B	5	0.25	7
C	8	0.40	15
D	3	0.15	18
F	2	0.10	20
Total	20	1.00	20

26.

Rating	Freq.	Rel. freq.	Cum. freq.
5-star	5	0.09	5
4-star	10	0.18	15
3-star	20	0.36	35
2-star	15	0.27	50
1-star	5	0.09	55
Total	55	0.99*	55

*Due to rounding.

27. Hair color is qualitative data because it describes a non-numerical quality of hair.
28. Average service time is quantitative data because it is a numerical measurement of time.
29. The taste of sausage is qualitative data because it describes a non-numerical quality of sausage (the numbers used are really just labels for the taste).
30. The lowest high temperature is quantitative data because temperatures are numerical data.
31. The responses to the question are qualitative data because they are non-numerical responses.
32. Total income is quantitative data because it is a numerical measurement of money.
33. The dessert selections are qualitative data because they are non-numerical choices in the poll.
34. The number of people voting is quantitative data because it is a numerical measurement of the number of votes cast.

35.

Bin	Freq.	Rel. freq.	Cum. freq.
95–99	3	0.15	3
90–94	2	0.10	5
85–89	3	0.15	8
80–84	2	0.10	10
75–79	4	0.20	14
70–74	1	0.05	15
65–69	4	0.20	19
60–64	1	0.05	20
Total	20	1.00	20

36.

Bin	Freq.	Rel. freq.	Cum. freq.
90–99	5	0.25	5
80–89	5	0.25	10
70–79	5	0.25	15
60–69	5	0.25	20
Total	20	1.00	20

37.

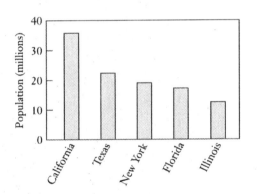

38.

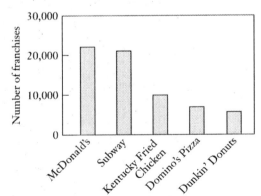

39.

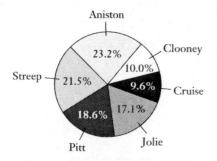

40.

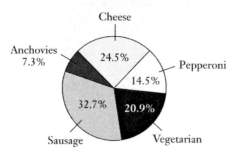

41.

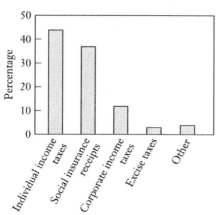

42.

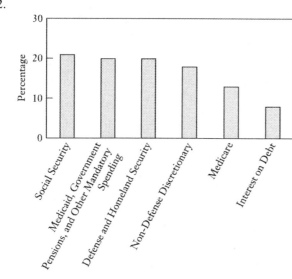

43.

Bin	Frequency
20–29	0
30–39	12
40–49	13
50–59	5
60–69	3
70–79	1
Total	34

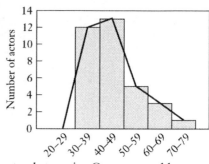

44. Actors tend to win Oscars at older ages than actresses.
45. Answers will vary.
46. Answers will vary.

FURTHER APPLICATIONS

47. a. The ages are quantitative categories.
    b.

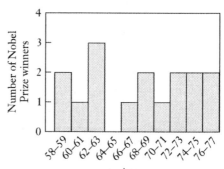

c. People who win the Nobel Prize (in literature) do so rather late in their career, and the data are evenly distributed (this would be more apparent if half as many bins were used).

48. a. The companies are qualitative categories.

b.

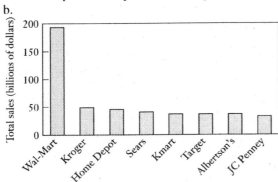

c. Walmart sales are nearly as much as the sum of all the others.

49. a. The ethnic groups are qualitative categories.

b.

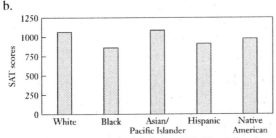

c. With the exception of Asian/Pacific Islanders, minority students don't do as well on the SAT as White students.

50. a. The groups are qualitative categories.

b.

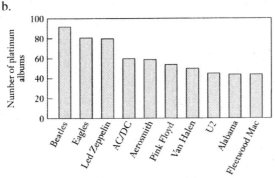

c. Wow! That's a lot of albums sold.

51. a. The land masses are qualitative categories.

b.

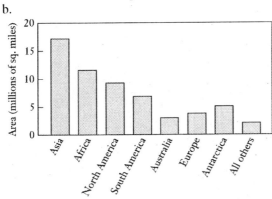

c. Together, Asia and Africa make up almost one-half of the worlds land masses.

52. a. The energy sources are qualitative categories.

b.

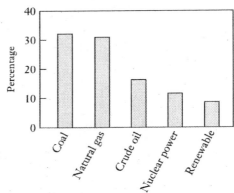

c. Nuclear power accounts for only 11.7% of the energy produced in the U.S.

53. a. The religions are qualitative categories.

b.

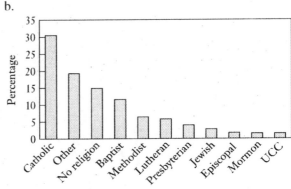

c. Catholics outnumber every category by a significant percentage.

54. a. The age groups are quantitative categories.

b.

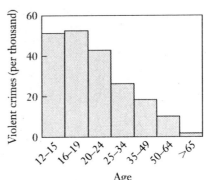

c. Victims of violent crimes are much more likely to be young (12–24 years old).

55. a. The years are quantitative categories.

b.

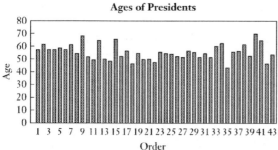

c. Families are getting smaller in the U.S.

56. a. There were about 26,000 alcohol related fatalities in 1982, and about 17,500 in 2003.

b. The percent change is (17,500 – 26,000)/26,000 = –33%.

c. In 1982, the percent of auto fatalities that involved alcohol was about 26,000/43,945 = 59%. The percent in 2003 was about 17,500/42,643 = 41%.

d. There are likely many variables that contributed to the trend, among them: people are better educated about the dangers of driving under the influence of alcohol (due to educational efforts on the part of many organizations); law enforcement agencies have increased patrols that deal exclusively with drunk driving (especially on certain weekends and holidays); and cars have become safer with the addition of airbags.

57. a.

Ages of Presidents

b. President 35 (Kennedy) could claim to be the youngest.

c. President 40 (Reagan) could claim to be the oldest.

UNIT 5D

QUICK QUIZ

1. **a**. Adding the data to a multiple bar graph simply requires a third bar for each year.

2. **b**. The height of the Tuberculosis wedge at 1950 is about 20 years.

3. **a**. The color of Oregon corresponds to the $25,000 – $29,999 category.

4. **c**. Iowa is contained between contour lines that are marked 30°F and 40°F, so the temperature there is between these values.

5. **b**. The color within the small loop matches the band between contour lines marked by 40°F and 50°F, and thus the temperature there is between those values.

6. **c**. When contour lines are close together, the data they represent change more rapidly compared to areas where the lines are far apart.

7. **c**. The height of the center of the pie charts corresponds to the number of women attending, and the height of the 1948 pie chart is about 450.

8. **b**. Because the scale on the y-axis is exaggerated, the changes appear to be larger than they really were.

9. **c**. Each tick mark represents another power of ten.

10. **b**. For all of the years shown in the figure, there is a positive percent change, which means the cost of college was increasing; it increases at a smaller rate when the graph is decreasing.

DOES IT MAKE SENSE?

19. Does not make sense. Using three-dimensional bars for two-dimensional data is a cosmetic change; it adds no information.

20. Makes sense. When the spread of your data values is very large, it is sometimes difficult to draw a reasonable linear scale on the y-axis. An exponential scale overcomes this difficulty.

21. Makes sense. Experimenting with different scales on the axes of graphs allows you to highlight certain aspects of the data.

22. Makes sense. As long as the graph shows a positive rate of increase, then the number of users is rising.

BASIC SKILLS & CONCEPTS

23. a. China, India and Russia all had to import grain because their net grain production is negative.

b. China, India, and Russia are all expected to need grain imports because their projected 2030 net grain production is negative.

c. The graph shows that both China and India will require significant grain imports, and thus (based only on the information shown in the graph), it's likely world grain production will need to increase.

24. a. The set of bars corresponding to the year 2000 shows the median income for various levels of education attained, and the other sets show the same information for different years (1995, 1985).

b. The 15-year absolute change for college graduates is much larger than the absolute change for high school graduates. The percent change is also higher for college graduates, though the comparison is not as stark.

c. The third dimension is purely cosmetic; it relays no information.

25. a. The death rate for pneumonia, cardiovascular disease, and tuberculosis decreased from 1900 to 2003; it increased for cancer.

b. The death rate was the greatest around 1950, where it was about 500 deaths per 100,000.

c. The death rate for cancer in 2000 was about 200 deaths per 100,000.

d. Deaths due to cardiovascular diseases will likely be responsible for the most deaths in 2050, as long as cancer levels out (as it has in the years following the mid-1990s).

26. a. In 1930, about 75,000 degrees were awarded to men, and about 50,000 were awarded to women. In 2005, a little less than 600,000 degrees were awarded to men, and around 800,000 degrees were awarded to women.

b. Men earned slightly more degrees in 1980, and women earned more degrees in 2005.

c. The steepest portion of the upper line occurred in the 1960s, and the upper line can be interpreted as the total number of degrees awarded.

d. In 1950, about 450,000 degrees were awarded, and in 2005, about 1.35 million degrees were awarded.

e. A multiple bar graph would probably be easier to read, and to answer questions of the sort from steps **a** through **d**.

27. a. About 15% of the budget went to net interest in 1990 and 1995; it dropped to about 8% in 2005.

b. In 1962, about 52% of the budget went to defense. The percentage dropped to about 23% in 1980, and dropped again in 2005, to about 20%.

c. In 1980, about 47% of the budget went to payments to individuals. This figure was about 57% in 2000, and about 54% in 2005.

28. Payments to individuals, as a percent of the total budget, increased. Defense spending decreased. Net interest slowly increased, and then decreased.

29. There are significant regional differences: the probability that a black student had white classmates is much higher in the northern states. It's difficult to make a blanket statement about the differences between urban and rural areas, but it certainly appears that the probability is lower in many urban areas (look at San Francisco/Oakland, Los Angeles and San Diego, Chicago, Detroit, Miami, and the larger cities along the eastern seaboard, and compare these with adjoining rural areas).

30. With no elevations marked on the contours, we can't be sure whether the two oval contours near the center of the map are pits or peaks, but given this is Colorado, it's a safe bet they are peaks. In fact, it's a safe bet these are Green and Bear Mountains, the summits in the foothills that form the backdrop to the University of Colorado where I teach. These mountains are steeper on their eastern slopes than on their western slopes, as evidenced by the close contour lines on the eastern side, and the region on the right side of the map is much flatter than on the left side of the map (it's the eastern plains that lead up to the foothills).

31. The height of each bar corresponds to the percent of the population for a particular age group and for a given year. For example, in Figure 5.34a, we can see that in 1960, children less than 5 years in age made up about 10% of the population.

32. The graph displays true three-dimensional data: each bar has a percent, year, and age group associated with it.

33. The percent of the youngest Americans has decreased.

34. In 1960, 5 to 17-year-olds constituted 24% of the population. By 2000, this figure had dropped to about 16%.

35. The percentage of 45 to 65-year-olds was about 20% in 1960, and is projected to be about 27% in 2010.

36. The 25 to 44-year-old group was largest in 1990.

37. The 45 to 65-year old group is projected to be largest in 2010.

38. The over-65-year-old group is expected to see the greatest increase.

39. The population is aging as evidenced by the increase in the over-65 category, and the decrease in the under-5 category.

40. You would need to know the total number of participants, the total number of women participants, the number of events for women, and whether the games were held for a particular year.

42. The area of the screen on the 2005 TV is larger than the area of the 1980 TV by a factor of about 16, and the volume of the 2005 TV is larger than the volume of the 1980 TV by a factor of about 64, and yet the actual number of homes with cable in 2005 is larger than the 1980 level by a factor of just over 4 (73/18 = 4.06).

43. In a flat pie chart, a wedge with central angle of, say, 60° represents 1/6 of the total area of the circle, no matter where it is located in the circle. In the distorted version shown, the face of the pie is an ellipse, and 60° wedges in ellipses don't necessarily have equal areas, and thus they won't correspond to the percentages they are attempting to depict.

44. The zero point for earnings is not on the graph, and thus it appears that women earn about 10% of what men earn. A more intellectually honest way to display the data is shown below.

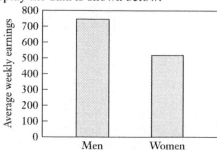

45. Note that the zero point for braking distance is not on the graph, and because of this, it looks like the breaking distance of an Oldsmobile is about half that of a Lincoln. In reality, the breaking distance of Lincolns is about 11% greater than the breaking distance of Oldsmobiles. A fairer graph (not shown) would start from zero.

46.

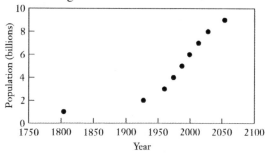

47. a. Public college costs rose by about 13% in the 2003-04 academic year.

b. The percentage increase in private college costs in the 2003-04 year was about 5%.

c. Private college costs rose more in dollars, because 5% of the '02–'03 costs for private colleges is more than 13% of the '02–'03 costs for public colleges.

48. Most of the growth occurred after 1950.

FURTHER APPLICATIONS

49. Two graphs work best for this data. Both men and women are waiting much longer to get married for the first time.

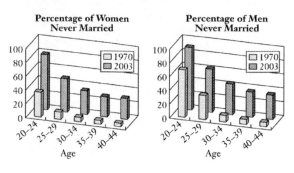

50. Using a three-dimensional graph, and splitting the statistics into categories of "Alcohol" and "No Alcohol," allows an easy visual comparison between the two.

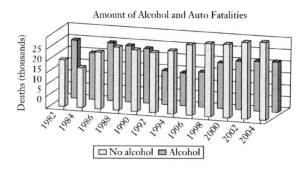

51. A simple multiple bar graph works well for this data.

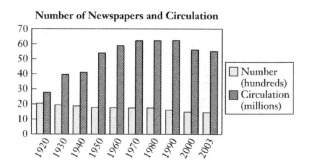

52. Combing the ideas of a stack plot with a bar graph allows all of the data to be displayed in a way that makes comparisons easy.

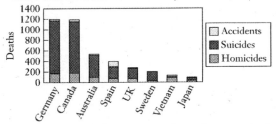

Annual Deaths Due to Firearms (excluding U.S., which has 30 times more deaths than Germany and Canada)

53. a. The change from one month to the next looks less significant when zero is included.

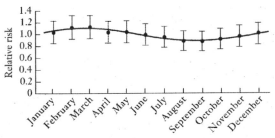

Month of birth

b. The claim is not justified because the error bars are large enough that the true values of relative risk may form a straight line across all months (which would mean the risk does not vary with season).

54.

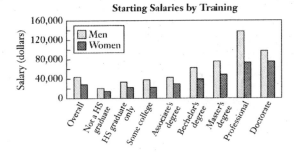

Starting Salaries by Training

UNIT 5E

QUICK QUIZ

1. **c.** When one variable is correlated with another, an increase in one goes with either increasing values of the other, or decreasing values of the other.

2. **b.** The dot representing Russia has a horizontal coordinate of about 63 years.

3. **a.** When points on a scatter diagram all lie near a line, there is a strong correlation between the variables represented. We call it a positive correlation when an increase in one variable goes along with an increase in another (and this is what produces a positive slope).

4. **b.** A negative correlation exists between two variables when an increase in one goes with a decrease in the other, and this is what produces a negative slope. That the points described fall in a broad swath, rather than a tight configuration that more closely resembles a line, means the correlation between the variables is weak.

5. **a.** Correlation is a necessary condition for causation.

6. **c.** When wages (adjusted for inflation) go higher, there's more incentive for people to work, which leads to lower unemployment. Or, looking at it from the other side, when unemployment rates fall, employers are forced to offer higher wages to attract good people from the small pool of available labor.

7. **a.** When establishing causation, look for evidence that larger amounts of the suspected cause produce larger amounts of the effect.

8. **c.** Values before humans peaked at a little less than 300 ppm, while values today are a little less than 400 ppm, and this is a 30% change.

9. **b.** From 1960 to 2000 (a span of 40 years), CO_2 concentration increased by about 50 ppm, and if that trend continues for another 40 years, to the year 2040, we can expect another increase of about 50 ppm, which will result in CO_2 levels near 420 ppm.

10. **c.** The courts have proclaimed that a member of the jury should find the defendant guilty when the jury member is firmly convinced the defendant is guilty of the crime charged.

DOES IT MAKE SENSE?

17. Makes sense. A strong negative correlation means that a decrease in the price goes along with an increase in the number of tickets sold.

18. Makes sense. A strong positive correlation means that an increase in time spent studying goes along with higher grades.

19. Does not make sense. Despite the fact that A and B are strongly correlated, we cannot be sure that A causes B (there may be an underlying effect that causes both A and B).

20. Does not make sense. A strong negative correlation between C and D does not mean that C must be the cause for D (there may be an underlying effect that causes the correlation between C and D).

21. Makes sense. If it were true that an increase in E caused a decrease in F, then a negative correlation would exist.

22. Does not make sense. It is very difficult to establish absolute proof, but if we find that increasing helmet use tends to decrease injury rates (and you agree that kids should wear helmets in situations where helmet use decreases injury rates), then you should support the requirement that kids wear helmets.

BASIC SKILLS & CONCEPTS

23. a. We seek a correlation between a car's *weight* and its *city gas mileage*.
    b. The diagram shows a moderately strong negative correlation.
    c. Heavier cars tend to get lower gas mileage.
24. a. We seek a correlation between *unemployment rate* and *voter turnout* during a presidential election.
    b. It appears that there is no correlation between the variables.
    c. There's not much regarding the relationship between the two variables that we can conclude from this diagram, as no correlation exists. We could reasonably conclude that unemployment ranged from 4% to 8% between the years of 1964 to 2004, and that voter turnout was between 50% and 70% for those years, though we have only a sample of the years (every fourth year, to be specific).
25. a. We seek a correlation between *salary level* and *percent of income given to charity* for employees of Big Co.
    b. At first glance, there's no correlation (which is a reasonable answer), though one could also argue for a very weak negative correlation based on the light representation of data points in the upper right corner of the scatter diagram.
    c. There's a slight indication that lower-salary employees give a larger percentage of their income to charity, but it's very weak.
26. a. We seek a correlation between *number of farms* and *size of farms in acres*.
    b. There is a strong negative correlation.
    c. The fewer farms there are in America, the larger the farms are.
27. Use degrees of latitude and degrees of temperature as units. There is a strong negative correlation, because as you move north from the equator, the temperatures in June tend to decrease.
28. Use inches and dollars as units. If one considered that children (short individuals) don't have much pocket change, then a weak positive correlation might exist. However, if adult heights (fully grown individuals) are considered, it's likely no correlation between height and pocket change exists.

29. Use years and hours as units. If the population studied consists of people from teen years to the elderly, one may find a weak negative correlation, because teens probably spend more time on their cell phones than adults, particularly older adults.
30. Use feet and pounds per square inch as units. There is a strong negative correlation because air pressure decreases as one increases altitude.
31. Use people and dollars as units. There is no correlation because the average salary of a school teacher varies considerably from one region of the country to another, and this variation isn't in lock step with the population.
32. Use people and percentage as units. There is a weak positive correlation, because foreign-born residents are more likely to be found in big cities.
33. Use children per woman and years as units. There is a strong negative correlation, because an increase in the life expectancy of a country goes along with a decrease in the number of children born.
34. Use dollars and years as units. There is likely a weak positive correlation, because most teachers are attracted to better schools, and these tend to be schools where the family incomes are higher.

FURTHER APPLICATIONS

35. a.

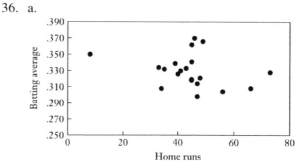

b. It appears there is a weak negative correlation.
c. In those countries where per capita GNP is high, there's more money available to spend on various government programs, and thus the per capita expenditure on defense decreases.

36. a.

b. There does not appear to be any correlation.

c. Hitting a home run and getting a hit are different skills, and thus some players who are able to hit for power don't have particularly impressive batting averages, and some players (e.g. Ichiro Suzuki) are very good at getting a hit, but aren't as able to send one out of the park.

37. a.

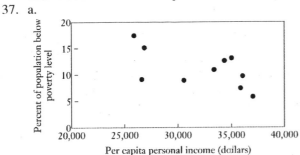

b. There is a weak negative correlation between the variables.

c. When the per capita income is higher, the average person is further away from poverty level, and the percent of the population below the poverty level decreases.

38. a.

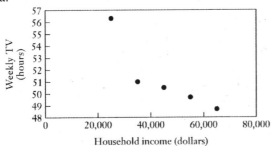

b. There is a strong negative correlation between the variables.

c. As people work more and earn more money, they have less time to spend in front of the TV.

39. a.

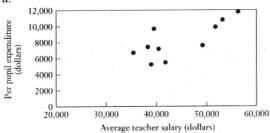

b. There is a strong positive correlation.

c. The per pupil expenditure almost certainly includes teacher salaries (that is, salaries are part of the cost of educating the students), and thus in those districts where the teacher salaries are high, the per pupil expenditure is also high.

40. a.

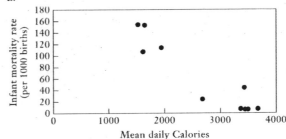

b. There is a strong negative correlation.

c. Sufficient caloric intake has much to do with the ability for an infant to survive, and is also related to the relative wealth of a country (those countries where caloric intake is low are generally poor countries, so not only are its inhabitants lacking in the basic needs, but also in advanced health care).

41. There is a positive correlation between the crime rate and the number of tourists. There may be direct cause and effect here: with more tourists, there are more targets for opportunistic crimes against them.

42. There is a positive correlation between the number of miles of freeway in Los Angeles and the amount of traffic congestion. There is likely a common underlying cause here: an increase in population.

43. There is a negative correlation between the cost of gas and the number of SUVs sold. There may be a direct cause at work here, because when gas prices increase, people are more conscious about the gas mileage for the car they purchase.

44. Sales of ice cream are positively correlated with sales of swimming suits. The common underlying cause is most likely a change in season.

45. Gas mileage is positively correlated with tire pressure. This is a direct cause: when tire pressure goes down, gas mileage also goes down.

46. The number of ministers and priests is positively correlated with movie ticket sales. There is a common underlying cause: an increase in population.

47. a. When the suspected cause (bad air in the building in which you work) is removed, the afternoon headaches go away. This is guideline 2.

b. Even when you vary other factors, such as drinking Coke, the headaches are still present, suggesting that Coke isn't the cause, but rather bad air in the building is to blame. This is guideline 1.

c. When the suspected cause is decreased, the headaches are less frequent. This is guideline 3.

d. The observations suggest that your headaches are caused by bad air at your work environment.

48. The causes of cancer are often random. A cancer cell is produced when the growth control mechanisms of a normal cell are altered by a

random mutation. Smoking may increase the chance of such a mutation occurring, but the mutation will not occur in all individuals. Therefore, by chance, some smokers escape cancer.

49. People do not decide to become conductors until relatively late in life, say, 30 years of age or over. Having already survived this many years, a person has a longer-than-average life expectancy.

50. You cannot conclude that the high-voltage line is the cause of cancer because a mechanism for the cause must be established. There may be an underlying cause.

51. A plausible explanation is that many youth soccer leagues around the world use age divisions. Those children born earlier in a given year are slightly older than others born in the same year. Being slightly stronger and better developed, they survive and move on to more advanced leagues.

UNIT 6A

QUICK QUIZ

1. **b**. The mean of a data set is the sum of all the data values divided by the number of data points.

2. **b**. The median of a data set is the middle value when the data are placed in numerical order.

3. **c**. Outliers are data values that are much smaller or larger than the other values.

4. **a**. Outliers that are larger than the rest of the data set tend to pull the mean to the right of the median, and this is the case for all possible data sets that satisfy the conditions given.

5. **c**. Because the mean is significantly higher than the median, the distribution is skewed to the right, which implies some students drink considerably more than 12 sodas per week. Specifically, it can be shown that at least one student must drink more than 16 sodas per week.

6. **c**. The high salaries of a few superstars pull the tail of this distribution to the right.

7. **a**. High outliers tend to pull the mean to the right of the median, and thus you would hope to get a salary near the mean. There are data sets with high outliers that can be constructed where the median is higher than the mean, but these are rare.

8. **a**. In general, data sets with a narrow central peak typically have less variation than those with broad, spread out values (the presence of outliers can confound the issue).

9. **c**. Driving in rush hour can go quickly on some days, but is agonizingly slow on others, so the time it takes to get downtown has high variation.

10. **b**. The mayor would like to see a high median and low variation because that means there's a tight, central peak in the distribution that corresponds to support for her.

DOES IT MAKE SENSE?

17. Makes sense. The two highest grades may be large enough to balance the remaining seven lower grades so that the third highest is the mean.

18. Does not make sense. The median for this exam is, by definition, the mean of the two middle scores (the fifth and sixth scores), and thus it could not be the third highest score.

19. Makes sense. When very high outliers are present, they tend to pull the mean to the right of the median (right-skewed).

20. Does not make sense. The word "average" has several meanings in mathematics, and the management and employees may be using different measures of the average (the mean and the median, for example).

21. Does not make sense. When the mean, median, and mode are all the same, it's a sign that you have a symmetric distribution of data.

22. Makes sense. Suppose the mean age of the general population is 32 years. There's no reason why a college extension class (which typically attracts older students) could not share the same mean.

BASIC SKILLS & CONCEPTS

23. The mean, median, and mode are 2.2698, 2.270, and 2.271, respectively. Because there is an even number of data points, the median is calculated by taking the mean of the middle two values (add 2.269 and 2.271, and divide by 2).

24. The mean, median, and mode are 98.44, 98.4, and 98.4, respectively. Because there is an even number of data points, the median is calculated by taking the mean of the middle two values (add 98.4 and 98.4, and divide by 2).

25. The mean, median, and mode are 0.215, 0.21, and 0.24, respectively.

26. The mean and median are 78.4 and 79, respectively. This is a multi-modal data set, with modes of 70, 73, 76, and 81.

27. The mean and median are 89.9 and 90, respectively. This is a bimodal data set, with modes of 87 and 91.

28. The mean and median are 0.9194 and 0.920, respectively. There is no mode.

29. The mean and median are 0.81237 and 0.8161, respectively. The outlier is 0.7901, because it varies from the others by a couple hundredths of a pound, while the rest vary from each other only by a few thousandths of a pound. Without the outlier, the mean is 0.81608, and the median is 0.8163.

30. The mean is 36 years, and the median is 36.7 years. Utah is an outlier. Eliminating Utah, the mean and median are 37.38 and 37, respectively.

31. The median would be a better representation of the average. A small number of households with high earnings skew the distribution to the right, affecting the mean.

32. This distribution is probably skewed to the right by a small percentage of men who marry (for the first time) very late in life. Therefore the median would do a better job representing the average age (the outliers affect the mean).

33. This distribution is probably skewed to the right by a small percentage of people who change jobs many times. Thus the median would do a better job of representing the average, as the outliers affect the mean.

34. More likely than not, this distribution is skewed to the right by a few flights where many pieces of

luggage were lost. Because of this, the mean is probably higher than the median, and thus the airline would want to use the median as the best representation of the average. Customers of the airline might argue that the mean is a better descriptor for the average.

35. This is a classic example of a symmetric distribution, and thus the mean and the median are almost identical (in a perfectly symmetric distribution, they are identical) – either the mean or the median could be used.

36. This distribution is probably skewed to the right by those times when the wait is long, and therefore the median is a better representation of the average (certainly from the view of an advertisement for the bank – customers might claim the mean is a more honest way of describing the average wait time).

37. a. There is one peak on the far left due to all the people who scored low.
 b. The distribution is right-skewed because the scores tail off to the right.
 c. The variation is large (relative to the data in exercise 38, for example).

38. a. There is one peak in the middle, representing the people who got Cs.
 b. This distribution is best described as symmetric, as there are even numbers of grades on either side of the peak. However, because the grade of F represents a much larger numerical category (say, 0 to 59%) than the other grades, its possible a few low outliers could make this a left-skewed distribution.
 c. The variation is moderate (relative to the data in exercise 37, for example).

39. a. There are likely two peaks in such a distribution, one for the women, and one for the men.
 b. The distribution is symmetric because one would find a tail on the left representing the lightest people on the team, and a tail on the right representing the heaviest people on the team.
 c. Relative to a single-gendered set of athletes, the variation would be large.

40. a. The last two digits of a 5-digit ZIP code correspond to a small town or delivery unit within a metropolitan area or sectional center (which, in turn, is designated by the second and third digits). As long as the U.S. Postal Service does not use some special method to come up with these last two digits (that is, as long as the process of selecting the last digit is essentially random), one would expect this to be a uniform distribution, with no peaks. If, on the other hand, the last two digits are selected sequentially whenever a new ZIP code needs to be introduced (because of

increasing population within a particular delivery area), it may be that 0s, 1s, and 2s outnumber the later digits by a large enough margin that one would see a less-than uniform distribution. (Curious to find whether this was so, I looked at the 695 ZIP codes in Colorado – sure enough, the 0s, 1s, and 2s outnumbered the 7s, 8s, and 9s by a significant margin. 35.7% of the ZIP codes ended in 0, 1, or 2, while only 22.5% ended in 7, 8, or 9. There was an interesting peak at the 1s that I can't explain).

b. This is a symmetric distribution because it is uniform (see, however, the discussion in part **a**) – that is, all digits 0–9 have nearly the same frequency in the case where the last digit is selected randomly.

c. The data values are spread out evenly across the distribution, so there is large variation. Note that the data set could be interpreted another way, resulting in different answers for all of these questions. If "the number of people with particular last digits" is taken to mean a data set with ten values, each describing the number of people who have a particular last digit in their ZIP code, then one would expect each value to be about 30 million people (there are 300 million people in the U.S.). This answer assumes the digits are randomly selected, and that each ZIP code represents roughly the same number of people. The frequency histogram for this set would be symmetric, with one peak (best described as a spike), and low variation.

41. a. Consider a typical data set for the monthly sales: we expect the sales to be high in the winter months, with very low sales (or even no sales) in the summer. The number of shovels sold each month, beginning in January, might look like this: {25, 20, 15, 3, 0, 0, 0, 0, 0, 3, 15, 20}. To picture this data set as a distribution, we create a frequency histogram.

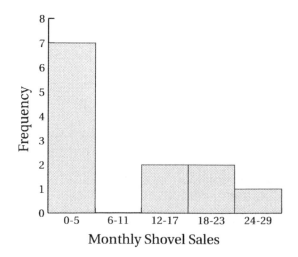

This histogram has two peaks, the second not as dramatic as the first. Realize that although the histogram would look different if we varied the bin sizes or the hypothetical sales data, its basic shape is captured in the diagram above. This is due to the fact that a majority of the monthly sales figures are expected to be low (corresponding to the left peak), and the winter monthly sales figures would be high (corresponding to the right peak).

b. The histogram shown in part **a** is right-skewed.

c. The variation is large because of the difference between low sales in the summer, and high sales in the winter.

42. a. Similar to exercise 41, the best way to visualize the distribution of monthly milk sales is to create a hypothetical data set. Milk sales are very likely uniform throughout the year, and thus any variation in the data would be due to the length of the month. Therefore, the monthly sales data (beginning from January) might look like this: {31, 28, 31, 30, 31, 30, 31, 31, 30, 31, 30, 31}. Here the numbers represent units of milk sold per month (where the unit would be dependent upon the daily volume of milk sold at the store). A frequency histogram for this data (not shown) would be best described as a spike (a single column corresponding to the bin that included sales numbers from 28-31 units). As in exercise 41, the histogram would take on a slightly different form if we binned the data differently, or varied the hypothetical sales data, but in all cases, the distribution could be described as a single, narrow peak.

b. The frequency histogram in part **a** would be symmetric.

c. The variation in monthly milk sales would be small because all the monthly sales figures are nearly the same.

43. a. There would be one peak in the distribution, corresponding to the average price of detergent.

b. More likely than not, there would be no extreme outliers in this data set, and it would be symmetric.

c. There would be moderate variation in the data set because we don't expect outliers. (The detergent may not sell well next to 19 other brands if its price is radically different. Of course this begs the question, "But what if it's much cheaper than the other brands?" That's not too likely to happen for a commodity like detergent, because once one company begins selling its detergent at a low price, the others would be forced to lower their prices to compete).

44. a. One would expect a single peak for this data set, representing the mean batting average for ball players.

b. Distributions that measure athletic ability tend to be symmetric.

c. The variation would be large, as some players (particularly pitchers) have low batting averages, and some have high batting averages.

FURTHER APPLICATIONS

45. The distribution has two peaks (bimodal), with no symmetry, and large variation. For tourists who want to watch the geyser erupt, it means they may have to wait around for a while (most likely between 25 and 40 minutes, though perhaps as long as 50 to 90 minutes, depending on when they arrive at the site).

46. The distribution has one peak, and is right-skewed. Most of the data is clustered around its peak, though it has considerable spread, so it has moderate variation. The histogram tells us that if a computer chip is going to fail, it will most likely fail soon, rather than late.

47. This distribution has one peak, is symmetric, and has moderate variation. The graph says that weights of rugby players are usually near the mean weight, but that there are some light and some heavy players.

48. a. As shown, the graph is not symmetric (though the idea it represents – uniform distribution of randomly chosen numbers – is symmetric).

b. No, the peaks appear randomly (though, again, the smooth distribution one envisions when numbers are chosen randomly could be described as a distribution with no peaks).

c. No, the distribution would look different because the numbers are chosen at random, and the ups and downs of the graph would appear at random (and different) locations.

d. The histogram would get smoother, approaching a uniform distribution.

49. a. We cannot be sure of the exact shape of the distribution with the given parameters, as we don't have all the raw data. However, because the mean is larger than the median, and because the data set has large outliers, it would likely be right-skewed, with a single peak at the mode.

b. About 150 families (50%) earned less than $35,000 because that value is the median income.

c. We don't have enough information to be certain how many families earned more than $41,000, but it is likely a little less than half, simply because the mean is a measure of center for all distributions. (Note that it is a little less than half because the outliers tend to pull the mean right of the median).

50. a. Because the mode is 0 minutes, and the distribution is right skewed (its mean is right of the median, and there are high outliers), the graph would have a single peak at 0 and would decrease

to the right. (Note that planes do not typically depart earlier than scheduled – it would be unwise to leave passengers behind – and thus there are no negative delays).

b. 50% of the flights were delayed less than the median time of 6 minutes due to the definition of the median.

c. 50% of the flights were delayed more than the median time of 6 minutes due to the definition of the median.

UNIT 6B

QUICK QUIZ

1. **a**. The range is defined as the high value – low value.

2. **c**. The five-number summary includes the low value, the first quartile, median, and third quartile, and the high value. Unless the mean happens to be the same as the median, it would not be part of the five-number summary.

3. **a**. Roughly half of any data set is contained between the lower and upper quartiles ("roughly" because with an odd number of data values, one cannot break a data set into equal parts).

4. **b**. Consider the set {0, 0, 0, 0, 0, 0, 0, 0, 0, 100}. Its mean is 10, which is larger than the upper quartile of 0.

5. **b**. You need the high and low values to compute the range, and you need all of the values to compute the standard deviation, so the only thing you can compute is a single deviation.

6. **b**. The standard deviation is defined in such a way that it can be interpreted as the average distance of a random value from the mean.

7. **c**. The standard deviation is defined as the square root of the variance, and thus is always non-negative.

8. **a**. Using the range rule of thumb, we see that the standard deviation is about four times as large as the range. (The worst-case scenario is when the range and standard deviation are both zero).

9. **b**. Newborn infants and first grade boys have similar heights, whereas there is considerable variation in the heights of all elementary school children.

10. **c**. Because the standard deviation for Garcia is the largest, the data are more spread out, so Professor Garcia must have had very high grades from more students than the other two.

DOES IT MAKE SENSE?

17. Does not make sense. The range depends upon only the low and high values, not on the middle values.

18. Makes sense. The upper quartile includes the highest score.

19. Makes sense. Consider the case where the 15 highest scores were 80, the next score was 68, and the lowest 14 scores were 40. There are numerous such cases that satisfy the conditions given.

20. Makes sense. Using the range rule of thumb, the range is approximately four times as large as the standard deviation. The only instance where the range would not be larger than the standard deviation is the case where both were 0.

21. Makes sense. The standard deviation describes the spread of the data, and one would certainly expect the heights of 5-year old children to have less variation than the heights of children aged 3 to 15.

22. Does not make sense. The standard deviation carries the same units as the mean.

BASIC SKILLS & CONCEPTS

23. The mean waiting time at Big Bank is (4.1 + 5.2 + 5.6 + 6.2 + 6.7 + 7.2 + 7.7 + 7.7 + 8.5 + 9.3 + 11.0) ÷ 11 = 79.2 ÷ 11 = 7.2. Because there are 11 values, the median is the sixth value = 7.2.

24. The mean waiting time at Best Bank is (6.6 + 6.7 + 6.7 + 6.9 + 7.1 + 7.2 + 7.3 + 7.4 + 7.7 + 7.8 + 7.8) ÷ 11 = 79.2 ÷ 11 = 7.2. Because there are 11 values, the median is the sixth value = 7.2.

25. a. For the East Coast, the mean, median, and range are 134.97, 123.45, and 117.8, respectively. For the West Coast, the mean, median, and range are 145.82, 150.3, and 69.2, respectively.

b. For the East Coast, the five-number summary is (98.2, 108.7, 123.45, 140.0, 216.0). For the West Coast, it is (113.2, 122.7, 150.3, 156.0, 182.4). The boxplots are not shown.

c. The standard deviation for the East Coast is 42.86. For the West Coast, it is 25.06.

d. For the East Coast, the standard deviation is approximately 117.8 ÷ 4 = 29.45, which is a far cry from the actual value of 42.86. This is due, in part, to the outlier of New York City (216.0). For the West Coast, the standard deviation is approximately 69.2 ÷ 4 = 17.3, which is also well off the mark.

e. The cost of living index is smaller, on average, for the East Coast cities shown, though the variation is higher (due in part to the outlier of New York City).

26. a. For the coastal cities, the mean, median, and range are 4943.4, 4906.5, and 3034, respectively.

The mean, median, and range for the non-coastal cities are 3952.9, 4125, and 3414, respectively.

b. For the coastal cities, the five-number summary is (3232, 4245, 4906.5, 5709, 6266). For the non-coastal cities, it is (1832, 3296, 4125, 4579, 5246). The boxplots are not shown.

c. The standard deviation for the coastal cities is 961.3. It is 1010.5 for the non-coastal cities.

d. The standard deviation for the coastal cities is approximately 3034 ÷ 4 = 758.5, which underestimates the actual value of 961.3. For the non-coastal cities, the standard deviation is approximately 3414 ÷ 4 = 853.5, which also underestimates the actual value of 1010.5.

e. The mean and median taxes for non-coastal cities are considerably smaller than the taxes paid in coastal cities, though the variation is slightly larger.

27. a. In San Francisco, the mean, median, and range are 65.1, 65, and 13, respectively. In Chicago, the mean, median, and range are 58.3, 60, and 54, respectively.

b. The five-number summary for San Francisco is (58, 62, 65, 68.5, 71). It is (30, 40.5, 60, 76.5, 84) in Chicago. The boxplots are not shown.

c. The standard deviation in San Francisco is 4.3; in Chicago, it is 19.6.

d. The standard deviation in San Francisco is approximately 13 ÷ 4 = 3.25, which underestimates the actual value of 4.3. In Chicago, the standard deviation is approximately 54 ÷ 4 = 13.5, which is considerably lower than the actual value of 19.6.

e. The average high temperatures in San Francisco are a little warmer than those in Chicago, though the variation of temperatures is much smaller in San Francisco.

28. a. The mean, median, and range for Beethoven's symphonies are 38.8, 36, and 42 minutes, respectively. For Mahler, these numbers are 75, 80, and 44 minutes.

b. Beethoven's five-number summary is (26, 29, 36, 45, 68). Mahler's is (50, 62, 80, 87.5, 94). The boxplots are not shown.

c. The standard deviation for Beethoven's symphonies is 13.13 minutes. It is 15.44 for Mahler's symphonies.

d. The standard deviation for Beethoven's symphonies is approximately 42 ÷ 4 = 10.5, which underestimates the actual value of 13.13. For Mahler, the standard deviation is approximately 44 ÷ 4 = 11, which underestimates the actual value of 15.44.

e. Mahler wrote symphonies that were significantly longer, on average, than Beethoven's,

and the variation is slightly larger for Mahler's symphonies.

FURTHER APPLICATIONS

29. a.

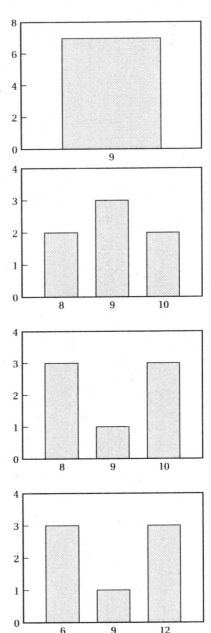

b. The five-number summaries for each of the sets shown are (in order): (9, 9, 9, 9, 9); (8, 8, 9, 10, 10); (8, 8, 9, 10, 10); and (6, 6, 9, 12, 12). The boxplots are not shown.

c. The standard deviations for the sets are (in order): 0.000, 0.816, 1.000, and 3.000.

d. Looking at just the answers to part **c**, we can tell that the variation gets larger from set to set.

30. a.

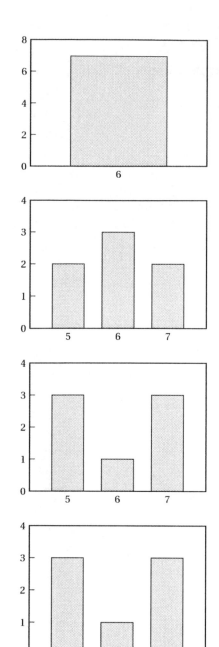

b. The five-number summaries for each of the sets shown are (in order): (6, 6, 6, 6, 6); (5, 5, 6, 7, 7); (5, 5, 6, 7, 7); and (3, 3, 6, 9, 9). The boxplots are not shown.

c. The standard deviations for the sets are (in order): 0.000, 0.816, 1.000, and 3.000.

d. Looking at just the answers to part c, we can tell that the variation gets larger from set to set.

31. The first pizza shop has a slightly larger mean delivery time, but much less variation in delivery time when compared to the second shop. If you want a reliable delivery time, choose the first shop. If you don't care when the pizza arrives, choose the shop that offers cheaper pizza (you like them equally well, so you may as well save some money).

32. While Skyview Airlines runs a little ahead of schedule (on average), it can also have long delays (late arrivals). SkyHigh Airlines on average runs slightly behind schedule, but it tends to have smaller delays. If you want to avoid the possibility of long delays, SkyHigh might be the better choice.

33. A lower standard deviation means more certainty in the return, and a lower risk.

34. Factory A has the lower average defect rate per day, but on some days, it can be expected to produce more defective chips than Factory B. The process in Factory B is more uniform and consistent, and thus one might argue that it is more reliable.

35. Batting averages are less varied today than they were in the past. Because the mean is unchanged, batting averages above .350 are less common today.

UNIT 6C

QUICK QUIZ

1. **b**. A normal distribution is symmetric with one peak, and this produces a bell-shaped curve.

2. **a**. The mean, median and mode are equal in a normal distribution.

3. **a**. Data values farther from the mean correspond to lower frequencies than those close to the mean, due to the bell-shaped distribution.

4. **c**. Since most of the workers earn minimum wage, the mode of the wage distribution is on the left, and the distribution is right-skewed.

5. **a**. Roughly 68% of data values fall within one standard deviation of the mean, and 68% is about 2/3.

6. **c**. In a normally distributed data set, 99.7% of all data fall within 3 standard deviations of the mean.

7. **a**. Note that 43 mpg is 1 standard deviation above the mean. Since 68% of the data lies within one standard deviation of the mean, the remaining 32% is farther than 1 standard deviation from the mean. The normal distribution is symmetric, so half of 32%, or 16%, lies above 1 standard deviation.

8. **c**. The z-score for 84 is $(84 - 75)/6 = 1.5$.

9. **c**. If your friend said his IQ was in the 75th percentile, it would mean his IQ is larger than 75% of the population. It is impossible to have an IQ that is larger than 102% of the population.

10. **b.** Table 6.3 shows that the percentile corresponding with a standard score of –0.60 is 27.43%.

DOES IT MAKE SENSE?

15. Makes sense. Physical characteristics are often normally distributed, and college basketball players are tall, though not all of them, so it makes sense that the mean is 6'3", with a standard deviation of 3" (this would put approximately 95% of the players within 5'9" to 6'9").

16. Makes sense. Physical characteristics are often normally distributed, and these statistics say that approximately 95% of babies born at Belmont are between 4.4 and 9.2 pounds (which is reasonable).

17. Does not make sense. With a mean of 6.8 pounds, and a standard deviation of 7 pounds, you would expect that a small percentage of babies would be born 2 standard deviations above the mean. But this would imply that some babies weigh more than 20.8 pounds, which is much too heavy for a newborn.

18. Does not make sense. The standard score is computed for an individual data value, not for an entire set of exams scores. Furthermore, a standard score of 75 for a particular data value would mean that value is 75 standard deviations away from the mean, which is virtually impossible (almost all data in a normally distributed data set is within 3 standard deviations of the mean).

19. Makes sense. A standard score of 2 or more corresponds to percentiles of 97.72% and higher, so while this could certainly happen, the teacher is giving out As (on the final exam) to only 2.28% of the class

20. Makes sense. If Jack is in the 50th percentile, he is taller than half of the population (to which he is being compared), and by definition, he is at the median height.

BASIC SKILLS & CONCEPTS

21. Diagrams **a** and **c** are normal, and diagram **c** has a larger standard deviation because its values are more spread out.

22. Diagrams **b** and **c** are normal, and diagram **b** has a larger standard deviation because its values are more spread out.

23. Most trains would probably leave near to their scheduled departure times, but a few could be considerably delayed, which would result in a right-skewed (and non-normal) distribution.

24. This distribution would be normal because a machine fills the bags with approximately 30 pounds of dog food, and the variation in these weights would be random, which typically results in normal distributions.

25. Random factors would be responsible for the variation seen in the distances from the bull's-eye, so this distribution would be normal.

26. There are many factors that go into the price of a pound of oranges, and this usually results in a normal distribution.

27. Exams such as the SAT are designed to produce scores that are normally distributed, and most difficult exams have scores that are similarly normally distributed.

28. Performances in athletic events are often normally distributed.

29. a. Half of any normally distributed data set lies below the mean, so 50% of the scores are less than 100.
b. Note that 120 is one standard deviation above the mean. Since 68% of the data lies within one standard deviation of the mean (between 80 and 120), half of 68%, or 34%, lies between 100 and 120. Add 34% to 50% (the answer to part **a**) to find that 84% of the scores are less than 120.
c. Note that 140 is two standard deviations above the mean. Since 95% of the data lies within two standard deviations above the mean (between 60 and 140), half of 95%, or 47.5%, lies between 100 and 140. Add 47.5% to 50% (see part **a**) to find that 97.5% of the scores are below 140.
d. Note that 60 is two standard deviations below the mean. Since 95% of the data lies within two standard deviations of the mean (between 60 and 140), 5% of the data lies outside this range. Because the normal distribution is symmetric, half of 5%, or 2.5%, lies in the lower tail below 60.
e. A sketch of the normal distribution would show that the amount of data lying above 60 is equivalent to the amount of data lying below 140, so the answer is 97.5% (see part **c**).
f. Note that 160 is three standard deviations above the mean. Since 99.7% of the data lies within three standard deviations of the mean (between 40 and 160), 0.3% of the data lies outside this range. Because the normal distribution is symmetric, half of 0.3%, or 0.15%, lies in the upper tail above 160.
g. A sketch of the normal distribution shows that the percent of data lying above 80 is equivalent to the percent lying below 120, so the answer is 84% (see part **b**).
h. The percent of data between 60 and 140 is 95%, because these are each two standard deviations from the mean.

30. a. A heart rate of 55 is one standard deviation below the mean. Since 68% of the data lies between 55 and 85, 32% lie outside that range,

which implies 16% lies below 55 (due to symmetry).

b. A heart rate of 40 is two standard deviations below the mean. Since 95% of the data lies between 40 and 100, 5% lie outside that range, which implies 2.5% lies below 40 (due to symmetry).

c. Half of 68% (or 34%) lies between 70 and 85, 50% lies below the mean of 70, so 84% of the data is less than 85.

d. Half of 95% (or 47.5%) lies between 70 and 100, and 50% lies below the mean of 70, so 97.5% of the data lies below 100.

e. This portion of the distribution is equal to the portion less than 55 because of symmetry, so the answer is 16% (see part **a**).

f. The portion of the distribution greater than 55 is equal to the portion less than 85 because of symmetry, so the answer is 84% (see part **c**).

g. The portion of the distribution more than 40 is equal to the portion less than 100 because of symmetry, so the answer is 97.5% (see part **d**).

h. Both 55 and 85 are one standard deviation from the mean, and thus 68% of the data lies between them.

31. A score of 75 is one standard deviation above the mean. Since 68% of normally distributed data lies within one standard deviation of the mean, half of 68%, or 34%, lies between 67 and 75 due to symmetry. The percent of data lying below 67 is 50%, so we add these two results to find that 84% of the scores lie below 75.

32. A score of 83 is two standard deviations above the mean. Since 95% of normally distributed data lies within two standard deviations of the mean (between 51 and 83), 5% lies outside this range. Half of 5%, or 2.5%, will be in the upper tail, above 83.

33. Subtract two standard deviations from the mean to get the cutoff score of $67 - 16 = 51$. Since 95% of the data lies within two standard deviations of the mean, 5% lies outside this range. Half of 5%, or 2.5%, will be below 51, and will fail the exam.

34. A score of 75 is one standard deviation above the mean. Since 68% of the data lies within one standard deviation of the mean (between 59 and 75), 32% of the data is outside this range. Half of 32%, or 16%, will be in the upper tail of the distribution, so 160 students will score above 75.

35. The standard score for 67 is $z = (67 - 67)/8 = 0$.

36. The standard score for 59 is $z = (59 - 67)/8 = -1$.

37. The standard score for 55 is $z = (55 - 67)/8 = -1.5$.

38. The standard score for 88 is $z = (88 - 67)/8 = 2.625$.

39. a. The data value is one standard deviation below the mean, so $z = -1$. The corresponding percentile is 15.87%.

b. $z = 1.5$, and the corresponding percentile is 93.32%.

c. $z = 2$, and the corresponding percentile is 97.72%.

40. a. $z = -0.5$, and the corresponding percentile is 30.85%.

b. $z = 1$, and the corresponding percentile is 84.13%.

c. $z = -1.9$, and the corresponding percentile is 2.87%.

41. a. The 15th percentile corresponds to a standard score of about $z = -1$, which means the data value is one standard deviation below the mean.

b. The 75th percentile corresponds to a standard score of about $z = 0.70$, which means the data value is 0.7 standard deviations above the mean.

c. The 23rd percentile corresponds to a standard score of about $z = -0.75$, which means the data value is 0.75 standard deviations below the mean.

42. a. The 69th percentile corresponds to a standard score of about $z = 0.50$, which means the data value is 0.5 standard deviations above the mean.

b. The 8th percentile corresponds to a standard score of about $z = -1.4$, which means the data value is 1.4 standard deviations below the mean.

c. The 48th percentile corresponds to a standard score of about $z = -0.05$, which means the data value is 0.05 standard deviations below the mean.

FURTHER APPLICATIONS

43. About 68% of births occur within 15 days of the mean, because this range is one standard deviation from the mean.

44. Within one month of the due date corresponds to two standard deviations on either side of the mean, which implies 95% of the births occur within one month of the mean.

45. Since 68% of births occur within 15 days of the due date, 32% occur outside this range, and half of 32%, or 16%, occur more than 15 days before the due date. It's probably a bad idea to travel that close to one's due date, because there's about a 1/6 chance of going into labor.

46. The standard score for 45 days before the due date is $z = -3$, which corresponds to a percentile of 0.13% (using the 68-95-99.7 Rule, this number is 0.15%). There would be relatively low risk in taking a trip 45 days before the due date.

47. a. The standard score is $z = (66 - 63.6)/2.5 = 0.96$, which corresponds to an approximate percentile of 83%.

b. $z = (62 - 63.6)/2.5 = -0.64$, which corresponds to an approximate percentile of 26%.

c. $z = (61.5 - 63.6)/2.5 = -0.84$, which corresponds to an approximate percentile of 20%.

d. $z = (64.7 - 63.6)/2.5 = 0.44$, which corresponds to an approximate percentile of 67%.

48. a. The standard score is $z = (275 - 268)/15 = 0.47$, which corresponds to an approximate percentile of 68%.

    b. $z = (255 - 268)/15 = -0.87$, which corresponds to an approximate percentile of 19%.

    c. $z = (280 - 268)/15 = 0.8$, which corresponds to an approximate percentile of 79%.

    d. $z = (245 - 268)/15 = -1.53$, which corresponds to an approximate percentile of 6%.

49. It is not likely because heights of eighth-graders would be normally distributed, and a standard deviation of 40 inches would imply some of the eighth graders (about 16%) are taller than 95 inches, which is preposterous.

50. Assuming the scores are out of 100, it is not likely. A standard deviation of 50 would imply some of the scores are higher than 100.

51. The 90th percentile corresponds to a z-score of about 1.3, which means a data value is 1.3 standard deviations above the mean. For the verbal portion of the GRE, this translates into a score of $469 + 1.3(120) = 625$. For the quantitative portion, it translates into a score of $597 + 1.3(148) = 789$.

52. The standard score for 600 is $z = (600 - 469)/120 = 1.09$, which corresponds to about the 86th percentile. This is the percent of students who score below 600, so the percent that score above 600 is 14%.

53. The standard score for 600 is $z = (600 - 597)/148 = 0.02$, which corresponds to about the 51st percentile. This is the percent of students who score below 600, so the percent that score above 600 is 49%.

54. The standard score for 700 is $z = (700 - 597)/148 = 0.7$, which is 0.7 standard deviations above the mean. Your verbal score would also need to be 0.7 standard deviations above the mean to be in the same percentile, which translates to a score of $469 + 0.7(120) = 553$.

55. The z-score for an 800 on the quantitative exam is $z = (800 - 597)/148 = 1.37$, or about 1.4. This corresponds to the 91.92 percentile, so about 92% score below 800, which means 8% score 800.

56. The z-score for an 800 on the verbal exam is $z = (800 - 469)/120 = 2.76$, which corresponds to an approximate percentile of 99.7%. Since 99.7% score below 800, about 0.3% score 800.

57. For the verbal exam, $z = (400 - 469)/120 = -0.575$. This is exactly between two entries on Table 6.3: $z = -0.60$, and $z = -0.55$. The percentiles corresponding to these z-scores are 27.43% and 29.12% (respectively), so about 28% score below 400. For the quantitative exam, $z = (400 - 597)/148 = -1.33$, which corresponds to an approximate percentile of 9%. Thus about 9% score below 400.

UNIT 6D

QUICK QUIZ

1. **c.** A divorce rate of 60% is statistically significant because such large variation from the national rate of 30% is not likely to occur by chance alone.

2. **b.** In order to determine whether a result is statistically significant, we must be able to compare it to a known quantity (such as the effect on a control group in this case).

3. **a.** Statistical significance at the 0.01 level means an observed difference between the effectiveness of the remedy and the placebo would occur by chance in fewer than 1 out of 100 trials of the experiment.

4. **c.** If the statistical significance is at the 0.05 level, we would expect that 1 in 20 experiments would show the pill working better than the placebo by chance alone.

5. **b.** The confidence interval is found by subtracting and adding 3% to the results of the poll (65%).

6. **c.** The central limit theorem tells us that the true proportion is within the margin of error 95% of the time.

7. **c.** The margin of error is approximately $\frac{1}{\sqrt{n}}$. Set this equal to 4% (0.04), and solve for n to find that the sample size was 625. If we quadruple the sample size to 2500, the margin of error will be approximately $\frac{1}{\sqrt{2500}} = 0.02$, or 2%.

8. **a.** The null hypothesis is often taken to be the assumption that there is no difference in the things being compared.

9. **c.** If you cannot reject the null hypothesis, the only thing you can be sure of is that you don't have evidence to support the alternative hypothesis.

10. **b.** If the difference in gas prices can be explained by chance in only 1 out of 100 experiments, you've found a result that is statistically significant at the 0.01 level.

DOES IT MAKE SENSE?

19. Makes sense. If the number of people cured by the new drug is not significantly larger than the number cured by the old drug, the difference could be explained by chance alone, which means the results are not statistically significant.

20. Does not make sense. While results significant at the 0.05 level offer some evidence that the Magic Diet Pill works, we cannot remove all doubt that the results came about by chance alone.

21. Does not make sense. The margin of error is based upon the number of people surveyed (the sample size), and thus both Agency A and B should have the same margin of error.

22. Makes sense. The margin of error is based upon the number of people surveyed (the sample size), and because it is approximately $\frac{1}{\sqrt{n}}$, it decreases as n increases.

23. Makes sense. The alternative hypothesis is the claim that is accepted if the null hypothesis is rejected.

24. Does not make sense. One cannot prove the null hypothesis – it can be rejected, in which case there is evidence for the alternative hypothesis, or we can not reject it, which only means we do not have evidence to support the alternative hypothesis.

BASIC SKILLS & CONCEPTS

25. Most of the time you would expect around 25 tails in 50 tosses of a coin. It would be very rare to get only 3 tails, and thus this is statistically significant.

26. Most of the time you would expect around 50 heads in 100 tosses of a coin, and since 52 is well within the bounds of what would be expected by chance alone, this is not statistically significant.

27. Note that 11/200 is about 5% – this is exactly what you would expect by chance alone from an airline that has 95% of its flights on time.

28. Note that 50/250 is 20% – this is much larger than the 5% you would expect if 95% of the flights were on time, so this is statistically significant.

29. There aren't many winners in the Power Ball lottery, and yet there are a good number of 7-11 stores. It would be very unlikely that ten winners in a row purchased their tickets at the same store, so this is statistically significant.

30. The likelihood of 42 people in a group of 45 all sharing the same birthday is extremely small, so this is statistically significant.

31. The result is significant at far less than the 0.01 level (which means it is significant at both the 0.01 and 0.05 level), because the probability of finding the stated results is less than 1 in 1 million by chance alone. This gives us good evidence to support the alternative hypothesis that the accepted value for temperature is wrong.

32. This result is significant at the 1/10,000 = 0.0001 level, so it is significant at both the 0.01 and 0.05 levels. Because chance alone does not do a good job of explaining the difference found in length of hospital stays, it would be reasonable to conclude that seat belts reduce the severity of injuries (assuming that the severity of injury is directly correlated with length of hospital stay).

33. The results of the study are significant at neither the 0.05 level nor the 0.01 level, and thus the improvement is not statistically significant.

34. The difference found in the weights would be expected by chance alone in only 1 out of 100 such surveys.

35. The margin of error is $1/\sqrt{1012} = 0.03$, or 3%, and the 95% confidence interval is 29% to 35%. This means we can be 95% confident that the actual percentage is between 29% and 35%.

36. The margin of error is $1/\sqrt{2085} = 0.02$, or 2%, and the 95% confidence interval is 71% to 75%. This means we can be 95% confident that the actual percentage is between 71% and 75%.

37. The margin of error is $1/\sqrt{1002} = 0.03$, or 3%, and the 95% confidence interval is 27% to 33% for the satisfied group, and 64% to 70% for the dissatisfied group.

38. The margin of error is $1/\sqrt{1013} = 0.03$, or 3%, and the 95% confidence interval is 39% to 45%.

39. The margin of error is $1/\sqrt{1003} = 0.03$, or 3%, and the 95% confidence interval is 45% to 51%.

40. The margin of error is $1/\sqrt{2818} = 0.02$, or 2%, and the 95% confidence intervals are 71% to 75% and 49% to 53%.

41. The margin of error is $1/\sqrt{2435} = 0.02$, or 2%, and the 95% confidence intervals are 15% to 19% and 12% to 16%.

42. The margin of error is $1/\sqrt{1229} = 0.03$, or 3%, and the 95% confidence intervals are 25% to 31% and 12% and 18%.

43. a. Null hypothesis: percentage of high school graduates = 85%. Alternative hypothesis: percentage of high school students > 85%.
    b. Rejecting the null hypothesis means there is evidence that the percentage of high school graduates exceeds 85%. Failing to reject the null hypothesis means there is insufficient evidence to conclude that the percentage of high school graduates exceeds 85%.

44. a. Null hypothesis: vitamin C in tablets = 500 mg. Alternate hypothesis: vitamin C in tablets < 500 mg.
    b. Rejecting the null hypothesis means that there is evidence that the tablets contain less than 500 mg. Failing to reject the null hypothesis means there is insufficient evidence to conclude that the tablets contain less than 500 mg.

45. a. Null hypothesis: mean teacher salary = $47,750. Alternative hypothesis: mean teacher salary > $47,750.
    b. Rejecting the null hypothesis means there is evidence that the mean teacher salary in the state exceeds $47,750. Failing to reject the null hypothesis means there is insufficient evidence to conclude that the mean teacher salary exceeds $47,750.

46. a. Null hypothesis: water usage = 1675 gallons per month. Alternative hypothesis: water usage > 1675 gallons per month.
    b. Rejecting the null hypothesis means there is evidence that the water usage exceeds 1675 gallons per month. Failing to reject the null hypothesis means there is insufficient evidence to conclude that water usage exceeds 1675 gallons per month.

47. a. Null hypothesis: percentage of underrepresented students = 20%. Alternative hypothesis: percentage of underrepresented students < 20%.
    b. Rejecting the null hypothesis means there is evidence that the percentage of underrepresented students is less than 20%. Failing to reject the null hypothesis means there is insufficient evidence to conclude that the percentage of underrepresented students is less than 20%.

48. a. Null hypothesis: pollution levels = EPA minimum. Alternative hypothesis: pollution levels < EPA minimum.
    b. Rejecting the null hypothesis means there is evidence that the pollution levels are less than the EPA minimum. Failing to reject the null hypothesis means there is insufficient evidence to conclude that the pollution levels are less than the EPA minimum.

49. Null hypothesis: mean annual mileage of cars in the fleet = 11,725 miles. Alternative hypothesis: mean annual mileage of cars in the fleet > 11,725. The result is significant at the 0.01 level, and provides good evidence for rejecting the null hypothesis.

50. Null hypothesis: proportion of supporting voters = 0.5. Alternative hypothesis: proportion of supporting voters > 0.5. The result is not significant at the 0.05 level, and there are no grounds for rejecting the null hypothesis.

51. Null hypothesis: mean stay = 2.1 days. Alternative hypothesis: mean stay > 2.1 days. The result is not significant at the 0.05 level, and there are no grounds for rejecting the null hypothesis.

52. Null hypothesis: mean gas mileage = 21.4 miles per gallon. Alternative hypothesis: mean gas mileage < 21.4 miles per gallon. The result is significant at the 0.01 level, and provides good evidence for rejecting the null hypothesis.

53. Null hypothesis: mean income = $40,000. Alternative hypothesis: mean income > $40,000. The result is significant at the 0.01 level, and provides good evidence for rejecting the null hypothesis.

54. Null hypothesis: mean ownership = 7.5 years. Alternative hypothesis: mean ownership < 7.5 years. The result is not significant at the 0.05 level, and there are no grounds for rejecting the null hypothesis.

FURTHER APPLICATIONS

55. The margin of error is $1/\sqrt{13,000} = 0.009$, or 0.9%, and the 95% confidence interval is 64.1% to 65.9%. This means we can be 95% confident that the actual percentage of viewers who watched *American Idol* was between 64.1% and 65.9%.

56. The margin of error is $1/\sqrt{1400} = 0.027$, or 2.7%, and the 95% confidence interval is 77.3% to 82.7%. This means we can be 95% confident that the actual percentage of athletes hazed was between 77.3% and 82.7%.

57. The margin of error is approximately $1/\sqrt{n}$. If we want to decrease the margin of error by a factor of 2, we must increase the sample size by a factor of 4, because $\dfrac{1}{\sqrt{4n}} = \dfrac{1}{2\sqrt{n}} = \dfrac{1}{2} \cdot \dfrac{1}{\sqrt{n}}$.

58. The margin of error is approximately $1/\sqrt{n}$. If we want to decrease the margin of error by a factor of 10, we must increase the sample size by a factor of 100, because $\dfrac{1}{\sqrt{100n}} = \dfrac{1}{10\sqrt{n}} = \dfrac{1}{10} \cdot \dfrac{1}{\sqrt{n}}$.

59. The margin of error, 3%, is consistent with the sample size because $1/\sqrt{1019} = 0.03 = 3\%$.

UNIT 7A

QUICK QUIZ

1. **b**. HHT is a different outcome than HTH due to the order in which the heads appear, but both are the same event because each has two heads.

2. **b**. This is a probability based on observations about the number of free throws Shawna attempted and made, and so it is empirical.

3. **a**. This is a theoretical probability because we are assuming each outcome is equally likely, and no experiment is being carried out to determine the probability.

4. **c**. If the probability of an event is $P(A)$, the probability it does not occur is $1 - P(A)$.

5. **b**. Table 7.3 shows that the probability Mackenzie wins is 5/36, whereas the probability that Serena wins is 4/36.

6. **c**. There are six possible outcomes for each of the four dice, and the multiplication principle says we multiply these outcomes together to get the total number of outcomes when all four dice are rolled.

7. **b**. The lowest sum that could occur when four dice are rolled is 4, and the highest is 24, and every sum in between is possible.

8. **a**. The sum of all the probabilities for a probability distribution is always 1.

9. **a**. If Triple Treat's probability of winning is 1/4, then the probability he loses is 3/4. This implies the odds that he wins is $(1/4) \div (3/4)$, or 1 to 3, which, in turn, means the odds against are 3 to 1.

10. **c**. The most likely outcome when a coin is tossed several times is that half of the time heads will appear.

DOES IT MAKE SENSE?

17. Makes sense. The outcomes are HTTT, THTT, TTHT, TTTH.

18. Does not make sense. The probability of any event is always between 0 and 1.

19. Makes sense. This is a subjective probability, but it's as good as any other guess one might make.

20. Does not make sense. The two outcomes in question are not equally likely.

21. Does not make sense. The sum of $P(A)$ and $P(\text{not } A)$ is always 1.

22. Makes sense. This is the method we use to compute empirical probabilities.

BASIC SKILLS & CONCEPTS

23. There are $12 \times 3 = 36$ choices.

24. There are $8 \times 6 \times 7 = 336$ packages.

25. There are $4 \times 6 \times 10 \times 12 = 2880$ systems.

26. Assuming each district elects exactly one representative, there are $2 \times 3 \times 4 = 24$ possible commissions.

27. There are $28 \times 4 = 112$ combinations.

28. There are $4 \times 3 \times 5 \times 2 \times 3 = 360$ sets.

29. There are $10 \times 5 \times 8 = 400$ systems.

30. There are $2 \times 2 \times 2 \times 8 = 64$ versions.

31. There are 4 kings in a standard deck, so the probability is $4/52 = 1/13$. We are assuming that each card is equally likely to be chosen.

32. There are 26 red cards, so the probability is $26/52 = 1/2$. We are assuming each card is equally likely to be chosen.

33. The probability is $2/6 = 1/3$. We are assuming equally likely outcomes.

34. There are $6 \times 6 = 36$ possible outcomes, and 3 of these sum to 4 (see Table 7.3), so the probability is $3/36 = 1/12$. It is assumed that each outcome is equally likely to occur.

35. There are 12 royalty cards, so the probability is $12/52 = 3/13$. It is assumed that each card is equally likely to be chosen.

36. There are 3 odd numbers on a die, so the probability is $3/6 = 1/2$. We are assuming equally likely outcomes.

37. The probability is $2/52 = 1/26$ because there are 2 black jacks. We are assuming equally likely outcomes.

38. There are 6 ways to get the same number on both dice, and 36 possible outcomes, so the probability is $6/36 = 1/6$. It is assumed that all outcomes are equally likely.

39. There are ten possible outcomes for the last digit in a phone number, and one of these is a 5, so the probability is 1/10. It is assumed that each digit is equally likely to occur at the end of a phone number.

40. The probability is 1/7, assuming that births are uniformly distributed over the days of the week.

41. There are 4 possible outcomes (BB, BG, GB, GG), and one of these consists of two boys, so the probability is 1/4. This assumes each outcome is equally likely.

42. Assuming that people are equally likely to be born during any hour of the day, the probability is 1/24.

43. There are 8 possible outcomes with a 3-child family (BBB, BBG, BGB, GBB, GGB, GBG, BGG, GGG), and 3 of these have exactly one boy, so the probability is 3/8. This assumes each outcome is equally likely to occur.

44. The probability is 1/4, assuming each answer is equally likely to be the correct one.

45. There are 22 pairs of socks, and 8 are white, so the probability is $8/22 = 4/11$, assuming that each pair of socks is equally likely to be chosen.

46. There are 12 months in the year, so the probability is 1/12, assuming births are uniformly distributed across the months of the year.

47. Your address ends in one of ten digits, and the probability that a randomly selected person has the same ending digit is 1/10. This assumes that each digit is as likely as the others to be at the end of an address, and it assumes that addresses end in digits.

48. You will wait longer than 15 minutes if you arrive at any of the first 15 minutes of a given half hour (30 minutes), so the probability is 15/30 = 1/2. This assumes your arrival times are uniformly distributed across any given half-hour.

49. The probability is 18/30 = 3/5 = 0.6.

50. The probability is 1/100 = 0.01.

51. The probability is 76% = 0.6.

52. The probability of a head is 42/100, so the probability of a tail is 58/100 = 0.58.

53. The probability is 225/250 = 0.9.

54. The probability is 1/200 = 0.05.

55. Answers will vary.

56. Answers will vary.

57. The probability is 5/6, because there are 5 outcomes that aren't 6s. It is assumed that each outcome is equally likely.

58. There are 8 possible outcomes when 3 heads are tossed (HHH, HHT, HTH, THH, TTH, THT, HTT, TTT), and only one of them consists of all 3 heads. Thus the probability of tossing 3 heads is 1/8, and the probability of not tossing 3 heads is 1 − 1/8 = 7/8. Equally likely outcomes are assumed.

59. The probability he will make the next free throw is 86% = 0.86, so the probability he will miss is 1 − 0.86 = 0.14, or 14%. The probabilities computed here are based on his past performance.

60. The probability that the next person you meet was born on a Sunday is 1/7 (assuming each day is equally likely), so the probability that the person was not born on a Sunday is 1 − 1/7 = 6/7.

61. The probability of rolling a sum of 7 is 6/36 (see Table 7.3), so the probability of not rolling a sum of 7 is 1 − 6/36 = 30/36 = 5/6. Equally likely outcomes are assumed.

62. The probability is 100% − 40% = 60% = 0.6. This answer assumes that "not rain" means "sunny day" (rather than, say, a cloudy day with no rain), and it assumes the subjective/empirical probability of rain is a reasonable prediction.

63. The probability of having a 100-year flood is 1/100, so the probability of not having one is 1 − 1/100 = 99/100 = 0.99. This assumes that each year the probability of a 100-year flood is 1/100.

64. The probability of meeting someone born in May or June is 2/12, so the probability that this does not

occur is 1 − 2/12 = 10/12 = 5/6. This assumes births are uniformly distributed across the year.

65.

Result	Probability
0 H	1/16
1 H	4/16
2 H	6/16
3 H	4/16
4 H	1/16

66.

Sum	Probability
2	1/16
3	2/16
4	3/16
5	4/16
6	3/16
7	2/16
8	1/16

67. The probability of getting a 1 or a 2 is 2/6 = 1/3, and the probability of not getting a 1 or a 2 is 2/3. Thus the odds for the event are (1/3) ÷ (2/3) = 1 to 2, and the odds against are 2 to 1.

68. The probability of getting two tails is 1/4, so the probability of not getting two tails is 3/4. Thus the odds for the event are (1/4) ÷ (3/4) = 1 to 3, and the odds against are 3 to 1.

69. This problem is similar to exercise 67, except that we are focusing on getting a 5 or a 6 (instead of a 1 or a 2) – the probabilities and odds remain the same. Thus the odds for the event are 1 to 2, and odds against are 2 to 1.

70. The probability of getting a head and a tail is 2/4 = 1/2, and the probability of not getting a head and a tail is 1/2. Thus the odds for the event are (1/2) ÷ (1/2) = 1 to 1, and the odds against are 1 to 1.

71. Since the odds on your bet are 3 to 4, you'll win $3 for every $4 you bet. A $20 bet is five $4 bets, so you will gain $15.

72. Since the odds on your bet are 5 to 4, you'll win $5 for every $4 you bet. A $20 bet is five $4 bets, so you will gain $25.

FURTHER APPLICATIONS

73. a. There are 52 women at the convention, so the probability a random delegate is a woman is 52/100 = 0.52.

b. There are 10 Independents, so the probability is 10/100 = 0.1.

c. There are 41 Democrats, and thus 59 non-Democrats, which means the probability is 59/100 = 0.59.

d. There are 21 female Republicans, so the probability is 21/100 = 0.21.

e. There are 16 male Democrats, so the probability you meet one is 16/100 = 0.16. Thus the probability that you meet a someone who is not a male Democrat is 1 – 0.16 = 0.84.

74. The probability in 2006 is 37 million ÷ 299 million = 0.12, and the probability in 2050 is 82 million ÷ 404 million = 0.20. Thus the probability is greater in 2050.

75. The empirical probabilities for 0 heads, 1 head, 2 heads, and 3 heads are (respectively): 260/1000 = 0.26, 495/1000 = 0.495, 245/1000 = 0.245, and 0/1000 = 0.0. The 8 possible outcomes when 3 coins are tossed are (HHH, HHT, HTH, THH, TTH, THT, HTT, TTT), and thus the theoretical probabilities for 0 heads, 1 head, 2 heads, and 3 heads are (respectively): 1/8 = 0.125, 3/8 = 0.375, 3/8 = 0.375, and 1/8 = 0.125. The differences between the empirical and theoretical probabilities are large enough to suspect that the coins are unfair.

76. The probability, as shown in the table, is 4.5% = 0.045. The table already *is* a probability distribution: it shows the probabilities (expressed as percents) that a randomly selected person will be in each of the categories.

77. The odds for event *A* are (0.99) ÷ (0.01) = 99 to 1, and the odds for event *B* are (0.96) ÷ (0.04) = 24 to 1. The odds for *A* are much higher, even though the probabilities for *A* and *B* are relatively close to one another.

UNIT 7B

QUICK QUIZ

1. **c.** The probability of getting a double-2 on at least one of the rolls is $1 - (35/36)^2$.

2. **c.** The rule works only when *A* and *B* are independent events.

3. **b.** The probability of choosing a pink rose on the second pick is dependent upon what happens on the first pick (because there will be fewer roses in the vases).

4. **c.** Since these are dependent events, the rule *P(A* and *B* and *C)* = *P(A) P(B* given *A) P(C* given *A* and *B)* must be used.

5. **c.** A person can be born on both a Wednesday and in July, so the events are overlapping.

6. **c.** *P*(5 or 6 or 7 or 8) = *P*(5) + *P*(6) + *P*(7) + *P*(8) = 4/36 + 5/36 + 6/36 + 5/36 = 20/36 > 0.5.

7. **a.** Since these events are independent, we have *P(sum of* 3 and *sum of* 4) = *P(sum of* 3) × *P(sum of* 4) = 2/36 × 3/36.

8. **b.** The probability of getting at least one success in ten trials of the experiment is 1 – [*P*(not two heads)]^{10}, so you need first to compute the probability of not two heads.

9. **c.** This answer shows the correct application of the *at least once* rule.

10. **c.** This answer shows the correct application of the *at least once* rule.

DOES IT MAKE SENSE?

15. Makes sense. You can't get both heads and tails on a single flip of a coin, but you must get one or the other.

16. Does not make sense. The events of flipping a coin several times in a row are independent, and thus the outcome of the first three do not affect the result of the fourth flip.

17. Does not make sense. The probability of drawing an ace or a spade is 16/52, but the probability of drawing the ace of spades is 1/52.

18. Does not make sense. The numbers in a lottery are randomly chosen, and each outcome is as equally likely (or equally unlikely) as the others.

19. Does not make sense. The chance of getting at least one 5 is $1 - (5/6)^3 \neq 3/6$.

20. Makes sense. The calculation described is a correct application of the *at least once* rule.

BASIC SKILLS & CONCEPTS

21. The events are independent. *P*(6 and 6 and 1 and 1) = *P*(6) × *P*(6) × *P*(1) × *P*(1) = $(1/6)^4$ = 1/1296.

22. The events are independent. *P(ace* and *ace* and *ace)* = *P(ace)* × *P(ace)* × *P(ace)* = $(4/52)^3$ = 1/2197.

23. The events are dependent. *P(A₁* and *A₂* and *A₃)* = *P(A₁)* × *P(A₂* given *A₁)* × *P(A₃* given *A₁* and *A₂)* = (4/52) × (3/51) × (2/50) = 0.00018.

24. The events are independent. Because the probability of rolling an odd result is the same on each throw (1/2), the probability of getting an odd result on all four dice is $(1/2)^4$ = 1/16.

25. The events are independent. Because the probability of rolling a 6 is the same on each throw (1/6), the probability of getting all 6s is $(1/6)^3 = 1/216 = 0.0046$.

26. The events are independent. This is similar to exercise 22, with an answer of $(13/52)^3 = 1/64$.

27. The events are dependent. This is similar to exercise 23, with an answer of $(13/52) \times (12/51) \times (11/50) = 0.0129$.

28. The events are dependent. This is also similar to exercise 23, with an answer of $(26/52) \times (25/51) \times (24/50) \times (23/49) \times (22/48) = 0.0253$.

29. The events are most likely independent (there may be some situations where one could argue dependence, such as the case where a woman gives birth to quintuplets, and these happen to be the next five births – but we can't solve the problem without assuming independence). Assuming the probability of giving birth to a girl is 1/2, the answer is $(1/2)^5 = 1/32$.

30. The events are independent. The probability of all four tickets being winners is $(1/8)^4 = 1/4096$.

31. The events are dependent. The probability is $(18/30) \times (17/29) \times (16/28) \times (15/27) = 0.1117$.

32. The events are dependent, and the probability is $(15/30) \times (14/29) \times (13/28) \times (12/27) \times (11/26) \times (10/25) = 0.0084$.

33. The events are independent. The probability is $(1/12)^3 = 1/1728 = 0.00058$.

34. The events are independent for all practical purposes, because the batch from which the chips are chosen is large. The probability is $(0.98)^3 = 0.9412$.

35. The events are independent for all practical purposes (as long as the student population is large). The probability is $(1/12)^3 = 1/1728$.

36. The events may be independent, and we'll have to assume as much to solve the problem. The probability is $(0.20)^4 = 0.0016$.

37. The events are non-overlapping. $P(red\ 6\ or\ black\ 8) = P(red\ 6) + P(black\ 8) = 2/52 + 2/52 = 1/13$.

38. The events are non-overlapping. $P(6\ or\ 8) = P(6) + P(8) = 5/36 + 5/36 = 5/18 = 0.278$.

39. The events are non-overlapping. $P(2\ or\ 3\ or\ 4) = P(2) + P(3) + P(4) = 1/36 + 2/36 + 3/36 = 1/6$.

40. The events are overlapping. $P(Q\ or\ club) = P(Q) + P(club) - P(Q\ and\ club) = 4/52 + 13/52 - 1/52 = 16/52 = 4/13$.

41. The events are non-overlapping. $P(Q\ or\ K) = P(Q) + P(K) = 4/52 + 4/52 = 2/13$.

42. The events are overlapping. $P(\#\ or\ diamond) = P(\#) + P(diamond) - P(\#\ and\ diamond) = 36/52 + 13/52 - 9/52 = 40/52 = 10/13$.

43. The events are overlapping. The probability is $1/6 + 3/6 - 1/6 = 3/6 = 1/2$.

44. The events are non-overlapping. The probability is $1/6 + 3/6 = 4/6 = 2/3$.

45. The events are overlapping. $P(W\ or\ R) = P(W) + P(R) - P(W\ and\ R) = 70/100 + 60/100 - 40/100 = 90/100 = 0.9$.

46. The events are overlapping. $P(M\ or\ A) = P(M) + P(A) - P(M\ and\ A) = 40/100 + 30/100 - 10/100 = 60/100 = 0.6$.

47. The events are non-overlapping. The easiest way to solve the problem is to look at the set of possible outcomes for a three child family, (GGG, GGB, GBG, BGG, BBG, BGB, GBB, BBB), and count the number of outcomes with either 1 or 2 girls. The probability is 6/8 = 3/4. One could also use the formulas for *or* probabilities.

48. The events are overlapping, and the probability is $18/34 + 12/34 - 6/34 = 24/34 = 12/17$.

49. The probability of not getting a 3 on a single roll is 5/6, so $P(\text{at least one } 3) = 1 - (5/6)^4 = 0.518$.

50. The probability of not getting a 6 on a single roll is 5/6, so $P(\text{at least one } 6) = 1 - (5/6)^6 = 0.665$.

51. $P(\text{at least one } 2) = 1 - (5/6)^3 = 0.421$.

52. $P(\text{at least one } H) = 1 - (1/2)^8 = 0.996$.

53. $P(\text{at least one ace}) = 1 - (48/52)^{10} = 0.551$.

54. $P(\text{at least one ace}) = 1 - (48/52)^{30} = 0.909$.

55. $P(\text{rain at least once}) = 1 - (0.80)^5 = 0.672$.

56. $P(\text{rain at least once}) = 1 - (0.90)^{10} = 0.651$.

57. $P(\text{at least one flu encounter}) = 1 - (0.96)^{10} = 0.335$.

58. $P(\text{at least one lefty}) = 1 - (0.89)^5 = 0.442$.

59. $P(\text{at least one ticket}) = 1 - (0.7)^5 = 0.832$.

60. $P(\text{at least one false test}) = 1 - (0.97)^{10} = 0.263$.

FURTHER APPLICATIONS

61. a. $P(G\ or\ P) = P(G) + P(P) - P(G\ and\ P) = 956/1028 + 450/1028 - 392/1028 = 0.986$.
    b. $P(NG\ or\ NP) = P(NG) + P(NP) - P(NG\ and\ NP) = 72/1028 + 578/1028 - 14/1028 = 0.619$.

62. a. The probability is 100/300 + 120/300 = 220/300 = 0.733.
    b. The probability is 80/300 + 145/300 – 50/300 = 175/300 = 0.583.
    c. The probability is 50/300 = 0.167.
    d. The probability is 50/145 = 0.345.
    e. The probability is 50/80 = 0.625.
    f. Yes, the drug appears to have some effect because the improvement rate for people who took the drug (50/80) is greater than both the improvement rate for the placebo group (55/100) and the control group (40/120).

63. a. These events are dependent because there are fewer people to choose from on the second and subsequent calls, and this affects the probability that a Republican is chosen.
    b. $P(R_1\ and\ R_2) = P(R_1) \times P(R_2\ given\ R_1) = (25/45) \times (24/44) = 0.303$.
    c. If the events are treated as independent, then the pollster is selecting a person from random and not

crossing that person off the list of candidates for the second call. The probability of selecting two Republicans is then $P(R_1 \text{ and } R_2) = P(R_1) \times P(R_2)$ $= (25/45) \times (25/45) = 0.309$.

d. The probabilities are nearly the same. This is due to the fact that the list of names is large, and removing one person from the list before making the second call doesn't appreciably change the probability that a Republican will be chosen.

64. $P(\text{AA}) = 1/4$; $P(\text{Aa}) = 1/2$; $P(\text{aa}) = 1/4$. The probability that the child will have the dominant trait is 3/4, and the probability for the recessive trait is 1/4.

65. The probability of winning would be $1 - (35/36)^{25} = 0.506$. Since this is larger than 50%, he should come out ahead over time.

66. a. These events are non-overlapping, so the probability is $1/10 + 1/50 + 1/500 = 0.122$. This is not much larger than the probability of getting only a \$2 winner (1/10) because the other probabilities are so low they don't contribute much to the overall probability.

   b. $P(\text{at least one \$5 winner}) = 1 - (49/50)^{50} = 0.636$.

   c. $P(\text{at least one \$10 winner}) = 1 - (499/500)^{500} = 0.632$.

67. a. The probability is 1/20.

   b. $P(H_1 \text{ and } H_2) = P(H_1) \times P(H_2) = (1/20) \times (1/20) = 1/400 = 0.0025$.

   c. $P(\text{at least one hurricane}) = 1 - (19/20)^{10} = 0.401$.

68. a. $P(\text{at least one HIV}) = 1 - (0.97)^{10} = 0.263$.

   b. $P(\text{at least one HIV}) = 1 - (0.97)^{20} = 0.456$.

UNIT 7C

QUICK QUIZ

1. **b**. The law of large numbers says that the proportion of years should be close to the probability of a hurricane on a single year (and $100/1000 = 0.1$).

2. **c**. The expected value is $-\$1 \times 1 + \$75 \text{ million} \times 1/100,000,000 = -\$0.25$.

3. **c**. If you purchase 1/10 of the available number of lottery tickets, there's a 1 in 10 chance that you have the winning ticket. But this means that 90% of the time you have purchased 1 million losing tickets.

4. **c**. The expected value can be understood as the average value of the game over many trials.

5. **b**. The expected value of a \$2000 fire insurance policy from the point of view of the insurance company is $\$2000 \times 1 + (-\$100,000) \times 1/50 = 0$,

so they can expect to lose money if they charge less than \$2000 per policy.

6. **a**. The shortcut saves 5 minutes 90% of the time, but it loses 20 minutes 10% of the time.

7. **c**. The results of the previous five games have no bearing on the outcome of the next game.

8. **c**. The results of the previous five games have no bearing on the next game.

9. **c**. In order to compute the probability of winning on any single trial, you would need to know the probability of winning on each of the various payouts.

10. **c**. 97% of \$10 million is \$9.7 million, which leaves \$300,000 in profit for the casino (over the long haul).

DOES IT MAKE SENSE?

17. Makes sense. An organization holding a raffle usually wants to raise money, which means the expected value for purchasers of raffle tickets will be negative.

18. Does not make sense. The expected value comes into play for large increases in sales.

19. Does not make sense. Each of the 16 possible outcomes when four coins are tossed is equally likely.

20. Does not make sense. The slot machine doesn't remember what happened on the previous 25 pulls, and your probability of winning remains the same for each pull.

21. Does not make sense. The slot machine doesn't remember what happened on the previous 25 pulls, and your probability of winning remains the same for each pull.

22. Does not make sense. You lost \$750 because roulette is a losing proposition (for players, and over the long haul). If you keep playing, it's most likely that you'll continue to lose.

BASIC SKILLS & CONCEPTS

23. You should not expect to get exactly 5000 heads (the probability of that happening is quite small), but you should expect to get a result near to 5000 heads. The law of large numbers says that the proportion of a large number of coin tosses that result in heads is near to the probability of getting heads on a single toss. Since the probability of getting heads is 1/2, you can expect that around one-half of the 10,000 tosses will result in heads.

24. The phrase means that over the long run, the person will most likely get a traffic citation. While it is true that the probability of getting a traffic citation for a single instance of speeding is low, it is also true that the probability of getting at least

one citation (or perhaps several) is rather high over many instances of speeding.

25. The probability of tossing three heads is 1/8, and that of not tossing three heads is 7/8. Thus the expected value of the game is $6 × 1/8 + (−$1) × 7/8 = −$0.125. Though one can assign a probability to the outcome of a single game, the result cannot be predicted, so you can't be sure whether you will win or lose money in one game. However, over the course of 100 games, the law of averages comes into play, and you can expect to lose money.

26. The expected value is $10 × 1/8 + (−$1) × 7/8 = $0.375 (see exercise 25). The outcome of one game cannot be predicted, though over 100 games, you should expect to win.

27. The probability of rolling two even numbers is 9/36 = 1/4 (of the 36 possible outcomes, 9 are "two even numbers"), and the probability of not rolling two even numbers is 27/36 = 3/4. Thus the expected value is $2 × 1/4 + (−$1) × 3/4 = −$0.25. The outcome of one game cannot be predicted, though over 100 games, you should expect to lose.

28. The probability of rolling doubles is 6/36 = 1/6 (of the 36 possible outcomes, 6 are "doubles"), and the probability of not rolling doubles is 30/36 = 5/6. Thus the expected value is $10 × 1/6 + (−$1) × 5/6 = $0.83. The outcome of one game cannot be predicted, though over 100 games, you should expect to win.

29. The expected value for a single policy is $800 × 1 + (−$10,000) × 1/50 + (−$20,000) × 1/100 + (−$50,000) × 1/250 = $200. The company can expect a profit of $200 × 10,000 = $2 million.

30. The expected value for a single policy is $500 × 1 + (−$5000) × 1/50 + (−$10,000) × 1/100 + (−$30,000) × 1/200 = $150. The company can expect a profit of $150 × 10,000 = $1.5 million.

31. For the sake of simplicity, assume that you arrive on the half-minute for each minute of the hour (that is, you arrive 30 seconds into the first minute of the hour, 30 seconds into the second minute of the hour, etc.). The probability that you arrive in any given minute in the first half-hour is 1/30, and your wait times (in minutes) for the first 30 minutes are 29.5, 28.5, 27.5, … , 0.5. Thus your expected wait time is 29.5 × 1/30 + 28.5 × 1/30 + 27.5 × 1/30 + … + 0.5 × 1/30 = 15 minutes. Of course the same is true for the second half-hour. (Note for instructors: if you wanted to allow for arrival at *any* time during a given minute, you would need to use calculus in order to solve the problem with any level of rigor, because the wait time function is continuous).

32. a. The probability that you will arrive between noon and 12:20 is 1/3 (because 20 minutes is one-third of an hour). Using a process similar to exercise 31, the mean waiting time is 10 minutes. (This is also the expected value for the wait time in the first 20 minutes as expected value is just a weighted mean – when the weights, or probabilities, are all the same, it is the mean).
b. Similar to part **a** and exercise 31, the probability that you arrive between 12:20 and 1:00 is 2/3, and the mean waiting time is 20 minutes.
c. The expected value for the wait time over the entire hour is 10 × 1/3 + 20 × 2/3 = 16.67 minutes.
d. The expected waiting time would be shorter, as shown in exercise 31.

33. a. Heads came up 46% of the time, and you've lost $8.
b. Yes, the increase in heads is consistent with the law of large numbers: the more often the coin is tossed, the more likely the percentage of heads is closer to 50%. Since 47% of 300 is 141, there have been 141 heads and 159 tails, and you are now behind $18.
c. You would need 59 heads in the next 100 tosses (so that the total number of heads would be 200) in order to break even. While it's possible to get 59 heads in 100 tosses, a number nearer to 50 is more likely.
d. If you decide to keep playing, the most likely outcome is that half of the time you'll see heads, and half the time you'll see tails, which means you'll still be behind.

34. a. You have lost $10.
b. You lost $6 in the second one hundred rolls, so you have now lost $16.
c. In the next 300 rolls, you lose $4, which means you are down $20.
d. You would need to roll 60 even numbers in the next 100 rolls in order to break even, and this is not as likely as rolling a number of evens closer to 50.
e. The percentages were 45% (45/100), 46% (92/200), and 48% (240/500), and this illustrates the law of large numbers because the percentages are approaching 50% as the number of rolls increases.

35. a. The probability of getting heads is the same as the probability of getting tails.
b. The most likely outcome after 1000 more flips is 500 heads and 500 tails (in which case the difference would remain at 16). The distribution of the number of heads is symmetric so that any deviation from "500 heads/500 tails" is as likely to be in the upper tail as the lower tail.

c. Once you have fewer heads than tails, the most likely occurrence after additional coin tosses is that the deficit of heads remains.

36. Both sets are equally likely as each is one of many possible outcomes when six numbers are drawn.

37. The probability of getting ten heads in ten tosses is $(1/2)^{10} = 1/1024$. There are many ten-toss sequences in the 1000 tosses (991 to be precise), and you should expect, on average, one streak of ten heads in every 1024 ten-toss sequences.

38. The probability of getting three hits in a row (in three at-bats) is $(1/3)^3 = 1/27$. It's typical for a starting player to have 5 at-bats in a game, which means there are three 3-at-bat sequences in each game you play, and thus approximately 75 such 3-at-bat sequences over the course of a season. You should expect to get three hits in a row once every 27 "3-at-bat" sequences, so it's not at all unlikely to find yourself getting three hits in a row, even in a game where you come to bat only three times.

39. a. Suppose you bet $1. Then your expected value is $1 \times 0.493 + (-\$1) \times 0.507 = -\$0.014$. In general, the expected value is –1.4% of your bet, which means the house edge is 1.4% (or 1.4¢ per dollar bet).
    b. You should expect to lose $100 \times \$0.014 = \$1.40$.
    c. You should expect to lose $500 \times 1.4\% = \$7$.
    d. The casino should expect to earn 1.4% of $1 million, which is $14,000.

40. The casino earns 7¢ to the dollar, or 7%, so it will earn 7% of $100 million, which is $7 million.

FURTHER APPLICATIONS

41. The expected value is $(-\$1) \times 1 + \$30,000,000 \times 1/80,089,128 + \$100,000 \times 1/1,953,393 + \$5000 \times 1/364,042 + \$100 \times 1/8466 + \$7 \times 1/605 + \$4 \times 1/188 + \$3 \times 1/74 = -\$0.48$. You can expect to lose $365 \times \$0.48 = \$175.20$ (or, if you don't round the intermediate answer of expected value, you can expect to lose around $173.45).

42. The expected value is $(-\$1) \times 1 + \$10,000,000 \times 1/80,089,128 + \$100,000 \times 1/1,953,393 + \$5000 \times 1/364,042 + \$100 \times 1/8466 + \$7 \times 1/605 + \$4 \times 1/188 + \$3 \times 1/74 = -\$0.73$. You can expect to lose $365 \times \$0.73 = \$266.45$ (or, if you don't round the intermediate answer of expected value, you can expect to lose around $264.63).

43. The expected value is $(-\$1) \times 1 + \$5,000,000 \times 1/76,275,360 + \$150,000 \times 1/2,179,296 + \$5000 \times 1/339,002 + \$150 \times 1/9686 + \$100 \times 1/7705 + \$5 \times 1/220 + \$2 \times 1/102 + \$1 \times 1/62 = -\$0.76$. You can expect to lose $365 \times \$0.76 = \$277.40$ (or, if you don't round the intermediate

answer of expected value, you can expect to lose around $278.84).

44. The expected value is $(-\$1) \times 1 + \$20,000,000 \times 1/76,275,360 + \$150,000 \times 1/2,179,296 + \$5000 \times 1/339,002 + \$150 \times 1/9686 + \$100 \times 1/7705 + \$5 \times 1/220 + \$2 \times 1/102 + \$1 \times 1/62 = -\$0.57$. You can expect to lose $365 \times \$0.57 = \$208.05$ (or, if you don't round the intermediate answer of expected value, you can expect to lose around $207.06).

45. The expected value for 1-point kicks is $1 \times 0.94 + 0 \times 0.06 = 0.94$ points. The expected value for 2-point attempts is $2 \times 0.37 + 0 \times 0.63 = 0.74$ points. In most cases, it makes sense to take the almost certain extra-point, rather than risk a failed 2-point attempt. One situation where most coaches will go for a 2-point attempt: if your team is down by 8 points late in the game, and you score a touchdown (6 points), you don't benefit much by taking the extra point. You'll still need a field goal (3 points) to win the game. However, if you go for a 2-point attempt, you may tie the game, and send it into overtime. If you miss the 2-point attempt, you'll still be able to win the game with a field goal.

46. The expected value of age is $6.5 \times 0.184 + 19 \times 0.155 + 29.5 \times 0.129 + 39.5 \times 0.131 + 54.5 \times 0.27 + 75 \times 0.131 = 37.7$ years. The expected value is a weighted mean, and as long as the age categories are uniformly distributed (so that their midpoints are representative of the categories), the expected value will be a good approximation to the mean.

47. The expected value for the number of people in a household is $1.5 \times 0.57 + 3.5 \times 0.32 + 6 \times 0.11 = 2.6$ people. The expected value is a weighted mean, and it is a good approximation to the actual mean as long as the midpoints are representative of the categories.

48. a. The expected value for earnings is $(-\$0.37) \times 1 + \$1,000,000 \times 1/10,000,000 = -\$0.27$.
    b. You paid an extra $7 that you could have saved, so the expected value is –$7.27. (The amount you paid for the magazines is immaterial as you get a return on that investment in the form of reading material and entertainment value).

49. a. For decision 1, the expected value for option A is $1,000,000, and the expected value for option B is $2,500,000 \times 0.1 + \$1,000,000 \times 0.89 + \$0 \times 0.01 = \$1,140,000$. For decision 2, the expected value for option A is $1,000,000 \times 0.11 + \$0 \times 0.89 = \$110,000$, and the expected value for option B is $2,500,000 \times 0.1 + \$0 \times 0.9 = \$250,000$.
    b. The responses in decision 1 are not consistent with the expected values, whereas they are for decision 2.

c. For decision 1, people aren't willing to risk it all and earn nothing, and thus they chose option A – there is a huge guaranteed payback (especially for people in the 1950s) that isn't much different from the expected value of option B. For decision 2, people realize that there's little chance for gaining anything, so they may as well go for the bigger prize at the expense of a slightly lowered chance of winning it.

UNIT 7D

QUICK QUIZ

1. **a.** The accident rate will go down because the numerator of the "accident rate per mile" ratio is decreasing while the denominator is increasing.

2. **a.** The death rate per mile went down because the number of miles driven increased.

3. **b.** Though there has been some variation in the number of deaths, the number of miles driven has steadily increased, and thus the death rate has generally decreased.

4. **c.** The death rate per person is the number of deaths due to AIDS divided by the population.

5. **c.** The death rate per person is $\dfrac{105,695}{300 \text{ million}}$, and this needs to be multiplied by 100,000 to get the death rate per 100,000 people.

6. **a.** The chart shows that children in their younger years have a significant risk of death.

7. **c.** Your life expectancy decreases as you age because the number of years before you die is decreasing.

8. **c.** Current life expectancies are calculated for current conditions – if these change, life expectancies can also change.

9. **b.** The life expectancies of men are consistently below those of women (and from the graph, the gap has widened a bit in the last several decades).

10. **a.** If life expectancy goes up, people will live longer, and will draw Social Security benefits for a longer period of time.

DOES IT MAKE SENSE?

15. Does not make sense. Automobiles are successfully sold in huge quantities despite the risks involved.

16. Does not make sense. Far fewer people drive motorcycles, so one would expect the number of deaths attributed to them is smaller. The death rate per mile driven on a motorcycle is probably higher than the death rate per mile driven in a car.

17. Does not make sense. Your life expectancy is an average life expectancy for people born when you were. Much more important is your genetic makeup, and the choices you make throughout life (your diet, your line of work, the activities you choose to participate in, etc.).

18. Makes sense. A 60-year old has about 15–25 years left on the meter, whereas a 20-year old has about 60 years left (on average).

BASIC SKILLS & CONCEPTS

19. The per-mile death rate was $\dfrac{42,646}{2.9 \times 10^{12}} = 1.5 \times 10^{-8}$.

Multiply by 100 million to get 1.5 deaths per 100 million vehicle-miles.

20. The per-person rate was $\dfrac{42,646}{2.94 \times 10^{8}} = 1.45 \times 10^{-4}$.

Multiply by 100,000 to get 14.5 fatalities per 100,000 people.

21. The per-driver rate was $\dfrac{42,646}{1.98 \times 10^{8}} = 2.15 \times 10^{-4}$.

Multiply by 100,000 to get 21.5 fatalities per 100,000 drivers.

22. In 1987, the per-person fatality rate was $\dfrac{46,390}{2.42 \times 10^{8}} = 1.92 \times 10^{-4}$. Multiply this by 100,000 to get 19.2 fatalities per 100,000 people. There were 28.6 fatalities per 100,000 drivers, and 2.4 fatalities per 100 million vehicle miles (the calculations are similar). In 2000, these figures were 14.9, 22.6, and 1.5, respectively. In all three measures, the death rates declined from 1987 to 2000.

23. There were $\dfrac{22}{1.87 \times 10^{7}} \times 10^{5} = 0.12$ death per 100,000 flight hours, $\dfrac{22}{7.7 \times 10^{9}} \times 10^{9} = 2.9$ deaths per 1 billion miles flown, and $\dfrac{22}{1.07 \times 10^{7}} \times 10^{5} = 0.21$ death per 100,000 departures. There were $\dfrac{32}{1.87 \times 10^{7}} \times 10^{5} = 0.17$ accident per 100,000 flight hours, $\dfrac{32}{7.7 \times 10^{9}} \times 10^{9} = 4.2$ accidents per 1 billion miles flown, and $\dfrac{32}{1.07 \times 10^{7}} \times 10^{5} = 0.30$ accident per 100,000 departures.

24. There were $\dfrac{562}{2.44 \times 10^{7}} \times 10^{5} = 2.3$ deaths per 100,000 flight hours, and $\dfrac{1669}{2.44 \times 10^{7}} \times 10^{5} = 6.8$ accidents per 100,000 flight hours. The risks in

commercial aviation are significantly lower than in general aviation.

25. The probability of death by diabetes is 73,249 ÷ 300 million = 0.00024. Since 73,249 ÷ 34,243 = 2.1, death by diabetes is 2.1 times more likely than death by septicemia.

26. Since 105,695 ÷ 42,536 = 2.5, death by accident is 2.5 times more likely than death by kidney disease.

27. The death rate is $\frac{63,343}{3 \times 10^8} \times 10^5 = 21.1$ deaths per 100,000 people.

28. The death rate is $\frac{684,462}{3 \times 10^8} \times 10^5 = 228$ deaths per 100,000 people.

29. The death rate due to stroke is $\frac{157,803}{3 \times 10^8} \times 10^5 = 52.6$ deaths per 100,000 people, so in a city of 500,000, you would expect 52.6 × 5 = 263 people to die from a stroke each year.

30. The death rate due to pulmonary disease is $\frac{126,128}{3 \times 10^8} \times 10^5 = 42$ deaths per 100,000 people, so in a city of 500,000, you would expect 42 × 5 = 210 people to die from pulmonary disease each year.

31. The death rate for 60-year-olds is about 13 per 1000, and for 65-year-olds, it's about 20 per 1000, so the death rate for the category of 60- to 65-year-olds is about 16 deaths per 1000 people. Multiply 16/1000 by 12.6 million to find the number of people in this category expected to die in a year: $\frac{16}{1000} \times 12.6 \times 10^6 = 201,600$ people.

32. The death rate for 25- to 35-year-olds is about 2 per 1000. Multiply 2/1000 by 40 million to find the number of people in this category expected to die in a year: $\frac{2}{1000} \times 40 \times 10^6 = 80,000$ people.

33. The life expectancy for a 40-year-old is about 40 years, so the average 40-year-old can expect to live to age 80.

34. The life expectancy for an 80-year-old is about 8 years, so an average 80-year-old can expect to die at age 88.

35. The death rate for a 50-year-old is about 5 per 1000, which means the probability that a randomly selected 50-year-old will die in the next year is 5/1000. Those that don't die will file no claim; the beneficiaries of those that do will file a $50,000 claim. Thus the expected value of a single policy (from the point of view of the insurance company) is $200 × 1 + (−$50,000) × 5/1000 + ($0) × 995/1000 = −$50. The company insures 1 million 50-year-olds, and expects to lose $50 per policy, so it can expect a loss of $50 million.

36. The death rate is 3 per 1000, which means the probability that a randomly selected 40-year-old will die in the next year is 3/1000. Those that don't die will file no claim; the beneficiaries of those that do will file a $50,000 claim. Thus the expected value of a single policy (from the point of view of the insurance company) is $200 × 1 + (−$50,000) × 3/1000 + ($0) × 997/1000 = $50. The company insures 5000 people, and expects to gain $50 per policy, so it can expect a profit of $250,000.

FURTHER APPLICATIONS

37. a. In Utah, about 49,870 ÷ 365 = 137 people were born per day.
   b. In Maine, about 13,861 ÷ 365 = 38 people were born per day.
   c. The birth rate in Utah was $\frac{49,870}{2.3 \times 10^6} \times 10^3 = 21.7$ births per 1000 people.
   d. The birth rate in Maine was $\frac{13,861}{1.3 \times 10^6} \times 10^3 = 10.7$ births per 1000 people.

38. a. In California, the death rate was $\frac{235,000}{35.1 \times 10^6} \times 10^3 = 6.7$ deaths per 1000 people. In Alaska it was $\frac{2990}{640,000} \times 10^3 = 4.7$ deaths per 1000.
   b. No, the death rates for various states are dependent upon not only the number of deaths, but also the population.

39. a. There were (13.5/1000) × 300 million = 4.05 million births in the U.S.
   b. There were (8.1/1000) × 300 million = 2.43 million deaths in the U.S.
   c. The population increased by 4.05 million – 2.43 million = 1.62 million people.
   d. About 3.0 million – 1.62 million = 1.38 million people immigrated to the U.S. (this estimate neglects to account for emigration, though the number of people who emigrate from the U.S. is relatively low). The proportion of the overall population growth due to immigration was 1.38/3.0 = 46%.

40. The category of young children (ages 0–5) has had a steady ratio of boys to girls that is slightly larger than 1 – this is due to the fact that more boys are born than girls. The category of older people (ages 65+) has had a marked decline in the ration of men to women, falling well below 1 – this is due to the fact that the life expectancy for women is larger than that for men, and the gap between the two has grown over the century (see Figure 7.9). The

category of "all ages" represents the happy medium between these other two categories.

41. a. The ratio of twins to people is about 125,000 ÷ 4,00,000 = 0.031.

b. The ratio of triplets (or higher) to people is about 7,000 ÷ 4,000,000 = 0.0018.

UNIT 7E

QUICK QUIZ

1. **b.** This is an arrangement with repetition, with 36 choices at each selection.

2. **c.** Assuming each person gets one entrée, this is a permutation of 3 items taken 3 at a time, and $_3P_3 = 3!/0! = 6$.

3. **c.** The order of selection is important when counting the number of ways to arrange the roles.

4. **b.** Once the five children have been chosen, we are arranging just those five (and all five) into the various roles, and thus this is a permutation of 5 items taken 5 at a time, or $_5P_5$.

5. **b.** The number of permutation of n items taken r at a time is always at least as large as the number of combinations of n items taken r at a time (by a factor of $r!$), and $_{15}P_7 = 32,432,400$ is much larger than $_7P_7 = 5040$.

6. **c.** The variable n stands for the number of items from which you are selecting, and the variable r stands for the number of items you select. Here, $n = 9$, and $r = 4$, and thus $(n - r)! = 5!$.

7. **c.** The number of combinations of 9 items taken 4 at a time is $_9C_4 = \dfrac{9!}{(9-4)!4!} = \dfrac{9 \times 8 \times 7 \times 6}{4 \times 3 \times 2 \times 1}$.

8. **b.** If there is a drawing, the probability that one person is selected is 100%.

9. **c.** The probability that it will be you is 1/100,000 = 0.00001, so the probability it will not be you is 1 − 0.00001 = 0.99999.

10. **c.** As shown in Example 8b, the probability is about 57%.

DOES IT MAKE SENSE?

15. Makes sense. The permutations formula is used when order of selection is important.

16. Makes sense. The order in which you receive the various cards of a poker hand is immaterial (this is true, at least, for 5-card stud – there are some variations of poker where the order in which you receive your cards can affect your decision to bet, fold, etc., and thus one could argue that the order of the cards is important).

17. Makes sense. The number of such batting orders is $_{25}P_9 = 7.4 \times 10^{11}$, which is nearly 1 trillion ways. Clearly there is no hope of trying all of them.

18. Does not make sense. Perhaps it is your lucky day, but some coincidence is bound to happen – of the millions of poker hands dealt to people around the world over the last, say, 24 hours, it's likely that someone will be dealt a low-probability hand. That it happened to be you is just coincidence.

19. Makes sense. This illustrates the general principle that *some* coincidence is far more likely that a *particular* coincidence.

20. Does not make sense. The probability of winning a state lottery is so low (typically 1 in several million) that you should not expect to win, even if you played every week of your life (there are only 4171 weeks in the life span of someone who makes it to age 80).

BASIC SKILLS & CONCEPTS

21. $6! = 720$

22. $12! = 479,001,600$.

23. $5! \div 3! = 20$.

24. $10! \div 8! = 90$.

25. $\dfrac{12!}{4!3!} = 3,326,400$.

26. $\dfrac{9!}{4!2!} = 7560$.

27. $\dfrac{11!}{3!(11-3)!} = 165$.

28. $\dfrac{30!}{29!} = 30$.

29. $\dfrac{8!}{3!(8-3)!} = 56$.

30. $\dfrac{30!}{28!} = 870$.

31. $\dfrac{6!8!}{4!5!} = 10,800$.

32. $\dfrac{15!}{2!13!} = 105$.

33. This is an arrangement with repetition, where we have 10 choices (the digits 0–9) for each of 5 selections, and thus there are $10^5 = 100,000$ possible zip codes.

34. This is an arrangement with repetition, where there are 36 choices for each of 4 selections, and thus there are $36^4 = 1,679,616$ passwords.

35. This is a permutation of 36 items taken 4 at a time because the order in which the characters are arranged is important (a different order results in a different password). Thus there are $_{36}P_4 = 1,413,720$ passwords.

36. This is a permutation (of 9 items taken 3 at a time) because once three committee members are chosen, the offices which they are to hold must be determined (and different orders produce different people in the various offices). The number of such executive committees is $_9P_3 = 504$.

37. This is a permutation of 8 items taken 8 at a time, and $_8P_8 = 40,320$.

38. The order of selection does not affect whether one is chosen for the committee, so this is a combination of 9 items taken 4 at a time, and $_9C_4 = 126$.

39. Because order of selection does not matter, this is a combination of 25 items taken 6 at a time, or $_{25}C_6 = 177,100$.

40. Since every player can be assigned to any position, the order of selection matters (perhaps it determines the position played, for example), and this is a permutation of 20 items taken 6 at a time. The number of such permutations is $_{20}P_6 = 27,907,200$.

41. Order matters, so this is a permutation of 6 items taken 6 at a time, which is $_6P_6 = 720$.

42. Assuming that the order in which the card is dealt is immaterial to the hand, this is a combination of 52 items taken 3 at a time, so there are $_{52}C_3 = 22,100$ hands.

43. This is an arrangement with repetition, so use the multiplication principle to find that there are $26^3 \times 10^4 = 175,760,000$ such license plates.

44. If we assume that the order in which the balls are selected do not affect the count, this is a combination of 36 items taken 5 at a time, and there are $_{36}C_5 = 376,992$ groups of five balls.

45. This is an arrangement with repetition, so use the multiplication principle to get $9 \times 10 \times 10 \times 9 \times 10 \times 10 \times 10 \times 10 \times 10 \times 10 = 8,100,000,000$. Note that with the first digit and the fourth digit, there are only 9 choices.

46. This is a permutation of 6 items taken 6 at a time, so there are $_6P_6 = 720$ anagrams.

47. If we assume that the letters can be repeated, this is an arrangement with repetition, and there are 4 choices for each of the 3 selections, which implies there are $4^3 = 64$ different "words."

48. The order of selection does not matter, so this is the number of combinations of 15 items taken 4 at a time, which is $_{15}C_4 = 1365$ teams.

49. The order in which the songs appear matters, so this is a permutation of 13 objects taken 13 at a time, and thus there are $_{13}P_{13} = 6,227,020,800$ different ways to order the songs.

50. The order in which the dogs are selected does not affect the 3-dog family you bring home, so this is a combination of 15 items taken 3 at a time. There are $_{15}C_3 = 455$ different dog families.

51. Following Example 8 in the text, the probability that no one has your birthday is $1 - \left(\frac{364}{365}\right)^{11} = 0.0297$. The probability that at least one pair shares a birthday is given by
$$1 - \frac{364 \times 363 \times ... \times 354}{365^{11}} = 1 - \frac{1.276 \times 10^{28}}{1.532 \times 10^{28}} = 0.167 .$$

52. Following Example 8 in the text, the probability that no one has your birthday is $1 - \left(\frac{364}{365}\right)^{19} = 0.0508$. The probability that at least one pair shares a birthday is given by
$$1 - \frac{364 \times 363 \times ... \times 346}{365^{19}} = 1 - \frac{2.8402 \times 10^{48}}{4.8257 \times 10^{48}} = 0.411 .$$

FURTHER APPLICATIONS

53. a. Use the multiplication principle to get $20 \times 8 = 160$ different sundaes.

b. This is an arrangement with repetition, so there are $20^3 = 8000$ possible triple cones.

c. Since you specify the locations of the flavors, the order matters, and you should use permutations. There are $_{20}P_3 = 6840$ possibilities.

d. The order of the flavors doesn't matter, so use combinations. There are $_{20}C_3 = 1140$ possibilities.

54. a. Since there are 8 choices for the first digit, and 10 choices for each digit thereafter, there are $8 \times 10^6 = 8$ million different 7-digit phone numbers. You don't add any phone numbers to the list by affixing a single area code, so each area code represents 8 million phone numbers. This might be enough to serve a city of 2 million people. (Several factors would need to be considered before coming up with a definitive answer. Are cell phones included in the count? How many phone numbers are used by businesses and government? What about pay phones, numbers for connecting to the Internet, fax lines, help and information lines, multiple lines at homes, etc.? Also realize that the phone company probably likes to have a good percentage of unused numbers – when a number goes out of service due to a family moving away or a business closing its doors, it remains unused for many months before it is reassigned to someone else. Considering that the state of Colorado has a population of about 4.5 million people, and is served by 4 area codes, the phone company, in any case, uses one area code for roughly one million people.)

b. A single three-digit exchange represents $10^4 = 10,000$ phone numbers, which would translate into 8 exchanges for a city of 80,000 if we assumed an average of one number for every person. However, given the enormous increase in the use of cell phones, fax lines, and the like (and considering the discussion in part **a**), the phone company probably uses more than 8 exchanges for such a city. Answers will vary.

55. This problem is best solved by trial and error. For Luigi, we know that 56 is the number of combinations of n items taken 3 at a time, and thus $_nC_3 = 56$. After a little experimentation, you will discover that $n = 8$; that is, Luigi uses 8 different toppings to create 56 different 3-topping pizzas. In a similar fashion, you can discover that Ramona uses 9 different toppings (solve $_nC_2 = 36$ for n).

56. a. As long as there are no rules that restrict the use of certain digits at various locations in the zip code, there are ten choices for each digit, and thus there are $10^5 = 100,000$ five-digit zip codes.
b. There are $300,000,000 \div 100,000 = 3000$ people per zip code.
c. There are $10^9 = 1$ billion nine-digit zip codes. Since there are only 300 million people in the U.S., everyone could have a personal zip code. In fact, in some sense, everyone already does: the Social Security number.

57. There are $_{32}C_6 = 906,102$ ways to choose the balls, and only one way to match all six numbers, so the probability is 1/906,102.

58. There are $_{40}C_5 = 658,008$ ways to choose the balls, and only one way to match all five numbers, so the probability is 1/658,008.

59. There are $_{52}C_5 = 2,598,960$ five-card hands. Four of those consist of the 10, J, Q, K, and A of the same suit, so the probability is $4/2,598,960 = 1/649,740$.

60. The order of selection matters, so there are $_8P_3 = 336$ ways to order the three top teams. There's only one way to pick the correct order, and thus the probability of doing so is 1/336.

61. There are $_{16}C_3 = 560$ ways to choose the top three spellers, and only one way to guess the correct three, so the probability is 1/560.

62. There are $_{16}C_4 = 1820$ ways to choose any four students, but only $_7C_4 = 35$ ways to pick four students from Ohio. Thus the probability is $35/1820 = 1/52 = 0.0192$.

63. There are $_{52}C_5 = 2,598,960$ five-card hands. In order to get four-of-a-kind in, say, aces, you need to select all four aces, and then any of the other remaining 48 cards. Thus there are 48 ways to get a four-of-a-kind in aces. This is true for the other 12 card values as well, so there are $13 \times 48 = 624$ different four-of-a-kind hands. The desired probability is then $624/2,598,960 = 0.00024$.

64. The intuitive answer is 1/2: half of the time you are in the first half of the program, and half of the time you are not. To prove it rigorously, count the number of ways to arrange the ten performers, and count the number of ways you could be in the first half of the program. There are $_{10}P_{10} = 3,628,800$ ways to arrange the ten performers. Now assume that you perform first: there are $_9P_9 = 362,880$ ways to arrange the other 9 performers, so there are 362,880 arrangements in the case where you go first. But there are also 362,880 arrangements in the case when you go second, third, fourth, or fifth. Thus there are $5 \times 362,880 = 1,814,400$ arrangements where you perform in the first half, and the probability of doing so is $1,814,400 \div 3,628,880 = 0.5$.

65. a. The probability of winning five games in a row is $0.48^5 = 0.025$, assuming you play only five games. It is considerably higher if you play numerous games.
b. The probability of winning ten games in a row is $0.48^{10} = 0.00065$, assuming you play only ten games. It is considerably higher if you play numerous games.
c. Once again, assuming all 2000 people play only five games, one would expect about 2.5% of them would win five games in a row (because the probability of five-in-a-row is 0.025, as shown in part **a**). This is $0.025 \times 2000 = 50$ people.
d. Assuming all 2000 people play only ten games, one would expect about $0.00065 \times 2000 = 1.3$ people to win all ten games.

66. a. The probability of not getting a hit on a single at-bat is 0.6, so the probability of getting at least one hit in four at-bats is $1 - 0.6^4 = 0.8704$.
b. Over the course of a particular 56 game sequence, the probability of getting a hit in all of those games is $0.8704^{56} = 0.00042$.
c. The probability that a player hitting .300 will get at least one hit in a game is $1 - 0.7^4 = 0.7599$, and thus the probability of a 56-game hitting streak (over a particular 56-game sequence) is $0.7599^{56} = 2.1 \times 10^{-7}$.
d. It's not too surprising that someone has hit for 56 games in a row as there have been many, many 56-game sequences where players had the chance to get a hit in all of them. This illustrates the idea that the probability of a particular coincidence may be small, but the probability that some coincidence occurs is large.

UNIT 8A

QUICK QUIZ

1. **b**. The absolute change in the population was 10,000 people, and if population grows linearly, the absolute change remains constant. Thus the population at the end of the second year will be 110,000 + 10,000 = 120,000.

2. **c**. Because the population increases exponentially, it undergoes constant percent change. Its population increases by 10% in the first year, and thus at the end of the second year, the population will be 110,000 × 10% + 110,000 = 121,000.

3. **a**. Because your money is growing exponentially, if it doubles in the first 6 months, it will double every 6 months.

4. **b**. The absolute change in the number of songs is 200, and this occurred over the span of 3 months. Because the number of songs is increasing linearly, it will grow by 200 every 3 months, and it will take 6 months to grow to 800 songs.

5. **c**. Exponential decay occurs whenever a quantity decreases by a constant percentage (over the same time interval).

6. **c**. Based on the results of Parable 1 in the text, the total number of pennies needed is $2^{64} - 1 = 1.8 \times 10^{19}$, which is equivalent to $\$1.8 \times 10^{17}$. The federal debt is about \$9 trillion ($\$9 \times 10^{12}$), which differs from the amount of money necessary by about a factor of 10,000.

7. **b**. Note that at 11:01, there are $2 = 2^1$ bacteria; at 11:02 there are $4 = 2^2$ bacteria; at 11:03 there are $8 = 2^3$, and so on. The exponent on the base of 2 matches the minute, and this pattern continues through 11:30, which means there are 2^{30} bacteria at that time.

8. **c**. At 11:31, there are 2^{31} bacteria, and as shown in exercise 7, there were 2^{30} bacteria at 11:30. The difference $2^{31} - 2^{30}$ is the number of bacteria added over that minute.

9. **a**. As with the population, the volume of the colony doubles every minute, so it only takes one minute for the volume to double from 1 to 2 m^3.

10. **b**. The growth of a population undergoing exponential change is comparatively slow in the initial stages, and then outrageously fast in the latter stages. This makes it difficult for members of the population to see that the growth they are currently experiencing is about to explode in short order.

DOES IT MAKE SENSE?

15. Makes sense. Any quantity that undergoes constant, positive percent change grows exponentially.

16. Makes sense. After only 20 days, the balance would be $\$2^{20} = \$1,048,576$.

17. Makes sense. Any quantity that grows exponentially will eventually become very large, so as long as the small town's rate of growth is large enough, it can become a large city within a few decades.

18. Does not make sense. Exponential growth cannot be sustained for any long period of time because the population will sooner or later outstrip its resources.

BASIC SKILLS & CONCEPTS

19. The population is growing linearly because its absolute change remains constant at 623 people per year. The population in four years will be 2500 + 4 × 623 = 4992.

20. The population is growing exponentially because its percent change remains constant at 3% per year. Each year, the population increases by a factor of 1.03, and thus in five years, the population will be $75,000(1.03)^5 = 86,946$ people.

21. This is exponential growth because the cost of food in increasing at a constant 30% per year. Each year, the cost increases by a factor of 1.30, so your food bill was $\$120(1.30)^3 = \$263.64$.

22. The price is growing linearly because its absolute change remains constant at 4¢ per week. In ten weeks, the price will be \$3.10 + 10 × 4¢ = \$3.50.

23. The price is decreasing exponentially because the percent change remains at a constant −12% per year. Each year, the price decreases by a factor of 0.88, so its price in three years will be $\$50(0.88)^3$ = \$34.07.

24. The car's value is decreasing exponentially because its percent change remains constant at −10% per year. Each year, the value decreases by a factor of 0.90, so the value in three years will be $\$12,000(0.90)^3 = \$8748$.

25. The house's value is increasing linearly because the price increases by the same amount each year. In five years, it will be worth \$100,000 + 5 × \$15,000 = \$175,000.

26. The house's value is increasing exponentially because it is increasing by the same percent each year. Its value increases by a factor of 1.08 each year, so in five years, it will be worth $\$100,000(1.08)^5 = \$146,933$.

27. There should be $2^{14} = 16,384$ grains placed on the 15th square. The total number of grains would be $2^{15} - 1 = 32,767$, and it would weigh $32,767 \times (1/7000) = 4.7$ pounds.

28. There should be $2^{29} = 536,870,912$ grains placed on the 30th square. The total number of grains would be $2^{30} - 1 = 1,073,741,823$, and it would weigh $1,073,741,823 \times (1/7000) = 153,392$ pounds.

29. When the chessboard is full, there are $2^{64} - 1$ grains, with total weight of $(2^{64} - 1) \times (1/7000) = 2.64 \times 10^{15}$ pounds, or about 1.3×10^{12} tons.

30. Divide the total weight of the wheat on the chessboard by the weight of the harvest ($1.3 \times 10^{12} \div 2 \times 10^9 = 650$) to find that the chessboard wheat weighs about 650 times more than the harvest.

31. After 20 days, you would have $2^{20} = 1,048,576$ pennies, or $10,485.76.

32. Assuming 1.5 mm per penny, the stack would reach $1,048,576¢ \times \dfrac{1.5 \text{ mm}}{1¢} \times \dfrac{1 \text{ m}}{1000 \text{ mm}} = 1573 \text{ m}$.

33. After experimenting with various values of n in 2^n, you'll find that the balance has grown to about $1.4 billion after 37 days.

34. Experiment with various values of n in the conversion $2^n ¢ \times \dfrac{1.5 \text{ mm}}{1¢} \times \dfrac{1 \text{ m}}{1000 \text{ mm}} \times \dfrac{1 \text{ km}}{1000 \text{ m}}$.

    When you get to $n = 65$, the height of the stack would be about 5.5×10^{13} km, enough to reach the star.

35. At 11:50, there are $2^{50} = 1.1 \times 10^{15}$ bacteria in the bottle. The bottle is full at 12:00 noon, so it was half-full at 11:59, 1/4-full at 11:58, 1/8-full at 11:57, and so on. Continuing in this manner, we find the bottle was 1/1024-full at 11:50. This could also be expressed as $1/2^{10}$-full at 11:50.

36. At 11:10, there are $2^{10} = 1024$ bacteria in the bottle, and it is $1/2^{50}$-full at that time (refer to exercise 35).

37. As discussed in the text, the volume of the colony of 2^{120} bacteria would occupy a volume of 1.3×10^{15} m^3. Divide this by the surface area of the earth to get an approximate depth:
$$1.3 \times 10^{15} \text{ m}^3 \div 5.1 \times 10^{14} \text{ m}^2 = 2.5 \text{ m}.$$
This is quite a bit more than knee-deep (it's more than 8 feet).

38. Experiment with various values of n in the conversion $2^n \times 10^{-21}$ m^3. When you get to $n = 333$ days, the volume of the colony would be about 1.75×10^{79} m^3. Note that many calculators will have difficulty computing 2^{333}. One way around this is to first compute 2^{300}, and then multiply by 10^{-21}. This will buy you some "room" in your calculator's computing capacity, after which you can continue to multiply by factors of 2 until reaching 1.75×10^{79} m^3.

39. a. (Only 100-year intervals are shown here).

Year	Population
2000	6.0×10^9
2100	2.4×10^{10}
2200	9.6×10^{10}
2300	3.8×10^{11}
2400	1.5×10^{12}
2500	6.1×10^{12}
2600	2.5×10^{13}
2700	9.8×10^{13}
2800	3.9×10^{14}
2900	1.6×10^{15}
3000	6.3×10^{15}

b. In the year 2800, there would be 3.9×10^{14} people, each occupying one square meter, and in 2850, there would be 7.9×10^{14} people (again, each occupying one square meter). Since 5.1×10^{14} m^2 is in between these two values, it would happen between 2800 and 2850.

c. We would reach the limit when the earth's population reached $5.1 \times 10^{14} \div 10^4 = 5.1 \times 10^{10}$ people. This would happen shortly after the year 2150.

d. If by 2150 we've already reached the limit of 10^4 m^2 per person on earth, it will take only three more doubling periods to increase our need for space eight-fold. Since the doubling period is 50 years, this would take only 150 years, at which point we would have already exceeded the additional space available in the solar system (there is only five times more area out there).

40. a. You should take the penny. After only 5 days, the penny would have grown to $2^5 = 32¢$, whereas the dime has grown to only $20¢$.

b. The penny will grow to 2^n ¢ in n days. Since $1000 is 100,000¢, and since it doubles only every 2 days, it will grow to $100,000 \times 2^{n/2}$ ¢ after n days. After experimenting with various values of n, you will find that the penny has grown to a balance larger than the $1000 in just 34 days.

c. Based on parts **a** and **b**, it should be apparent that doubling time is more important in the long run than initial amount.

UNIT 8B

QUICK QUIZ

1. **a**. The factor by which an exponentially growing quantity grows is $2^{t/T_{double}}$.

2. **b**. The approximate doubling time formula says that a quantity's doubling time is about 70/r, where r is the growth rate.

3. **a**. The approximate doubling time formula does not do a good job when the growth rate r goes higher than 15%.

4. **b**. The approximate doubling time formula, T_{double} = 70/r, can be rearranged to say r = 70/T_{double}.

5. **c**. During the first 12 years, half of the tritium decays, and during the second 12 years, half of that, or 1/4 decays.

6. **b**. Note that 2.8 billion years/4 = 700 million years. This implies the uranium-235 decayed by a factor of 2 four times, which means $1/2^4$ = 1/16 of the uranium-235 remains.

7. **b**. The half-life can be approximated by T_{half} = 70/r.

8. **c**. A property of logarithms states $\log_{10}(10^x) = x$.

9. **c**. The decimal equivalent of 20% is 0.2, though you should set r = −0.2 because the population is decreasing.

10. **a**. The doubling time formula states $T_{double} = \dfrac{\log_{10} 2}{\log_{10}(1+r)}$.

DOES IT MAKE SENSE?

19. Does not make sense. In 50 years, the population will increase by a factor of 4.

20. Makes sense. The approximate doubling time formula reads T_{double} = 70/r, so in this case, T_{double} = 70/7 = 10 years.

21. Does not make sense. While it's true that half will be gone in ten years, over the next ten years, only half of what remains will decay, which means there will still be 1/4 of the original amount.

22. Makes sense. After 100,000 years, the plutonium will have decayed by a factor of 2 about four times, which means there will still be about 1/16 of the original quantity left.

BASIC SKILLS & CONCEPTS

23. True. $10^0 = 1$, and $10^1 = 10$, so $10^{0.928}$ should be between 1 and 10 (because 0.928 is between 0 and 1).

24. False. $10^3 = 1000$, so $10^{3.334}$ must be larger than 1000 (because 3.334 is larger than 3).

25. False. $10^{-5.2} = \dfrac{1}{10^{5.2}}$, which is quite small.

26. True. $10^{-2} = 0.01$, and $10^{-3} = 0.001$, so $10^{-2.67}$ is between 0.01 and 0.001 (because −2.67 is between −2 and −3).

27. False. While it is true that π is between 3 and 4, $\log_{10} \pi$ is not (it's between 0 and 1).

28. False. $\log_{10} 10 = 1$, and $\log_{10} 100 = 2$, so $\log_{10} 96$ is between 1 and 2.

29. False. $\log_{10}(10^6) = 6$, and $\log_{10}(10^7) = 7$. Because 1,600,000 is between 10^6 and 10^7, $\log_{10} 1,600,000$ is between 6 and 7.

30. True. $\log_{10}(10^9) = 9$, and $\log_{10}(10^{10}) = 10$, so $\log_{10}(8 \times 10^9)$ is between 9 and 10, because 8×10^9 is between 10^9 and 10^{10}.

31. True. Since $\log_{10}\left(\dfrac{1}{4}\right) = \log_{10}\left(4^{-1}\right) = -\log_{10} 4$, we know $\log_{10}\left(\dfrac{1}{4}\right)$ is between −1 and 0 because $\log_{10} 4$ is between 0 and 1.

32. False. Note that 0.00045 = 4.5×10^{-4}, which is between 10^{-4} and 10^{-5}. This implies that $\log_{10}(0.00045)$ is between −5 and −4.

33. a. $\log_{10} 8 = \log_{10}(2^3) = 3\log_{10} 2 = 3 \times 0.301 = 0.903$.

b. $\log_{10} 2000 = \log_{10} 2 + \log_{10} 10^3 = 0.301 + 3 = 3.301$.

c. $\log_{10} 0.5 = \log_{10} 1 - \log_{10} 2 = 0 - 0.301 = -0.301$.

d. $\log_{10} 64 = \log_{10} 2^6 = 6\log_{10} 2 = 6 \times 0.301 = 1.806$.

e. $\log_{10}\left(\dfrac{1}{8}\right) = \log_{10} 2^{-3} = -3\log_{10} 2 = -3 \times 0.301 = -0.903$.

f. $\log_{10} 0.2 = \log_{10}\left(\dfrac{2}{10}\right) = \log_{10} 2 - \log_{10} 10 = 0.301 - 1 = -0.699$.

34. a. $\log_{10} 50 = \log_{10} 5 + \log_{10} 10 = 0.699 + 1 = 1.699$.

b. $\log_{10} 5000 = \log_{10} 5 + \log_{10} 100 = 0.699 + 3 = 3.699$.

c. $\log_{10} 0.05 = \log_{10}\left(\dfrac{5}{100}\right) = \log_{10} 5 - \log_{10} 100 = 0.699 - 2 = -1.301$.

d. $\log_{10} 25 = \log_{10} 5^2 = 2\log_{10} 5 = 2 \times 0.699 = 1.398$.

e. $\log_{10} 0.2 = \log_{10}\left(\dfrac{1}{5}\right) = \log_{10} 1 - \log_{10} 5 = 0 - 0.699 = -0.699$.

f. $\log_{10} 0.04 = \log_{10}(5^{-2}) = -2\log_{10} 5 = -2 \times 0.699 = -1.398$.

35. In 12 hours, the fly population will increase by a factor of $2^{12/4} = 2^3 = 8$. Since one week is 168 hours, the population will increase by a factor of $2^{168/4} = 2^{42} = 4.4 \times 10^{12}$ in one week.

36. The balance of the account grows by a factor of $2^{30/10} = 2^3 = 8$ in 30 years. In 50 years, it grows by a factor of $2^{50/10} = 2^5 = 32$.

37. The population will increase by a factor of four (quadruple) in 30 years because $2^{30/15} = 4$.

38. One year is 52 weeks, so prices will rise by a factor of $2^{52/4} = 2^{13} = 8192$.

39. In 12 years, the population will be $3500 \times 2^{12/10} = 8041$. In 24 years, it will be $3500 \times 2^{24/10} = 18,473$.

40. In 12 years, the population will be $15,600 \times 2^{12/8} = 44,123$. In 24 years, it will be $15,600 \times 2^{24/8} = 124,800$.

41. Note that 3 years is 36 months, and 4 years is 48 months. In 3 years, the number of cells will be $1 \times 2^{36/2.5} = 21,619$. In 4 years, the number will be $1 \times 2^{48/2.5} = 602,249$.

42. Three years is 36 months, so there will be $1 \times 2^{36/6} = 64$ cells in 3 years. In 6 years (72 months), there will be $1 \times 2^{72/6} = 4096$ cells.

43. The year 2016 is 10 years later than 2006, so the population will be $6.5 \times 2^{10/45} = 7.6$ billion. In 2056 (50 years later), the population will be $6.5 \times 2^{50/45} = 14.0$ billion. In 2106 (100 years later), it will be $6.5 \times 2^{100/45} = 30.3$ billion.

44. The year 2016 is 10 years later than 2006, so the population will be $6.5 \times 2^{10/60} = 7.3$ billion. In 2056 (50 years later), the population will be $6.5 \times 2^{50/60} = 11.6$ billion. In 2106 (100 years later), it will be $6.5 \times 2^{100/60} = 20.6$ billion.

45.

Month	Population
0	100
1	$100 \times (1.07)^1 = 107$
2	$100 \times (1.07)^2 = 114$
3	$100 \times (1.07)^3 = 123$
4	$100 \times (1.07)^4 = 131$
5	$100 \times (1.07)^5 = 140$
6	$100 \times (1.07)^6 = 150$
7	$100 \times (1.07)^7 = 161$
8	$100 \times (1.07)^8 = 172$
9	$100 \times (1.07)^9 = 184$
10	$100 \times (1.07)^{10} = 197$
11	$100 \times (1.07)^{11} = 210$
12	$100 \times (1.07)^{12} = 225$
13	$100 \times (1.07)^{13} = 241$
14	$100 \times (1.07)^{14} = 258$
15	$100 \times (1.07)^{15} = 276$

Because the population after ten months is 197, which is almost twice the initial population of 100, the doubling time is just over 10 months. The approximate doubling time formula claims that $T_{\text{double}} = 70/7 = 10$ months, which is pretty close to what we can discern from the table. Neither answer is exact, though.

46.

Month	Population
0	1000
1	$1000 \times (1.20)^1 = 1200$
2	$1000 \times (1.20)^2 = 1440$
3	$1000 \times (1.20)^3 = 1728$
4	$1000 \times (1.20)^4 = 2074$
5	$1000 \times (1.20)^5 = 2488$
6	$1000 \times (1.20)^6 = 2986$
7	$1000 \times (1.20)^7 = 3583$
8	$1000 \times (1.20)^8 = 4300$
9	$1000 \times (1.20)^9 = 5160$
10	$1000 \times (1.20)^{10} = 6192$
11	$1000 \times (1.20)^{11} = 7430$
12	$1000 \times (1.20)^{12} = 8916$
13	$1000 \times (1.20)^{13} = 10,699$
14	$1000 \times (1.20)^{14} = 12,839$
15	$1000 \times (1.20)^{15} = 15,407$

Because the population after four months is 2074, which is a little more than twice the initial population of 1000, the doubling time is just under 4 months. The approximate doubling time formula claims that $T_{double} = 70/20 = 3.5$ months, which in not in perfect agreement from what we could discern from the table – this is due to the fact that the approximate doubling time formula doesn't work as well once r is greater than 15%.

47. $T_{double} \sim 70/4 = 17.5$ years. Prices will increase by a factor of $(1.04)^3 = 1.12$ in three years. Using the doubling time formula, prices would increase by a factor of $2^{3/17.5} = 1.13$, so the approximate doubling time formula does a reasonable job.

48. $T_{double} \sim 70/3.5 = 20$ years. The population will increase by a factor of $(1.035)^{50} = 5.58$. Using the doubling time formula, the population would increase by a factor of $2^{50/20} = 5.66$, so the approximate doubling time formula does a reasonable job.

49. $T_{double} \sim 70/0.9 = 78$ months. Prices will increase by a factor of $(1.009)^{12} = 1.11$ in one year, and by a factor of $(1.009)^{96} = 2.36$ in eight years. Using the doubling time formula, prices would increase by a factor of $2^{12/78} = 1.11$ in one year, and by a factor of $2^{96/78} = 2.35$ in eight years, so the approximate doubling time formula does a reasonable job.

50. $T_{double} \sim 70/2.1 = 33$ years. Oil consumption will increase by a factor of $(1.021)^{10} = 1.23$ in ten years. Using the doubling time formula, consumption would increase by a factor of $2^{10/33} = 1.23$, so the approximate doubling time formula does a reasonable job.

51. After 140 years, the fraction of radioactive substance that remains is $\left(\dfrac{1}{2}\right)^{140/70} = \dfrac{1}{4}$. After 280 years, the fraction remaining is $\left(\dfrac{1}{2}\right)^{280/70} = \dfrac{1}{16}$.

52. After 120 years, the fraction of radioactive substance that remains is $\left(\dfrac{1}{2}\right)^{120/500} = 0.85$. After 2500 years, the fraction remaining is $\left(\dfrac{1}{2}\right)^{2500/500} = \dfrac{1}{32}$.

53. The concentration of the drug decreases by a factor of $\left(\dfrac{1}{2}\right)^{24/18} = 0.40$ after 24 hours, and by a factor of $\left(\dfrac{1}{2}\right)^{36/18} = \dfrac{1}{4}$ after 36 hours.

54. The concentration of the drug decreases by a factor of $\left(\dfrac{1}{2}\right)^{24/4} = \dfrac{1}{64}$ after 24 hours, and by a factor of $\left(\dfrac{1}{2}\right)^{36/4} = 2^{-9} = \dfrac{1}{512}$ after 36 hours.

55. In 40 years, the population will be $1{,}000{,}000 \times \left(\dfrac{1}{2}\right)^{40/20} = 250{,}000$, and it will be $1{,}000{,}000 \times \left(\dfrac{1}{2}\right)^{70/20} = 88{,}388$ in 70 years.

56. In 20 years, the population will be $1{,}000{,}000 \times \left(\dfrac{1}{2}\right)^{20/25} = 574{,}349$, and it will be $1{,}000{,}000 \times \left(\dfrac{1}{2}\right)^{30/25} = 435{,}275$ in 30 years.

57. In 150 days, $1 \times \left(\dfrac{1}{2}\right)^{150/77} = 0.26$ kg of cobalt will remain, and $1 \times \left(\dfrac{1}{2}\right)^{300/77} = 0.067$ kg of cobalt will remain after 300 days.

58. In 1000 years, $1 \times \left(\dfrac{1}{2}\right)^{1000/1600} = 0.65$ kg of radium will remain, and $1 \times \left(\dfrac{1}{2}\right)^{10{,}000/1600} = 0.013$ kg of radium will remain after 10,000 years.

59. $T_{half} \sim 70/8 = 8.75$ years. The fraction of the forest that will remain after 30 years is $(1 - 0.08)^{30} = 0.082$. Using the half-life formula, the fraction that will remain is $\left(\dfrac{1}{2}\right)^{30/8.75} = 0.093$, so the approximate half-life formula is doing a reasonable job.

60. $T_{half} \sim 70/13 = 5.4$ weeks. The fraction of the pollutant that will remain after 52 weeks is $(1 - 0.13)^{52} = 0.00072$. Using the half-life formula, the fraction that will remain is $\left(\dfrac{1}{2}\right)^{52/5.4} = 0.0013$, so the approximate half-life formula isn't giving a very accurate answer – this is due to the fact that the percent decrease is near the 15%-cutoff for the approximate half-life formula, and because we are making a prediction 52 weeks into the future.

61. $T_{half} \sim 70/9 = 7.8$ years. After 50 years, the population will be $10{,}000(1 - 0.09)^{50} = 90$ elephants. Using the half-life formula, the population will be $10{,}000 \times \left(\dfrac{1}{2}\right)^{50/7.8} = 118$

elephants, so the approximate half-life formula is doing a reasonable job.

62. The annual production will be $4000(1-0.06)^{15} = 1581$ kg in 15 years. If you use the approximate half-life formula to find that $T_{half} \sim 70/6 = 11.7$ years, the annual production would be $4000 \times \left(\frac{1}{2}\right)^{15/11.7} = 1645$ kg, which shows that the approximate half-life formula does a reasonable job in making the prediction.

63. The approximate doubling time is $T_{double} \sim 70/12 = 5.8$ years. (A rounded value for) the exact doubling time is $\dfrac{\log_{10} 2}{\log_{10}(1+0.12)} = 6.11$ years. The price of a \$500 item in four years will be $\$500 \times 2^{4/6.11} = \$787.12$. (Note that this answer is using the rounded value for the "exact" doubling time – if you use all the digits your calculator stores, you should get a price of \$786.76).

64. The approximate doubling time is $T_{double} \sim 70/80 = 0.875$ month. (A rounded value for) the exact doubling time is $\dfrac{\log_{10} 2}{\log_{10}(1+0.80)} = 1.18$ months. The price of a \$1000 item in one year (12 months) will be $\$1000 \times 2^{12/1.18} = \$1,151,654$. (Note that this answer is using the rounded value of the "exact" doubling time – if you use all the digits your calculator stores, you should get a price of \$1,156,831).

65. The approximate doubling time is $T_{double} \sim 70/4 = 17.5$ years. (A rounded value for) the exact doubling time is $\dfrac{\log_{10} 2}{\log_{10}(1+0.04)} = 17.67$ years. The nation's population in 30 years will be $1,000,000 \times 2^{30/17.67} = 324,404,283$. (Note that this answer is using the rounded value for the "exact" doubling time – if you use all the digits your calculator stores, you should get a population of 324,339,751).

66. The approximate doubling time is $T_{double} \sim 70/20 = 3.5$ weeks. (A rounded value for) the exact doubling time is $\dfrac{\log_{10} 2}{\log_{10}(1+0.20)} = 3.8$ weeks. The termite population in 52 weeks will be $100 \times 2^{52/3.8} = 1,316,309$. (Note that this answer is using the rounded value for the "exact" doubling time – if you use all the digits your calculator stores, you should get a population of 1,310,463).

FURTHER APPLICATIONS

67. The amount of plutonium found today would be $10^{12} \times \left(\frac{1}{2}\right)^{4.6 \times 10^9 / 24,000} = 0$ tons. The reason there is no plutonium left is that 4.6 billion ÷ 24,000 is nearly 200,000, which means whatever amount of plutonium was originally present has undergone about 200,000 halving periods, and that's enough to reduce any amount imaginable to 0 (even if the entire mass of the earth were radioactive plutonium at the outset, it would have all decayed to other elements in 4.6 billion years).

68. After 50 years, there will be $1 \times \left(\frac{1}{2}\right)^{50/12} = 0.056$ kg of tritium remaining. If the weapons aren't maintained, but just stored for 50 years, they won't have the potency for which they were designed, as most of the radioactive material would have decayed.

UNIT 8C

QUICK QUIZ

1. **c.** Convert 75 million people per year into people per minute: $\dfrac{75 \times 10^6 \text{ people}}{\text{yr}} \times \dfrac{1 \text{ yr}}{365 \text{ d}} \times \dfrac{1 \text{ d}}{24 \text{ h}} \times \dfrac{1 \text{ hr}}{60 \text{ min}}$ = 143 people per minute (or about 140 people/min).

2. **b.** The text states the population is 6.5 billion people in 2006, growing at 1.2% per year. This implies a 2009 population of $6.5 \times 10^9 (1.012)^3 = 6.7$ billion.

3. **b.** The birth rate peaked in 1960, and has seen a significant decline since then, but it is not the primary reason for the rapid growth – the decreasing death rate has played the most important role over the last three centuries.

4. **b.** This answer gives the correct definition of carrying capacity.

5. **c.** Answers **a** and **b** would tend to decrease the carrying capacity, while developing a cheap source of energy would allow us to solve some of the barriers to population growth, such as clean water for all.

6. **a.** The bacteria in a bottle exhaust their resources, at which point the population collapses.

7. **c.** The logistic model looks like exponential growth at the outset, but then the growth rate declines, and the population levels out to a level at (or below) the carrying capacity.

8. **a**. The birth rate in 1950 was quite high, and with no change in the death rate, this would lead to rapid exponential growth.

9. **a**. The approximate doubling time of a population growing at 1.2% per year is 70/1.2 = 58.3 years.

10. **c**. Answers **a** and **b** would be required in order for the population to level out (the birth rate must decline to equal the death rate if population is to remain steady, and a population of 9 billion is 50% larger than the current level of 6 billion, and thus we would need an increase of 50% in food production). This leaves answer **c**, which is not necessary to sustain a population of 9 billion.

DOES IT MAKE SENSE?

17. Makes sense. If the current growth rate of 1.2% remains steady for the next decade, we can expect a population of $6.5 \times 10^9 (1.012)^{10} = 7.3$ billion, which is an increase of 800 million people (i.e. more than twice the size of the current U.S. population of 300 million).

18. Makes sense. Growth rate is equal to birth rate – death rate, so if the birth rate declines by a greater margin than the death rate, the difference between them will decrease, which means the growth rate will decrease.

19. Does not make sense. The carrying capacity depends upon many factors, such as our ability to produce food for the current population.

20. Does not make sense. The carrying capacity is influenced by a very complex set of parameters, and the best we can do is estimate its value, despite advances in computer technology.

21. Does not make sense. Predator/prey models often include the idea of overshoot and collapse.

22. Does not make sense. While past history gives us some indication that the human population is on a path toward logistic growth, some measures (such as the high growth rate in the 1960s) do not fit in well with the logistic model.

BASIC SKILLS & CONCEPTS

23. $T_{\text{double}} \sim 70/0.9 = 78$ years. Under this assumption, the population in 2050 would be $6 \times 2^{50/78} = 9.4$ billion.

24. $T_{\text{double}} \sim 70/1.8 = 39$ years. Under this assumption, the population in 2050 would be $6 \times 2^{50/39} = 14.6$ billion.

25. $T_{\text{double}} \sim 70/1.6 = 44$ years. Under this assumption, the population in 2050 would be $6 \times 2^{50/44} = 13.2$ billion.

26. $T_{\text{double}} \sim 70/0.7 = 100$ years. Under this assumption, the population in 2050 would be $6 \times 2^{50/100} = 8.5$ billion.

27. a. The growth rate in 1985 was 14.5 − 11.8 = 2.7 per 1000 people. In 1995, it was 9.3 − 11.4 = −2.1 per 1000 people. In 2003, it was 9.0 − 11 = −2.0 per 1000 people.
b. The birth rate decreased while the death rate remained fairly constant, which results in a declining growth rate. In this case, the growth rate became negative, which implies a declining population. If these trends continue, we can expect a decreasing population in the Czech Republic, though because there are so many factors that influence the growth rate of a country, it would be unwise to put much faith in these predictions 20 years hence.

28. a. The growth rate in 1985 was 23.8 − 6.6 = 17.2 per 1000 people. In 1995, it was 21.0 − 6.3 = 14.7 per 1000 people. In 2003, it was 19.0 − 6.0 = 13.0 per 1000 people.
b. The birth rate decreased while the death rate remained fairly constant, which results in a declining growth rate. In this case, the growth rate is still positive, which implies a population that is growing more slowly. If these trends continue, we can expect an increasing population in Israel, though because there are so many factors that influence the growth rate of a country, it would be unwise to put much faith in these predictions 20 years hence.

29. a. The growth rate in 1985 was 11.8 − 11.3 = 0.5 per 1000 people. In 1995, it was 11.7 − 11.0 = 0.7 per 1000 people. In 2003, it was 11.0 − 10.0 = −1.0 per 1000 people.
b. The birth rate decreased, as did the death rate, though the difference between the two was small (but positive), which results in a slowly growing population. If these trends continue, we can expect a slowly growing population in Sweden, though because there are so many factors that influence the growth rate of a country, it would be unwise to put much faith in these predictions 20 years hence.

30. a. The growth rate in 1985 was 15.7 − 8.7 = 7.0 per 1000 people. In 1995, it was 15.1 − 8.8 = 6.3 per 1000 people. In 2003, it was 14.0 − 8.0 = 6.0 per 1000 people.
b. The birth rate decreased, as did the death rate, though the difference between the two was small (it was, however, positive). This implies a slowly growing population. If these trends continue, we can expect a slowly growing population in the United States, though because there are so many factors that influence the growth rate of a country, it would be unwise to put much faith in these predictions 20 years hence.

31. When the population is 10 million, the actual growth rate is $4\% \times \left(1 - \dfrac{10,000,000}{60,000,000}\right) = 3.3\%$. When

the population is 30 million, the actual growth rate is $4\% \times \left(1 - \dfrac{30,000,000}{60,000,000}\right) = 2.0\%$. When the population is 50 million, the actual growth rate is $4\% \times \left(1 - \dfrac{50,000,000}{60,000,000}\right) = 0.67\%$.

32. When the population is 10 million, the actual growth rate is $6\% \times \left(1 - \dfrac{10,000,000}{80,000,000}\right) = 5.25\%$. When the population is 50 million, the actual growth rate is $6\% \times \left(1 - \dfrac{50,000,000}{80,000,000}\right) = 2.25\%$. When the population is 70 million, the actual growth rate is $6\% \times \left(1 - \dfrac{70,000,000}{80,000,000}\right) = 0.75\%$.

FURTHER APPLICATIONS

33. $T_{\text{double}} \sim 70/0.7 = 100$ years. In 2056, the population will be $3 \times 10^8 \times 2^{50/100} = 424$ million. In 2106, the population will be $3 \times 10^8 \times 2^{100/100} = 600$ million.

34. $T_{\text{double}} \sim 70/0.5 = 140$ years. In 2056, the population will be $3 \times 10^8 \times 2^{50/140} = 384$ million. In 2106, the population will be $3 \times 10^8 \times 2^{100/140} = 492$ million.

35. $T_{\text{double}} \sim 70/1.0 = 70$ years. In 2056, the population will be $3 \times 10^8 \times 2^{50/70} = 492$ million. In 2106, the population will be $3 \times 10^8 \times 2^{100/70} = 808$ million.

36. $T_{\text{double}} \sim 70/0.4 = 175$ years. In 2056, the population will be $3 \times 10^8 \times 2^{50/175} = 366$ million. In 2106, the population will be $3 \times 10^8 \times 2^{100/175} = 446$ million.

37. Answers will vary depending on your age.

38. Answers will vary depending on your age.

39. We must first compute the base growth rate r in the logistic model, using the 1960s data:
$$r = \frac{2.1\%}{\left(1 - \dfrac{3 \text{ billion}}{8 \text{ billion}}\right)} = 3.36\%.$$

The current growth rate can now be predicted using a population of 6.5 billion:
$$\text{growth rate} = 3.36\% \times \left(1 - \frac{6.5 \text{ billion}}{8 \text{ billion}}\right) = 0.63\%.$$

This is lower than the actual current growth rate of 1.1%, which indicates the assumed carrying capacity of 8 billion is too low to fit well with the data from the 1960s to present.

40. We must first compute the base growth rate r in the logistic model, using the 1960s data:
$$r = \frac{2.1\%}{\left(1 - \dfrac{3 \text{ billion}}{10 \text{ billion}}\right)} = 3\%.$$

The current growth rate can now be predicted using a population of 6.5 billion:
$$\text{growth rate} = 3\% \times \left(1 - \frac{6.5 \text{ billion}}{10 \text{ billion}}\right) = 1.05\%.$$

This is lower than the actual current growth rate of 1.1%, which indicates the assumed carrying capacity of 10 billion is too low to fit well with the data from the 1960s to present.

41. We must first compute the base growth rate r in the logistic model, using the 1960s data:
$$r = \frac{2.1\%}{\left(1 - \dfrac{3 \text{ billion}}{15 \text{ billion}}\right)} = 2.625\%.$$

The current growth rate can now be predicted using a population of 6.5 billion:
$$\text{growth rate} = 2.625\% \times \left(1 - \frac{6.5 \text{ billion}}{15 \text{ billion}}\right) = 1.5\%.$$

This is higher than the actual current growth rate of 1.1%, which indicates the assumed carrying capacity of 15 billion is too high to fit well with the data from the 1960s to present.

42. We must first compute the base growth rate r in the logistic model, using the 1960s data:
$$r = \frac{2.1\%}{\left(1 - \dfrac{3 \text{ billion}}{20 \text{ billion}}\right)} = 2.47\%.$$

The current growth rate can now be predicted using a population of 6.5 billion:
$$\text{growth rate} = 2.47\% \times \left(1 - \frac{6.5 \text{ billion}}{20 \text{ billion}}\right) = 1.7\%.$$

This is higher than the actual current growth rate of 1.1%, which indicates the assumed carrying capacity of 20 billion is too high to fit well with the data from the 1960s to present.

43. With an annual growth rate of 2%, the approximate doubling time would be $T_{\text{double}} \sim 70/2 = 35$ years. The population of the city in the year 2000 (ten years beyond 1990) would have been about $100,000(2)^{10/35} = 122,000$. The predicted population in 2010 and 2050 would be 149,000 and 328,000, respectively (the computation is similar to the 2000 prediction). With an annual growth rate of 5%, the approximate doubling time would be $T_{\text{double}} \sim 70/5 = 14$ years. The population of the city in the year 2000 would have been $100,000(2)^{10/14} = 164,000$. The predicted population in 2010 and 2050 would be 269,000 and 1,950,000, respectively.

UNIT 8D

QUICK QUIZ

1. **a**. Each magnitude on the Richter scale represents about 32 times as much energy as the previous magnitude.

2. **b**. Most deaths in earthquakes are caused by the collapse of buildings, landslides, and tsunamis.

3. **a**. By definition, a sound of 0 dB is the softest sound audible by a human.

4. **b**. From the definition of the decibel scale, we have

$$\frac{\text{intensity of sound}}{\text{intensity of softest audible sound}} = 10^{(95/10)} = 10^{9.5}.$$

The ratio on the left tells us this sound has intensity $10^{9.5}$ times as large as the softest audible sound.

5. **a**. From the definition of the decibel scale, we have $\frac{\text{intensity of sound}}{\text{intensity of softest audible sound}} = 10^{(10/10)} = 10.$

The ratio on the left tells us a 10-dB sound is ten times as large as the softest audible sound, which is 0 dB.

6. **c**. Gravity follows the inverse square law, so its strength is proportional to the square of the distance between the objects. Thus if this distance is tripled (multiplied by 3), the strength of the force of gravity is decreased by a factor of $3^2 = 9$.

7. **c**. On the pH scale, a lower number corresponds to higher acidity.

8. **b**. Because $[H^+] = 10^{-pH}$, we have $[H^+] = 10^{-0} = 1$, so the hydrogen ion concentration is 1 mole per liter.

9. **c**. Because $pH = -\log_{10}[H^+]$, we have pH = $-\log_{10} 10^{-5} = -(-5) = 5$.

10. **a**. A lake damaged by acid rain has a relatively low pH. To bring it back to health, you want to raise the pH.

DOES IT MAKE SENSE?

15. Does not make sense. Each unit on the Richter scale represents an increase of nearly 32 fold in the amount of energy released, and thus an earthquake of magnitude 8 releases about 32^4 (close to 1 million) times as much energy as an earthquake of magnitude 4. This does not imply that a magnitude 8 earthquake will do 1 million times as much damage, but it's not likely it will do only twice the damage of a magnitude 4 quake.

16. Does not make sense. As shown in Table 8.5, a 120-dB sound is 10^{12} times as loud as the softest audible sound, and a 100-dB sound is 10^{10} times as loud. This implies a 120-dB sound is 100 times as loud as a 100-dB sound.

17. Does not make sense. The pH of water is related to its hydrogen ion concentration, which is not affected by its volume.

18. Does not make sense. Lakes that have been affected by acid rain often have clear water because nothing is able to grow in them.

BASIC SKILLS & CONCEPTS

19. $E = (2.5 \times 10^4) \cdot 10^{1.5 \times 6} = 2.5 \times 10^{13}$ joules.

20. Because each unit on the Richter scale represents an increase of nearly 32 fold in the amount of energy released, we can expect that a magnitude 7 quake is about 32^2 (1024) times as large as a magnitude 5 quake. To find the exact factor, one can compute the energy released by each quake. $E = (2.5 \times 10^4) \cdot 10^{1.5 \times 7} = 2.5 \times 10^{14.5}$ joules for the magnitude 7 quake, and $E = (2.5 \times 10^4) \cdot 10^{1.5 \times 5} = 2.5 \times 10^{11.5}$ joules for the magnitude 5 quake. Note that the energy released by the magnitude 7 quake is $10^3 = 1000$ times as large as the magnitude 5 quake.

21. $E = (2.5 \times 10^4) \cdot 10^{1.5 \times 9} = 7.9 \times 10^{17}$ joules.

22. $E = (2.5 \times 10^4) \cdot 10^{1.5 \times 7.9} = 1.8 \times 10^{16}$ joules.

23. The energy released by a magnitude 6 quake is 2.5×10^{13} joules (see exercise 19), and since $5 \times 10^{15} \div 2.5 \times 10^{13} = 200$, the bomb releases 200 times as much energy.

24. Use the relationship $\log_{10} E = 4.4 + 1.5M$, where $E = 5 \times 10^{15}$ joules (the energy of the bomb) and M is the magnitude of the earthquake.

$$\log_{10}(5 \times 10^{15}) = 4.4 + 1.5M$$
$$15.7 = 4.4 + 1.5M$$
$$M = 7.53$$

Assuming the bomb was deployed for the use it was designed, it would cause more destruction. Nuclear bombs are detonated above ground, and their blast cones wipe out entire cities. A significant amount of the energy released by an earthquake is absorbed by the earth.

25. As shown in Table 8.5, ordinary conversation is around 60 dB, and is $10^6 = 1,000,000$ times as loud as the softest audible sound.

26. As shown in Table 8.5, a siren at 30 meters is around 100 dB, and is $10^{10} = 10$ billion times as loud as the softest audible sound.

27. The loudness is $10 \log_{10}(20 \times 10^6) = 73$ dB.

28. The loudness is $10\log_{10}(18\times10^{12}) = 133$ dB.

29. As with Example 4 in the text, we can compare the intensities of two sounds using the following:
$$\frac{\text{intensity of sound 1}}{\text{intensity of sound 2}} = 10^{(45-10)/10} = 3162 \,.$$
Thus a 45-dB sound is 3162 times as loud as a 10-dB sound.

30. According to Table 8.5, a whisper is 20 dB, and is 10^2 times as loud as the softest audible sound. A 40 dB sound is 10^4 times as loud as the softest audible sound, and thus is 100 times as loud as a 20-dB sound.

31. The distance has decreased by a factor of 5, which means the intensity of sound will increase by a factor of $5^2 = 25$.

32. The distance has decreased by a factor of 100, which means the intensity of sound will increase by a factor of $100^2 = 10,000$.

33. The distance has decreased by a factor of 2, which means the intensity of sound will increase by a factor of $2^2 = 4$.

34. The distance has decreased by a factor of 4, which means the intensity of sound will increase by a factor of $4^2 = 16$.

35. Each unit of increase on the pH scale corresponds to a decrease by a factor of 10 in the hydrogen ion concentration. Thus an increase of 3 on the pH scale corresponds to a decrease in the hydrogen ion concentration by a factor of $10^3 = 1000$. This makes the solution more basic.

36. Each unit of decrease on the pH scale corresponds to an increase by a factor of 10 in the hydrogen ion concentration. Thus a decrease of 2.5 on the pH scale corresponds to an increase in the hydrogen ion concentration by a factor of $10^{2.5} = 316$. This makes the solution more acidic.

37. $[H^+] = 10^{-7.5} = 3.2\times10^{-8}$ mole per liter.

38. $[H^+] = 10^{-2.5} = 3.2\times10^{-3}$ mole per liter.

39. $pH = -\log_{10}(0.01) = 2$. This is an acid, as is any solution with pH less than 7.

40. $pH = -\log_{10}(10^{-10}) = 10$. This is a base, as is any solution with pH greater than 7.

41. Acid rain (pH = 2) is $10^4 = 10,000$ times more acidic than ordinary water (pH = 6). See exercise 35.

42. Acid rain (pH = 2.5) is $10^{3.5} = 3162$ times more acidic than ordinary water (pH = 6). See exercise 35.

FURTHER APPLICATIONS

43. According to Table 8.4, earthquakes with magnitudes between 2 and 3 are labeled "very minor," and they occur about 1000 times per year worldwide. The glasses in the cupboards of the Los Angeles residents near the epicenter may rattle around a bit, but nothing serious would be expected to happen.

44. A 160-dB sound is 10,000 times as intense as a 120-dB sound, and 120 dB is the level at which there is a strong risk of damage to the human ear, according to Table 8.5. This would be decidedly bad: a burst eardrum, bleeding from the ear, and a permanent loss of hearing could ensue.

45. A solution with a pH of 12 is very basic: 100,000 times more basic than pure water. When children ingest such liquids, the mouth, throat, and digestive tracts are often burned. One would hope that a secondary effect of the incident would be that an adult would call the poison center immediately.

46. According to Table 8.4, an earthquake of magnitude 8.5 is in the "great" category; only 1 per year (on average) occurs worldwide. Such a quake could conceivably cause much death and destruction in Tokyo (though it is a modern city, with buildings designed to diminish the effects of an earthquake).

47. You probably would not be able to hear your friend (the noise of the sirens is louder). If your friend is shouting: "Watch out for that falling piano above you!" you might die.

48. The forest will suffer the serious effects of acid rain (which, with a pH of 4, is 100 times more acidic than normal rain of pH 6).

49. a. The distance has increased by a factor of 100, so the intensity of the sound will decrease by a factor of $100^2 = 10,000$ times (this is due to the inverse square law). According to Table 8.5, busy street traffic is 80 dB, and is 10^8 times as loud as the softest audible sound. Note that a 40-dB sound is 10^4 times as loud as the softest sound, and thus is 10,000 times less intense than an 80-dB sound.
    b. As with Example 4 in the text, we can compare the intensities of two sounds using the following:
    $$\frac{\text{intensity of sound 1}}{\text{intensity of sound 2}} = 10^{(135-120)/10} = 31.6 \,.$$
    Thus a 135-dB sound is 31.6 times as loud as a 120-dB sound. In order to reduce the intensity of the sound by a factor of 31.6, you need to increase the distance from the speaker by a factor of $\sqrt{31.6} = 5.6$, so you should sit 5.6×10 m = 56 meters away.
    c. The distance from you to the booth (8 meters) is 8 times as much as the distance between the people talking (1 meter), so the intensity of the sound will have decreased by a factor of 64 by the time it reaches you. A 20-dB sound is 100 times

louder than the softest audible sound, and when decreased by a factor of 64, it becomes (100/64) times as loud as the softest sound. Therefore its loudness in decibels is $10\log_{10}\left(\dfrac{100}{64}\right) = 1.94$ dB.

Note that a 60-dB sound is 10,000 times as loud as a 20-dB sound (Table 8.5). If you wanted to amplify the sound that reaches you to 60 dB, you would need to increase it by a factor of 64 to overcome the loss of intensity due to distance (this would bring it back to 20 dB), and increase it again by a factor of 10,000 to raise it to the 60-dB level. This is equivalent to amplifying the sound by a factor of 640,000. Pray that the waiter doesn't come to your table and say a loud "hello" while your earpiece is in.

50. a. The distance has decreased by a factor of 300, so the intensity of the sound will increase by a factor of $300^2 = 90,000$.

b. A siren at 30 meters is 10^{10} times as loud as the softest audible sound. If the intensity is increased by a factor of 90,000, it will be $90,000 \times 10^{10} = 9 \times 10^{14}$ times as loud as the softest sound. This means its loudness in decibels is $10\log_{10}(9 \times 10^{14})$ = 149.5 dB.

c. Note that a 150-dB sound is $10^3 = 1000$ times as loud as a 120-dB sound, the level at which there is a strong risk of damage to the human ear. It is very likely your eardrum will be damaged.

51. a. $[H^+] = 10^{-4}$ mole per liter.

b. The lake water with pH = 7 has a hydrogen ion concentration of 10^{-7} mole per liter. There are 3.785 liters in a gallon, so a 100 million gallon lake has $378,500,000 = 3.785 \times 10^8$ liters in it. Multiplying the hydrogen ion concentration by the volume of the lake gives us 37.85 moles of hydrogen ions before the acid was added. In a similar fashion, we find that 100,000 gallons (378,500 liters) of acid with pH = 2 ($[H^+] = 10^{-2}$) has 3785 moles of hydrogen ions. Combining both the volumes of the liquids and the moles of hydrogen ions gives us a hydrogen ion concentration of $\dfrac{37.85 + 3785 \text{ mole}}{3.785 \times 10^8 + 378,500 \text{ L}} = 10^{-5}$ mole per liter. This implies the polluted lake has pH = $-\log_{10}(10^{-5}) = 5$.

c. Proceeding as in part **b**, the acid-rain lake (without added acid) has 37,850 moles of hydrogen ions. When the acid is added (increasing the number of moles by 3785), the hydrogen ion concentration becomes $\dfrac{37,850 + 3785 \text{ mole}}{3.785 \times 10^8 + 378,500 \text{ L}} =$

1.1×10^{-4} mole per liter. This implies the polluted lake has pH = $-\log_{10}(1.1 \times 10^{-4}) = 3.96$.

d. The pollution could be detected if the acid was dumped into a lake with pH = 7 (part **b**), but it could not be detected if it was dumped into a lake with pH = 4 (part **c**).

UNIT 9A

QUICK QUIZ

1. **a.** A function describes how a dependent variable changes with respect to one or more independent variables.

2. **a.** The variable s is the independent variable, upon which the variable r depends.

3. **c.** The DJIA changes with respect to the passage of time, and thus is a function of time.

4. **b.** It is customary to plot the values of the independent variable along the horizontal axis.

5. **b.** The dependent variable is normally plotted along the vertical axis, and in this case, the dependent variable is z (with an independent variable of w).

6. **b.** The range of a function consists of the values of the dependent variable.

7. **a.** The speed of the car is the independent variable (because gas mileage changes with respect to speed), and the domain of a function is the set of values of interest for the independent variable.

8. **c.** The range of a function is the set of values corresponding to the values in the domain, which in turn are the set of values that make sense in the function. If you used a function to predict values outside the range, you would be forced to use values outside the domain; these values don't make sense.

9. **c.** Traffic volume on an urban freeway peaks in the morning rush hour, peaks again in the evening rush hour, and typically repeats this pattern day after day. If weekend traffic were significantly different from the weekday pattern, we would still see a weekly pattern repeating itself – this is a hallmark of a periodic function.

10. **b.** A model that does not agree well with past data probably won't do a good job of predicting the future.

DOES IT MAKE SENSE?

15. Makes sense. Climatologists use mathematical models to predict and understand the nature of the earth's climate.

16. Makes sense. The demand for concert tickets changes with respect to the price of the ticket: in general, if the price goes up, demand will fall, and vice versa.

17. Does not make sense. If your heart rate depends upon your running speed, heart rate is the dependent variable, and the range is used to describe the values of the dependent variable.

18. Does not make sense. A model may fit observed data very well, but if it is used to extrapolate beyond the data set, there's no telling what may happen.

BASIC SKILLS & CONCEPTS

19.

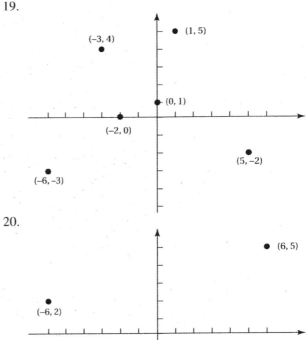

20.

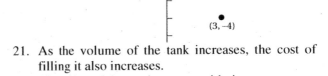

21. As the volume of the tank increases, the cost of filling it also increases.

22. The price of the car increases with time.

23. The speed of the skydiver increases with time until reaching constant terminal velocity. This describes the relationship of a skydiver falling a sufficient distance before opening his chute. When the chute is opened, the speed decreases to a different terminal velocity until the skydiver reaches the ground.

24. The intensity of the sound decreases as distance from the speaker increases.

25. As the average speed of the car increases, the travel time decreases.

26. In a particular gear, the faster you pedal a bike, the faster the bike will go.

27. As the gas mileage increases, the cost of driving a fixed distance decreases (assuming that gas costs remain constant).

28. The balance after a fixed period of time increases with the APR.

29. a. The pressure at 6000 feet is about 24 inches of mercury; the pressure at 18,000 feet is about 17 inches; and the pressure at 29,000 feet is about 11 inches.

    b. The altitude is about 8000 feet when the pressure is 23 inches of mercury; the altitude is about 14,000 feet when the pressure is 19 inches; and the altitude is about 25,000 feet when the pressure is 13 inches.

    c. It appears that the pressure reaches 5 inches of mercury at an altitude of about 50,000. The pressure approaches zero as one moves out of earth's atmosphere and into outer space.

30. a. On April 1, there's about 12.4 hours of daylight, and on October 31, about 10.7 hours. For all of these questions, your answers may vary somewhat from those given here, as it is difficult to read a graph of this sort with any level of precision.

    b. There are 13 hours of daylight around April 19 and August 20.

    c. There are 10.5 hours of daylight around January 31 and November 8.

    d. At 20°N latitude (closer to the equator), the graph would be flatter (the variation in the length of a day is not as pronounced). At 60°N latitude (closer to the North Pole), the graph would be steeper and taller (the variation in the length of the day is larger). At 40°S latitude, the graph would have a similar shape, except that the location of the peaks and valleys would be exchanged (the shortest day of the year in the southern hemisphere is around June 21).

31. a. The independent variable is time (in years), and the dependent variable is world population. The domain is the set of years from 1950 to 2000, and the range is the set of population values between roughly 2.5 billion and 6 billion people.

    b. The function shows a steadily increasing world population between 1950 and 2000.

32. a. The independent variable is age (measured in years), and the dependent variable is weight (measured in pounds). The domain is the set of ages between 0 and 40 years, and the range is all weights between about 8 pounds and 130 pounds.

33. a. The variables are (*time, temperature*), or (*date, temperature*). The domain is all days over the course of a year, and the range is the set of temperatures between 38°F and 85°F.

    b.

    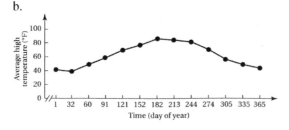

34. a. The independent variable is altitude (in feet), and the dependent variable is boiling temperature (in °F). The domain is the set of altitudes between 0 and 9000 feet. The range is the set of temperatures between 193.6°F and 212°F.

    b.

    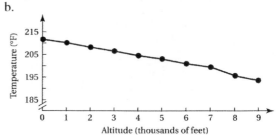

    c. The boiling point of water decreases with altitude.

35. a. The variables are (*year, tobacco production*). The domain is the set of years between 1975 and 1990, and the range is the set of weights between 1.2 and 2.2 billion pounds.

    b.

    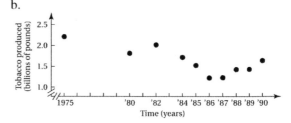

    c. In this case, because the data consist of yearly figures for production, it would not be appropriate to fill in the graph between the data points. The function, then, is simply the production numbers associated with each year.

36. a. The variables are (*time, projected population*). The domain is the set of years between 2010 and 2040. The range is the set of population values between 309 and 393 million people.

    b.

    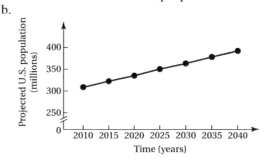

    c. The projected population increases steadily with time.

c. The temperature increases during the first half of the year, and then decreases during the second half of the year.

37. a. The domain of the function (*altitude, temperature*) is the set of altitudes of interest – say, 0 ft to 15,000 ft (or 0 m to 4000 m). The range is the set of temperatures associated with the altitudes in the domain; the interval 30°F to 90°F (or about 0°C to 30°C) would cover all temperatures of interest (this assumes a summer ascent of a mountain in the temperate zone of the earth).

    b.

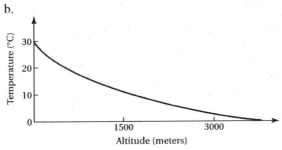

38. a. The domain of the function (*day of year, high temperature*) is the set of days over a two-year period. The days could be labeled (1, 2, 3, ... , 730). The range consists of the high temperatures on those days. In a temperate location, temperatures between 10°C and 30°C (about 50°F and 90°F) might work.

    b.

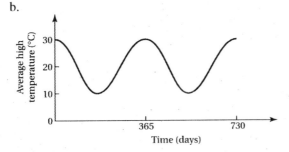

39. a. The domain of the function (*blood alcohol content, reflex time*) consists of all reasonable BACs (in gm/100 mL). For example, numbers between 0 and 0.25 would be appropriate. The range would consist of the reflex times associated with those BACs.

    b.

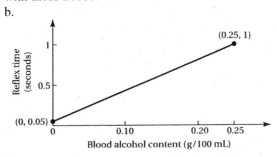

40. a. The domain of the function (*number of pages in a book, time to read the book*) consists of the lengths of most books – say, 30 pages to 1000 pages. The range consists of the reading times for these books for a specific individual; for example, it may consist of times between 1 hour and 20 hours (assuming the person reads at a rate of 50 pages per hour). The reading time should increase steadily with the length of the book (assuming the material being read is at a similar level), as shown in the figure.

    b.

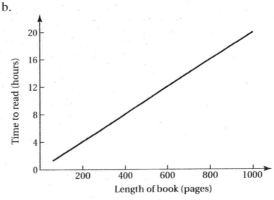

41. a. The domain of the function (*time of day, traffic flow*) consists of all times over a full day. The range consists of all traffic flows (in units of cars per minute) at the various times of the day. We would expect light traffic flow at night, medium traffic flow during the midday hours, and heavy traffic flow during the two rush hours.

    b.

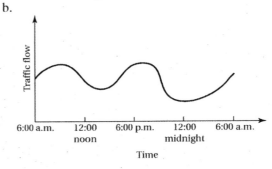

42. a. The domain of the function (*price of gasoline, number of tourists in Yellowstone*) would consist of all realistic gasoline prices, say, between $2 and $4 per gallon. The range includes all reasonable number of tourists in Yellowstone (the graph provides a qualitative model and general trend).

    b.

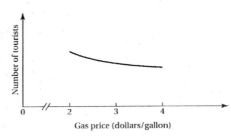

43. a. The domain of the function (*time, world record in the 100-meter dash*) consists of all years from 1970 to 2004. The range consists of the world records for the race at all times between 1970 and 2004. Some research would be needed to find the exact records and the days on which they were lowered. The graph shows a slow decrease (from about 10.2 seconds to 9.8 seconds for men, and from about 11.0 seconds to 10.4 seconds for women) over this period of time.

b.

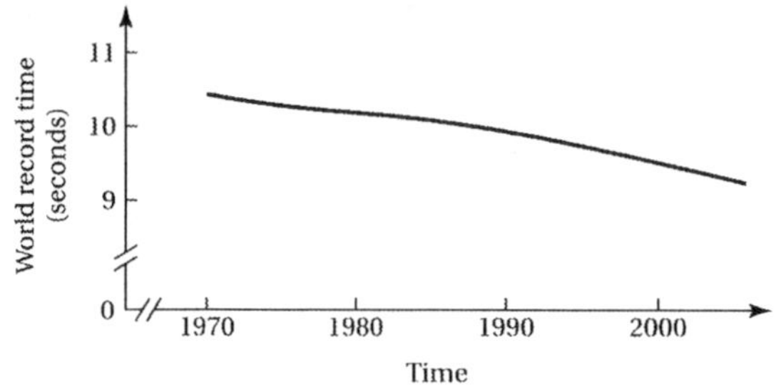

World record time (seconds) vs *Time* — a slowly decreasing curve from about 10.4 at 1970 to about 9.2 near 2004, with axis labels 9, 10, 11 on the vertical axis and 1970, 1980, 1990, 2000 on the horizontal axis.

44. a. The domain of the function (*minutes after lighting, length of candle*) consists of all times between 0 minutes and the time at which the candle would be expected to disappear – say, 0 minutes to 100 minutes. The range is the set of numbers between zero and the initial length of the candle, say 0 to 5 inches.

b.

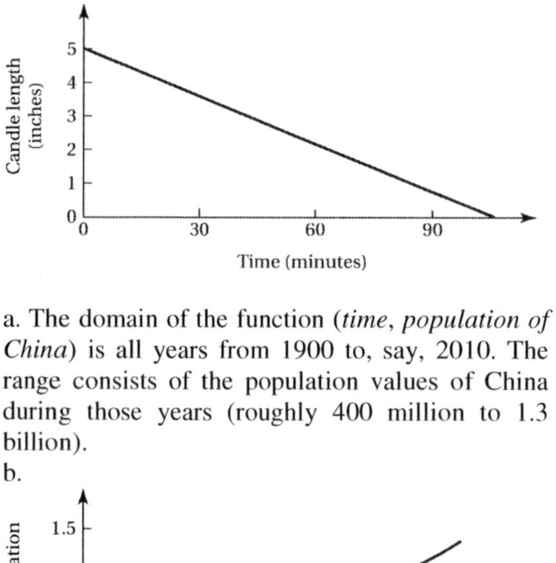

Candle length (inches) vs *Time (minutes)* — a straight line decreasing from 5 inches at 0 minutes to 0 near 100 minutes, with vertical axis labels 1–5 and horizontal axis labels 30, 60, 90.

45. a. The domain of the function (*time, population of China*) is all years from 1900 to, say, 2010. The range consists of the population values of China during those years (roughly 400 million to 1.3 billion).

b.

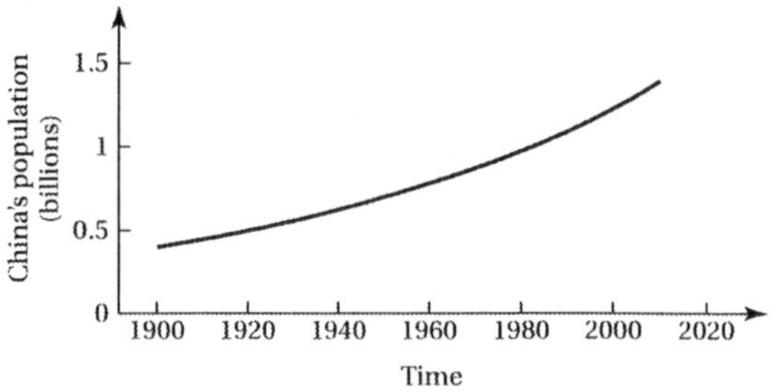

China's population (billions) vs *Time* — an increasing curve from about 0.4 at 1900 to about 1.4 near 2010, with vertical axis labels 0.5, 1, 1.5 and horizontal axis labels 1900, 1920, 1940, 1960, 1980, 2000, 2020.

46. a. The domain of the function (*time of day, elevation of tide*) consists of all times over a two-day period. The range consists of the heights of the tides over that two-day period. Some research would be needed to find the exact tide heights at a given location, but the graph would be periodic, rising and falling twice per day.

b.

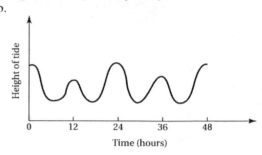

Height of tide vs *Time (hours)* — a periodic wave rising and falling, with horizontal axis labels 12, 24, 36, 48.

47. a. The domain of the function (*angle of cannon, horizontal distance traveled by cannonball*) is all cannon angles between 0° and 90°. The range would consist of all horizontal distances traveled by the cannonball for the various angles in the domain. It is well known that a projectile has maximum range when the angle is about 45°, so the graph shows a peak at 45°.

b.

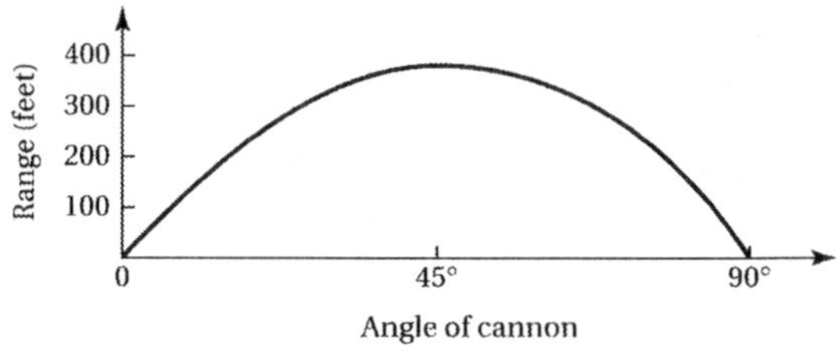

Range (feet) vs *Angle of cannon* — a symmetric arch peaking near 400 feet at 45°, returning to 0 at 0° and 90°, with vertical axis labels 100, 200, 300, 400.

48. a. The domain of the function (*weight of car, average gas mileage*) consists of the typical weights of cars – say, from 1000 pounds to 8000 pounds. The range consists of the average gas mileage for cars of various weights. This function should be roughly decreasing, because we expect gas mileage to decrease as the weight of the car increases. However, the function would probably not be a good model because of the many exceptions (heavy cars with good gas mileage, and vice versa).

b.

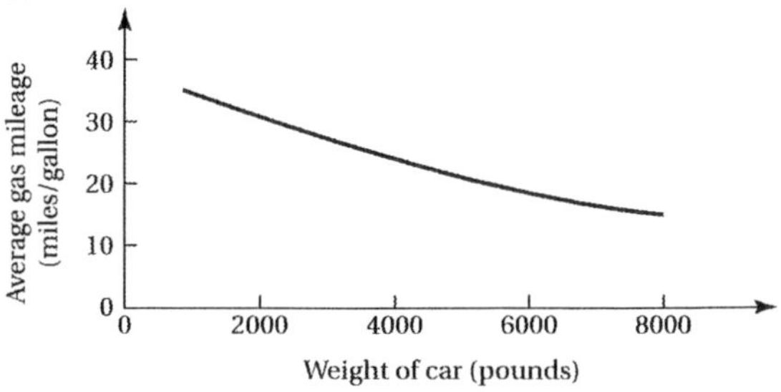

Average gas mileage (miles/gallon) vs *Weight of car (pounds)* — a decreasing curve from about 35 at 1000 pounds to about 15 at 8000 pounds, with vertical axis labels 10, 20, 30, 40 and horizontal axis labels 2000, 4000, 6000, 8000.

UNIT 9B

QUICK QUIZ

1. **c.** Constant absolute change over the same time interval (or other variable) gives rise to linear models, and this amounts to constant slope.

2. **b.** The slope of a linear function is the rate of change in the dependent variable with respect to the independent variable.

3. **c.** When a line slopes downward, the ratio of its change in y to change in x is negative, and this amounts to a negative slope or negative rate of change.

4. **c.** With only information about the first three miles of the trail, there's no knowing what will happen at mile 5.

5. **c.** Larger rates of change correspond with larger and steeper slopes.

6. **a.** The initial value corresponds with *time* = 0, and this results in an initial *price* = $100.

7. **c.** The coefficient on the independent variable is the slope, which also represents the rate of change. Since this coefficient is negative, we can expect a graph that slopes downward.

8. **a.** The y-intercept $b = 7$, and the slope $m = -2$, and thus the line, in the form $y = mx + b$, has equation $y = -2x + 7$.

9. **b.** A line in the form $y = mx + b$ has slope = m and y-intercept = b, so the slope of both $y = 12x - 3$ and $y = 12x + 3$ is $m = 12$, and they have different y-intercepts (-3 and 3).

10. **c.** Charlie picks $550 - 150 = 400$ apples over the span of two hours, so the slope of the function is $400/2 = 200$.

DOES IT MAKE SENSE?

17. Does not make sense. The graph of a linear function is always a line.

18. Makes sense. The rate of change is the slope.

19. Makes sense. The familiar relationship *distance* = *speed* × *time* can be solved for *speed* to produce *speed* = *distance* ÷ *time*, which is the rate of change in distance with respect to time.

20. Makes sense. To make a model connecting two data points, simply find the slope of the line segment that joins them, and compute the y-intercept.

BASIC SKILLS & CONCEPTS

21. **a.** Rain depth increases linearly with time.
    b. It appears that the change in depth over the first three hours is four inches, so the slope is 4/3 inches per hour.

c. The model is realistic if the rainfall rate is a constant 4/3 inches per hour over four hours.

22. **a.** Population increases linearly with time.
    b. It appears that the population has increased by 20,000 over the span of two years, so the slope is 10,000 people per year.
    c. As long as the population growth is a constant 10,000 people per year for eight years, this is a good model.

23. **a.** On a long trip, the distance from home decreases linearly with time.
    b. The distance has decreased by 500 miles over the span of 7 hours, so the slope is $-500 ÷ 7 = -71.4$ miles per hour.
    c. This is a good model if the speed of travel is a constant 71.4 miles per hour over 7 hours.

24. **a.** There is no profit from the first 1000 units sold, and then the profits increase linearly with sales.
    b. The profit changed by $10,000 when 1000 additional units were sold, so the slope is $10 per unit.
    c. This is a good model assuming 1000 units must be sold to recover fixed costs, and assuming each unit sold thereafter produces a profit of $10.

25. **a.** Shoe size increases linearly with the height of the individual.
    b. The change in shoe size was 11 while the change in height was 80 inches, and this produces a slope of $11 ÷ 80 = 0.1375$ size per inch.
    c. This model is a rough approximation at best, and it would be difficult to find realistic conditions where the relationship held.

26. **a.** As the length of the race increases, the average speed of the record-setting runner decreases linearly.
    b. The record pace decreases from about 38 km/hr to 20 km/hr as the length of the race increases from 0 km to 10 km, which results in a slope of $(38 - 20) ÷ (0 - 10) = -1.8$ km/hr.
    c. The model is a rough approximation to the actual record times, and it would be difficult to find actual conditions under which the model would be realistic.

27. The *water depth* decreases with respect to *time* at a rate of 1.5 in./day, so the rate of change is -1.5 in./day. In 6.5 days, the water depth decreases by 1.5 in./day × 6.5 days = 9.75 inches. In 12.5 days, it decreases by 1.5 in./day × 12.5 days = 18.75 in.

28. Your *distance traveled* increases with respect to *time* at a rate of 65 miles per hour. In 3.5 hours, you travel 65 mi/hr × 3.5 hr = 227.5 miles. In 6.8 hours, you travel 65 mi/hr × 6.8 hr = 442 miles.

29. The *height* of the plant increases with respect to *time* at a rate of 0.8 in./day. In 30 days, the height increases by 0.8 in./day × 30 days = 24 inches. In

60 days, the height increases 0.8 in./day × 60 days = 48 inches.

30. At this gas station, *sales* (in gal/wk) decrease with respect to *price* (in ¢/gal), and the rate of change is $-120\left(\dfrac{\text{gal}}{\text{wk}}\right)\bigg/\left(\dfrac{¢}{\text{gal}}\right)=-120\dfrac{\text{gal}^2}{¢\cdot\text{wk}}$. If the price is increased by 10 cents per gallon, the sales change by $-120\dfrac{\text{gal}^2}{¢\cdot\text{wk}}\times10\dfrac{¢}{\text{gal}}=-1200\dfrac{\text{gal}}{\text{wk}}$. If the price is decreased by 5 ¢/gal, the sales change by $-120\dfrac{\text{gal}^2}{¢\cdot\text{wk}}\times-5\dfrac{¢}{\text{gal}}=600\dfrac{\text{gal}}{\text{wk}}$.

31. The *snow depth* increases with respect to *time* at a rate of 3.5 inches per hour. In 6.3 hours, the snow depth will have increased by 3.5 in./hr × 6.3 hr = 22.05 inches. In 9.8 hours, the snow depth will have increased by 3.5 in./hr × 9.8 hr = 34.3 in.

32. Your *maximum heart rate* decreases with respect to your *age*, and the rate of change is –1 beat per minute per year. If your age changes from 25 to 40 (a change of 15 years), then your maximum heart rate decreases by $1\dfrac{\text{beat}}{\text{min}\cdot\text{yr}}\times15\text{yr}=15\dfrac{\text{beats}}{\text{min}}$ (from 195 beats/min to 180 beats/min). Your maximum heart rate at age 70 is 220 – 70 = 150 beats/min.

33. The independent variable is time *t*, measured in years, where *t* = 0 represents today. The dependent variable is price *p*. The equation for the price function is *p* = 15,000 + 800*t*. A new car will cost *p* = 15,000 + 800 × 3.5 = $17,800. This function does not give a good model for car prices.

34. The independent variable is time *t*, measured in years, where *t* = 0 represents the year 2006. The dependent variable is record time *R*. The equation of the record time function is *R* = 50.40 – 0.05*t*. The world record time in 2020 (*t* = 14) would be *R* = 50.40 – 0.05 × 14 = 49.70 seconds. This model may prove to be inaccurate.

35. The independent variable is snow depth *d*, measured in inches, and the dependent variable is maximum speed *s*, measured in miles per hour. The equation for the speed function is *s* = 40 – 1.1*d*. To find the depth at which the plow will not be able to move, set *s* = 0 and solve for *d*.
$$0 = 40 - 1.1d$$
$$1.1d = 40$$
$$d = 40/1.1 = 36 \text{ inches.}$$
The rate at which the speed decreases per inch of snow depth is probably not a constant, so this model is an approximation.

36. The independent variable is miles driven *m* and the dependent variable is rental cost *r*. The equation for the rental cost function is *r* = 40 + 0.08*m*. Neglecting the cost of gas, you can find out how far you can drive by setting *r* = 100 and solving for *m*.
$$100 = 40 + 0.08m$$
$$60 = 0.08m$$
$$m = 60/0.08 = 750 \text{ miles.}$$
This function gives a very good model of the rental costs.

37. The independent variable is time *t*, measured in minutes, and the dependent variable is rental cost *r*. As long as the copy business is willing to prorate rental charges per minute (rather than in 5-minute blocks), the change per minute is $1.50/5 = $0.30 per minute. This implies the rental cost function is *r* = 8 + 0.30*t*. To find out how many minutes can be rented for $25, set *r* = 25, and solve for *t*.
$$25 = 8 + 0.30t$$
$$17 = 0.30t$$
$$t = 17/0.30 = 56.7 \text{ minutes.}$$
This function gives a very good model of rental costs.

38. The independent variable is time *t*, measured in years, where *t* = 0 represents 1980. The dependent variable is population *p*. The population function is *p* = 2000 + 200*t*. The population in 2010 (*t* = 30) is *p* = 2000 + 200 × 30 = 8000 people. If the population grows at a constant absolute rate of change, at least in the average sense, then this model is reliable for as long as these conditions exist.

39. Let *W* represent the weight of the dog in pounds, and *t* the time in years. The slope of the model is (15 – 2.5) ÷ (1 – 0) = 12.5 pounds per year, so the linear function is *W* = 12.5*t* + 2.5. When the dog is 5 years old, its weight is *W* = 12.5 × 5 + 2.5 = 65 pounds, and at age 10, it weighs *W* = 12.5 × 10 + 2.5 = 127.5 pounds. The model is accurate only for small ages.

40. The cost of leasing the bike is *L* = 150*m* + 200, where *L* is the cost in dollars, and *m* is time, measured in months. Set *L* = 6500 and solve for *m* to find the length of the lease that costs as much as the purchase price of the bike.
$$6500 = 150m + 200$$
$$6300 = 150m$$
$$m = 6300/150 = 42 \text{ months.}$$
After 42 months, the cost of leasing the bike is more than the cost of buying it outright.

41. Let *P* represent the profit (or loss) realized when selling *n* raffle tickets. The initial cost of the raffle to the fundraisers is $350 (a negative profit), and the rate of change of the profit with respect to the number of tickets sold is $10 per ticket. Thus the profit function is *P* = 10*n* – 350. One can see by inspection that 35 tickets must be sold to break even.

42. Let *P* represent the profit (or loss) realized when selling *n* tickets. The initial cost to the fundraisers is $100 (a negative profit), and the rate of change of the profit with respect to the number of tickets sold is $4 per ticket. Thus the profit function is $P = 4n - 100$. One can see by inspection that 25 tickets must be sold to break even.

43. Let *V* represent the value of the washing machine, and let *t* represent time (in years). The value function is $V = -75t + 1200$. Set $V = 0$ and solve for *t* to find out how long it will take for the value to reach $0.

$$0 = -75t + 1200$$
$$75t = 1200$$
$$t = 1200/75 = 16 \text{ years.}$$

44. The daily cost of extracting 2000 tons of gold at $1000 per ton is $2,000,000. Each ton produces 3 ounces of gold, with revenue of 3*p*, so the daily revenue would be $2000 \times 3p = 6000p$. Thus the profit function is $P = 6000p - 2,000,000$. The profit will be $0 when the price of gold is $2,000,000/6000 = \$333.33$, so this is the minimum price that makes the mine profitable.

FURTHER APPLICATIONS

45. The slope is $m = 2$, and the *y*-intercept is (0, 6).

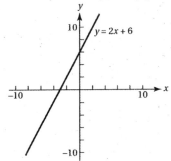

46. The slope is $m = -3$, and the *y*-intercept is (0, 3).

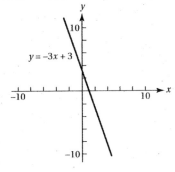

47. The slope is $m = -5$, and the *y*-intercept is (0, –5).

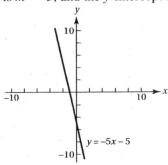

48. The slope is $m = 4$, and the *y*-intercept is (0, 1).

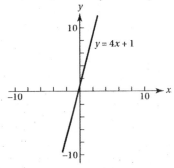

49. The slope is $m = 3$, and the *y*-intercept is (0, –6).
50. The slope is $m = -2$, and the *y*-intercept is (0, 5).
51. The slope is $m = -1$, and the *y*-intercept is (0, 4).
52. The slope is $m = 2$, and the *y*-intercept is (0, 4).

Graphs for Exercises 49–52:

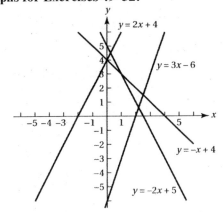

53. The independent and dependent variables are *time* and *elevation*, respectively.

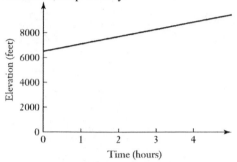

After 3.5 hours, the elevation of the climbers is 6500 + 600 × 3.5 = 8600 feet. The model is reasonable provided the rate of ascent is nearly constant.

54. The independent and dependent variables are *time* and *diameter*, respectively.

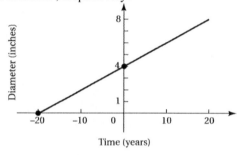

As shown in the graph, the tree needs 20 years to grow from 0 to 4 inches. This can be solved algebraically by creating an equation for the diameter of the tree: $d = 0.2t + 4$. Here it is understood that t is measured in years, beginning from the time you first measured the tree's diameter. Set $d = 0$ in the equation, and solve for t to find that $t = -20$, which means the tree began growing 20 years ago. The assumption that the tree grows linearly with respect to time would need to be evaluated by a biologist.

55. The independent and dependent variables are *number of posters* and *cost*, respectively.

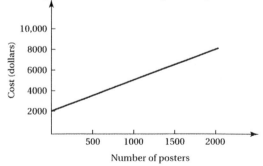

The cost of producing 2000 posters is 2000 + 2000 × 3 = $8000. This function probably gives a fairly realistic estimate of printing costs.

56. The independent and dependent variables are *time* and *amount of sugar*, respectively.

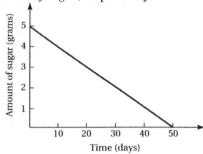

Solve $0 = -0.1t + 5$ for t to find that the sugar is gone in 50 days (this is also evident from the graph). A biologist (or beer master at a brewery) would need to assess the assumption that the sugar consumption rate is constant.

57. The independent and dependent variables are *time* and *cost*, respectively.

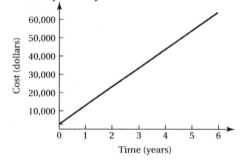

The cost of 6 years of school is 2000 + 10,000 × 6 = $62,000. Provided costs do not change during the six-year period, this function is an accurate model of the cost.

58. The independent and dependent variables are *load* and *maximum speed*, respectively.

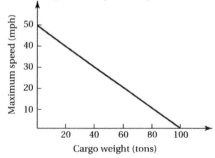

The maximum speed decreases by 10 mph for every additional 20 tons of cargo, so the slope of the graph is –0.5 mph/ton. To find the load at which the maximum speed is 0, solve $0 = -0.5w + 50$ for w (weight). This results in $w = 100$ tons.

Maximum truck speeds most likely don't decrease linearly with load, but the model probably gives a rough approximation.

59. a. Half of the fish caught in the second outing are tagged, and this means the proportion of those tagged in the entire population is 1/2. Thus $200/N = 1/2$, which implies $N = 400$ fish.

b. One-fourth of the fish caught in the second outing are tagged, and this means the proportion of those tagged in the entire population is 1/4. Thus $200/N = 1/4$, which implies $N = 800$ fish.

c. If p represents the proportion of those caught in the second outing that are tagged, we have $200/N = p$, which implies $N = f(p) = 200/p$.

d. Graph not supplied, though it looks similar to $y = 1/x$, with domain of $0 < p \leq 1$. When p is small, N is very large, and when p is close to 1, N is close to 200. Note that the above domain is the domain of the mathematical model, not the set of all possible values of p that could be observed in such a study. Consider a situation where only 200 fish are caught in the first outing from a very large lake with a large fish population. On the second outing, you may find that none of the 200 fish caught is tagged, in which case $p = 0$. This makes sense in the field, but it does not make sense in the mathematical model, because we cannot predict the fish population by using $N = 200/0$ (division by 0 is not allowed).

e. If $p = 15\% = 0.15$, $N = 200/0.15 = 1333$ fish.

UNIT 9C

QUICK QUIZ

1. **a.** Q_0 represents the initial value in the exponential model.

2. **b.** The variable r represents the growth rate, expressed as a decimal (and $3\% = 0.03$).

3. **c.** Because the value of the dollar is decreasing, r is negative.

4. **b.** The population of Boomtown at any time t is given by $10,000 \times 1.2^t$.

5. **c.** If you start out with a positive quantity, and remove half of it, half still remains (and it is a positive quantity, which can never equal 0).

6. **b.** If you know the initial amount and half-life of any exponentially decreasing quantity, you can use $Q = Q_0 \times \left(\dfrac{1}{2}\right)^{t/T_{half}}$ to predict the future amount after any time t.

7. **c.** You need to know both the initial amount Q_0 and the amount at some future time t in order to solve the exponential model $Q = Q_0 \times \left(\dfrac{1}{2}\right)^{t/T_{half}}$ for t (you must also know T_{half}, but we are given that).

8. **c.** Because 1/16 of the original uranium is present, we know it has undergone 4 halving periods, and since each of these is 700 million years, the rock is 4×700 million $= 2.8$ billion years old.

9. **a.** When you solve $\dfrac{1}{25}Q_0 = Q_0 \times \left(\dfrac{1}{2}\right)^{t/700,000,000}$ for t, you get the expression given in answer **a**.

10. **a.** We know $Q = Q_0(1+r)^t$, and $Q = Q_0 \times 2^{t/T_{double}}$, and thus $Q_0(1+r)^t = Q_0 \times 2^{t/T_{double}}$. Divide both sides by Q_0 to get the result shown in the answer.

DOES IT MAKE SENSE?

17. Does not make sense. After 100 years, the population growing at 2% per year will have increased by a factor of $1.02^{100} = 7.245$, whereas the population growing at 1% per year will have increased by a factor of $1.01^{100} = 2.705$. Under only very special circumstances will the first population grow by twice as many people as the second population. (Let Q_0 represent the initial amount of the population growing by 2%, and R_0 the initial amount of the population growing by 1%. After 100 years, Q_0 will have grown to $7.245Q_0$, and thus will have grown by $7.245Q_0 - Q_0 = 6.245Q_0$. In a similar fashion, it can be shown that R_0 will have grown by $1.705R_0$. We need $6.245Q_0 = 2 \times 1.705R_0$ in order to satisfy the condition that the first population will grow by twice as many people as the second population. This implies that the ratio $R_0/Q_0 = 6.245/3.41 = 1.83$. In other words, whenever the initial amount of the second population is 1.83 times as large as the initial amount of the first population, the first population will grow by twice as many people in 100 years. Try it with initial populations of 100 and 183.)

18. Makes sense. The growth rate for an exponentially decreasing quantity is always negative.

19. Makes sense. If we know the half-life of the radioactive material, we can create an exponential function that models the quantity remaining as time passes. In order to use this model to determine ages of bones, we only need to measure the amount of radioactive material present in the bone, and the amount it had originally (the latter is usually surmised by making assumptions about conditions present at the time of death).

20. Makes sense. Money invested in a bank grows at a constant rate of relative change as long as the APR is constant, and thus it is appropriate to use an exponential function.

BASIC CONCEPTS & SKILLS

21. $2^x = 128 \Rightarrow \log_{10} 2^x = \log_{10} 128 \Rightarrow x\log_{10} 2 = \log_{10} 128 \Rightarrow x = \dfrac{\log_{10} 128}{\log_{10} 2} = 7$.

22. $10^x = 23 \Rightarrow \log_{10} 10^x = \log_{10} 23 \Rightarrow x = 1.36$.

23. $3^x = 99 \Rightarrow \log_{10} 3^x = \log_{10} 99 \Rightarrow x\log_{10} 3 = \log_{10} 99 \Rightarrow x = \dfrac{\log_{10} 99}{\log_{10} 3} = 4.18$.

24. $5^{2x} = 240 \Rightarrow \log_{10} 5^{2x} = \log_{10} 240 \Rightarrow 2x\log_{10} 5 = \log_{10} 240 \Rightarrow x = \dfrac{\log_{10} 240}{2\log_{10} 5} = 1.70$.

25. $7^{3x} = 623 \Rightarrow \log_{10} 7^{3x} = \log_{10} 623 \Rightarrow 3x\log_{10} 7 = \log_{10} 623 \Rightarrow x = \dfrac{\log_{10} 623}{3\log_{10} 7} = 1.10$.

26. $3 \times 4^x = 180 \Rightarrow 4^x = 60 \Rightarrow \log_{10} 4^x = \log_{10} 60 \Rightarrow x\log_{10} 4 = \log_{10} 60 \Rightarrow x = \dfrac{\log_{10} 60}{\log_{10} 4} = 2.95$.

27. $9^x = 1748 \Rightarrow x = \dfrac{\log_{10} 1748}{\log_{10} 9} = 3.40$. (See exercise 23 for a similar process of solution.)

28. $3^{x/4} = 444 \Rightarrow x = \dfrac{4\log_{10} 444}{\log_{10} 3} = 22.19$. (See exercise 24 for a similar process of solution).

29. $\log_{10} x = 4 \Rightarrow 10^{\log_{10} x} = 10^4 \Rightarrow x = 10,000$.

30. $\log_{10} x = -3 \Rightarrow 10^{\log_{10} x} = 10^{-3} \Rightarrow x = 0.001$.

31. $\log_{10} x = 3.5 \Rightarrow x = 10^{3.5} = 3162.28$. (See exercise 29 for a similar process of solution).

32. $\log_{10} x = -2.2 \Rightarrow x = 10^{-2.2} = 0.0063$. (See exercise 30 for a similar process of solution).

33. $3\log_{10} x = 4.2 \Rightarrow \log_{10} x = 1.4 \Rightarrow x = 10^{1.4} = 25.12$.

34. $\log_{10} 3x = 5.1 \Rightarrow 3x = 10^{5.1} \Rightarrow x = 41,964.18$.

35. $\log_{10}(4 + x) = 1.1 \Rightarrow 4 + x = 10^{1.1} \Rightarrow x = 8.59$.

36. $4\log_{10}(4x) = 4 \Rightarrow \log_{10}(4x) = 1 \Rightarrow 4x = 10^1 \Rightarrow x = 2.50$.

37. a. $Q = 60,000 \times (1.025)^t$, where Q is the population of the town, and t is time (measured in years).

b.

Year	Population
0	60,000
1	61,500
2	63,038
3	64,613
4	66,229
5	67,884
6	69,582
7	71,321
8	73,104
9	74,932
10	76,805

c.

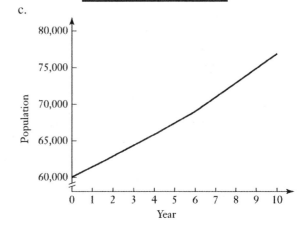

38. a. $Q = 800 \times (1.03)^t$, where Q is the number of restaurants, and t is time, measured in years, with $t = 0$ corresponding to 2001.

b.

Year	Restaurants
0	800
1	824
2	849
3	874
4	900
5	927
6	955
7	984
8	1013
9	1044
10	1075

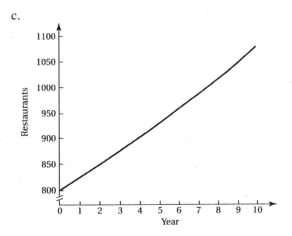

c.

40. a. $Q = 10,000 \times (0.997)^t$, where Q is the population of the town after t years.
b.

Month	Population
0	10,000
1	9970
2	9940
3	9910
4	9881
5	9851
6	9821
7	9792
8	9763
9	9733
10	9704

c.

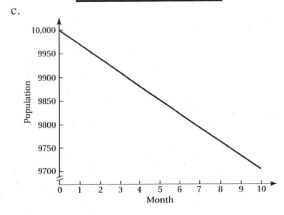

39. a. $Q = 1,000,000 \times (0.93)^t$, where Q is the number of acres of forest left after t years.
b.

Year	Acres ($\times 10^6$)
0	1.00
1	0.93
2	0.86
3	0.80
4	0.75
5	0.70
6	0.65
7	0.60
8	0.56
9	0.52
10	0.48

c.

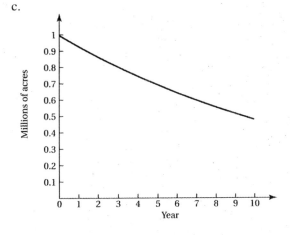

41. a. $Q = 175,000 \times (1.05)^t$, where Q is the average price of a home in dollars, and t is time, measured in years, with $t = 0$ corresponding to 2007.
b.

Year	Average price
0	$175,000
1	$183,750
2	$192,938
3	$202,584
4	$212,714
5	$223,349
6	$234,517
7	$246,243
8	$258,555
9	$271,482
10	$285,057

c.

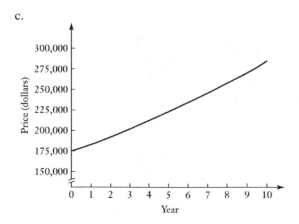

42. a. $Q = 8 \times (0.85)^t$, where Q is the amount of the drug remaining in the blood stream, measured in milligrams, and t is time, measured in hours.

b.

Hour	Drug (mg)
0	8.00
1	6.80
2	5.78
3	4.91
4	4.18
5	3.55
6	3.02
7	2.56
8	2.18
9	1.85
10	1.57

c.

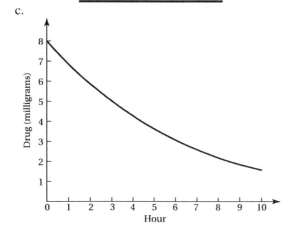

43. a. $Q = 2000 \times (1.05)^t$, where Q is your monthly salary in dollars, and t is time, measured in years.

b.

Year	Monthly Salary
0	$2000.00
1	$2100.00
2	$2205.00
3	$2315.25
4	$2431.01
5	$2552.56
6	$2680.19
7	$2814.20
8	$2954.91
9	$3102.66
10	$3257.79

c.

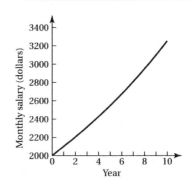

44. a. $Q = 10,000 \times (0.5)^t$, where Q is the value of the 100,000 rubles, measured in dollars, and t is time in years, with $t = 0$ corresponding to 1991.

b.

Year	Value of rubles
0	$10,000
1	$5000
2	$2500
3	$1250
4	$625
5	$313
6	$156
7	$78
8	$39
9	$20
10	$10

c.

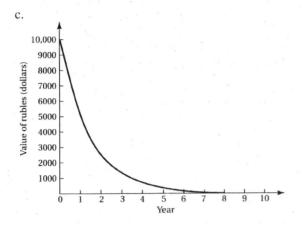

45. Over the span of a year, prices will increase by a factor of $(1.012)^{12} = 1.154$, which is a 15.4% increase.

46. Over the span of a year, the fraction by which the price of gold will change is $(0.995)^{12} = 0.942$, which implies a 5.8% decrease.

47. Over the course of a year, prices would have risen by a factor of $(1.8)^{12} = 1156.83$, or an annual increase of 115,683%. Assuming one day is 1/30 of a month, prices would rise by a factor of $(1.8)^{(1/30)} = 1.0198$ in one day, which is a 1.98% increase.

48. Over the course of a year, prices would have risen by a factor of $(1.9)^{12} = 2213.31$, or an annual increase of 221,331%. Assuming one day is 1/30 of a month, prices would rise by a factor of $(1.9)^{(1/30)} = 1.0216$ in one day, which is a 2.16% increase.

49. An exponential model for the animal population is $Q = 1500 \times (0.92)^t$. We need to find the time t that will produce a population $Q = 30$ animals, which amounts to solving $30 = 1500 \times (0.92)^t$ for t.

$$\frac{30}{1500} = 0.92^t \implies 0.02 = 0.92^t \implies \log_{10} 0.02 =$$

$$\log_{10} 0.92^t \implies \log_{10} 0.02 = t \log_{10} 0.92 \implies$$

$$t = \frac{\log_{10} 0.02}{\log_{10} 0.92} = 46.92 \text{ years.}$$

50. a. An exponential model for oil production, valid between 1950 and 1972, is $Q = 518 \times (1.07)^t$, where Q is measured in millions of tons, and $t = 0$ corresponds with 1950. In 1972, $t = 22$, so oil production was $Q = 518 \times (1.07)^{22} = 2295$ million tons, or about 2.3 billion tons.
b. In 1998, 26 years beyond 1972, oil production would have been $Q = 2295 \times (1.07)^{26} = 13,328$ million tons, or about 13.3 billion tons, assuming a constant growth rate of 7%. This is considerably larger than the actual 1998 level of 3.3 billion tons.
c. In 1998, 26 years beyond 1972, oil production would have been $Q = 2295 \times (1.03)^{26} = 4949$ million tons, or about 4.9 billion tons, assuming a constant growth rate of 3%. This is still larger than the actual 1998 level of 3.3 billion tons.
d. Based on the answer to part c, the average annual growth rate between 1972 and 1993 was less than 3%. Experiment with various values of r in $3300 = 2295 \times (1 + r)^{26}$ to find that $r \sim 1.4\%$ per year. One can also solve the equation using algebra: $3300 = 2295 \times (1 + r)^{26} \implies \frac{3300}{2295} = (1 + r)^{26}$

Now raise both sides to the reciprocal power of 26, i.e. to the 1/26 power, and then subtract 1 to find $r = \left(\frac{3300}{2295}\right)^{1/26} - 1 = 0.014 = 1.4\%$.

51. a. An exponential model for the amount of Valium in the bloodstream is $Q = 50 \times \left(\frac{1}{2}\right)^{t/36}$. After 12 hours, there will be $Q = 50 \times \left(\frac{1}{2}\right)^{12/36} = 39.7$ mg.
b. Ten percent of the initial amount is 5 mg, so solve $5 = 50 \times \left(\frac{1}{2}\right)^{t/36}$ for t:

$$0.1 = (0.5)^{t/36} \implies \log_{10} 0.1 = \log_{10}(0.5)^{t/36} \implies$$

$$\log_{10} 0.1 = \frac{t}{36} \log_{10} 0.5 \implies t = \frac{36 \log_{10} 0.1}{\log_{10} 0.5} \implies$$

$$t = 120 \text{ hours.}$$

52. a. At 6:00 p.m., there will be $Q = 300 \times \left(\frac{1}{2}\right)^{6/8} = 178.4$ mg. At midnight, $Q = 300 \times \left(\frac{1}{2}\right)^{12/8} = 106.1$ mg. At noon the next day, $Q = 300 \times \left(\frac{1}{2}\right)^{24/8} = 37.5$ mg.
b. Five percent of the original amount is 15 mg, so solve $15 = 300 \times \left(\frac{1}{2}\right)^{t/8}$ for t.

$$0.05 = (0.5)^{t/8} \implies \log_{10} 0.05 = \log_{10}(0.5)^{t/8} \implies$$

$$\log_{10} 0.05 = \frac{t}{8} \log_{10} 0.5 \implies t = \frac{8 \log_{10} 0.05}{\log_{10} 0.5} \implies$$

$$t = 35 \text{ hours.}$$

53. a. An exponential model for the amount of uranium left is $Q = Q_0 \times \left(\frac{1}{2}\right)^{t/4.5}$, where t is measured in billions of years. We want to determine t when the amount Q is equal to 65% of

the original amount, i.e. when $Q = 0.65Q_0$. Solve $0.65Q_0 = Q_0 \times \left(\frac{1}{2}\right)^{t/4.5}$ for t – begin by dividing both sides by Q_0:

$$0.65 = \left(\frac{1}{2}\right)^{t/4.5} \Rightarrow \log_{10} 0.65 = \log_{10}(0.5)^{t/4.5} \Rightarrow$$

$$\log_{10} 0.65 = \frac{t}{4.5}\log_{10} 0.5 \Rightarrow t = \frac{4.5\log_{10} 0.65}{\log_{10} 0.5} \Rightarrow$$

$$t = 2.8 \text{ billion years old.}$$

b. Following the same process shown in part **a**, we have $t = \dfrac{4.5\log_{10} 0.45}{\log_{10} 0.5} = 5.2$ billion years old.

54. a. An exponential model for the amount of carbon-14 left is $Q = Q_0 \times \left(\frac{1}{2}\right)^{t/5700}$, where t is measured in years. We want to determine t when the amount Q is equal to 63% of the original amount, i.e. when $Q = 0.63Q_0$. Solve $0.63Q_0 = Q_0 \times \left(\frac{1}{2}\right)^{t/5700}$ for t – begin by dividing both sides by Q_0:

$$0.63 = \left(\frac{1}{2}\right)^{t/5700} \Rightarrow \log_{10} 0.63 = \log_{10}(0.5)^{t/5700}$$

$$\log_{10} 0.63 = \frac{t}{5700}\log_{10} 0.5 \Rightarrow t = \frac{5700\log_{10} 0.63}{\log_{10} 0.5}$$

$$t = 3799 \text{ years.}$$

The cloth was painted 3799 years ago.

b. Following the same process shown in part **a**, we have $t = \dfrac{5700\log_{10} 0.123}{\log_{10} 0.5} = 17{,}233$ years ago.

c. The age of the earth is about 4.5 billion years old. The half-life of carbon-14 is only 5700 years, and thus carbon-14 present at the formation of the earth has long since decayed to immeasurably small amounts (it has undergone almost 800,000 halving periods, far more than necessary to decrease any imaginable amount of carbon-14 to an amount that is essentially zero).

FURTHER APPLICATIONS

55. An exponential model for the amount of radioactive substance is $Q = 3 \times \left(\frac{1}{2}\right)^{t/20}$, where Q is the density of the substance in mg/cm^2, and t is time in years, with $t = 0$ corresponding to the present. This model is valid for times in the past – we need only assign negative values for t. Thus 55 years ago corresponds with $t = -55$, so the density at that time was $Q = 3 \times \left(\frac{1}{2}\right)^{-55/20} = 20.2$ mg/cm^2.

One can also solve $3 = Q_0 \times \left(\frac{1}{2}\right)^{55/20}$ for Q_0 to produce the same result.

56. In 2020 ($t = 15$ years beyond 2005), the population will be $Q = 105{,}000 \times (1.03)^{15} = 163{,}587$. In 2100 ($t = 95$), $Q = 105{,}000 \times (1.03)^{95} = 1{,}740{,}707$.

57. The cart of groceries cost $Q = \$125 \times (1.035)^5 = \$148.46$.

UNIT 10A

QUICK QUIZ

1. **a**. As long as the points are distinct, two points are sufficient to determine a unique line.
2. **b**. The surface of a wall is similar to a plane, which is two-dimensional.
3. **a**. By definition, an acute angle has measure less than 90°.
4. **c**. By definition, a regular polygon is a many-sided figure where each side has the same length, and each internal angle is the same.
5. **b**. By definition, a right triangle has one 90° angle.
6. **a**. The formula for the circumference of a circle of radius r is $C = 2\pi r$.
7. **c**. The formula for the volume of a sphere of radius r is $V = \frac{4}{3}\pi r^3$.
8. **c**. Suppose the side length of a square is denoted by s. Its area is then s^2. If the lengths of the sides are doubled to $2s$, the area becomes $(2s) = 4s^2$, and this is 4 times as large as the original area.
9. **c**. The volume of a sphere whose radius has tripled from r to $3r$ is $V = \frac{4}{3}\pi(3r)^3 = 3^3 \cdot \frac{4}{3}\pi r^3$.
10. **a**. The volume of a block does not increase when it is cut into pieces, though its surface area does, which implies is surface-area-to-volume ratio does as well.

DOES IT MAKE SENSE?

21. Does not make sense. If the highways are, in fact, straight lines, they will not intersect more than once.
22. Does not make sense. A triangle can have no more than one right angle, as the sum of its three angles is 180° (and thus two right angles would leave no room for a third).
23. Makes sense. A rectangular prism is just a box.
24. Makes sense. The distance across a circle (its diameter) is smaller than the distance half way around it.
25. Does not make sense. Basketballs are in the shape of a sphere (a can is shaped like a right circular cylinder).
26. Makes sense. Construct the fence along the diagonal of the yard, and you'll have two triangular yards.

BASIC SKILLS & CONCEPTS

27. One-half of a circle is 180°.
28. One-sixth of a circle is 60°.
29. One-tenth of a circle is 36°.
30. Two-thirds of a circle is 240°.
31. One-sixtieth of a circle is 6°.
32. Five-sixths of a circle is 300°.
33. A 45° angle subtends 45°/360° = 1/8 circle.
34. A 6° angle subtends 6°/360° = 1/60 circle.
35. A 120° angle subtends 120°/360° = 1/3 circle.
36. A 90° angle subtends 90°/360° = 1/4 circle.
37. A 270° angle subtends 270°/360° = 3/4 circle.
38. An 18° angle subtends 18°/360° = 1/20 circle.
39. A 300° angle subtends 300°/360° = 5/6 circle.
40. A 225° angle subtends 225°/360° = 5/8 circle.
41. $C = 2\pi \times 8 = 16\pi$ m = 50.3 m. $A = \pi \cdot 8^2 = 64\pi = 201.1$ m^2.
42. $C = 2\pi \times 3 = 6\pi$ km = 18.8 km. $A = \pi \cdot 3^2 = 9\pi = 28.3$ km^2.
43. $C = 2\pi \times 8 = 16\pi$ cm = 50.3 cm. $A = \pi \cdot 8^2 = 64\pi = 201.1$ cm^2.
44. $C = 2\pi \times 4.5 = 9\pi = 28.3$ m. $A = \pi \cdot 4.5^2 = 20.25\pi = 63.6$ m^2.
45. $C = 2\pi \times 15 = 30\pi$ mm = 94.2 mm. $A = \pi \cdot 15^2 = 225\pi = 706.9$ mm^2.
46. $C = 2\pi \times 0.75 = 1.5\pi$ km = 4.7 km. $A = \pi \cdot 0.75^2 = 0.5625\pi = 1.8$ km^2.
47. The perimeter is 4 × 9 = 36 mi. The area is 9 × 9 = 81 mi^2.
48. The perimeter is 2 × 8 + 2 × 14 = 44 in. The area is 8 × 14 = 112 in.^{2}.
49. The perimeter is 2 × 12 + 2 × 30 = 84 ft. The area is 30 × 6 = 180 ft^2.
50. The perimeter is 4 × 1.4 = 5.6 cm. The area is 1.4 × 1.4 = 1.96 cm^2.
51. The perimeter is 2 × 2.2 + 2 × 2.0 = 8.4 cm. The area is 2.2 × 2.0 = 4.4 cm^2.
52. The perimeter is 2 × 4.5 + 2 × 12.2 = 33.4 ft. The area is 12.2 × 3.6 = 43.92 ft^2.
53. The perimeter is 6 + 8 + 10 = 24 units. The area is $\frac{1}{2} \times 8 \times 6 = 24$ units^2.
54. The perimeter is 3.125 + 1.875 + 2.5 = 7.5 units. The area is $\frac{1}{2} \times 3.125 \times 1.5 = 2.34$ units^2.
55. The perimeter is 8 + 5 + 5 = 18 units. The area is $\frac{1}{2} \times 8 \times 3 = 12$ units^2.
56. The perimeter is 13 + 13 + 24 = 50 units. The area is $\frac{1}{2} \times 24 \times 5 = 60$ units^2.
57. The two semicircular caps together make a single circle, whose radius is 3 feet. The perimeter, then, is 2 × 8 + 2π × 3 = 34.85 ft, and the area is $6 \times 8 + \pi \times 3^2 = 76.27$ ft^2.

58. The two semicircular ends of the track together make a single circle, whose radius is 30 yards. The perimeter, then, is $2 \times 100 + 2\pi \times 30 = 388.5$ yd, and the area is $60 \times 100 + \pi \times 30^2 = 8827.4$ yd^2.

59. The area is $\frac{1}{2} \times 12 \times 11 = 66$ ft^2.

60. The barn on the left has the greater area because the height of its triangular roof section is larger.

61. The area of the parallelogram is $180 \times 150 = 27,500$ yd^2.

62. The area of the park is $90 \times 60 = 5400$ m^2. The area of the playground is $20 \times 55 = 1100$ m^2. Thus the grassy area is 5400 m^2 $-$ 1100 m^2 $=$ 4300 m^2.

63. The pool holds $50 \times 30 \times 2.5 = 3750$ m^3.

64. The arena holds $30 \times 40 \times 8 = 9600$ m^3. One liter is 1000 cubic centimeters, and thus 0.001 cubic meters, which means each cubic meter holds 1000 liters. This implies the arena holds 9,600,000 liters.

65. The duct is in the shape of a cylinder, and so its volume is $\pi \times 1.5^2 \times 40 = 282.7$ ft^3 (note that 18 inches is 1.5 feet). The surface area of the duct is $2\pi \times 1.5 \times 40 = 377.0$ ft^2. We are assuming here that there are no circular end pieces on the duct that need to be painted. If there are end pieces, the area would increase by $2\pi \times 1.5^2 = 14.1$ ft^2.

66. The ball's circumference is 69 cm, so its radius is $r = 69 \div 2\pi = 10.98$ cm (rounded). Its volume is $\frac{4}{3} \times \pi \times r^3 = 5547.5$ cm^3 (using an un-rounded value for r), and its surface area is $4\pi \times r^2 = 1515.5$ cm^2.

67. The circumference is greater because it is π diameters (of a tennis ball) long, whereas the height is only 3 diameters tall.

68. When the canal is full, there are $3 \times 2 \times 30 = 180$ m^3 of water. If 60% of the water has evaporated, 40% of 180 cubic meters, or 72 cubic meters remain.

69. The volume of the reservoir is $250 \times 60 \times 12 = 180,000$ m^3. 30% of this volume, which is 54,000 m^3, must be added.

70. The first drum has greater volume ($\pi \times 2^2 \times 3 = 37.7$ ft^3), than the second drum (whose volume is $\pi \times 1.5^2 \times 4 = 28.3$ ft^3).

71. The first tree has greater volume ($\pi \times 2.1^2 \times 40 = 554.2$ ft^3) than the second tree (whose volume is $\pi \times 2.4^2 \times 30 = 542.9$ ft^3).

72. The height of the concert hall will be 30 times as large as the height of the model.

73. The surface area of the concert hall will be $30^2 = 900$ times as great as the surface area of the

model (because areas always scale with the square of the scale factor).

74. The volume of the concert hall will be $30^3 = 27,000$ times as large as the volume of the model (because volumes always scale with the cube of the scale factor).

75. The height of the office complex will be 80 times as large as the height of the model.

76. The amount of paint needed is a function of the surface area, so you will need $80^2 = 6400$ times as much paint for the office complex than for the model (areas scale with the square of the scale factor).

77. You would need $80^3 = 512,000$ times as many marbles to fill the office complex (volumes always scale with the cube of the scale factor).

78. Your arm length has increased by a factor of 4.

79. Your waist size is a measurement of length, so it has increased by a factor of 4.

80. The material required for your clothes is a function of surface area, so the amount needed has increased by a factor of 16.

81. Your weight is a function of your volume, so it has increased by a factor of 64.

82. Answers will vary. Example: I'm 70 inches tall, and Sam is 1.2 $\times$ 70 = 84 inches tall.

83. Answers will vary. Example: My waist size is 32 inches, and Sam's is 1.2 $\times$ 32 = 38.4 inches.

84. Answers will vary. Example: My weight is 155 lb, and Sam weighs $1.2^3 \times 155 = 268$ lb.

85. Think of a soup can (a squirrel) and a trash can (a human), compute their surface areas and volumes, find their surface-area-to-volume ratios, and you will discover that the surface-area-to-volume ratio for squirrels is larger than that of humans. Another way to understand this fact: surface area scales with the square of the scale factor, whereas volume scales with the cube of the scale factor. Thus the surface-area-to-volume ratio decreases when objects are scaled up (and in fact, it scales with the reciprocal of the scale factor).

86. Squirrels lose more heat for their volume (or weight) than humans because of their larger surface-area-to-volume ratio, so squirrels must maintain a higher metabolism and eat more food for their weight.

87. The moon's surface-area-to-volume ratio is four (i.e. the scale factor) times as large as Earth's, (see discussion at the end of exercise 85).

88. Based only upon the result of exercise 87, the earth should have a hotter interior today because its surface-area-to-volume ratio is lower, and thus it radiates less heat per unit volume than the moon. A hot interior leads to more volcanic activity. Note

that the earth also has the benefit of an atmosphere, which helps to retain heat.

89. If you understood the comment at the end of exercise 85, the surface-area-to-volume ratio of the bowling ball should be 1/3 the ratio of the softball, because the bowling ball is 3 times as large. Computing directly: The surface area of the softball is $4\pi \times 2^2 = 50.3$ in^2, its volume is $\frac{4}{3}\pi \times 2^3 = 33.5$ in^3, and its surface-area-to-volume ratio is 1.5. The surface area of the bowling ball is $4\pi \times 6^2 = 452.4$ in^2, its volume is $\frac{4}{3}\pi \times 6^3 = 904.8$ in^3, and its surface-area-to-volume ratio is 0.5. As expected, the ratio of the bowling ball is 1/3 the ratio of the softball.

90. The surface-area-to-volume ratio for any sphere is given by $\left(4\pi \times r^2\right) \div \left(\frac{4}{3}\pi \times r^3\right) = \frac{3}{r}$, so the ratio for the earth is $3 \div 6400 = 0.00047$, and for Mars it is $3 \div 3400 = 0.00088$ (Mars' ratio being larger). To compute these ratios from the surface areas and volumes of the planets, use the formulas shown above to find that the surface area for the Earth is 5.15×10^8 km^2, while its volume is 1.10×10^{12} km^3. The surface area of Mars is 1.45×10^8 km^2, while its volume is 1.65×10^{11} km^3.

FURTHER APPLICATIONS

91. a. The book occupies three-dimensional space, so three dimensions are needed to describe it.
    b. The cover of the book occupies a portion of a plane, so two dimensions are needed to describe it.
    c. An edge of the book lies along a line, so a single dimension is adequate for its description.
    d. A point is dimensionless, so anything on the book that corresponds to a point (such as a corner of a page) is of zero dimension.

92. Exactly one line can be drawn perpendicular to the first line through the given point. No other distinct parallel line can be drawn through the point.

93. The third line is necessarily perpendicular to both lines due to a theorem from geometry (when two parallel lines are cut by any other line, all three lying in the same plane, alternate interior angles are equal – this amounts to saying that if the angle between one of the parallel lines and the third line is 90°, the angle between the other parallel line and the third line is 90°).

94. The area of the backyard is $20 \times 10 = 200$ m^2, the area of the garden is $4 \times 4 = 16$ m^2, and the area of the patio is $\frac{1}{2}\pi \times 5^2 = 39.3$ m^2. Together these facts imply the area to be seeded is $200 - 16 - 39.3 = 144.7$ square meters.

95. a. The surface area of an individual sac is $4\pi \times \left(\frac{1}{6}\right)^2 = 0.349$ mm^2, and the total surface area is 300 million times this value, which is 1.05×10^8 mm$^2 = 105$ m^2. The volume of a single sac is $\frac{4}{3}\pi \times \left(\frac{1}{6}\right)^3 = 0.0194$ mm^3, so the total volume is 5.82×10^6 mm^3 (multiply the individual volume by 300 million).
    b. We need to solve $5.82 \times 10^6 = \frac{4}{3}\pi \times r^3$ for r to find the radius of such a sphere. Multiply both sides of the equation by $\frac{3}{4\pi}$ and take the cube root to find $r = 112$ mm (rounded). This sphere has surface area of $4\pi \times (111.572)^2 = 1.56 \times 10^5$ mm^2. The surface area of the air sacs is $1.05 \times 10^8 \div 1.56 \times 10^5 = 673$ times as large as the surface area of the hypothetical sphere.
    c. We need to solve $1.05 \times 10^8 = 4\pi \times r^2$ for r to find the radius of such a sphere. Divide both sides by 4π and take the square root to find $r = 2891$ mm, or about 2.9 meters (i.e. more than 9 feet). The human lung has a remarkable design as it is able to take advantage of large surface area despite its relatively small volume.

96. a. The engine is $6 \times \pi \times 2.22^2 \times 3.25 = 302$ in.^{3}.
    b. Convert 302 cubic inches into liters:

$$302 \text{ in.}^3 \times \left(\frac{2.54 \text{ cm}}{1 \text{ in.}}\right)^3 \times \frac{1 \text{ L}}{1000 \text{ cm}^3} = 4.95 \text{ L}.$$

The American engine is more than twice the size of the foreign engine.

97. The volume of one tunnel is $\frac{1}{2}\pi \times (4)^2 \times 50,000 = 1.26 \times 10^6$ m^3, so the volume of all three is 3.8×10^6 m$^3 = 0.0038$ km^3. Depending on whether the dimensions given are for a rough tunnel, or the structure that a motorist sees driving through it, the amount of earth removed may be considerably more than the answer provided.

UNIT 10B

QUICK QUIZ

1. **c.** Each degree contains 60 minutes.
2. **b.** Each degree contains 60 minutes, and each minute contains 60 seconds.

3. **a**. Lines of latitude run east and west on the globe, parallel to the equator.

4. **b**. That you are at 30°S means you are in the southern hemisphere (and thus not in North America). A check of the globe will reveal these coordinates lie in the south Pacific.

5. **b**. Angular size is a function of the distance from the object: when the distance from an object increases, its angular size decreases.

6. **b**. Imagine a solar eclipse, when the Moon is positioned between the Earth and the Sun, and think of the triangle that stretches from a point on Earth to the edges of the moon. Imagine another triangle that continues beyond the Moon to the edges of the Sun (a simple drawing will help you to visualize the situation). These two triangles are similar, and thus we can write the ratio $\frac{\text{diameter of Sun}}{\text{diameter of Moon}} = \frac{400x}{x}$, where x represents the distance from the Earth to the Moon. This ratio implies that the diameter of the Sun is 400 times the diameter of the Moon. One can also appeal to the angular size formula in the text to get the same result.

7. **a**. A 10% grade means the slope is 1/10, which implies a vertical change of 1 unit for every horizontal change of 10 units.

8. **a**. The Pythagorean theorem gives $x = \sqrt{6^2 + 9^2}$.

9. **a**. The statement in answer **a** is an application of the fact that the ratio of corresponding sides in a pair of similar triangles is equal to the ratio of a different set of corresponding sides.

10. **b**. As explained in Example 9 of the text, a circle is the solution to the problem of enclosing the largest possible area with a fixed perimeter.

DOES IT MAKE SENSE?

19. Does not make sense. Points south of the equator experience summer in December.

20. Does not make sense. We see the angular size of the Moon, not its physical size.

21. Makes sense. As long as the speaker can ride a bike, a 1% grade should pose no difficulty.

22. Does not make sense. The sum of the angles in all triangles is 180°, yet not all triangles are similar.

23. Makes sense. Triangle B is just a scaled up version of Triangle A, so they are similar.

24. Makes sense. As stated in Example 10 of the text, a cube-shaped box is the one with smallest surface area for a given volume.

BASIC SKILLS & CONCEPTS

25. $32.5° = 32° + 0.5° \times \frac{60'}{1°} = 32°30'$.

26. $280.1° = 280° + 0.1° \times \frac{60'}{1°} = 280°6'$.

27. $12.33° = 12° + 0.33° \times \frac{60'}{1°} = 12°19.8' = 12° + 19' + 0.8' \times \frac{60''}{1'} = 12°19'48''$.

28. $0.08° = 0.08° \times \frac{60'}{1°} = 0°4.8' = 0° + 4' + 0.8' \times \frac{60''}{1'} = 0°4'48''$.

29. $149.83° = 149° + 0.83° \times \frac{60'}{1°} = 149°49.8' = 149° + 49' + 0.8' \times \frac{60''}{1'} = 149°49'48''$.

30. $47.6723° = 47° + 0.6723° \times \frac{60'}{1°} = 47°40.338' = 47° + 40' + 0.338' \times \frac{60''}{1'} = 47°40'20''$.

31. $30°10' = 30° + 10' \times \frac{1°}{60'} = 30.17°$.

32. $60°30'30'' = 60° + 30' \times \frac{1°}{60'} + 30'' \times \frac{1°}{3600''} = 60.51°$.

33. $123°10'36'' = 123° + 10' \times \frac{1°}{60'} + 36'' \times \frac{1°}{3600''} = 123.18°$.

34. $2°2'2'' = 2° + 2' \times \frac{1°}{60'} + 2'' \times \frac{1°}{3600''} = 2.03°$.

35. $8°59'10'' = 8° + 59' \times \frac{1°}{60'} + 10'' \times \frac{1°}{3600''} = 8.99°$.

36. $150°14'28'' = 150° + 14' \times \frac{1°}{60'} + 28'' \times \frac{1°}{3600''} = 150.24°$.

37. A full circle is 360°, and each degree is 60', so there are $360° \times \frac{60'}{1°} = 21,600'$ in a circle.

38. $360° \times \frac{60'}{1°} \times \frac{60''}{1'} = 1,296,000''$.

39. Copenhagen is at 56°N, 12°E (or 12.5°E).

40. La Paz is at 16°S, 68°W.

41. The latitude changes from 36°N to 36°S. To find the longitude, move 180° east from 115°W to arrive at 65°E. (Note that after moving 115°, you'll be at the prime meridian, or 0°, and you still have 65° to go). Thus the point opposite Las Vegas is 36°S, 65°E.

42. The latitude changes from 43°N to 43°S. To find the longitude, move 180° east from 88°W to arrive at 92°E. (Note that after moving 88°, you'll be at the prime meridian, or 0°, and you still have 92° to go). Thus the point opposite Milwaukee is 43°S, 92°E.

43. Buenos Aires is farther from the North Pole because its latitude (35°S) is further south than the latitude of Capetown (34°S).

44. Guatemala City is further from the South Pole because it is north of the equator while Lusaka is south of the equator.

45. Buffalo is 17° north of Miami, and each degree is 1/360 of the circumference of the Earth. Since the circumference is about 25,000 mi, Buffalo is $\frac{17}{360} \times 25,000 = 1181$ mi, or about 1200 miles from Miami.

46. Washington is 50° north of Lima, and each degree is 1/360 of the circumference of the Earth. Since the circumference is about 25,000 mi, Washington is $\frac{50}{360} \times 25,000 = 3472$ mi, or about 3500 miles from Lima.

47. A quarter is about an inch in diameter, and 5 yards is 180 inches. Thus its angular size is $1 \text{ in.} \times \frac{360°}{2\pi \times 180 \text{ in.}} = 0.32°$.

48. A quarter is about an inch in diameter, and 25 yards is 900 inches. Thus its angular size is $1 \text{ in.} \times \frac{360°}{2\pi \times 900 \text{ in.}} = 0.064ß$.

49. The Sun's true diameter (physical size) is $0.5ß \times \frac{2\pi \times 150,000,000 \text{ km}}{360°} = 1.31 \times 10^6 \text{ km}$.

50. The tree's height (physical size) is $0.5ß \times \frac{2\pi \times 2640 \text{ ft}}{360°} = 23.0 \text{ ft}$. Note that 0.5 mile is 2640 feet.

51. A roof with a pitch of 1 in 4 has a slope of 1/4, which is steeper than a roof with a slope of 2/10.

52. A road with a 12% grade has a slope of 12/100 = 0.12, and a road with a pitch of 1 in 8 has as slope of 1/8 = 0.125, so the road with a pitch of 1 in 8 is steeper.

53. A railroad with a 3% grade has a slope of 3/100 = 0.03, which is not as steep as a railroad with a slope of 1/25 = 0.04.

54. A sidewalk with a pitch of 1 in 6 has a slope of 1/6 = 0.17. This is steeper than a sidewalk with a 15% grade, which has a slope of 0.15.

55. The slope of a 7 in 12 roof is 7/12. The roof will rise $\frac{7}{12} \times 15 = 8.75$ feet in a horizontal run of 15 feet.

56. A road with a 5% grade has a slope of 5/100 = 1/20, which means it rises 1/20 foot for each horizontal foot. Imagine the road as a right triangle, where the ratio of the height to the base is 1/20. If you drive 6 miles along the road, you've gone 31,680 feet along the hypotenuse of this triangle. Let x represent the height of the triangle; the base is then $20x$ (because the slope is 1/20). Using the Pythagorean theorem, we have

$x^2 + (20x)^2 = 31,680^2$, which yields $x = 1582$ ft. Note that if you take the 6 miles as the horizontal run (rather than the correct procedure of treating it as the hypotenuse), you get an answer little different from above: 1584 feet.

57. Think of a right triangle with side lengths of 6 and 6 – this produces an isosceles triangle, which implies the non-right angles are both 45°. It is possible to have a 7 in 6 roof: it's just a steep roof that rises 7 feet for every 6 feet of horizontal run.

58. The slope of such a path is 1500/5280 = 0.284, which is an approximate grade of 28%.

59. The slope of such a road is 20/150 = 0.133, so its grade is 13.3%.

60. A trail with a 22% grade has a slope of 22/100, so it rises $\frac{22}{100} \times 200$ yd = 44 yards.

61. a. Walk 6 blocks east (6/8 mi) and 1 block north (1/5 mi) for a total distance of 19/20 = 0.95 mi.
    b. The Pythagorean theorem gives the straight-line distance as $\sqrt{(6/8)^2 + (1/5)^2} = 0.78$ mi.

62. a. Walk 3 blocks east (3/8 mi) and 4 blocks north (4/5 mi) for a total distance of 47/40 = 1.175 mi.
    b. The Pythagorean theorem gives the straight-line distance as $\sqrt{(3/8)^2 + (4/5)^2} = 0.88$ mi.

63. a. Walk 2 blocks west (2/8 mi) and 3 blocks north (3/5 mi) for a total distance of 17/20 = 0.85 mi.
    b. The Pythagorean theorem gives the straight-line distance as $\sqrt{(2/8)^2 + (3/5)^2} = 0.65$ mi.

64. a. Walk 8 blocks east (8/8 mi) and 2 blocks south (2/5 mi) for a total distance of 7/5 = 1.4 mi.
    b. The Pythagorean theorem gives the straight-line distance as $\sqrt{(8/8)^2 + (2/5)^2} = 1.08$ mi.

65. a. Walk 3 blocks east (3/8 mi) and 3 blocks south (3/5 mi) for a total distance of 39/40 = 0.975 mi.
    b. The Pythagorean theorem gives the straight-line distance as $\sqrt{(3/8)^2 + (3/5)^2} = 0.71$ mi.

66. a. Walk 5 blocks west (5/8 mi) and 1 block south (1/5 mi) for a total distance of 33/40 = 0.825 mi.
    b. The Pythagorean theorem gives the straight-line distance as $\sqrt{(5/8)^2 + (1/5)^2} = 0.66$ mi.

67. The height of the triangle in Figure 10.31 is $\sqrt{800^2 - 150^2} = 785.8$ ft, and thus the area of the lot is $\frac{1}{2} \times 150 \times 785.8 = 58,936 \text{ ft}^2$, which is $58,936 \text{ ft}^2 \times \frac{1 \text{ acre}}{43,560 \text{ ft}^2} = 1.35$ acres.

68. The height of the triangle in Figure 10.31 is $\sqrt{1800^2 - 300^2} = 1774.8$ ft, and thus the area of the

lot is $\frac{1}{2} \times 300 \times 1774.8 = 266,224$ ft^2, which is

$266,224$ ft$^2 \times \dfrac{1 \text{ acre}}{43,560 \text{ ft}^2} = 6.11$ acres.

69. The height of the triangle in Figure 10.31 is $\sqrt{3800^2 - 600^2} = 3752.3$ ft, and thus the area of the

    lot is $\frac{1}{2} \times 600 \times 3752.3 = 1,125,700$ ft^2, which is

    $1,125,700$ ft$^2 \times \dfrac{1 \text{ acre}}{43,560 \text{ ft}^2} = 25.84$ acres.

70. Note that 0.45 mi is 2376 ft, and 1.2 miles is 6336 ft. The height of the triangle in Figure 10.31 is $\sqrt{6336^2 - 2376^2} = 5873.6$ ft, and thus the area of the

    lot is $\frac{1}{2} \times 2376 \times 5873.6 = 6,977,871$ ft^2, which is

    $6,977,871$ ft$^2 \times \dfrac{1 \text{ acre}}{43,560 \text{ ft}^2} = 160.19$ acres.

71. The larger triangle is just a scaled up version of the smaller triangle (or so it appears), and so they are similar.

72. The larger triangle is just a scaled up version of the smaller triangle (or so it appears), and so they are similar.

73. The triangle on the left appears to be an isosceles triangle, whereas the one on the right does not, which means the triangles don't have the same angle measure, and cannot be similar.

74. One triangle looks like a rotated version of the other, so they are similar.

75. 8/10 = x/5, which implies $x = 4$. Use the Pythagorean theorem to show that $y = 3$ (we know the triangles are right because the left triangle satisfies $6^2 + 8^2 = 10^2$).

76. x/9 = 2/3, which implies $x = 6$. Since the triangle on the left is isosceles, so is the one on the right, which means $y = 2$.

77. x/60 = 10/40, which implies $x = 15$. 50/60 = y/40, which implies $y = 100/3 = 33.3$.

78. a/3 = 12/9, which implies $a = 4$. 5/3 = c/9, which implies $c = 15$.

79. Refer to Figure 10.34, and note that a 12-ft fence that casts a 25-foot shadow is equivalent to a house of height h (set back 60 feet from the property line) that casts an 85-ft shadow. We can write the ratio 12/25 = h/85, which implies $h = 40.8$ ft.

80. As in exercise 79, we can write 12/20 = h/50, which implies $h = 30$ ft.

81. As in exercise 79, we can write 12/30 = h/80, which implies $h = 32$ ft.

82. As in exercise 79, we can write 12/10 = h/40, which implies $h = 48$ ft.

83. The radius of a circle with circumference of 60 m is 60/2π = 9.55 m, and so its area is $\pi \times (9.55)^2 = 286.5$ m^2. The side length of a square with perimeter of 60 m is 60/4 = 15 m, and so its area is $15 \times 15 = 225$ m^2. The area of the circular region is larger.

84. The radius of a circle with circumference of 800 ft is 800/2π = 127.32 ft, and so its area is $\pi \times (127.32)^2 = 50,930$ ft^2. The side length of a square with perimeter of 800 ft is 800/4 = 200 ft, and so its area is $200 \times 200 = 40,000$ ft^2. The area of the circular region is larger.

85. The radius of a circle with circumference of 240 m is 240/2π = 38.2 m, and so its area is $\pi \times (38.2)^2 = 4584$ m^2. The side length of a square with perimeter of 240 m is 240/4 = 60 m, and so its area is $60 \times 60 = 3600$ m^2. The area of the circular region is larger.

86. The radius of a circle with circumference of 0.27 mi is 0.27/2π = 0.043 mi, and so its area is $\pi \times (0.043)^2 = 0.0058$ mi^2. The side length of a square with perimeter of 0.27 mi is 0.27/4 = 0.0675 mi, and so its area is $0.0675 \times 0.0675 = 0.00456$ mi^2. The area of the circular region is larger.

87. For the first can described, the area of the top and bottom is $2 \times \pi \times 4^2 = 100.53$ in.^{2}, and the area of the side is $2\pi \times 4 \times 5 = 125.66$ in.^{2}. The cost of the can is 100.53 in.$^2 \times \dfrac{\$1.00}{\text{in.}^2} + 125.66$ in.$^2 \times \dfrac{\$0.50}{\text{in.}^2} =$ \$163.36. In a similar manner, it can be shown that the cost of the second can is 157.08 in.$^2 \times \dfrac{\$1.00}{\text{in.}^2} + 125.66$ in.$^2 \times \dfrac{\$0.50}{\text{in.}^2} = \$219.91$.

88. For the first bucket described, the area of the bottom is $\pi \times 6^2 = 113.1$ in.^{2}, and the area of the side is $2\pi \times 6 \times 18 = 678.58$ in.^{2}. The cost is $\left(2 \times 113.1 \text{ in.}^2 + 678.58 \text{ in.}^2\right) \times \left(\dfrac{1 \text{ ft}}{12 \text{ in.}}\right)^2 \times \dfrac{\$0.50}{\text{ft}^2} =$ \$3.14. In a similar manner, it can be shown that the cost of the second can is $\left(2 \times 254.47 \text{ in.}^2 + 848.23 \text{ in.}^2\right) \times \left(\dfrac{1 \text{ ft}}{12 \text{ in.}}\right)^2 \times \dfrac{\$0.50}{\text{ft}^2} =$ \$4.71.

89. Assuming a rectangular box, the most economical shape is a cube, with side length equal to 2 ft (see Example 10 in the text). Such a box has 6 faces, each with area of 4 ft^2, for a total area of 24 ft^2. At \$0.15 per square foot, the box would cost \$3.60.

90. The most economical shape of a rectangular prism is a cube (see Example 10 in the text). Since the volume of a cube with side length s is s^3, we must

have $s^3 = 4$ ft^3, which implies $s = \sqrt[3]{4} = 1.587$ ft. The surface area of a cube is $6s^2$, so the surface area of the safe is $6 \times \left(\sqrt[3]{4}\right)^2 = 15.12$ ft^2. At a cost of \$6.50 per square foot, the material for the safe would cost $15.12 \text{ ft}^2 \times \dfrac{\$6.50}{\text{ft}^2} = \$98.27$.

FURTHER APPLICATIONS

91. Begin by converting 0.1 second into degrees: $0.1'' \times \dfrac{1'}{60''} \times \dfrac{1°}{60'} = 2.78 \times 10^{-5}$ degree. Now use the angular size formula (solved for physical size) to compute the size of an object whose angular size is 0.1" at a distance of 350 km. The physical size is $2.78 \times 10^{-5°} \times \dfrac{2\pi \times 350 \text{ km}}{360°} \times \dfrac{1000 \text{ m}}{1 \text{ km}} \times \dfrac{100 \text{ cm}}{1 \text{ m}} =$ 17 cm. Thus the letter size would need to be 17 cm (almost 7 inches, much larger than the print in a newspaper) before you could read it with the Hubble, and this neglects the problems of peering through Earth's atmosphere.

92. The angular size of the star is $1.4 \times 10^6 \text{ km} \times \dfrac{360°}{2\pi \times 10^{14} \text{ km}} \times \dfrac{3600''}{1°} = 0.003''$, which is smaller than the resolution of a powerful telescope, so no surface details could be seen.

93. The throw goes along the hypotenuse of a right triangle, whose length is $\sqrt{90^2 + 90^2} = 127.3$ ft.

94. The cost of running the line along the edges of the field is $(1.5 \text{ mi} + 2.75 \text{ mi}) \times \dfrac{\$3500}{1 \text{ mi}} = \$14,875$. The cost of running the line along the hypotenuse is $\sqrt{(1.5 \text{ mi})^2 + (2.75 \text{ mi})^2} \times \dfrac{\$3500}{1 \text{ mi}} = \$10,964$, for a savings of $\$14,875 - \$10,964 = \$3911$.

95. For simplicity, assume you can row at a rate of 1.0 mph, and you can bike at a rate of 1.5 mph. Using $\text{time} = \dfrac{\text{distance}}{\text{rate}}$, the time it takes to bike along the edges of the reservoir is $\dfrac{1.2 \text{ mi} + 0.9 \text{ mi}}{1.5 \text{ mph}} = 1.4$ hr. The time it takes to row along the hypotenuse is $\dfrac{\sqrt{(1.2 \text{ mi})^2 + (0.9 \text{ mi})^2}}{1.0 \text{ mph}} = 1.5$ hr, so biking is faster.

96. The sidewalk connecting the library to humanities is $\sqrt{15^2 + 15^2} = 21.2$ m, the sidewalk between humanities and chemistry is $\sqrt{10^2 + 30^2} = 31.6$ m, and the sidewalk between chemistry and the library is $\sqrt{15^2 + 25^2} = 29.2$ m. Together, the total length of the sidewalks is 82.0 m.

97. a. The volume of the water in the bed is $8 \times 7 \times 0.75 = 42$ ft^3. Divide this volume by the area of the lower room (80 ft^2) to find that the depth of the water is 0.525 ft.
b. The weight of the water in the bed is $42 \text{ ft}^3 \times \dfrac{62.4 \text{ lb}}{1 \text{ ft}^3} = 2620.8$ lb.

98. The volume of the tank is $\dfrac{4}{3}\pi \times (25 \text{ ft})^3 \times \left(\dfrac{0.3048 \text{ m}}{1 \text{ ft}}\right)^3 = 1853$ m^3. The volume of the pool is $50 \text{ m} \times 25 \text{ m} \times 2 \text{ m} = 2500$ m^3, so the tank is not large enough to fill the pool.

99. The perimeter of a corral with dimensions of 10 m by 40 m is 100 m. One could use a square-shaped corral with side length of 20 m to achieve the desired area of 400 square meters; this corral would have a perimeter of 80 m, and would require less fencing.

100. The combined area of the right and left flaps of the box is $2 \times 0.75 \text{ m} \times 0.25 \text{ m} = 0.375$ m^2. The combined area for the top and bottoms flaps is $2 \times 1.25 \text{ m} \times 0.25 \text{ m} = 0.625$ m^2. The area of the base is $0.75 \text{ m} \times 1.25 \text{ m} = 0.9375$ m^2. The total surface area is 1.9375 square meters. The volume is $1.25 \text{ m} \times 0.75 \text{ m} \times 0.25 \text{ m} = 0.2344$ m^3. If the corner cuts were 0.3 m on a side, the volume would be $1.15 \text{ m} \times 0.65 \text{ m} \times 0.3 \text{ m} = 0.2243$ m^3 (smaller). The box of largest volume occurs when the corner cut length is about 0.24 m.

101. Your project will cost $3 \text{ mi} \times \dfrac{\$500}{1 \text{ mi}} + \sqrt{(2 \text{ mi})^2 + (1 \text{ mi})^2} \times \dfrac{\$1000}{1 \text{ mi}} = \$3736$. Using the plan suggested by your boss will cost $4 \text{ mi} \times \dfrac{\$500}{1 \text{ mi}} + \sqrt{(1 \text{ mi})^2 + (1 \text{ mi})^2} \times \dfrac{\$1000}{1 \text{ mi}} = \$3414$.

102. Following the hint in the exercise, if you draw a good diagram, you should see a pair of similar triangles that can be used to set up the ratio $\dfrac{10}{15} = \dfrac{h}{50}$, where h is the height of the building measured from the top of your head. Solving for h yields $h = 33.3$ ft – add your height to find the height of the building.

103. a. With a lot of work and patience, you might be able to come up with the dimensions of the can that has the lowest surface area (and thus lowest cost): $r = 3.8$ cm and $h = 7.7$ cm. One way to save time is to observe that $355 = \pi r^2 h$, which implies that $h = \dfrac{355}{\pi r^2}$. Insert this expression for h into the surface area formula $2\pi rh + 2\pi r^2$ to find that the surface area can be expressed as a function of r:

$A = \dfrac{710}{r} + 2\pi r^2$. Since the cost is directly proportional to the surface area, the object is to find the value of r that yields the smallest surface area A. If you graph A on a calculator, and use the trace function, you'll see that $r = 3.8$ at the low point of the graph.

b. The dimensions of the optimal can found above imply the can is as wide (diameter) as it is high. Soda cans aren't built that way, probably for a variety of reasons. (Among them: the can needs to fit into the hand of an average human, and the top and bottom of the can cost more because the aluminum is thicker).

104. The volume of the glacier is $100 \text{ m} \times 20 \text{ m} \times 3 \text{ m} = 6000 \text{ m}^3$. The surface area of the lake is $\pi \times (1000 \text{ m})^2 = 3.14 \times 10^6 \text{ m}^2$. Divide the volume by the surface area to find the amount by which the water level would rise: $6000 \text{ m}^3 \div 3.14 \times 10^6 \text{ m}^2 = 0.002$ meters, or about 2 millimeters. This solution assumes a cubic meter of ice melts into a cubic meter of water.

105. a. Note that the radius of the cone will be 6 ft (because the height is 1/3 the radius). The volume is $\dfrac{1}{3}\pi \times 6^2 \times 2 = 75.4 \text{ ft}^3$.

b. Again, note that $r = 3h$, and solve $1000 \text{ ft}^3 = \dfrac{1}{3}\pi \times (3h)^2 \times h = 3\pi \times h^3$ for h to find $h = 4.7$ ft.

c. Assuming 10,000 grains per cubic inch, there are $75.4 \text{ ft}^3 \times \left(\dfrac{12 \text{ in.}}{1 \text{ ft}}\right)^3 \times \dfrac{10{,}000 \text{ grains}}{\text{in.}^3} = 1.3$ billion grains. The figure of 10,000 grains per cubic inch is very much dependent upon the size of sand grain assumed, which varies.

106. The radius of the tank is 3.25 ft, so the water's weight is

$\pi \times (3.25 \text{ ft})^2 \times 22 \text{ ft} \times \left(\dfrac{12 \text{ in.}}{1 \text{ ft}}\right)^3 \times \dfrac{0.03613 \text{ lb}}{1 \text{ in.}^3} = 45{,}615\text{lb}$,

which is 22.8 tons. The empty tank weighs $1750 \div 2000 = 0.875$ ton. The truck's gross weight is $16.3 + 22.8 + 0.875$ tons, which is just shy of 40 tons. You can be confident in crossing the bridge because load limit signs always have a built-in safety margin.

107. a. The pyramid's height is $481 \div 3 = 160.3$ yards, which is about 1.6 times the length of a football field (excluding the end zones).

b. The volume of the pyramid is $\dfrac{1}{3} \times (756 \text{ ft})^2 \times 481 \text{ ft} = 91{,}636{,}272 \text{ ft}^3$, which is

$91{,}636{,}272 \text{ ft}^3 \times \left(\dfrac{1 \text{ yd}}{3 \text{ ft}}\right)^3 = 3{,}393{,}936 \text{ yd}^3$.

c. Divide the result in part **b** by 1.5 to get around 2,263,000 blocks.

d.

$2{,}263{,}000 \text{ blocks} \times \dfrac{2.5 \text{ min}}{\text{block}} \times \dfrac{1 \text{ hr}}{60 \text{ min}} \times \dfrac{1 \text{ d}}{12 \text{ hr}} \times \dfrac{1 \text{ yr}}{365 \text{ d}}$

$= 21.5$ years. This is comparable to the amount of time suggested in historical records, which indicates that Lehner's estimate is in error. However, we don't have all the facts – perhaps Lehner began with the assumption that with a work force of 10,000 laborers, one stone could be placed every 2.5 minutes, or maybe he assumed laborers worked on the project 24 hours per day.

e. The volume of the Eiffel tower is $\dfrac{1}{3} \times (120 \text{ ft})^2 \times 980 \text{ ft} = 4{,}704{,}000 \text{ ft}^3$, which is about 5% of the pyramid's volume.

UNIT 10C

QUICK QUIZ

1. **b**. As noted in the text, fractals successfully replicate natural forms, especially when random iteration is used.

2. **a**. A coastline can be modeled with fractal curves which have dimension between 1 and 2, and by the very definition of fractal dimension, we see that shortening the length of the ruler increases the number of elements (which, in turn, represents the length of the coastline).

3. **b**. The edge of a leaf (think of a maple leaf) has many of the properties of a fractal, such as self similarity, and a length that increases as one decreases the size of the ruler used to measure it.

4. **c**. Fractals often have the property of self similarity, which means that under greater magnification, the underlying pattern repeats itself.

5. **c**. The definition of the fractal dimension of an object leads to fractional values for the dimension.

6. **c**. Data suggest that most coastlines have a fractal dimension of about 1.25.

7. **a**. The curve labeled L_6 in Figure 10.53 is simply the sixth step (or iteration) of the process required to generate the snowflake curve. The snowflake curve itself is denoted by L_∞ (the end product of performing infinite iterations).

8. **c.** An area bounded by a finite curve (it is understood that by this we mean a closed curve of finite length) cannot possibly be of infinite area. If it were possible, we'd have to throw all of our notions about the areas of bounded plane regions out the door. How could the area of a region contained within a region of a finite area be infinitely large?

9. **a.** The definition of a self-similar fractal is that its patterns repeat themselves under greater magnification.

10. **b.** From previous units, we know that if you take, say, an ice cube, and break it into smaller pieces, the aggregate surface area of the pieces is larger than the surface area of the original cube of ice. The same idea is illustrated by the process of creating the Sierpinski sponge. In the first step, when the four subcubes are removed, it can be shown that the surface area increases by a factor of 4/3. In fact, this happens in every step, and thus the surface area becomes infinitely large as the process continues.

DOES IT MAKE SENSE?

19. Makes sense. The boundary of a rectangle is made of straight lines whose lengths are well defined, and so can be measured with a standard ruler (to a reasonable degree of accuracy).

20. Does not make sense. A mountain skyline is similar to a coastline in that it reveals ever more detail at greater magnification, and thus it is very difficult to define its length, let alone measure it with any degree of accuracy.

21. Does not make sense. The boundary of the snowflake island is infinitely long, and though its area is finite, it is not computed with a simple "length times width" formula.

22. Does not make sense. The measured length of a fractal increases as the ruler length *decreases*.

23. Makes sense. Data have been collected that shows many boundaries in nature, such as coastlines and edges of leaves, have fractal dimensions greater than one.

24. Makes sense. A leaf riddled with holes, whose boundaries are fractals, has some of the properties of the Sierpinski triangle, and this object has a fractal dimension between 1 and 2, with an area of 0. In the same way it is difficult to define the length of a coastline, it is difficult to compute the surface area of a leaf riddled with holes – our standard notions of surface area don't work well with regions that are bounded by fractals.

BASIC SKILLS & CONCEPTS

25. According to the definition of fractal dimension, R = 2 and N = 2, so we have $2 = 2^D$, where D is the fractal dimension. It is evident that $D = 1$ in this case, and thus the object is not a fractal (it behaves like an ordinary geometric object with regard to length measurements).

26. According to the definition of fractal dimension, R = 2 and N = 4, so we have $4 = 2^D$, where D is the fractal dimension. It is evident that $D = 2$ in this case, and thus the object is not a fractal (it behaves like an ordinary geometric object with regard to area measurements).

27. According to the definition of fractal dimension, R = 2 and N = 8, so we have $8 = 2^D$, where D is the fractal dimension. It is evident that $D = 3$ in this case, and thus the object is not a fractal (it behaves like an ordinary geometric object with regard to volume measurements).

28. According to the definition of fractal dimension, R = 2 and N = 3, so we have $3 = 2^D$, where D is the fractal dimension. Solving for D using logarithms produces a value of $D = \dfrac{\log_{10} 3}{\log_{10} 2} = 1.585$, and thus the object is a fractal (it does not behave like an ordinary geometric object with regard to length measurements).

29. According to the definition of fractal dimension, R = 2 and N = 6, so we have $6 = 2^D$, where D is the fractal dimension. Solving for D using logarithms produces a value of $D = \dfrac{\log_{10} 6}{\log_{10} 2} = 2.585$, and thus the object is a fractal (it does not behave like an ordinary geometric object with regard to area measurements).

30. According to the definition of fractal dimension, R = 2 and N = 12, so we have $12 = 2^D$, where D is the fractal dimension. Solving for D using logarithms produces a value of $D = \dfrac{\log_{10} 12}{\log_{10} 2} = 3.585$, and thus the object is a fractal (it does not behave like an ordinary geometric object with regard to volume measurements).

31. According to the definition of fractal dimension, R = 5 and N = 5, so we have $5 = 5^D$, where D is the fractal dimension. It is evident that $D = 1$ in this case, and thus the object is not a fractal (it behaves like an ordinary geometric object with regard to length measurements).

32. According to the definition of fractal dimension, R = 5 and N = 25, so we have $25 = 5^D$, where D is the fractal dimension. It is evident that $D = 2$ in this case, and thus the object is not a fractal (it

behaves like an ordinary geometric object with regard to area measurements).

33. According to the definition of fractal dimension, R = 5 and N = 125, so we have $125 = 5^D$, where D is the fractal dimension. It is evident that D = 3 in this case, and thus the object is not a fractal (it behaves like an ordinary geometric object with regard to volume measurements).

34. According to the definition of fractal dimension, R = 5 and N = 7, so we have $7 = 5^D$, where D is the fractal dimension. Solving for D using logarithms produces a value of $D = \dfrac{\log_{10} 7}{\log_{10} 5} = 1.209$, and thus the object is a fractal (it does not behave like an ordinary geometric object with regard to length measurements).

35. According to the definition of fractal dimension, R = 5 and N = 30, so we have $30 = 5^D$, where D is the fractal dimension. Solving for D using logarithms produces a value of $D = \dfrac{\log_{10} 30}{\log_{10} 5} = 2.113$, and thus the object is a fractal (it does not behave like an ordinary geometric object with regard to area measurements).

36. According to the definition of fractal dimension, R = 5 and N = 150, so we have $150 = 5^D$, where D is the fractal dimension. Solving for D using logarithms produces a value of $D = \dfrac{\log_{10} 150}{\log_{10} 5} = 3.113$, and thus the object is a fractal (it does not behave like an ordinary geometric object with regard to volume measurements).

37. a. Suppose that the original line segment has length of 1 unit. When we measure the length of the first iteration of the quadratic Koch curve with a ruler of length 1 unit (or one element), we find the length is 1 unit, the distance from one endpoint to the other. When we shorten the ruler by a factor of R = 4 so that its length is 1/4 unit, the length of the first iteration is N = 8 elements (i.e., the length is 8/4 = 2 units). This is true at every stage of the process.
b. According to the definition of fractal dimension, we have $8 = 4^D$. Solving for D yields $D = \dfrac{\log_{10} 8}{\log_{10} 4} = 1.5$. The length of the quadratic Koch curve is infinite, because at each iteration, the length increases by a factor of 2, and thus its length grows without bound as the process continues.
c. Consider what happens to the area of the quadratic Koch island as we go from the first stage

(a square) to the second stage. Along the upper boundary, the area is increased by a small square drawn above the boundary, but it is decreased by a small square drawn below the boundary. This is true along every edge of the original square, and the net effect is no change in the area. The same is true for every step of the process, so the area of the final island is equal to the area of the original square. The coastline of the island is infinite, as noted above in part **b**.

38. a.

$\log_{10} r$	2	1	0	−1	−2	−3
$\log_{10} L$	2.5	3.1	3.7	4.3	4.9	5.5

b. Graph not shown.
c. The graph is a straight line if you use the rounded values shown in the above table, which indicates the coastline is a self-similar fractal.
d. The slope s is –0.6, so the fractional dimension is D = 1 – (–0.6) = 1.6.

FURTHER APPLICATIONS

39. When the ruler is reduced by a factor of R = 9, there will be N = 4 elements found (each of length 1/9). This gives $4 = 9^D$, which when solved leads to $D = \dfrac{\log_{10} 4}{\log_{10} 9} = 0.631$. (Note that this is the answer you get no matter what stage of the process you choose to analyze). The dimension is less than 1 due to the fact that the end result of the process of constructing the Cantor set is a set of isolated points. Though there are infinitely many points, there aren't "enough" of them to constitute a line segment of measurable length (that is, this fractal object does not behave like an ordinary geometric object with regard to length).

40. a. Start with a meter stick and measure the length of the sidewalk, counting the number of times you lay the stick down on the sidewalk. Now reduce the length of the stick to 0.1 meter – a reduction by a factor of R = 10. Repeat the measurement of the sidewalk, counting the number of times you lay the stick down on the sidewalk. You should find that the number of elements for this second measurement is about N = 10 times the number of elements of the first sidewalk. If this pattern continues (every time the ruler is decreased in length by a factor of 10, the number of elements increases by an approximate factor of N = 10), then the sidewalk is a one-dimensional object. To illustrate the process, imagine a sidewalk that is about 5.724 meters in length. In the first measurement, you'll find 5 full elements because the last placement of the 1-meter stick would extend beyond the end of the walk. On the second

measurement, you'll find 57 full elements, again because the last element will extend beyond the end of the walk. On a third measurement, you'll find 572 elements, and on the fourth measurement, you'll find about 5724 elements, depending upon the exact length of the walk. In each step, N is approximately 10, and in fact, N gets closer and closer to 10 as you repeat the process. If you compute N for each step of the process just described, you'll find the following values: $N = 57/5 = 11.4$; $N = 572/57 = 10.035$; and $N = 5724/572 = 10.007$. In then end, we can conclude that N is very close to R, and so we have $10 = 10^D$, which implies $D = 1$.

b. Start with a meter stick and measure the length and width of the room, counting the number of square elements with an area of 1 m^2 that you create in the process (exclude the rectangles of less than 1 m^2 that will likely occur at the edges of the room, as described in part **a**). Now reduce the length of the stick to 0.1 meter – a reduction by a factor of $R = 10$. Repeat the measurement of the room, counting the number of elements with an area of 0.01 m^2 that you create. You should find that the number of elements for this second measuring is approximately $N = 100$ times the number of elements in the first measurement. If this pattern continues (every time the ruler is decreased in length by a factor of $R = 10$, the number of elements increases by an approximate factor of $N = R^2 = 100$), then the room is a two-dimensional object.

c. The process used to determine that $N = R^3$ is very similar to that described in parts **a** and **b**, except that you will measure the length, width, and depth of the pool at each stage, and find with each reduction of length in the ruler by a factor of $R = 10$, the number of cubical elements will increase by an approximate factor of $N = 1000$.

41. a. Note that every time the ruler is decreased in length by a factor of $R = 10$, the number of elements increases by a factor of $N = 20$, which leads to $20 = 10^D$. This implies the fractal dimension is $D = \dfrac{\log_{10} 20}{\log_{10} 10} = 1.301$.

b. Note that every time the ruler is decreased in length by a factor of $R = 2$, the number of area elements increases by a factor of $N = 3$, which leads to $3 = 2^D$. This implies the fractal dimension is $D = \dfrac{\log_{10} 3}{\log_{10} 2} = 1.585$. The fractal dimension is less than two because the standard notion of surface area for ordinary objects does not carry over to the surface area of fractal objects.

c. Note that every time the ruler is decreased in length by a factor of $R = 2$, the number of volume elements increases by a factor of $N = 6$, which leads to $6 = 2^D$. This implies the fractal dimension is $D = \dfrac{\log_{10} 6}{\log_{10} 2} = 2.585$. A fractal dimension between 2 and 3 is reasonable because such a rock exhibits the same properties as the Sierpinski sponge – it is somewhat "less" than a solid three-dimensional cube because material has been removed in a fractal pattern.

42. Answers will vary, but patterns seen in leaves, the branches of trees, lungs, capillaries, coastlines, rock formations, and clouds are good examples.

43. The branching in many natural objects has the same pattern repeated on many different scales. This is the process by which self-similar fractals are generated. Euclidean geometry is not equipped to describe the repetitions of patterns on many scales.

UNIT 11A

QUICK QUIZ

1. **b**. Instruments with strings (guitar, violin, piano), woodwinds with reeds (clarinet, bassoon), and instruments with a column of air in a tube (organ pipe, horn, flute) – all produce their sound with an object that vibrates.

2. **a**. In the case of a string vibrating, a single cycle of vibration corresponds to the string moving to its high point and to its low point, so 100 cps means the string is at its high point (and low point) 100 times each second.

3. **a**. Higher pitches go hand in hand with higher frequencies.

4. **c**. The fundamental frequency of a string occurs when the string vibrates up and down along its entire length, and this produces the lowest possible pitch from that string. (Though the text does not discuss it, you may know that a longer wavelength produces a lower frequency – the wavelength can't get any longer for a particular string than the wave associated with the fundamental frequency).

5. **a**. Every time you raise the pitch of a sound by an octave, the pitch doubles.

6. **c**. The 12-tone scale uses twelve equally spaced (in the sense described below) notes for every octave. The factor f by which the frequency changes in moving from one note to the next is constant, which means that in multiplying an initial frequency by f 12 times in a row, you've moved an octave up the scale, and doubled the frequency. This gives us the relationship $f^{12} = 2$, which in turn implies that $f = \sqrt[12]{2}$.

7. **c**. Table 11.1 shows the frequencies of each of the notes in a particular octave; the names of the notes repeat every octave. As you can see in the table, increasing the frequency of middle C by a factor of 1.5 moves you to a G, so if you increase the frequency of the next higher C by a factor of 1.5, you'll end up at the next higher G.

8. **b**. The frequency of each note in the 12-tone scale is related to the note one half-step below it by a multiplicative factor of $f = \sqrt[12]{2} = 1.05946$. This means the frequencies increase by about 5.9% every half-step, which is exponential growth.

9. **b**. The mathematician Fourier discovered that musical sounds are the sum of several constant-frequency waves.

10. **a**. The process of digitizing analog sound changes wave forms that represent sound waves into lists of numbers that can be stored on CDs, and reinterpreted by a CD player to produce a musical sound.

DOES IT MAKE SENSE?

17. Does not make sense. The pitch of a string is a function of the length of the string, not the number of times the string is plucked.

18. Makes sense. When the length of a string is halved, its frequency doubles, and a doubling in frequency corresponds to an increase in pitch of one octave. Decrease the length of the string by a factor of 4, and its pitch will increase by a factor of 4, which corresponds to two octaves.

19. Makes sense. The frequency of each note in the 12-tone scale increases by a factor of $f = \sqrt[12]{2} = 1.05946$, and this is exponential growth.

20. Makes sense. Each key on a piano corresponds to a note one half-step above the preceding key, and as there are 12 half-steps in an octave, there are 88/12, or about 7 octaves on a standard piano (some pianos have even more than 88 keys).

21. Does not make sense. The scratch on the record would be difficult to repair. However, if it is a minor scratch, one might be able to digitize the sound the record produces, and at that point a digital filter could be used to reduce or remove the effects of the scratch.

BASIC SKILLS & CONCEPTS

22. The next higher octave corresponds to a doubling in frequency, so the requested frequencies are 440 cps, 880 cps, 1760 cps, and 3520 cps.

23. The next lower octave corresponds to a halving in frequency, so the requested frequencies are 880 cps, 440 cps, 220 cps, and 110 cps.

24.

Note	Frequency (cps)
F	347
F#	368
G	389
G#	413
A	437
A#	463
B	491
C	520
C#	551
D	584
D#	618
E	655

The table can be generated beginning with the initial frequency of 347 cps, and multiplying by

$f = \sqrt[12]{2}$ to produce each successive note. Realize that you will get slightly different values for some of the entries in the table if you generate it from middle C, whose frequency is 260 cps. This is due to rounding errors, and it explains the different values shown in this table and in Table 11.1 at the middle G entry. We began with an initial value of 347 cps to generate this table, but that's a rounded value for the true frequency of middle F.

25.

Note	Frequency (cps)
G	390
G#	413
A	438
A#	464
B	491
C	521
C#	552
D	584
D#	619
E	656
F	695
F#	736

The table can be generated beginning with the initial frequency of 390 cps, and multiplying by $f = \sqrt[12]{2}$ to produce each successive note. Realize that you will get slightly different values for some of the entries in the table if you generate it from middle C, whose frequency is 260 cps. This is due to rounding errors, and it explains the different values shown in this table and in Table 11.1 at the A, A#, and C entries. We began with an initial value of 390 cps to generate this table, but that's a rounded value for the true frequency of middle G. If we had used an exact value for middle G, we should find that the frequency of the C in this table, which is one octave higher than middle C, is 520 (because frequencies double every octave).

26. Raise A by a fifth to produce a frequency of $437 \text{ cps} \times \frac{3}{2} = 655.5 \text{ cps}$. Raise this by a fifth to produce $655.5 \text{ cps} \times \frac{3}{2} = 983.25 \text{ cps}$. Lower this by a sixth to produce $983.25 \text{ cps} \times \frac{3}{5} = 589.95 \text{ cps}$. Finally, lower this by a fourth to produce $589.95 \text{ cps} \times \frac{3}{4} = 442.4625 \text{ cps}$, or about 442 cps. We have not returned to the same frequency, because the ratios used to increase or decrease by the various intervals are approximations to the actual ratio between the given intervals. In essence, we began with 437 and multiplied it by $\frac{3}{2} \times \frac{3}{2} \times \frac{3}{5} \times \frac{3}{4} = \frac{81}{80}$, which is just over 1.

27. a. $260 \times \left(\sqrt[12]{2}\right)^7 = 390$ cps.

b. $260 \times \left(\sqrt[12]{2}\right)^9 = 437$ cps.

c. An octave is 12 half-steps, so use a total of 19 half-steps. $260 \times \left(\sqrt[12]{2}\right)^{19} = 779$ cps.

d. $260 \times \left(\sqrt[12]{2}\right)^{25} = 1102$ cps.

e. An octave is 12 half-steps, so use a total of 39 half-steps. $260 \times \left(\sqrt[12]{2}\right)^{39} = 2474$ cps.

28. a. $390 \times \left(\sqrt[12]{2}\right)^6 = 552$ cps.

b. $390 \times \left(\sqrt[12]{2}\right)^4 = 491$ cps.

c. An octave is 12 half-steps, so use a total of 17 half-steps. $390 \times \left(\sqrt[12]{2}\right)^{17} = 1041$ cps.

d. $390 \times \left(\sqrt[12]{2}\right)^{25} = 1653$ cps.

e. An octave is 12 half-steps, so use a total of 26 half-steps. $390 \times \left(\sqrt[12]{2}\right)^{26} = 1751$ cps.

29. To compute the frequency for a note one half-step below a particular frequency, we simply divide by $f = \sqrt[12]{2}$, which is equivalent to multiplying by the factor f raised to the power of -1. Thus to find the note 7 half steps below middle A, use $437 \times \left(\sqrt[12]{2}\right)^{-7} = 292$ cps. Ten half-steps below middle A is $437 \times \left(\sqrt[12]{2}\right)^{-10} = 245$ cps.

30. a. $\left(\sqrt[12]{2}\right)^7 = 2^{7/12}$.

b. From part **a**, it raises by a factor of $\left(2^{7/12}\right)^2 = 2^{14/12} = 2.245$.

c.

Note	Frequency (cps)
C	260
G	390
D	584
A	875
E	1310
B	1963
F#	2942
C#	4407
G#	6604
D#	9894
A#	14,825
F	22,212
C	33,280

The table can be generated beginning with the initial frequency of 260 cps, and multiplying by a factor of $2^{7/12}$ to produce successive notes.

d. As shown in the table in part **c**, you need 12 fifths to return to a C, which is 7 octaves. You can also understand this by analyzing the factor $2^{7/12}$.

e. The ratio is 33,280/260 = 128. This, too, can be understood in the context of the multiplicative factor $2^{7/12}$ used to raise a note by a fifth. If you use this factor 12 times, you will have increased the frequency of the initial note by a factor of $\left(2^{7/12}\right)^{12} = 2^7 = 128$. Another way to look at it: move one octave up, and you double the frequency. Here we have moved up 7 octaves, so the frequency has increased by a factor of 2^7.

31. The factor by which the tone has increased is $\left(\sqrt[12]{2}\right)^5 = 2^{5/12} = 1.335$. Because $\left(2^{5/12}\right)^{12} = 2^5$, you need 12 fourths. This is the first time the factor of $2^{5/12}$ turns into a factor of 2, and that is what is necessary to return to the same-named note (raising an octave is a doubling in frequency). There are 5 octaves in the circle of fourths, as evidenced by the factor by which the initial frequency has changed: 2^5.

32. There are 2 half notes in a 4/4-time measure, 8 eighth notes, and 16 sixteenth notes.

UNIT 11B

QUICK QUIZ

1. **b**. The principal vanishing point in a painting is the point of intersection of those lines in the painting that are parallel in the real scene, and perpendicular to the canvas. We are assuming here that the tracks are, in fact, perpendicular to the canvas, and that they are straight.

2. **b**. The *horizon line* is the line (horizontal, of course) though the principal vanishing point. According to the principals of perspective, all sets of parallel lines in the real scene intersect at some point along the horizon line in the painting.

3. **a**. Not only does the painting show this fact, but the parallel beams in the ceiling are perpendicular to the canvas, so they should intersect at the principal vanishing point.

4. **c**. There is a vertical line of symmetry in the center of da Vinci's sketch, as both sides of the drawing are nearly identical on either side of this line.

5. **c**. If the letter **W** were reflected across this line, it would appear unchanged from the original.

6. **b**. Rotate the letter **Z** through 180°, and it remains unchanged in appearance.

7. **a**. Because a circle can be rotated through any angle and remain unchanged, it has rotation symmetry. It also has reflection symmetry over any line through its center, for the same reason.

8. **c**. The only regular polygons that admit complete tilings are equilateral triangles, squares, and regular hexagons.

9. **a**. Refer to Figure 11.23 in the text.

10. **c**. A periodic tiling is one where a pattern repeats itself throughout the tiling.

DOES IT MAKE SENSE?

19. Does not make sense. The principal vanishing point is often very apparent in paintings that are rendered in proper perspective (see Figures 11.6 and 11.8, for example).

20. Does not make sense. Real landscapes are never so perfectly flat that perspective needn't be considered. Bands of color and light that are nearer to the artist need to be painted wider than bands of equal width (in the real world) that are farther away, due to the laws of perspective. Good artists paint even the dim shadows of a slowly rolling desert floor in perspective. One might argue that the statement makes sense if the desert really *is* a flat, monochrome surface, with nothing in it to indicate depth, and meeting the horizon in a straight line. But such a painting would be exceedingly dull (two fat strips of paint, with sand-colored paint at the bottom, and sky-blue paint on the top), and no one would recognize it as a realistic desert scene.

21. Makes sense. It is the science and art of perspective painting that allows talented artists to render realistic three-dimensional scenes on a two-dimensional canvas.

22. Does not make sense. Perhaps Kenny prefers the letter **R** over the letter **O**, but not out of any sense of symmetry. The letter **R** has none.

23. Does not make sense. Only equilateral triangles, squares, and regular hexagons allow for complete tilings. Susan should rent a tile saw.

24. Makes sense. The Washington Monument's shape has both rotation symmetry and reflection symmetry.

BASIC SKILLS & CONCEPTS

25. a. The only obvious vanishing point is depicted in the diagram below. It is not the principal vanishing point because the lines of the road do not meet the canvas at right angles. However, it does lie on the horizon line.

    b.

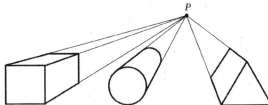

26. The box on the left is drawn in proper perspective because the edges of the box that recede into the distance converge at a vanishing point.

27.

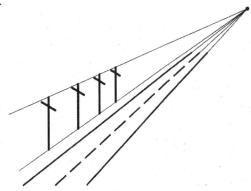

28.

29. a. In order to draw the equally spaced poles, first draw a perspective line along the bases of the existing poles, and draw one along the tops. These two lines should intersect at a vanishing point

(directly on, or very near to the horizon). Now measure 2.0 cm along the base line, and draw a vertical pole to meet the top perspective line. Repeat this procedure for the second pole.

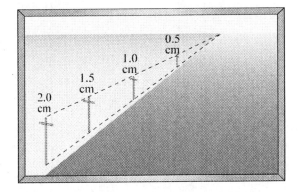

b. The heights of the poles can be measured directly with a ruler. You should find the first pole you drew is about 1.0 cm, and the second about 0.5 cm. Notice that the lengths of the poles are decreasing in a linear fashion (2.0, 1.5, 1.0, and 0.5 cm). This is due to the fact that the poles are sandwiched between two lines of constant slope, and that the distances between them are equal. (Also note that the diagram in part **a** is not to scale).

c. If your drawing is an accurate depiction of the scene, the poles are not equally spaced in the actual scene. This is due to perspective: equal distances on the canvas do not correspond with equal distances in the real scene. Because the heights of the poles are assumed to be equal, the short pole you drew in the background is much farther away from you than the first pole you drew, despite the fact that they are equally spaced in the drawing.

30.

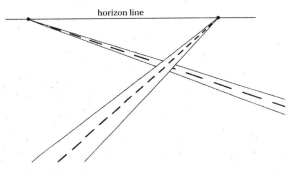

31. a. The letters with right/left reflection symmetry are A, H, I, M, O, T, U, V, W, X, and Y.
    b. The letters with top/bottom reflection symmetry are B, C, D, E, H, I, K, O, and X.

c. The letters with both of these symmetries are H, I, O, and X.

d. The letters with rotational symmetry are H, I, N, O, S, X, and Z.

32. a. There are four reflection symmetries and three rotational symmetries.

b. There are seven reflection symmetries and six rotational symmetries.

33. a. Rotating the triangle about its center 120° or 240° will produce an identical figure.

b. Rotating the square about its center 90°, 180°, or 270° will produce an identical figure.

c. Rotating the pentagon around its center 72°, 144°, 216°, or 288° will produce an identical figure.

d. Rotating an *n*-gon about its center 360°/*n* (and multiples of this angle less than 360°) will produce an identical figure. There are *n* − 1 different angles of rotational symmetry for an *n*-gon.

34. The figure has reflection symmetries (about vertical and horizontal lines drawn though its center, and either of its diagonals), and it has rotation symmetries (angles of 90°, 180°, and 270°).

35. The figure has reflection symmetries (about vertical and horizontal lines drawn through its center), and it has rotation symmetry (an angle of 180°).

36. The figure has reflection symmetry (about a horizontal line through its center, and about a vertical line through its center if we could locate its left-to-right center), and it has translation symmetry.

37. The figure has reflection symmetries (about 6 diagonal lines drawn through its center; these lines go through the spaces between the petals), and it has rotation symmetries (angles of 60°, 120°, 180°, 240°, and 300°).

38.

39.

40.

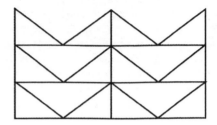

41.

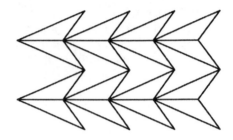

42.

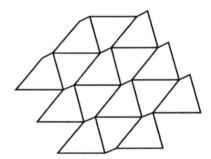

43.

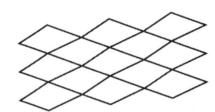

44. Answers will vary.

45. The angles around a point *P* are precisely the angles that appear inside of a single quadrilateral. Thus, the angles around *P* have a sum of 360°, and the quadrilaterals around *P* fit perfectly together.

46.

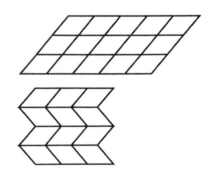

UNIT 11C

QUICK QUIZ

1. **c.** The value of the golden ratio can be derived by solving $\frac{L}{1} = \frac{L+1}{L}$ for L. This equation comes from the idea that the most aesthetically pleasing way to divide a line is one where the ratio of the length of the long piece (L) to the length of the short piece (1) is equal to the ratio of the length of the entire line ($L + 1$) to the length of the long piece L, and it is this idea that produces the golden ratio.

2. **c.** The fourth number in the Fibonacci series is 3, which is not the value for the golden ratio.

3. **c.** The value of ϕ is about 1.6, and the ratio of the long piece to the short piece should be around 1.6 before claiming the line is divided into the golden ratio. Since $0.6/0.4 = 1.5$, these are roughly the correct lengths for a golden ratio.

4. **b.** A golden rectangle is defined to be a rectangle whose ratio of its long side to short side is ϕ.

5. **b.** A golden rectangle is defined to be a rectangle whose ratio of its long side to short side is ϕ. Note than $10 \div 6.25 = 1.6$.

6. **a.** The golden rectangle became a cornerstone of their philosophy of aesthetics.

7. **a.** Refer to Figure 11.46.

8. **b.** Because the ratio of successive Fibonacci numbers converges to $\phi \sim 1.62$, each Fibonacci number is about 62% larger than the preceding number.

9. **b.** The 21st number in the series is the sum of the preceding two numbers.

10. **b.** Refer to Table 11.3.

DOES IT MAKE SENSE?

17. Does not make sense. The ratio of lengths of Maria's two sticks is $2/2 = 1$, which is not the golden ratio.

18. Makes sense. The dimensions of a standard domino are close to the dimensions of a golden rectangle.

19. Does not make sense. While circles have a lot of symmetry, they do not embody the golden ratio.

20. Does not make sense. Each year, Juliet's age increases by one, and the Fibonacci numbers do not increase like that.

BASIC SKILLS & CONCEPTS

21. The longer segment should have a length of 3.71 inches, and the shorter segment a length of 2.29 inches.

22. The ratio of the length of the longer piece (call it L) to the shorter piece should be ϕ, which implies $L \div 5 = \phi$. Thus $L = 5\phi$, and the length of the entire line is $5 + 5\phi = 13.1$ meters.

23. The middle and right rectangles are golden rectangles.

24. If 2.7 in. is the longer side, and S the shorter side, we have $2.7 \div S = \phi$, which means $S = 2.7 \div 1.62 = 1.67$ in. If 2.7 in. is the shorter side, and L the longer side, we have $L \div 2.7 = \phi$, which means $L = 2.7\phi = 4.37$ in.

25. If 5.8 m is the longer side, and S the shorter side, we have $5.8 \div S = \phi$, which means $S = 5.8 \div 1.62 = 3.58$ m. If 5.8 m is the shorter side, and L the longer side, we have $L \div 5.8 = \phi$, which means $L = 5.8\phi = 9.40$ m.

26. If 12.6 km is the longer side, and S the shorter side, we have $12.6 \div S = \phi$, which means $S = 12.6 \div 1.62 = 7.78$ km. If 12.6 km is the shorter side, and L the longer side, we have $L \div 12.6 = \phi$, which means $L = 12.6\phi = 20.41$ km.

27. If 0.66 cm is the longer side, and S the shorter side, we have $0.66 \div S = \phi$, which means $S = 0.66 \div 1.62 = 0.41$ cm. If 0.66 cm is the shorter side, and L the longer side, we have $L \div 0.66 = \phi$, which means $L = 0.66\phi = 1.07$ cm.

FURTHER APPLICATIONS

29. **a.** Begin with $\frac{L}{1} = \frac{L+1}{L}$, and multiply both sides by L to arrive at $L^2 = L + 1$, which can be rearranged to produce $L^2 - L - 1 = 0$.

   b. The two roots are
   $$L = \frac{-(-1) + \sqrt{(-1)^2 - 4(1)(-1)}}{2(1)} = \frac{1 + \sqrt{5}}{2} \text{ and}$$
   $$L = \frac{-(-1) - \sqrt{(-1)^2 - 4(1)(-1)}}{2(1)} = \frac{1 - \sqrt{5}}{2}.$$
   The first is $\phi = 1.618034\ldots$.

30. **a.** $\frac{1}{\phi} = \frac{1}{1.618034} = 0.618034 = \phi - 1$.

   b. $\phi^2 = 1.618034^2 = 2.618034 = \phi + 1$.

32. a. The second column in the table below shows the first ten Lucas numbers.

n	L_n	L_n/L_{n-1}
1	1	–
2	3	3
3	4	1.33
4	7	1.75
5	11	1.57
6	18	1.64
7	29	1.61
8	47	1.62
9	76	1.617
10	123	1.618

b. The ratios of successive Lucas numbers are shown in the right column of the table above. It appears that the ratio is approaching the golden ratio ϕ .

UNIT 12A

QUICK QUIZ

1. **b**. In a three-candidate race, it's possible that none of the candidates receives a majority of the votes.

2. **c**. Gore won 48.38% of the vote, which is not a majority, only a plurality.

3. **b**. A 60% vote is required to end a filibuster, which means 41% of the senators (a minority) can prevent a bill from coming to a vote by staging a filibuster.

4. **a**. In a runoff, the two candidates with the most votes go in a head-to-head competition, and Perot would be eliminated at this stage.

5. **b**. A preference schedule is a ballot where voters list, in order of their preference, the choices before them.

6. **c**. In an election where preference schedules are used, a voter is expected to fill in all choices.

7. **a**. Look at the second row of Figure 12.3.

8. **c**. Candidate D showed up in third place on 12 + 4 + 2 = 18 ballots.

9. **b**. Candidate E received only 6 first-place votes.

10. **b**. As shown in the text, a different winner would be declared for each of the five methods discussed (plurality, runoff, sequential runoff, a Borda count, and the Condorcet method).

DOES IT MAKES SENSE?

19. Does not make sense. If both candidates received more than 50% of the vote, the total vote would exceed 100%.

20. Makes sense. In an election with more than two candidates, the candidate that wins the most votes has won a plurality of the votes (in some cases this might also be a majority of votes).

21. Makes sense. Imagine a race with three candidates. Herman could win a plurality of the votes in the first election, with Hanna coming in second, in which case a runoff election would ensue. Hanna would win the election if she beat Herman in the runoff.

22. Makes sense. As shown in the analysis of the preference schedule outcomes of Table 12.3, there are scenarios where one candidate beats the other using a particular method of election, but the situation is reversed when using a different method of election.

23. Makes sense. This is the way most U.S. presidential elections are decided – a candidate wins both the popular and electoral vote.

24. Does not make sense. In the situation described, a hung jury would be declared, and the defendant would not be found guilty. (To be found guilty of a criminal offense in most states, a unanimous vote is often required).

BASIC SKILLS & CONCEPTS

25. Although Tilden narrowly won the popular vote, Hayes narrowly won the electoral vote, and became president.

26. Although Harrison narrowly won the popular vote, Cleveland easily won the electoral vote, and became president.

27. Garfield narrowly won the popular vote, and easily won the electoral vote to become president.

28. Wilson narrowly won both the popular and electoral vote to become president.

29. Carter narrowly won the popular vote, and comfortably won the electoral vote to become president.

30. George W. Bush lost the popular vote by a small margin, but he won the electoral vote by a small margin to become president.

31. George W. Bush won the popular vote by a close margin, and comfortably won the electoral vote to become president.

32. a. 62/100 = 62% of the senators would vote to end the filibuster, so the filibuster will likely end, and the bill could come to a vote where it would pass.
    b. A 2/3 vote of an 11-member jury requires at least 8 votes (because 7/11 = 63.6% < 2/3), so there will be no conviction in this trial. (A hung jury is likely).
    c. Only 72% of the states support the amendment (75% is required), so it will fail to pass.
    d. It is not likely to become law because 68/100 = 68% of the Senate will support it, and 270/435 = 62% of the House will support it, and this isn't enough for the veto to be overturned.

33. a. The percentage of shareholders favoring the merger is 6650/10,100 = 65.84%, which is just shy of the required 2/3 = 66.67% vote needed.
    b. A 3/4 vote of a 12-member jury requires at least 9 votes; thus, there will be no conviction.
    c. Only 70% of the states support the amendment (75% is required), so it will fail to pass.
    d. It is likely to become law because 68/100 = 68% of the Senate will support it, and 292/435 = 67.1% of the House will support it, so the veto can be overturned.

34. a. Wilson earned 6,286,214/13,896,156 = 45.24% of the popular vote, Roosevelt won 29.69%, and Taft won 25.07%. Wilson won the popular vote by a plurality, but no one won a majority.
    b. Wilson won 435/531 = 81.92% of the electoral vote, Roosevelt won 16.57%, and Taft won 1.51%. Wilson won both a plurality and a majority of the electoral vote.

c. If Taft had dropped out of the election, and Roosevelt had won most of Taft's popular votes, then Roosevelt could have won the popular vote. For Roosevelt to win the presidency, his additional popular votes would need to have been distributed among the states in a way that put him ahead of Wilson in many of the states that Wilson had won – Roosevelt would have needed Taft's 8 electoral votes, plus 170 of Wilson's electoral votes to win.

d. If Roosevelt had dropped out of the election and Taft had won most of Roosevelt's popular votes, then Taft could have won the popular vote. However, his additional popular votes would need to have been distributed among states in a way that allowed him to win the electoral vote.

35. a. A total of 66 votes were cast.

b. Candidate D is the plurality winner (22 first-place votes), but not by a majority.

c. In a runoff, candidate D would win, because 40 voters prefer D to B (who finished in second place in part **b**), while only 26 prefer B to D.

d. In a sequential runoff, the candidate with the fewest votes is eliminated at each stage. Candidate A received the fewest first-place votes in the original results (only 8), so A is eliminated, and those votes are redistributed among the other candidates. Recounting the votes after A has been eliminated, we find that B has 20 first-place votes, C has 16, and D has 30. Thus C is now eliminated, and the votes counted again. In this final stage, we find that B has 26 first-place votes, and D has 40 votes (as in part **b**), so D wins the sequential runoff.

e. In a Borda count, first-place votes receive a value of 4, second-place votes receive a value of 3, and so on. Working through each column of the table, and noting the number of voters who cast such ballots, the count for candidate A is computed as follows:

$$20 \times 1 + 15 \times 3 + 10 \times 2 + 8 \times 4 + 7 \times 3 + 6 \times 3 = 156.$$

The count for candidate B is

$$20 \times 4 + 15 \times 1 + 10 \times 1 + 8 \times 1 + 7 \times 2 + 6 \times 2 = 139.$$

The count for candidate C is

$$20 \times 2 + 15 \times 2 + 10 \times 4 + 8 \times 2 + 7 \times 1 + 6 \times 4 = 157.$$

The count for candidate D is

$$20 \times 3 + 15 \times 4 + 10 \times 3 + 8 \times 3 + 7 \times 4 + 6 \times 1 = 208.$$

Candidate D wins in this case.

f. Since there are 4 candidates, there are 6 pairings to consider. The results for each pairing are shown below.

A beats B, 46 to 20.   C beats A, 36 to 30.
D beats A, 52 to 14.   C beats B, 39 to 27.
D beats B, 40 to 26.   D beats C, 50 to 16.

Since D wins more pairwise comparisons than any other candidate, D is the winner.

g. As the winner by all five methods, candidate D is clearly the winner of the election.

36. a. A total of 29 votes were cast.

b. Candidate D is the plurality winner (13 first-place votes), but not by a majority.

c. In a runoff, candidate D would win, because 16 voters prefer D to B (who finished in second place in part **b**), while only 13 prefer B to D.

d. Using the process illustrated in exercise 35d, it can be shown that D wins a sequential runoff.

e. Using the process illustrated in exercise 35e, the counts of the five candidates are A = 91, B = 115, C = 76, D = 100, and E = 53. Candidate B has the highest count, so B wins in this case.

f. Checking all 10 possible pairwise comparisons (AB, AC, AD, AE, BC, BD, BE, CD, CE, and DE), you should find that each of candidates A, B, and D wins 3 of the match-ups, so no winner can be declared by this method.

g. Candidates B and D both win by at least one method, so the outcome is in contention. However, D won three of the five methods, so one could argue the election should go to D.

37. a. A total of 100 votes were cast.

b. Candidate C is the plurality winner (40 first-place votes), but not by a majority.

c. In a runoff, candidate A would win, because 55 voters prefer A to C.

d. With only three candidates, the sequential runoff method is the same as the standard runoff between the top two candidates, and thus A would win.

e. Using the process illustrated in exercise 35e, the counts of the three candidates are A = 200, B = 210, and C = 190. Candidate B has the highest count, so B wins a Borda count.

f. Since there are 3 candidates, there are 3 pairings to consider. The results of each pairing are:
B beats A, 55 to 45.   A beats C, 55 to 45.
B beats C, 55 to 45.
Since B wins two of the pairwise comparisons, B is the winner.

g. Candidate A wins by runoff, B wins by a Borda count and pairwise comparisons, and C is the plurality winner. Thus there is no clear winner.

38. a. A total of 30 votes were cast.

b. Candidates A, B, and D tie by the plurality method, all with 10 first-place votes.

c. The runoff method does not produce a winner, because only one candidate can be eliminated based on fewest first-place votes. The remaining three candidates (A, B, and D) tie.

d. Like the runoff method, the sequential runoff method fails to produce a winner: candidates A, B, and D tie.

e. Using the process illustrated in exercise 35e, the counts of the candidates are A = 80, B = 90, C = 60, and D = 70. Candidate B wins in this case.

f. Checking all 6 possible pairwise comparisons (AB, AC, AD, BC, BD, and CD), you should find that candidate B wins more head-to-head match-ups (3) than any other candidate, so B is the winner.

g. As the winner by the only two conclusive methods, candidate B is the winner of the election.

39. a. A total of 90 votes were cast.

b. Candidate E is the plurality winner (40 first-place votes), but not by a majority.

c. Candidate B wins a runoff, because 50 voters prefer B over E, who would receive 40 votes (D is eliminated at the beginning).

d. With only three candidates earning first-place votes, the sequential runoff method is the same as the standard runoff between the top two candidates, and thus B would win.

e. Using the process illustrated in exercise 35e, the counts of the candidates are A = 260, B = 290, C = 200, D = 290, and E = 310. Candidate E has the highest count, so E wins a Borda cont.

f. Since there are 5 candidates, there are 10 pairings to consider. The results for each pairing are shown below.

A beats B, 60 to 30.　　A beats C, 60 to 30.
D beats A, 60 to 30.　　E beats A, 70 to 20.
B beats C, 90 to 0.　　D beats B, 60 to 30.
B beats E, 50 to 40.　　D beats C, 60 to 30.
C beats E, 50 to 40.　　E beats D, 70 to 20.

Since D wins more pairwise comparisons than any other candidate (3), D is the winner.

g. Candidates B and E each win two of the five methods, and D wins one method, so all have some claim on the prize. The outcome is debatable.

40. Since there are 4 candidates, there are 6 pairings to consider. The results for each pairing are shown below.

B beats A, 60 to 50.　　A beats C, 110 to 0.
A beats D, 110 to 0.　　B beats C, 60 to 50.
B beats D, 60 to 50.

At this point, we don't even need to check the last pairing because we have already found the solution: candidate B wins all three of his head-to-head races, and thus is the Condorcet winner. (If you are curious, C beats D, 60 votes to 50 votes).

41. The results of the three head-to-head races are shown below.

A beats B, 18 to 9.　　B beats C, 19 to 8.
C beats A, 17 to 10.

No winner can be determined, and the curious situation where voters prefer A to B, B to C, and C

to A is called the *Condorcet paradox*, or *voting paradox*.

FURTHER APPLICATIONS

42. a. Best won a plurality, because he won more votes than the other candidates, but no one won a majority, as more than 50% of the vote is required before a majority winner can be claimed.

b. Able needs just over 15 percentage points to gain a majority and win a runoff. Since 15%/23% = 0.652, Able needs just over 65.2% of Crown's votes.

43. a. Fillipo won a plurality, because he won more votes than the other candidates, but no one won a majority, as more than 50% of the vote is required before a majority win can be claimed.

b. Earnest needs just over 23 percentage points to gain a majority and win a runoff. Since 23%/26% = 0.8846, Earnest needs just over 88.46% of Davis's votes.

44. a. Irving won a plurality because he won more votes than the other candidates, but no one won a majority (Irving won 205/485 = 42.3% of the vote, which isn't enough).

b. To overtake Irving, Heyduke needs 83 additional votes (this would give Heyduke a total of 243 votes, with Irving winning only 242 votes).

45. a. King won a plurality because he won more votes than the other candidates, but no one won a majority (King won 382/943 = 40.5% of the vote, which isn't enough).

b. To overtake King, Lord needs 166 additional votes (this would give Lord a total of 472 votes, with King winning only 471 votes).

46.

First	A	A	C	C
Second	B	C	A	B
Third	C	B	B	A
	4	2	3	1

47.

First	A	A	C	C	D
Second	B	C	A	B	A
Third	C	D	D	A	B
Fourth	D	B	B	D	C
	5	1	2	2	2

48. a. Label the four candidates as A, B, C, and D. It is easy enough to list all possible pairings: AB, AC, AD, BC, BD, and CD, for a total of 6 pairings. Note that this list is a list of combinations of four objects taken two at a time, so there should be $_4C_2$ = 6 pairings.

b. With 5 candidates, there are $_5C_2$ = 10 pairings.

c. With 6 candidates, there are $_6C_2 = 15$ pairings.

49. Each voter will record a first, second, third, fourth, fifth and sixth place vote. The points for these places total $6 + 5 + 4 + 3 + 2 + 1 = 21$ points. With 30 voters, there are $30 \times 21 = 630$ total points.

50. Each voter will record a first, second, third, and fourth place vote. The points for these places total $4 + 3 + 2 + 1 = 10$ points. With 30 voters, there are $30 \times 10 = 300$ total points. Candidate D has $300 - 125 - 80 - 75 = 20$ points, and thus candidate A wins the election.

UNIT 12B

QUICK QUIZ

1. **b**. An election isn't declared fair until all four fairness criteria are satisfied.

2. **a**. Berman wins a plurality because he has the most votes.

3. **b**. Goldsmith won the least number of first-place votes, and so is eliminated in a runoff. Freedman wins Goldsmith's 18 votes, and so beats Berman.

4. **c**. Criterion 1 is only applicable when a candidate wins a majority of votes.

5. **b**. Freedman wins both head-to-head races, and thus by Criterion 2, Freedman should win if this is a fair election.

6. **a**. See exercise 5.

7. **a**. Candidate X (Freedman) needs to be declared the winner of the first election before Criterion 4 comes into play.

8. **b**. There are plenty of elections where all four fairness criteria are satisfied. Arrow's theorem says only that no election system can be satisfied in *all* circumstances.

9. **b**. The text gives examples of approval voting scenarios that are not fair (and Arrow's theorem guarantees there are such cases).

10. **c**. In a small state, the number of voters per senator is much smaller than in a large state, and thus each voter has more voting power.

DOES IT MAKE SENSE?

15. Makes sense. Karen feels that because she won all head-to-head races, she should win the election so that Criterion 2 is satisfied – otherwise, it's not a fair election.

16. Makes sense. Kai feels the election is not fair, because under Criterion 1, he should win.

17. Does not make sense. Assuming the plurality method is used to decide the second election, Table 12.12 claims Criterion 3 is always satisfied (and thus Wendy could not have managed to win).

18. Does not make sense. Arrow's impossibility theorem states that no voting system can satisfy all four fairness criteria all of the time (see Example 4 in the text).

BASIC SKILLS & CONCEPTS

19. A candidate who wins a majority is the only person to receive a plurality. Thus the candidate will win the election, and Criterion 1 is satisfied.

20. Candidate A is the plurality winner, but candidate B wins in head-to-head races against both A and C. This implies the plurality method violates Criterion 2.

21. The following preference schedule is just one possible example.

First	B	A	C	C
Second	A	B	A	B
Third	C	C	B	A
	2	4	2	3

C is the plurality winner, but A beats both C and B, which means Criterion 2 is violated.

22. Suppose a candidate wins by the plurality method, and in a second election, moves up in at least one ranking (while the other candidates keep their relative rankings). That candidate's first-place votes must either remain the same or increase, so that candidate will win the second election.

23. Candidate A would win by the plurality method. However if candidate C were to drop out of the election, then B would win by the plurality method, and Criterion 4 would be violated.

24. The following preference schedule is just one possible example.

First	A	B	C
Second	B	A	B
Third	C	C	A
	3	2	4

Candidate C would win by plurality. However, if candidate A drops out, candidate B wins by plurality.

25. Assume a candidate receives a majority. In either runoff method, votes are redistributed as candidates are eliminated. But it is impossible for another candidate to accumulate enough votes to overtake a candidate who already has a majority.

26. By the sequential runoff method (which is the same as the top two runoff method with three candidates), candidate C is eliminated, and A wins the runoff. Candidate A also wins head-to-head races against B and C, so Criterion 2 is satisfied.

27. By the sequential runoff method (which is the same as the top two runoff method with three candidates), candidate B is eliminated, and C wins the runoff. However, candidate B wins head-to-head races against A and C, so Criterion 2 is violated.

28. The following preference schedule is just one possible example.

First	B	A	C
Second	A	C	A
Third	C	B	B
	3	2	4

Candidate C wins in a sequential runoff. But A beats B and C in head-to-head races, violating Criterion 2.

29. In the sequential runoff method, candidate B is eliminated first, then candidate A, making C the winner. Now suppose that the 4 voters on the third ballot (ACB) move C up and vote for the ranking CAB. Now A is eliminated first, and B wins the election. Thus criterion 3 is violated.

30. After candidate C is eliminated, candidate B wins the runoff. However, if A were to drop out, C would win the election. So Criterion 4 is violated.

31. The following preference schedule is just one possible example.

First	A	B	C
Second	B	A	B
Third	C	C	A
	4	3	5

After candidate B is eliminated, A wins the runoff. However, if C were to drop out, B would win the election. So Criterion 4 is violated.

32. We see that candidate A has a majority of votes (3/5 = 60%). By the point system (using 2, 1, and 0 points), A has 6 points, B has 7, and C has 2. So B wins by the point system, and Criterion 1 is violated, since the majority winner lost.

33. The following preference schedule is just one possible example.

First	A	B	C
Second	B	C	B
Third	C	A	A
	4	2	1

Candidate A has a majority of the votes, but loses in a Borda count (A gets 8 points, B gets 9, and C gets 4, using 2, 1, and 0 points).

34. Using the point system (with 2, 1, and 0 points), candidate A receives 10 points, B receives 11 points, and C receives 6 points. However, A beats B and C in head-to-head races, violating Criterion 2.

35. The following preference schedule is just one possible example.

First	A	D	C
Second	B	B	B
Third	C	A	D
Fourth	D	C	A
	4	8	3

Using the Borda count (with 3, 2, 1, and 0 points), A gets 20 points, B gets 30, C gets 13, and D gets 27 points, making B the winner. However, D wins head-to-head races against all other candidates, and thus Criterion 2 is violated.

36. Suppose a candidate wins by the point system, and in a second election, that candidate moves up in at least one ranking. That candidate's point total must increase at the expense of other candidates, and so will he win the second election.

37. Using the point system (with 2, 1, and 0 points), candidate A gets 11 points, B gets 11 points, and C gets 14 points, which makes C the winner. However, if Candidate A were to drop from the race, then B would receive 7 points and C would receive 5 points (notice that the point values become 1 and 0 with only two candidates). Thus Criterion 4 is violated.

38. The following preference schedule is just one possible example.

First	A	B
Second	C	A
Third	B	C
	2	3

Using the point system (with 2, 1, and 0 points), Candidate A gets 7 points, B gets 6, and C gets 2 points, which makes A the winner. However, if C were to drop from the race, then B would receive 3 points, and B would receive 2 (notice that the point values become 1 and 0 with only two candidates). Thus criterion 4 is violated.

39. Assume candidate A wins a majority of first-place votes. Then in every head-to-head race with another candidate, A must win (by a majority). Thus, A wins every head-to-head race and is the winner by pairwise comparisons, so Criterion 1 is satisfied.

40. If a candidate wins every head-to-head contest against other candidates then that candidate wins by the method of pairwise comparisons, so Criterion 2 is satisfied.

41. Suppose candidate A wins by the method of pairwise comparisons, and in a second election, moves up above candidate B in at least one ballot. A's position relative to B remains the same or improves, and A's position and B's position relative to the other candidates remains the same, so A must win the second election.

42. With the pairwise comparison method, A beats C, D, and E; B beats A; C beats B and D; D beats B and E; and E beats B and C. Thus A wins with three points. If C, D, and E drop out, then B beats A on three of the five ballots and wins the election. The outcome of the election is changed when C, D, and E drop out, which violates Criterion 4.

43. The following preference schedule is just one possible example.

First	B	C	D
Second	A	A	C
Third	D	D	B
Fourth	C	B	A
	2	2	2

By the pairwise comparison method, A would beat D, B would beat A, C would beat A and B, and D would beat B and C. This would lead to a tie between C and D. However, if A were to drop out of the election, then D would have two pairwise wins, and C would have one pairwise win. Criterion 4 is violated because the outcome of the election is changed when A drops out.

44. a. Voting only for their first choices, candidate C wins by plurality with 40% of the vote.
    b. By an approval vote, 30% + 29% = 59% of the voters approve of candidate B, 30% + 29% + 1% = 60% approve of candidate A, and 40% of the voters approve of candidate C. The winner is A.

45. a. Voting only for their first choices, candidate C wins by plurality with 42% of the vote.
    b. By an approval vote, 28% + 29% = 57% of the voters approve of A, 28% + 29% +1% = 58% approve of B, and 42% of the voters approve of C. The winner is B.

46. Imagine that there is a vote of the four shareholders. Regardless of how the three largest shareholders (26%, 26%, 25%) vote, their votes will give a majority to one side or the other (try all combinations). The vote of the third shareholder (23%) cannot change the outcome.

47. The electoral votes per person for each of the states can be computed by dividing the number of electoral votes by the population. The results are as follows:

New York 1.61×10^{-6} Illinois 1.65×10^{-6}

Rhode Island 3.70×10^{-6} Alaska 4.58×10^{-6}

It is evident that voters in Alaska have more voting power than those in Illinois.

48. The voters in Alaska have more voting power than those in New York (see exercise 47).

49. The voters in Rhode Island have more voting power than those in Illinois (see exercise 47).

50. The voters in Illinois have more voting power than those in New York (see exercise 47).

51. From the least to greatest voting power, the ranking is: New York, Illinois, Rhode Island, Alaska.

FURTHER APPLICATIONS

52. The winner by plurality, but not majority, is A. So Criterion 1 does not apply. Candidate A beats all other candidates one-on-one and is also declared winner by the plurality method, so Criterion 2 is satisfied. The plurality method always satisfies Criterion 3. If C were to drop out of the election, then B would win by plurality, violating Criterion 4.

53. A single runoff would eliminate C and D. Candidate A would win the runoff, 23 to 18. There is no majority winner, so Criterion 1 does not apply. Candidate A beats all other candidates one-on-one, and is also declared winner in a single runoff, so Criterion 2 is satisfied. If A is moved up in any of the rankings, it doesn't affect the outcome of the election, so Criterion 3 is satisfied. If any combination of {B, C, D} drops out of the race, the outcome is not changed. So in this case (though not in general), Criterion 4 is satisfied.

54. A sequential runoff eliminates candidate D, followed by B and C, leaving A as the winner. There is no majority winner, so Criterion 1 does not apply. Candidate A beats all other candidates one-to-one, and is also declared winner by the sequential runoff method, so Criterion 2 is satisfied. If A is moved up in any of the rankings, it doesn't affect the outcome of the election, so Criterion 3 is satisfied. If any combination of {B, C, D} drops out of the race, the outcome is not changed. So in this case (though not in general), Criterion 4 is satisfied.

55. Candidate A wins the point system (using 3, 2, 1, and 0 points) with 83 points. There is no majority winner, so Criterion 1 does not apply. Candidate A beats all other candidates one-on-one, and is also declared winner by the point system, so Criterion 2 is satisfied. The point system always satisfies Criterion 3. If any combination of {B, C, D} drops out of the race, the outcome is not changed. So in this case (though not in general), Criterion 4 is satisfied.

56. Candidate A wins by the pairwise comparison method because A beats all other candidates in head-to-head races. There is no majority winner, so Criterion 1 does not apply. Candidate A beats all other candidates one-on-one and is automatically declared winner by the pairwise comparison method, so Criterion 2 is satisfied. The pairwise comparison method always satisfies Criterion 3. Since A beats all other candidates, the removal of any other candidate cannot affect the outcome of the election, and thus Criterion 4 is satisfied.

57. Candidate A wins by a plurality, but not by a majority. There is no majority winner, so Criterion 1 does not apply. Candidate E beats all other candidates one-on-one, but loses by the plurality method, so Criterion 2 is violated. The plurality method always satisfies Criterion 3. If any of B, C, or D were to drop out of the election, the outcome of A winning would change, so Criterion 4 is violated.

58. After candidates C, D, and E are eliminated, B wins the runoff. There is no majority winner, so Criterion 1 does not apply. Candidate E beats all other candidates one-to-one, but loses by the runoff method, so Criterion 2 is violated. If B were to move up in any of the rankings, it would not affect the outcome of the election (in this case), so Criterion 3 is satisfied. If candidate A were to drop out of the race, then D would win, so Criterion 4 is violated.

59. The candidates E, D, and B are eliminated sequentially, leaving a final runoff between A and C, which C wins. There is no majority winner, so Criterion 1 does not apply. Candidate E beats all other candidates one-on-one, but loses in the sequential runoff method, so Criterion 2 is violated. If candidate C moved up in any of the rankings, the outcome is not affected, so Criterion 3 is satisfied. If A were to drop out of the election, D would win instead of C, so Criterion 4 is violated.

60. Candidate D wins the election by the Borda count (using 4, 3, 2, 1, and 0 points) with 136 points. There is no majority winner, so Criterion 1 does not apply. Candidate E beats all other candidates one-on-one, but loses by the point system, so Criterion 2 is violated. The point system always satisfies Criterion 3. If C drops out of the race, then the winner is no longer D, but E – this is a violation of Criterion 4.

61. We have seen that E beats all other candidates in pairwise races (see exercise 57) and is the winner by the pairwise comparison method. There is no majority winner, so Criterion 1 does not apply. The pairwise comparison method always satisfies Criteria 2 and 3. It can be shown that if any combination of {A, B, C, D} drops out of the race, the winner is still E, so Criterion 4 is satisfied.

62. If the two major parties deadlock at 49 votes apiece, then the deciding votes are held by the Independents. If both Independents vote with one party, that party wins the vote.

UNIT 12C

QUICK QUIZ

1. **c.** The Constitution does not specify the number of representatives, and the House has, in fact, had 435 members only since 1912. The number briefly rose by two when Hawaii and Alaska were granted statehood (1959), but dropped back to 435 in the next apportionment (and will likely remain at that level, unless a 1941 law is changed).

2. **b.** Apportionment is a process used to divide the available seats among the states.

3. **a.** The standard divisor is defined to be the total U.S. population divided by the number of seats in the House.

4. **b.** The standard quota is defined to be the population of a state divided by the standard divisor. In this case, the standard divisor is 1 million.

5. **b.** In this scenario, the standard divisor would be defined as the population of students divided by the number of teachers, or $25,000 \div 1000 = 25$.

6. **b.** In this scenario, the standard quota would be defined as the population of the school divided by the standard divisor computed in exercise 5. Thus it would be $220 \div 25 = 8.8$.

7. **c.** Parks Elementary would get the eight teachers because the Hamilton method assigns the extra teacher to the school with the highest standard quota.

8. **c.** The Hamilton, Jefferson, Webster, and Hill-Huntington methods are the only four methods of apportionment that have been used (to date) to assign the seats in the House to various states.

9. **c.** At present, the law states that the Hill-Huntington method is to be used to reapportion seats at every census.

10. **a.** M. L. Balinsky and H. P. Young proved that it is impossible to devise a method of apportionment that satisfies the fairness criteria in all cases.

DOES IT MAKE SENSE?

19. Makes sense. If the number of staff support persons needed in a division depends on the

number of employees in that division, an apportionment method would be a good idea.

20. Does not make sense. The points allocated to the skaters should be determined by the merits of their performances. Apportionment methods are used in situations in which the population or size of various groups determines how much representation each group should receive.

21. Does not make sense. All apportionment methods have deficiencies, and no single method (of those discussed in the text) is better than the others due to the level of math required to carry it out.

22. Makes sense. This is an example of the Alabama paradox. Ideally, a fair apportionment method should not be prone to the paradox.

BASIC SKILLS & CONCEPTS

23. The number of people per representative would be $350,000,000 \div 435 = 804,598$. If the constitutional limit were observed, the number of representatives would be $350,000,000 \div 30,000 = 11,667$.

24. The number of people per representative would be $400,000,000 \div 500 = 800,000$. If the constitutional limit were observed, the number of representatives would be $400,000,000 \div 30,000 = 13,333$.

25. In order to compute the standard quota, the standard divisor must first be computed. The standard divisor is $\frac{294 \text{ million}}{435} = 676,000$. For Connecticut, the standard quota is $\frac{3,504,000}{676,000} = 5.18$, which is larger than the 5 seats the state actually has, so Connecticut is underrepresented.

26. The standard divisor is 676,000 (see exercise 25). For Georgia, the standard quota is $\frac{8,829,000}{676,000} = 13.06$, which is larger than the 13 seats the state actually has, so Georgia is underrepresented.

27. The standard divisor is 676,000 (see exercise 25). For Florida, the standard quota is $\frac{17,397,000}{676,000} = 25.74$, which is larger than the 25 seats the state actually has, so Florida is underrepresented.

28. The standard divisor is 676,000 (see exercise 25). For Ohio, the standard quota is $\frac{11,459,000}{676,000} = 16.95$, which is smaller than the 18 seats the state actually has, so Ohio is overrepresented.

29. The total number of employees is $250 + 320 + 380 + 400 = 1350$. The standard divisor is then $\frac{1350}{35} = 38.57$. For the first division, the standard quota is $\frac{250}{38.57} = 6.48$. The standard quotas for the other divisions are 8.30, 9.85, and 10.37, respectively (computed in a similar fashion).

30. The total student population is $560 + 1230 + 1490 + 1760 + 2340 = 7380$. The standard divisor is then $\frac{7380}{18} = 410$. For the first college, the standard quota is $\frac{560}{410} = 1.37$. The standard quotas for the other divisions are 3.00, 3.63, 4.29, and 5.71, respectively (computed in a similar fashion).

31. Refer to exercise 29. Using Hamilton's method for the assignments, round each standard quota down to get $6 + 8 + 9 + 10 = 33$ technicians. Since the first and third divisions have the highest remainders, the extra two technicians will be assigned to them, giving a final apportionment of 7, 8, 10, and 10 technicians to each of the four divisions.

32. Refer to exercise 30. Using Hamilton's method for the assignments, round each standard quota down to get $1 + 3 + 3 + 4 + 5 = 16$ advisors. Since the third and fifth colleges have the highest remainders, the extra two advisors will be assigned to them, giving a final apportionment of 1, 3, 4, 4, and 6 advisors to each of the five colleges.

33. The total population is $950 + 670 + 246 = 1866$, so with 100 seats to be apportioned, the standard divisor is $1866 \div 100 = 18.66$. This is used to compute the standard quota and the minimum quotas in the table below. Hamilton's method applied to these three states yields:

State	A	B	C	Total
Pop.	950	670	246	1866
Std. Q.	50.91	35.91	13.18	100
Min. Q.	50	35	13	98
Frac. R.	0.91	0.91	0.18	2
Final A.	51	36	13	100

Assuming 101 delegates, Hamilton's method yields:

State	A	B	C	Total
Pop.	950	670	246	1866
Std. Q.	50.42	35.26	13.32	101
Min. Q.	51	36	13	100
Frac. R.	0.42	0.26	0.32	1
Final A.	52	36	13	101

No state lost seats as a result of the additional available seat, so the Alabama paradox does not occur here.

34. The total population is 2540 + 1140 + 6330 = 10,010, so with 100 seats to be apportioned, the standard divisor is 10,010 ÷ 100 = 100.10. This is used to compute the standard quota and the minimum quotas in the table below. Hamilton's method applied to these three states yields:

State	A	B	C	Total
Pop.	2540	1140	6330	10,010
Std. Q.	25.37	11.39	63.24	100
Min. Q.	25	11	63	99
Frac. R.	0.37	0.39	0.24	1
Final A.	25	12	63	100

Assuming 101 delegates, Hamilton's method yields:

State	A	B	C	Total
Pop.	2540	1140	6330	10,010
Std. Q.	25.63	11.50	63.87	101
Min. Q.	25	11	63	99
Frac. R.	0.63	0.50	0.87	2
Final A.	26	11	64	101

State B lost a seat as a result of the additional available seat, so the Alabama paradox does occur here.

35. The total population is 770 + 155 + 70 + 673 = 1668, so with 100 seats to be apportioned, the standard divisor is 1668 ÷ 100 = 16.68. This is used to compute the standard quota and the minimum quotas in the table below. Hamilton's method applied to these four states yields:

State	A	B	C	D	Total
Pop.	770	155	70	673	1668
Std. Q.	46.16	9.29	4.20	40.35	100
Min. Q.	46	9	4	40	99
Frac. R.	0.16	0.29	0.20	0.35	1
Final A.	46	9	4	41	100

Assuming 101 delegates, Hamilton's method yields:

State	A	B	C	D	Total
Pop.	770	155	70	673	1668
Std. Q.	46.62	9.39	4.24	40.75	101
Min. Q.	46	9	4	40	99
Frac. R.	0.62	0.39	0.24	0.75	2
Final A.	47	9	4	41	101

No state lost seats as a result of the additional available seat, so the Alabama paradox does not occur here.

36. The total population is 562 + 88 + 108 + 242 = 1000, so with 100 seats to be apportioned, the standard divisor is 1000 ÷ 100 = 10. This is used to compute the standard quota and the minimum quotas in the table below. Hamilton's method applied to these four states yields:

State	A	B	C	D	Total
Pop.	562	88	108	242	1000
Std. Q.	56.20	8.80	10.80	24.20	100
Min. Q.	56	8	10	24	98
Frac. R.	0.20	0.80	0.80	0.20	2
Final A.	56	9	11	24	100

Assuming 101 delegates, Hamilton's method yields:

State	A	B	C	D	Total
Pop.	562	88	108	242	1000
Std. Q.	56.76	8.89	10.91	24.44	101
Min. Q.	56	8	10	24	98
Frac. R.	0.76	0.89	0.91	0.44	3
Final A.	57	9	11	24	101

No state lost seats as a result of the additional available seat, so the Alabama paradox does not occur here.

37. The total population is 98 + 689 + 212 = 999, so with 100 seats to be apportioned, the standard divisor is 999 ÷ 100 = 9.99. This is used to compute the standard quota and the minimum quotas in the table below. Using a modified divisor of 9.83 instead, we get the modified quotas listed, and the new minimum quotas. Jefferson's method then yields:

State	A	B	C	Total
Pop.	98	689	212	999
Std. Q.	9.81	68.97	21.22	100
Min. Q.	9	68	21	98
Mod. Q.	9.97	70.09	21.57	101.63
N. Min. Q.	9	70	21	100

Since the new minimum quota successfully apportions all 100 seats, we can stop. Note, however, that the quota criterion is violated, because state B's standard quota is 68.97, yet it was given 70 seats.

38. The total population is 1280 + 631 + 2320 = 4231, so with 100 seats to be apportioned, the standard divisor is 4231 ÷ 100 = 42.31. This is used to compute the standard quota and the minimum quotas in the table below. Using a modified

divisor of 42.00 instead, we get the modified quotas listed, and the new minimum quotas. Jefferson's method then yields:

State	A	B	C	Total
Pop.	1280	631	2320	4231
Std. Q.	30.25	14.91	54.83	100
Min. Q.	30	14	54	98
Mod. Q.	30.48	15.02	55.24	100.74
N. Min. Q.	30	15	55	100

Since the new minimum quota successfully apportions all 100 seats, we can stop. The quota criterion is satisfied.

39. The total population is 979, so with 100 seats to be apportioned, the standard divisor is $979 \div 100 = 9.79$. This is used to compute the standard quota and the minimum quotas in the table below. Using a modified divisor of 9.60 instead, we get the modified quotas listed, and the new minimum quotas. Jefferson's method then yields:

State	A	B	C	D	Total
Pop.	69	680	155	75	979
Std. Q.	7.05	69.46	15.83	7.66	100
Min. Q.	7	69	15	7	98
Mod. Q.	7.19	70.83	16.15	7.81	101.98
NMQ	7	70	16	7	100

Since the new minimum quota successfully apportions all 100 seats, we can stop. The quota criterion is satisfied.

40. The total population is 9400, so with 100 seats to be apportioned, the standard divisor is $9400 \div 100 = 94.00$. This is used to compute the standard quota and the minimum quotas in the table below. Using a modified divisor of 92.00 instead, we get the modified quotas listed, and the new minimum quotas. Jefferson's method then yields:

State	A	B	C	D	Total
Pop.	1220	5030	2460	690	9400
Std. Q.	12.98	53.51	26.17	7.34	100
Min. Q.	12	53	26	7	98
Mod. Q.	13.26	54.67	26.74	7.50	102.17
NMQ	13	54	26	7	100

Since the new minimum quota successfully apportions all 100 seats, we can stop. The quota criterion is satisfied.

41. After trial and error, a modified divisor of 38.4 was found to work. The results are summarized in the table below.

Division	I	II	III	IV
Number in division	250	320	380	400
Modified Quota	6.51	8.33	9.90	10.42
Number assigned	7	8	10	10

42. No modified divisor is necessary in this case. The standard quotas from exercise 30 are 1.37, 3.00, 3.63, 4.29, and 5.71, respectively, and Webster's method directs us to round quotas using standard rounding rules. This yields an apportionment of 1, 3, 4, 4, and 6 advisors to the respective colleges. Since this apportionment leaves no extra advisors, we have found a suitable apportionment.

43. An interesting situation arises in this problem: if the standard divisor, standard quotas, and geometric means are computed without rounding, it turns out a modified divisor is not necessary. That is, after computing said values, the Hill-Huntington method immediately produces an apportionment with no leftover technicians, and it is not necessary to seek a modified divisor. The results are summarized in the table below.

Division	I	II	III	IV
Number in division	250	320	380	400
Standard Quota	6.4815	8.30	9.85	10.37
Geometric Mean	$\sqrt{6 \times 7}$ 6.4807	$\sqrt{8 \times 9}$ 8.49	$\sqrt{9 \times 10}$ 9.49	$\sqrt{10 \times 11}$ 10.49
Number assigned	7	8	10	10

Division I is the culprit – the standard quota and geometric mean are so close to one another that it is hard to determine whether one should round up or down (note that the values at the other entries in the table are not shown to the same precision, because the decision about whether to round up or down can be made with less precise values). If the rounded values from exercise 30 are used, you will need to use a modified divisor in order to find an apportionment that uses all 35 technicians. A divisor of 38.4 is suitable (and realize that modified divisors are not unique, in that divisors close to one another produce the same results).

44. No modified divisor is necessary in this case. The standard quotas from exercise 30 are 1.37, 3.00, 3.63, 4.29, and 5.71, respectively, and the Hill-Huntington method directs us to round quotas based on geometric means. The required geometric means are (respectively): $\sqrt{1 \times 2} = 1.414$; $\sqrt{3 \times 4} = 3.464$; $\sqrt{3 \times 4} = 3.464$; $\sqrt{4 \times 5} = 4.472$; and $\sqrt{5 \times 6} = 5.477$. This yields an apportionment of 1, 3, 4, 4, and 6 advisors to the respective colleges. Since this apportionment leaves no extra advisors, we have found a suitable apportionment.

FURTHER APPLICATIONS

45. The total population is 7710, so with 100 seats to be apportioned, the standard divisor is $7710 \div 100 = 77.10$. This is used to compute the standard quota and the minimum quotas in the table below. Hamilton's method applied to these three states yields:

State	A	B	C	Total
Pop.	1140	6320	250	7710
Std. Q.	14.79	81.97	3.24	100
Min. Q.	14	81	3	98
Frac. R.	0.79	0.97	0.24	2
Final A.	15	82	3	100

With the addition of a new state D of population 500, for whom 5 new delegates are added, Hamilton's method (with a new standard divisor of $8210 \div 105 = 78.19$) yields:

State	A	B	C	D	Total
Pop.	1140	6320	250	500	8210
Std. Q.	14.58	80.83	3.20	6.39	105
Min. Q.	14	80	3	6	103
Frac. R.	0.58	0.83	0.20	0.39	2
Final A.	15	81	3	6	105

Even though 5 new seats were added with state D representation in mind, Hamilton's method assigned 6 seats to this state, 1 of them at the expense of state B. Since B lost a seat as a result of the additional seats for the new state, the New State paradox occurs here.

46. The total population is 9948, so with 100 seats to be apportioned, the standard divisor is $9948 \div 100 = 99.48$. This is used to compute the standard quota and the minimum quotas in the table below. Hamilton's method applied to these three states yields:

State	A	B	C	Total
Pop.	5310	1330	3308	9948
Std. Q.	53.38	13.37	33.25	100
Min. Q.	53	13	33	99
Frac. R.	0.38	0.37	0.25	1
Final A.	54	13	33	100

With the addition of a new state D of population 500, for whom 5 new delegates are added, Hamilton's method (with a new standard divisor of $10,448 \div 105 = 99.50$) yields:

State	A	B	C	D	Total
Pop.	5310	1330	3308	500	10,448
Std. Q.	53.36	13.37	33.24	5.02	105
Min. Q.	53	13	33	5	104
Frac. R.	0.36	0.37	0.24	0.02	1
Final A.	53	14	33	5	105

While Hamilton's method assigned 5 seats to the new state, as intended, it also gave State B an additional state at the expense of state A. Since A lost a seat as a result of the additional seats for the new state, the New State paradox occurs here.

47. a. The total population is 999, so with 100 seats to be apportioned, the standard divisor is $999 \div 100 = 99.9$. This is used to compute the standard quota and the minimum quotas in the table below. Hamilton's method yields:

State	A	B	C	Total
Pop.	535	334	120	999
Std. Q.	53.55	34.43	12.01	100
Min. Q.	53	34	12	99
Frac. R.	0.55	0.43	0.01	1
Final A.	54	34	12	100

b. Jefferson's method begins as with Hamilton's. As noted in part **a**, the standard divisor is 9.99, so we try lower modified divisors until the apportionment comes out just right. By trial and error, the modified divisor 9.90 is found to work, as documented in the last two rows of the table below. Note that this choice of the modified divisor is not unique, as other nearby values also work.

State	A	B	C	Total
Pop.	535	334	120	999
Std. Q.	53.55	34.43	12.01	100
Min. Q.	53	34	12	98
Mod. Q.	54.04	34.75	12.12	100.91
N. Min. Q.	54	34	12	100

c. Webster's method requires us to find a modified divisor such that the corresponding modified quotas round (not truncate) to numbers that sum to the desired 100 delegates. Inspecting the table in part **a**, we see that the standard divisor and standard quotas are already adequate – we don't need to seek a modified divisor in this case.

State	A	B	C	Total
Pop.	535	334	120	999
Std. Q.	53.55	34.43	12.01	100
Min. Q.	53	34	12	99
Rou. Q.	54	34	12	100

d. The Hill-Huntington method requires us to find a modified divisor such that the corresponding modified quotas, *rounded relative to the geometric mean*, yield numbers which sum to the required 100 delegates. As in part **c**, the standard divisor and standard quotas are already sufficient because they round (per the geometric means) to the desired apportionment. Thus there is no need to seek out a modified divisor in this case.

State	A	B	C	Total
Pop.	535	334	120	999
Std. Q.	53.55	34.43	12.01	100
Min. Q.	53	34	12	99
Geo. M.	53.50	34.50	12.49	-
Rou. Q.	54	34	12	100

The geometric means are for the whole numbers bracketing the standard quotas, namely: $\sqrt{53 \times 54}$ = 53.50, $\sqrt{34 \times 35}$ = 34.50, and $\sqrt{12 \times 13}$ = 12.49. The modified quotas (in this case the standard quotas) are compared to these, and hence 34.43 and 12.01 are rounded down to 34 and 12, respectively, whereas 53.55 is rounded up to 54.

e. All four methods gave the same results.

48. Refer to exercise 47 for a detailed explanation of the method of solution that yields the following apportionments.

a. Standard divisor = 9.76.

State	A	B	C	Total
Pop.	144	443	389	976
Std. Q.	14.75	45.39	39.86	100
Min. Q.	14	45	39	98
Frac. R.	0.75	0.39	0.86	2
Final A.	15	45	40	100

b. Modified divisor = 9.63.

State	A	B	C	Total
Pop.	144	443	389	976
Std. Q.	14.75	45.39	39.86	100
Min. Q.	14	45	39	98
Mod. Q.	14.95	46.00	40.39	101.35
N. Min. Q.	14	46	40	100

c. Modified divisor not necessary.

State	A	B	C	Total
Pop.	144	443	389	976
Std. Q.	14.75	45.39	39.86	100
Min. Q.	14	45	39	98
Rou. Q.	15	45	40	100

d. Modified divisor not necessary.

State	A	B	C	Total
Pop.	144	443	389	976
Std. Q.	14.75	45.39	39.86	100
Min. Q.	14	45	39	99
Geo. M.	14.49	45.50	39.50	-
Rou. Q.	15	45	40	100

e. The Hamilton, Webster, and Hill-Huntington methods all give the same result, so one could argue that these yield the best apportionment.

49. Refer to exercise 47 for a detailed explanation of the method of solution that yields the following apportionments.

a. Standard divisor = 100.

State	A	B	C	D	Total
Pop.	836	2703	2626	3835	10,000
Std. Q.	8.36	27.03	26.26	38.35	100
Min. Q.	8	27	26	38	99
Frac. R.	0.36	0.03	0.26	0.35	1
Final A.	9	27	26	38	100

b. Modified divisor = 98.3.

State	A	B	C	D	Total
Pop.	836	2703	2626	3835	10,000
Std. Q.	8.36	27.03	26.26	38.35	100
Min. Q.	8	27	26	38	99
Mod. Q.	8.50	27.50	26.71	39.01	101.73
NMQ	8	27	26	39	100

c. Modified divisor = 99.5.

State	A	B	C	D	Total
Pop.	836	2703	2626	3835	10,000
Std. Q.	8.36	27.03	26.26	38.35	100
Min. Q.	8	27	26	38	99
Mod. Q.	8.40	27.17	26.39	38.54	100.50
Rou. Q.	8	27	26	39	100

d. Modified divisor = 99.5.

State	A	B	C	D	Total
Pop.	836	2703	2626	3835	10,000
Std. Q.	8.36	27.03	26.26	38.35	100
Min. Q.	8	27	26	38	99
Mod. Q.	8.40	27.17	26.39	38.54	100.49
Geo. M.	8.49	27.50	26.50	38.50	-
Rou. Q.	8	27	26	39	100

e. The Jefferson, Webster, and Hill-Huntington methods all gave the same result, so one could argue that these yield the best apportionment.

50. Refer to exercise 47 for a detailed explanation of the method of solution that yields the following apportionments.

a. Standard divisor = 125.57.

State	A	B	C	D	Total
Pop.	1234	3498	2267	5558	12,557
Std. Q.	9.83	27.86	18.05	44.26	100
Min. Q.	9	27	18	44	98
Frac. R.	0.83	0.86	0.05	0.26	2
Final A.	10	28	18	44	100

b. Modified divisor = 123.5.

State	A	B	C	D	Total
Pop.	1234	3498	2267	5558	12,557
Std. Q.	9.83	27.86	18.05	44.26	100
Min. Q.	9	27	18	44	98
Mod. Q.	9.99	28.32	18.36	45.00	101.68
NMQ	9	28	18	45	100

c. Modified divisor not necessary.

State	A	B	C	D	Total
Pop.	1234	3498	2267	5558	12,557
Std. Q.	9.83	27.86	18.05	44.26	100
Min. Q.	9	27	18	44	98
Rou. Q.	10	28	18	44	100

d. Modified divisor not necessary.

State	A	B	C	D	Total
Pop.	1234	3498	2267	5558	12,557
Std. Q.	9.83	27.86	18.05	44.26	100
Min. Q.	9	27	18	44	98
Geo. M.	9.49	27.50	18.49	44.50	-
Rou. Q.	10	28	18	44	100

e. The Hamilton, Webster, and Hill-Huntington methods all give the same results, so one could argue that these yield the best apportionment.

51. a. The total population is 390 students, so with 10 committee positions to be apportioned, the standard divisor is $390 \div 10 = 39$. This is used to compute the standard quota and the minimum quotas in the table below. Hamilton's method yields:

Group	Soc.	Pol.	Ath.	Total
Pop.	48	97	245	390
Std. Q.	1.23	2.49	6.28	10
Min. Q.	1	2	6	9
Frac. R.	0.23	0.49	0.28	1
Final A.	1	3	6	10

b. Jefferson's method begins as with Hamilton's. As noted in part **a**, the standard divisor is 39, so we try lower modified divisors until the apportionment comes out just right. By trial and error, the modified divisor of 35 is found to work. Note that this choice of the modified divisor is not unique, as other nearby values also work.

Group	Soc.	Pol.	Ath.	Total
Pop.	48	97	245	390
Std. Q.	1.23	2.49	6.28	10
Min. Q.	1	2	6	9
Mod. Q.	1.37	2.77	7.00	11.14
NMQ	1	2	7	10

c. Webster's method requires us to find a modified divisor such that the corresponding modified quotas round (not truncate) to numbers that sum to the desired 10 members. Inspecting the tables in parts **a** and **b**, we see that neither the standard nor modified quotas there work, so we must try other modified divisors. This time, we find that 38 is a suitable modified divisor. Note that this choice of the modified divisor is not unique, as other nearby values also work.

Group	Soc.	Pol.	Ath.	Total
Pop.	48	97	245	390
Std. Q.	1.23	2.49	6.28	10
Min. Q.	1	2	6	9
Mod. Q.	1.26	2.55	6.45	10.26
Rou. Q.	1	3	6	10

d. The Hill-Huntington method requires us to find a modified divisor such that the corresponding modified quotas, *rounded relative to the geometric mean*, yield numbers that sum to the desired 10 members. The standard divisor of 39 and standard quotas are already sufficient because they round (per the geometric means) to the desired apportionment. Thus there is no need to seek out a modified divisor in this case.

Group	Soc.	Pol.	Ath.	Total
Pop.	48	97	245	390
Std. Q.	1.23	2.49	6.28	10
Min. Q.	1	2	6	9
Geo. M.	1.41	2.45	6.48	-
Rou. Q.	1	3	6	10

The geometric means are for the whole numbers bracketing the standard quotas, namely: $\sqrt{1\times2}$ = 1.41, $\sqrt{2\times3}$ = 2.45, and $\sqrt{6\times7}$ = 6.48. The modified quotas (in this case the standard quotas) are compared to these, and hence 1.23 and 6.28 are rounded down to 1 and 6, respectively, whereas 2.49 is rounded up to 3.
e. The Hamilton, Webster, and Hill-Huntington methods all give the same result, and thus one could argue that these yield the best apportionment.

52. Refer to exercise 51 for a detailed explanation of the method of solution that yields the following apportionments.
a. Standard divisor = 62.75.

Dept.	Pol.	Fire	Para.	Total
Pop.	485	213	306	1004
Std. Q.	7.73	3.39	4.88	16
Min. Q.	7	3	4	14
Frac. R.	0.73	0.39	0.88	2
Final A.	8	3	5	16

b. Modified divisor = 60.

Dept.	Pol.	Fire	Para.	Total
Pop.	485	213	306	1004
Std. Q.	7.73	3.39	4.88	16
Min. Q.	7	3	4	14
Mod. Q.	8.08	3.55	5.10	16.73
NMQ	8	3	5	16

c. Modified divisor not necessary.

Dept.	Pol.	Fire	Para.	Total
Pop.	485	213	306	1004
Std. Q.	7.73	3.39	4.88	16
Min. Q.	7	3	4	14
Rou. Q.	8	3	5	16

d. Modified divisor not necessary.

Dept.	Pol.	Fire	Para.	Total
Pop.	485	213	306	1004
Std. Q.	7.73	3.39	4.88	16
Min. Q.	7	3	4	14
Geo. M.	7.48	3.46	4.47	-
Rou. Q.	8	3	5	16

e. All four methods give the same results.
53. Refer to exercise 51 for a detailed explanation of the method of solution that yields the following apportionments.
a. Note that the total "population" is 2.5 + 7.6 + 3.9 + 5.5 = 19.5 (million dollars).
Standard divisor = 0.78.

Store	Bou.	Den.	Bro.	F. C.	Total
Pop.	2.5	7.6	3.9	5.5	19.5
Std. Q.	3.21	9.74	5.00	7.05	25
Min. Q.	3	9	5	7	24
Frac. R.	0.21	0.74	0.00	0.05	1
Final A.	3	10	5	7	25

b. Modified divisor = 0.76.

Store	Bou.	Den.	Bro.	F. C.	Total
Pop.	2.5	7.6	3.9	5.5	19.5
Std. Q.	3.21	9.74	5.00	7.05	25
Min. Q.	3	9	5	7	24
Mod. Q.	3.29	10.00	5.13	7.24	25.66
NMQ	3	10	5	7	25

c. Modified divisor not necessary.

Store	Bou.	Den.	Bro.	F. C.	Total
Pop.	2.5	7.6	3.9	5.5	19.5
Std. Q.	3.21	9.74	5.00	7.05	25
Min. Q.	3	9	5	7	24
Rou. Q.	3	10	5	7	25

d. Modified divisor not necessary.

Store	Bou.	Den.	Bro.	F. C.	Total
Pop.	2.5	7.6	3.9	5.5	19.5
Std. Q.	3.21	9.74	5.00	7.05	25
Min. Q.	3	9	5	7	24
Geo. M.	3.46	9.49	5.48	7.48	-
Rou. Q.	3	10	5	7	25

e. All four methods give the same results.
54. Refer to exercise 51 for a detailed explanation of the method of solution that yields the following apportionments.
a. Standard divisor = 1143.33.

Nbrhd.	G	W	C	Total
Pop.	4300	3040	2950	10,290
Std. Q.	3.76	2.66	2.58	9
Min. Q.	3	2	2	7
Frac. R.	0.76	0.66	0.58	2
Final A.	4	3	2	9

b. Modified divisor = 1000.

Nbrhd.	G	W	C	Total
Pop.	4300	3040	2950	10,290
Std. Q.	3.76	2.66	2.58	9
Min. Q.	3	2	2	7
Mod. Q.	4.30	3.04	2.95	10.29
NMQ	4	3	2	9

c. Modified divisor = 1200.

Nbrhd.	G	W	C	Total
Pop.	4300	3040	2950	10,290
Std. Q.	3.76	2.66	2.58	9
Min. Q.	3	2	2	7
Mod. Q.	3.58	2.53	2.49	8.58
Rou. Q.	4	3	2	9

d. Modified divisor = 1220.

Nbrhd.	G	W	C	Total
Pop.	4300	3040	2950	10,290
Std. Q.	3.76	2.66	2.58	9
Min. Q.	3	2	2	7
Mod. Q.	3.52	2.49	2.42	8.43
Geo. M.	3.46	2.45	2.45	-
Final A.	4	3	2	9

e. All four methods give the same results.

UNIT 12D

QUICK QUIZ

1. **c**. The process of redrawing district boundaries is called redistricting.
2. **b**. This answer does the best job in summarizing the political importance of redistricting.
3. **b**. The number of Republican and Democratic voters is close to the same in most states, so districts where there was a large margin of victory are likely to be districts where there is a heavy concentration of Republican voters.
4. **c**. If district boundaries were drawn in a random fashion, one would expect that Republicans would win about 56% of the house seats. Since they won only 15/32 = 47% of the seats, it appears that the district boundaries were set in a way that favored Democrats.
5. **b**. If district boundaries were drawn in a random fashion, one would expect that Republicans would win about 58% of the house seats. Since they won 21/32 = 66% of the seats, it appears that the district boundaries were set in a way that favored Republicans.
6. **c**. Gerrymandering is the drawing of district boundaries so as to serve the political interests of the politicians in charge of the drawing process.
7. **a**. If you concentrate most of the Republicans in a few districts (and essentially concede that they will win in those districts), you will stack the deck in the favor of the Democrats in all the remaining districts.
8. **b**. The courts have generally allowed even very convoluted district boundaries to stand as long as they don't violate existing laws.
9. **a**. If district lines are drawn in such a way as to maximize the number of, say, Democratic seats in the House, they must concentrate the Republican voters in a few districts, and these districts are going to elect Republican representatives (assuming voters vote along party lines).
10. **b**. In an election for a seat that, say, a Democrat is almost guaranteed to win, the real contest occurs in the primary election, rather than the general election. Primaries tend to draw smaller numbers of voters, and those with more clearly partisan interests, and this results in the election of a representative with more extreme partisan views.

DOES IT MAKE SENSE?

17. Makes sense. The district lines in that state are most likely drawn in such a way as to favor Democrats.
18. Makes sense. The practice of gerrymandering often produces districts where the percentage of voters in a particular party is not the same as the overall percentage of those voters in the state.
19. Does not make sense. If the practice of gerrymandering is alive and well in your state, you probably shouldn't expect that the percentage of voters from the various political parties is accurately reflected in the percentage of representatives from those parties that win elections.
20. Does not make sense. It is against the law to draw district lines where the populations differ by a large margin. In a state with 8 million people and 8 House seats, there should be roughly 1 million people per district.
21. Does not make sense. Current laws require that district lines should be drawn to produce contiguous districts.
22. Makes sense. To the extent that the practice of gerrymandering produces districts where the elections are noncompetitive (and therefore these districts elect representatives with more extreme views), the removal of the practice would presumably produce more districts that are competitive, which would result in a smaller number of representatives who hold extreme views.

BASIC SKILLS & CONCEPTS

23. a. In 1998, the percentage of votes cast for Republicans was $\frac{574}{574 + 407} = 59\%$, and for

Democrats it was $\frac{407}{574+407}=41\%$. In 2004, the percentage of votes cast for Republicans was $\frac{1126}{1126+598}=65\%$, and for Democrats it was $\frac{598}{1126+598}=35\%$.

b. In 1998, the percentage of House seats won by Republicans was 5/6 = 83%, and for Democrats it was 1/6 = 17%. In 2004, the percentage of House seats won by Republicans was 6/8 = 75%, and it was 2/8 = 25% for Democrats.

c. In both 1998 and 2004, the percentage of House seats won by Republicans was significantly larger than the percentage of votes they received, though the disparity was not as pronounced in 2004.

d. Because of the change noted in part **c**, it's plausible that redistricting had an effect on the distribution of representatives.

24. a. In 1998, the percentage of votes cast for Republicans was $\frac{558}{558+581}=49\%$, and for Democrats it was $\frac{581}{558+581}=51\%$. In 2004, the percentage of votes cast for Republicans was $\frac{3319}{3319+2212}=60\%$, and for Democrats it was $\frac{2212}{3319+2212}=40\%$.

b. In 1998, the percentage of House seats won by Republicans was 15/23 = 65%, and for Democrats it was 8/23 = 35%. In 2004, the percentage of House seats won by Republicans was 18/25 = 72%, and it was 7/25 = 28% for Democrats.

c. In both 1998 and 2004, the percentage of House seats won by Republicans was significantly larger than the percentage of votes they received.

d. It appears as though the district lines in 1998 were set up to favor Republicans, because roughly half of the votes cast were for Republicans, yet they won 65% of the seats. It's difficult to determine whether redistricting had an effect on the 2004 outcomes – more voters chose Republican candidates, and this would lead to more seats in the House.

25. a. In 1998, the percentage of votes cast for Republicans was $\frac{1040}{1040+592}=64\%$, and for Democrats it was $\frac{592}{1040+592}=36\%$. In 2004, the percentage of votes cast for Republicans was

$\frac{1914}{1914+1366}=58\%$, and for Democrats it was $\frac{1366}{1914+1366}=42\%$.

b. In 1998, the percentage of House seats won by Republicans was 8/11 = 73%, and for Democrats it was 3/11 = 27%. In 2004, the percentage of House seats won by Republicans was 7/13 = 54%, and it was 6/13 = 46% for Democrats.

c. In 1998, the percentage of House seats won by Republicans was significantly larger than the percentage of votes they received. In 2004, the percentage of votes and seats were pretty close to one another.

d. Because of the change noted in part **c**, it's plausible that redistricting had an effect on the distribution of representatives.

26. a. In 1998, the percentage of votes cast for Republicans was $\frac{1608}{1608+2180}=42\%$, and for Democrats it was $\frac{2180}{1608+2180}=58\%$. In 2004, the percentage of votes cast for Republicans was $\frac{2209}{2209+3457}=39\%$, and for Democrats it was $\frac{3457}{2209+3457}=61\%$.

b. In 1998, the percentage of House seats won by Republicans was 13/31 = 42%, and for Democrats it was 18/31 = 58%. In 2004, the percentage of House seats won by Republicans was 9/29 = 31%, and it was 20/29 = 69% for Democrats.

c. In 1998, the percentage of House seats won by Republicans was the same as the percentage of votes they received. In 2004, the percentage of seats was a little lower.

d. Because of the change noted in part **c**, it's plausible that redistricting had an effect on the distribution of representatives.

27. a. In 1998, the percentage of votes cast for Republicans was $\frac{1472}{1472+1381}=52\%$, and for Democrats it was $\frac{1381}{1472+1381}=48\%$. In 2004, the percentage of votes cast for Republicans was $\frac{2565}{2565+2478}=51\%$, and for Democrats it was $\frac{2478}{2565+2478}=49\%$.

b. In 1998, the percentage of House seats won by Republicans was 10/21 = 48%, and for Democrats it was 11/21 = 52%. In 2004, the percentage of House seats won by Republicans was 12/19 = 63%, and it was 7/19 = 37% for Democrats.

c. In 1998, the percentage of House seats won by Republicans was very close to the percentage of votes they received. In 2004, the percentage of votes changed only by a small amount, yet the percentage of seats won went up by a significant margin.

d. Because of the change noted in part **c**, it's plausible that redistricting had an effect on the distribution of representatives.

28. a. The most likely distribution would be 5 Republican and 5 Democrat seats.

b. The maximum number of Republican seats that could be won is 9. In order to get a majority of Republican voters in as many districts as possible, you need to load up one district with Democrats. Each district has 600,000 people – imagine drawing district lines so that all 600,000 people were Democrats in a particular district. That district would elect a Democrat for its representative, but the remaining 9 districts could be drawn to have Republican majorities, and they would elect Republicans. (Note: With the assumption that voting is to take place along party lines, all you'd really need to do is move 1 Democrat from each of 9 districts into the remaining district, and then take 9 Republicans from that district and distribute them evenly across the other 9 districts. This would produce a Republican majority in 9 districts. Of course this assumes that each district begins with exactly 300,000 Republicans, and 300,000 Democrats). Reverse the above logic to convince yourself that the minimum number of Republican representatives is 1.

29. a. The most likely distribution would be 8 Republican and 8 Democrat seats.

b. The maximum number of Republican seats that could be won is 15. In order to get a majority of Republican voters in as many districts as possible, you need to load up one district with Democrats. Each district has 625,000 people – imagine drawing district lines so that all 625,000 people were Democrats in a particular district. That district would elect a Democrat for its representative, but the remaining 15 districts could be drawn to have Republican majorities, and they would elect Republicans. (Note: With the assumption that voting is to take place along party lines, all you'd really need to do is move 1 Democrat from each of 15 districts into the remaining district, and then take 15 Republicans from that district and distribute them evenly across the other 15 districts. This would produce a Republican majority in 15 districts. Of course this assumes that each district begins with exactly 312,500 Republicans, and 312,500 Democrats).

Reverse the above logic to convince yourself that the minimum number of Republican representatives is 1.

30. a. The most likely distribution would be 5 Republican and 5 Democrat seats.

b. The maximum number of Republican seats is 9, and the minimum number is 1. (Refer to exercise 28b; the logic is the same).

31. a. The most likely distribution would be 6 Republican and 6 Democrat seats.

b. The maximum number of Republican seats is 11, and the minimum number is 1. (Refer to exercise 29b; the logic is the same).

32. a. The most likely distribution would be 10 Republican and 0 Democrat seats. This is due to the fact that with random district lines, one would expect a 70% majority in favor of Republicans in every single district, and as long as voting takes place along party lines, all of these districts will elect Republican representatives.

b. From part **a**, we see that the maximum number of Republican seats is 10. In order to find the minimum number, first observe that each district has 500,000 people, and the entire state has 1,500,000 Democrats. A particular district will elect a Democrat only when the district has a Democrat majority. This requires at least 250,001 Democrats (and 249,999 Republicans), with the assumption that voting takes place along party lines (and that everyone votes). However, there are only 1,500,000 Democrats to spread around, and since $1,500,000 \div 250,001 = 5.999976$, the maximum number of districts where one could find a Democrat majority is 5. This implies that the minimum number of Republican seats is 5.

33. a. The most likely distribution would be 15 Republican and 0 Democrat seats. This is due to the fact that with random district lines, one would expect an 80% majority in favor of Republicans in every single district, and as long as voting takes place along party lines, all of these districts will elect Republican representatives.

b. From part **a**, we see that the maximum number of Republican seats is 15. In order to find the minimum number, first observe that each district has 500,000 people, and the entire state has 1,500,000 Democrats. A particular district will elect a Democrat only when the district has a Democrat majority. This requires at least 250,001 Democrats (and 249,999 Republicans), with the assumption that voting takes place along party lines (and that everyone votes). However, there are only 1,500,000 Democrats to spread around, and since $1,500,000 \div 250,001 = 5.999976$, the maximum number of districts where one could find a Democrat majority is 5. This implies that the minimum number of Republican seats is 10.

34. There are several solutions. Perhaps the easiest to describe is one where the boundaries divide the state into eight rectangles, each 2 blocks wide and 4 blocks high.

35. There are several solutions. Perhaps the easiest to describe is one where the boundaries divide the state into 8 rectangles, each 4 blocks wide and 2 blocks high.

36. There are several solutions. Perhaps the easiest to describe is one where the boundaries divide the state into eight rectangles, each 2 blocks wide and 4 blocks high.

37. There are several solutions. Perhaps the easiest to describe is one where the boundaries divide the state into 8 rectangles, each 4 blocks wide and 2 blocks high.

38. Answers will vary, though it is certainly possible to find the required boundaries.

39. It is not possible to draw district boundaries that satisfy the conditions given. Three Democrats are needed in a single district for a Democrat majority, and thus a valid solution would require three Democrats in each of three districts, for a total of nine Democrats. But there are only eight Democrats in the state.

40. Answers will vary (there are several solutions).

41. Answers will vary (there are several solutions).

42. Yes, it is possible – draw boundaries so that three districts have 3 Republicans, and 2 Democrats (these districts will elect a Republican), and the other two will automatically elect a Democrat.

FURTHER APPLICATIONS

43. Answers will vary for the first three cases (there are several solutions). The last case, where 4 Republicans are elected, is not possible. Five Republicans are needed in a single district for a Republican majority, and thus a valid solution would require five Republicans in each of four districts, for a total of 20 Republicans. But there are only 18 Republicans in the state.

44. Answers will vary for the first three cases (there are several solutions). The last case, where 4 Republicans are elected, is not possible. Five Republicans are needed in a single district for a Republican majority, and thus a valid solution would require five Republicans in each of four districts, for a total of 20 Republicans. But there are only 18 Republicans in the state.

45. There are many solutions.

46. Solutions will vary.

47. It is not possible for one party to win every House seat for the situation described. To show this for the example provided (20 voters and four

districts), note that 3 voters of the same party are required for a majority in a single district. Thus a majority in all four districts would require 12 voters of the same party, which is impossible, because there are only 10 such voters. This argument can be generalized to give a proof of the statement in the exercise.

UNIT 13A

QUICK QUIZ

1. **c.** In going from the East Island to the south shore, one crosses the bridge (or edge) labeled *e*.

2. **a.** If you begin on the north shore, and cross bridge *b*, you arrive on the West Island. Walk across bridge *g*, and you arrive on the East Island.

3. **b.** The edges in the network represent borders with other countries.

4. **c.** All Euler circuits begin and end at the same vertex, so that vertex (at the very least) is touched twice.

5. **b.** An Euler circuit exists for a network if and only if each vertex has an even number of edges.

6. **c.** The path described is not a circuit because it traverses two edges more than once.

7. **b.** A tree contains no circuits.

8. **a.** There are two edges for every vertex.

9. **a.** This is not a spanning network because it does not include the vertex *C*.

10. **a.** Using Kruskal's algorithm, it can be shown that the minimum cost spanning network has a cost of 4.

DOES IT MAKE SENSE?

21. Makes sense. A network could be used to represent those countries (vertices) that trade with other countries.

22. Makes sense. Erin could represent teams with vertices, and games played between teams as edges (using multiple edges between vertices if teams play each other more than once, or using weights along the edges for the same purpose).

23. Does not make sense. An Euler circuit guarantees the salesman will visit the town in which he begins at least twice.

24. Makes sense. A tree network could be used to represent which teams (vertices) play each other in the tournament. Because teams are eliminated after one loss, there will be no closed loops (circuits) in the network.

25. Does not make sense. A minimum cost spanning network may not give an optimal walking route.

26. Does not make sense. In a complete network of order *n*, each vertex is connected to $n - 1$ vertices, which means that the degree of each vertex ($n - 1$) is less than the order.

BASIC SKILLS & CONCEPTS

27. a.

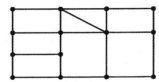

b. The network would look the same as in part **a**, except that every edge would be replaced by two edges (each edge representing a sidewalk).

28.

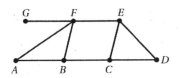

29.

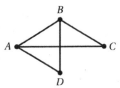

Rather than thinking of Amy, Beth, Cate, and Daniel and the baseball cards they trade, think of various countries and the commodities that they trade.

30. a. Five vertices are needed to represent the land masses, and 8 edges are needed to represent the bridges.

b.

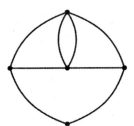

c. No, it is not possible, as the path described would be an Euler circuit. But no Euler circuit exists for this network, because two of the vertices have an odd number of edges.

31. a. Four vertices are needed to represent the land masses, and five edges are needed to represent the ferry routes.

b.

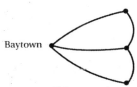

c. No, it is not possible, as the path described would be an Euler circuit. But no Euler circuit exists for this network, because two of the vertices have an odd number of edges.

32. a.

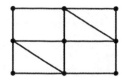

b. Yes, the network has an Euler circuit because each vertex has an even number of edges (there are many ways to draw the Euler circuit).

c. Following the Euler circuit is a very efficient way for the meter reader to do his job.

33. Intersections are represented by vertices, and sidewalks by edges in the network pictured below.

Because every vertex has an even degree, an Euler circuit can be found (there are, in fact, many in this network).

34. a. There are seven vertices, so the network is of order 7.

b. Vertices *A*, *D*, and *G* have degree 2; vertices *B*, *C*, *E*, and *F* have degree 3.

c. The network has no special form.

d. With vertices of odd degree, there are no Euler circuits.

35. a. There are eight vertices, so the network is of order 8.

b. Vertices *A*, *D*, *E*, *F*, *G*, and *H* have degree 3; vertices *B* and *C* have degree 4.

c. The network has no special form.

d. With vertices of odd degree, there are no Euler circuits.

36. a. There are twelve vertices, so the network is of order 12.

b. Vertices *A*, *B*, *G*, *H*, *I*, *J*, *K*, and *L* have degree 1; vertices *D*, *E*, and *F* have degree 3: vertex *C* has degree 5.

c. The network is a tree (no circuits or closed paths).

d. With vertices of odd degree, there are no Euler circuits.

37. a. There are eight vertices, so the network is of order 8.

b. All vertices have degree 4.

c. The network has no special form that was mentioned in the text (it's called a *bipartite* since every vertex of the top set of four vertices is joined to every vertex of the bottom set of four vertices).

d. Because all vertices have even degree, there are Euler circuits.

e. One Euler circuit is *A*, *E*, *B*, *F*, *C*, *G*, *D*, *H*, *C*, *E*, *D*, *F*, *A*, *G*, *B*, *H*, *A*.

38. a. There are six vertices; the network is of order 6.

b. Vertices *B* and *E* have degree 2; vertices *C* and *D* have degree 3; vertices *A* and *F* have degree 4.

c. The network has no special form.

d. With vertices of odd degree, there are no Euler circuits.

39. a. There are five vertices, so the network is of order 5.

b. Vertex *A* has degree 1; vertices *C* and *D* have degree 2; vertex *E* has degree 3; vertex *B* has degree 4.

c. The network has no special form.

d. With vertices of odd degree, there are no Euler circuits.

40. Network I has the lowest cost of 24. Network II costs 29, and Network III costs 31.

41. To carry out Kruskal's algorithm, highlight edges of lowest cost to highest cost until a spanning network has been found. In those cases where a closed circuit exists, delete edges of highest cost. Following the algorithm for this circuit results in edges *AB*, *BC*, *BE*, *EF*, and *BD*, with a cost of 14. Note that the edge *BD* could be replaced by *ED*, and you'd still have a minimum cost spanning network (these networks are not always unique).

42. To carry out Kruskal's algorithm, highlight edges of lowest cost to highest cost until a spanning network has been found. In those cases where a closed circuit exists, delete edges of highest cost. Following the algorithm for this circuit results in edges *AC*, *AB*, *CE*, *EG*, *ED*, and *CF*, with a cost of 16.

43. To carry out Kruskal's algorithm, highlight edges of lowest cost to highest cost until a spanning network has been found. In those cases where a closed circuit exists, delete edges of highest cost. Following the algorithm for this circuit results in edges *d*, *b*, *f*, *h*, *a*, and *c*, with a length of 13 km.

44. To carry out Kruskal's algorithm, highlight edges of lowest cost to highest cost until a spanning network has been found. In those cases where a closed circuit exists, delete edges of highest cost. Following the algorithm for this circuit results in edges *c*, *f*, *i*, *e*, and *j*, with a cost of 45.

FURTHER APPLICATIONS

45. Answers may vary.

a.

b.

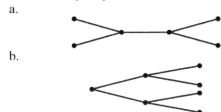

c.

46. Answers may vary.
a.

b.

c.

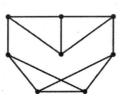

47. The complete network of order 5 is shown below.

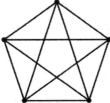

The network has 10 edges, which agrees with the rule

$$\frac{n \times (n-1)}{2} = \frac{5 \times (5-1)}{2} = 10.$$

48. The complete network of order 6 is shown below.

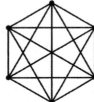

The network has 15 edges, which agrees with the rule

$$\frac{n \times (n-1)}{2} = \frac{6 \times (6-1)}{2} = 15.$$

49. The order of the network is 9, because 8 states border Tennessee, and for the same reason, the degree of the Tennessee vertex is 8.

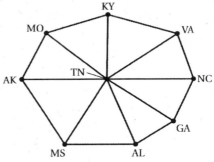

50. The order of the network is 9, because 8 states border Missouri, and for the same reason, the degree of the Missouri vertex is 8.

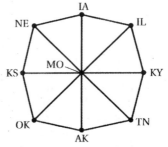

51. a.

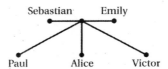

b.

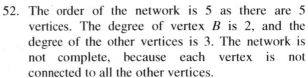

52. The order of the network is 5 as there are 5 vertices. The degree of vertex B is 2, and the degree of the other vertices is 3. The network is not complete, because each vertex is not connected to all the other vertices.

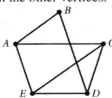

53.

–	A	B	C	D	E	F
A	–	X	X	X	X	
B	X	–	X		X	X
C	X	X	–	X		X
D	X		X	–	X	X
E	X	X		X	–	X
F		X	X	X	X	–

54. a. The traversing path can start at one of the vertices with an odd degree, and end at the other vertex with an odd degree. All of the other vertices must have an even degree, so that the path can both enter and leave those vertices.

b. The network in exercise 34 has four vertices with an odd degree, so it is not traversable. The network in exercise 35 has six vertices with an odd degree, so it is not traversable. The network in exercise 36 has vertices of odd degree, so it is not traversable. The network in exercise 37 has only vertices of even degree, so it is traversable (in fact, it has Euler circuits). The network in exercise 38 has two vertices with an odd degree, so it is traversable. The network in exercise 39 has two vertices with an odd degree, so it is traversable.

UNIT 13B

QUICK QUIZ

1. **c**. A Hamiltonian circuit is a closed path through a network that passes through every vertex exactly once, and returns to the starting vertex.

2. **a**. This path is not Hamiltonian because the path passes though the vertex A more than once.

3. **b**. In a complete network, every vertex is connected to every other vertex.

4. **b**. The order of a network is its number of vertices.

5. **b**. There are $\dfrac{(6-1)!}{2} = 5 \times 4 \times 3$ Hamiltonian circuits in a complete network of order 6.

6. **a**. The traveling salesman problem seeks to find the shortest Hamiltonian circuit.

7. **c**. In general, there is no known algorithm that produces the optimal solution to a traveling salesman problem, other than checking every possible Hamiltonian circuit.

8. **c**. Assuming a complete network connecting all the cities, the number of Hamiltonian circuits is given by $\dfrac{(20-1)!}{2} = 6.08 \times 10^{16}$, which is much more than a trillion.

9. **a**. A near-optimal solution is one where we don't check every conceivable circuit, but we use an algorithm (such as the nearest neighbor method) to produce an answer that is close to the optimal solution.

10. **a**. Phoenix is the closest city to San Diego.

DOES IT MAKE SENSE?

15. Does not make sense. Justin might want to visit cousin Jed, return to his house, visit cousins Jean and Jorge, and once again return to his house, followed by visits to his other cousins, in which case the traveling salesman problem would not apply (because Justin would be traveling through the vertex of his house several times). There's nothing in the statement of the problem that clearly delineates the need for a traveling salesman approach.

16. Makes sense. Justin's plan to visit each house exactly once, returning to his own house, is an apt description of the traveling salesman problem.

17. Makes sense. Roger need only test $\dfrac{(5-1)!}{2} = 12$ circuits, which would be reasonable task to attempt in an evening.

18. Does not make sense. The traveling salesman problem is relevant to many problems beyond sales, many of which impact our lives.

BASIC SKILLS & CONCEPTS

19. The circuit shown is not a Hamiltonian circuit because it doesn't return to the starting point. It can be made into a Hamiltonian circuit by rotating the arrow along the vertical edge so that it points to the leftmost vertex.

20. The circuit shown is a Hamiltonian circuit; it passes through every vertex once and returns to its starting point.

21. The circuit shown is not a Hamiltonian circuit because it doesn't return to the starting point. It cannot be made into a Hamiltonian circuit.

22. The circuit shown is not a Hamiltonian circuit because it doesn't return to the starting point. It can be made into a Hamiltonian circuit by including one more edge between the two leftmost vertices.

23. a. There are $\dfrac{(7-1)!}{2} = 360$ Hamiltonian circuits in a complete network of order 7.

b. There are $\dfrac{(15-1)!}{2} = 4.36 \times 10^{10}$ Hamiltonian circuits in a complete network of order 15.

c. It would take $360 \text{ s} \times \dfrac{1 \text{ min}}{60 \text{ s}} = 6$ minutes to check the circuits in part **a**. For part **b**, it would take about $4.36 \times 10^{10} \text{ s} \times \dfrac{1 \text{ hr}}{3600 \text{ s}} \times \dfrac{1 \text{ d}}{24 \text{ hr}} \times \dfrac{1 \text{ yr}}{365 \text{ d}} = 1383$

years. (Note that this answer uses the rounded value of 4.36×10^{10} circuits – using a more exact number would produce a rounded answer of 1382 years).

24. a. There are $(9 - 1)! \div 2 = 20{,}160$ Hamiltonian circuits in a complete network of order 9.

b. There are $\dfrac{(25-1)!}{2} = 3.10 \times 10^{23}$ Hamiltonian circuits in a complete network of order 25.

c. It would take $20{,}160 \text{ s} \times \dfrac{1 \text{ hr}}{3600 \text{ s}} = 5.6$ hours to check the circuits in part **a**. For part **b**, it would take $3.10 \times 10^{23} \text{ s} \times \dfrac{1 \text{ hr}}{3600 \text{ s}} \times \dfrac{1 \text{ d}}{24 \text{ hr}} \times \dfrac{1 \text{ yr}}{365 \text{ d}} = 9.8 \times 10^{15}$ years.

25. a. The network will look exactly like Figure 13.35b of the text except that the vertex for Zion would be missing, along with all of the edges connected to it. The resulting network would have four vertices, and a total of six edges.

b. The length of the trip is $136 + 75 + 151 + 108 = 470$ miles.

c. Travel from Grand Canyon to Bryce to Capitol Reef to Canyonlands, and return to Grand Canyon, for a total distance of $108 + 69 + 75 + 202 = 454$ miles.

d. Travel from Bryce to Capitol Reef to Canyonlands to Grand Canyon, and return to Bryce for a total distance of $69 + 75 + 202 + 108 = 454$ miles.

e. There are three different Hamiltonian circuits possible in this network of order four. They have lengths of 454, 470, and 558 miles, so we have found the Hamiltonian circuit with the shortest length in parts **c** and **d**.

26. a. There are $\dfrac{(9 - 1)!}{2} = 20{,}160$ circuits.

b. It will take $20{,}160 \text{ circuits} \times \dfrac{1 \text{ s}}{1{,}000{,}000 \text{ circuits}} = 0.02$ second.

c. That's less time than needed for the eye to blink.

27. a. There are $(12 - 1)! \div 2 = 19{,}958{,}400$ circuits.

b. It will take $19{,}958{,}400 \text{ circuits} \times \dfrac{1 \text{ s}}{1{,}000{,}000 \text{ circuits}} = 19.96$, or about 20 seconds.

c. That's about the time needed to take two breaths.

28. a. There are $\dfrac{(16 - 1)!}{2} = 6.54 \times 10^{11}$ circuits.

b. It will take $6.54 \times 10^{11} \text{ circuits} \times \dfrac{1 \text{ s}}{1{,}000{,}000 \text{ circuits}} = $ about 650,000 seconds, or 7.6 days.

c. That's about one week.

29. a. There are $\dfrac{(20 - 1)!}{2} = 6.08 \times 10^{16}$ circuits.

b. It will take $6.08 \times 10^{16} \text{ circuits} \times \dfrac{1 \text{ s}}{1{,}000{,}000 \text{ circuits}} = $ about 60 billion seconds, or about 1930 years.

c. That's almost two millennia.

30. a.

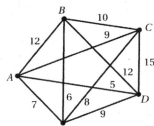

Not drawn to scale!

b. One way to find the shortest route is to check every possible circuit. Since this is a complete network of order 5, there are $(5 - 1) \div 2 = 12$ different networks to check. If you begin at A, and use the nearest neighbor method, you will find that the circuit $ADEBCA$ has length 39, and it turns out this is the shortest possible circuit. (Note that if you found a solution of, say, $BCADEB$, this is the same circuit described above, with a different starting point).

31. Note that because this network is not complete, it is difficult to determine exactly how many Hamiltonian circuits exist, unless you spend the time to count them all. Also true is that the nearest neighbor method does not always work for networks that aren't complete (see below). The six circuits that the exercise asks us to check – those beginning at each city, and using the nearest neighbor method – follow here.

Circuit $AEFBCDX$ fails to produce a complete circuit when the nearest neighbor method is applied. All goes well until we get to vertex D, at which point we cannot return to A (because the network is not complete).

The circuit beginning at city B also fails to produce a Hamiltonian circuit. Using the nearest neighbor method, we travel along the path $BFEAX$, at which point we are stuck, because we cannot go from A to a vertex not yet visited.

Beginning at city C, we follow the path CDF, at which point we have a decision to make: it is 2 hours to both cities E and B. Choosing the first option leads us to the first complete circuit available (again, using the nearest neighbor method): $CDFEABC$, which would take 23 hours to traverse. The other option ($CDFBEAX$) runs into a dead end at vertex A, because we cannot return to C from there.

The circuit beginning at D is just a repeat of the circuit beginning at C. We come to a decision point at *F*; one way produces the circuit *DFEABCD* (which has length 23, and is the same circuit as described above, with a different initial point), and the other way produces the dead end circuit *DFBEAX*.

Starting at *E*, we run into a dead end: *EFBAX* (this is similar to what happened with the circuit beginning at *B*).

Finally, the circuit starting at *F* gives us *FEABCDF*, a circuit of length 23, and identical to the Hamiltonian circuits beginning at *C* and *D* (with different initial point). The nearest neighbor method also produces the dead end circuit *FBEAX*. If you break from convention and don't follow the nearest neighbor rule, you can find circuits that are as good as those found above (*ABFCDEA*, with length 23, for example).

FURTHER APPLICATIONS

32. Beginning at St. Louis, the nearest neighbor method gives the circuit SL, KC, Memphis, Louisville, Chicago, and back to St. Louis, which has a length of 1684 miles. All other circuits, found by trial and error, give longer routes. If all connections were included (such as a direct connection from Memphis to Chicago), making the circuit complete, it's not likely that a new, shorter circuit could be found. This is due to the fact that St. Louis is centrally located, and the missing connections would be significantly longer than those already shown on the map.

33. There are three possible Hamiltonian circuits in this complete network of order 4. These are *ACBDA*, with length 15; *ACDBA*, with length 14; and *ABCDA*, with length 17. Abe should, of course, use the second route to minimize travel distance, though the nearest neighbor method produces the first route (recall that the nearest neighbor method usually produces a near optimal solution). The other drivers should use the second route, beginning and ending at their respective houses.

34. The nearest neighbor method gives the shortest time of 75 minutes for the route *AEDCB*, beginning and ending at the station. An equally fast route of *EDCBA* can be found by trial and error.

35. The company will fly for 30 fewer hours each day, for a savings of $15,000 × 30 = $450,000 per day. Multiply this by 365 to find a savings of $164,250,000 per year.

36. The current cost per day is 75,000 × $0.95 = $71,250, which translates to $26,006,250 per year. A reduction of 2% in driving means that annual costs will be 0.98 × $26,006,250 = $25,486,125.

This would produce an annual savings of $26,006,250 − $25,486,125 = $520,125.

UNIT 13C

QUICK QUIZ

1. **b.** One objective in using CPM (critical path method) to solve scheduling problems is to find the most efficient way to carry out a plan.

2. **a.** The vertices in a scheduling network represent completion points for various tasks (in this case, the completion point for the design phase).

3. **c.** When two (or more) tasks can occur at the same time between two stages of the project, the task that requires the most time is called the limiting task.

4. **c.** The limiting task between vertices *B* and *C* is finance, because that task takes the most time between the vertices.

5. **b.** The amount of slack time for *deliver construction materials* is 1 month, because it takes two months to complete the *finance* task.

6. **a.** The critical path through a network includes all the limiting tasks. The limiting task between vertices *C* and *F* is *construction* because it takes 4 months compared to 3 for the other tasks.

7. **a.** Changing *design* to 1.5 months would save 1.5 months, whereas changing *construction* to 2 months would save only 1 month as the other simultaneous tasks between those vertices take 3 months. Changing *finance* would also save only 1 month.

8. **c.** It takes 5 months along the critical path to get to vertex *C*, and one month to order paint, so the EST for *order appliances* is 6 months.

9. **a.** The EFT for any task is its EST added to the amount of time it takes to complete the task (and in this case, that amounts to 7 months).

10. **a.** When arranging the schedule for the NFL, one doesn't have to worry about limiting tasks, EST, EFT, or the like: the games are all played on Sunday (excepting a few games on Mondays and Thursdays), and there's ample time for all teams to travel back home and regroup before it is necessary to travel again. On the other hand, using CPM might yield worthwhile results for the scheduling of Major League Baseball games. These are played nearly every day during the season, and the schedulers need to be mindful of the earliest time at which a team can be expected to leave one city so that a game in the next city is not scheduled too early. There may be some component of CPM that would be useful for scheduling NFL games on a particular Sunday.

The NFL receives much revenue from the networks televising the games, and must be certain that the games are set up in such a way as to meet the needs of the networks.

DOES IT MAKE SENSE?

17. Does not make sense. Vacations are usually sequential affairs in which one stop/city occurs at a time. The critical path method applies to problems that require concurrent tasks.
18. Makes sense. Remodeling the upstairs of a home is just a small-scale version of the example used in the text regarding the building of a home.
19. Does not make sense. A delay in tasks that are included in the critical path always delays the entire project.
20. Makes sense. Two weeks of slack time means a two-week delay can occur without delaying the entire project.

BASIC SKILLS & CONCEPTS

21. Tasks $a, e, f,$ and g are on the critical path between A and F because these take the longest time.
22. Tasks $f, g, i,$ and k are on the critical path between D and H because these take the longest time.
23. Tasks $a, e, f, g, i,$ and h are on the critical path for the entire project because these take the longest time.
24. The critical path has length of 10.5 hours.
25. Tasks $a, d, e,$ and g are on the critical path between A and F because these take the longest time.
26. Tasks $d, e,$ and g are on the critical path between B and F because these take the longest time.
27. Tasks $a, d, e, g,$ and h are on the critical path for the entire project because these take the longest time.
28. The critical path has length of 19 months.
29. a. The EST for task e is 2 hours, and for i it is 7.5 hours.
   b. The LST for task e is 2 hours, and for i it is 7.5 hours.
30. a. The EST for task h is 4.5 hours, and for k it is 9.5 hours.
   b. The LST for task h is 5.5 hours, and for k it is 9.5 hours.
31. a. The EFT for task e is 2.5 hours, and for i it is 9.5 hours.
   b. The LFT for task e is 2.5 hours, and for i it is 9.5 hours.
32. a. The EFT for task h is 6.5 hours, and for k it is 10.5 hours.
   b. The LFT for task h is 7.5 hours, and for k it is 10.5 hours.

33. a. The EST for task e is 4 months, and for h it is 15 months.
   b. The LST for task e is 4 months, and for h it is 15 months.
34. a. The EST for task c is 3 months, and for g it is 7 months.
   b. The LST for task c is 5 months, and for g it is 7 months.
35. a. The EFT for task e is 7 months, and for h it is 19 months.
   b. The LFT for task e is 7 months, and for h it is 19 months.
36. a. The EFT for task c is 5 months, and for g it is 15 months.
   b. The LFT for task c is 7 months, and for g it is 15 months.
37. Since task h is not on the critical path, and since it has a slack time of 1 hour, there is no effect on the overall schedule if it is delayed by 1 hour.
38. Since task f is on the critical path, a one-hour delay in this task will delay the entire project by one hour.
39.

Task	EST	LST	EFT	LFT	Slack
a	0.0	0.0	2.0	2.0	0.0
b	0.0	1.0	1.0	2.0	1.0
c	0.0	1.5	1.0	2.5	1.5
d	1.0	2.0	1.5	2.5	1.0
e	2.0	2.0	2.5	2.5	0.0
f	2.5	2.5	4.5	4.5	0.0
g	4.5	4.5	7.5	7.5	0.0
h	4.5	5.5	6.5	7.5	1.0
i	7.5	7.5	9.5	9.5	0.0
j	9.5	10.0	10.0	10.5	0.5
k	9.5	9.5	10.5	10.5	0.0

40. Since task f is not on the critical path, and since it has a slack time of 10 months, there is no effect on the overall schedule if it is delayed by 1 month.
41. Since task e is on the critical path, a one-month delay in this task will delay the entire project by one month.

42.

Task	EST	LST	EFT	LFT	Slack
a	0	0	3	3	0
b	0	10	2	12	10
c	3	5	5	7	2
d	3	3	4	4	0
e	4	4	7	7	0
f	2	12	5	15	10
g	7	7	15	15	0
h	15	15	19	19	0

43. The slack time for a task is LST − EST (or, equivalently, LFT − EFT). For this job, the slack times are $a = 0$; $b = 0$; $c = 10$; $d = 0$; $e = 15$; $f = 30$; $g = 0$; and $h = 0$.

44. The critical path includes the tasks a, b, d, g, and h.

45. The critical path has a length of 150 minutes.

46. Tasks (b, c), (d, e), and (f, g) take place at the same time. Tasks a and h must be done alone.

47.

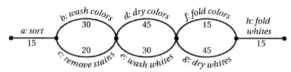

48. The slack time for a task is LST − EST (or, equivalently, LFT − EFT). For this job, the slack times are $a = 0$; $b = 1$; $c = 0$; $d = 2$; $e = 3$, and $f = 0$.

49. The critical path includes the tasks a, c, and f.

50. The critical path has a length of 22 minutes.

51. Tasks (a, b) and (c, d, e) take place at the same time. Task f must be done alone.

52.

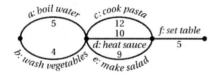